This book deals with the transformation of labour markets in Indonesia over 30 years of New Order government under President Soeharto. It traces the impact of rapid economic growth on employment, wages and labour productivity in an initially poor labour surplus economy. Key elements of the process include a growing industrial and informal sector work force, rising labour incomes, increasing mobility of rural labour, regional integration and greater female participation in the economy. Challenges include high rates of urban unemployment, dissatisfaction with tight controls imposed on industrial workers and rising aspirations created by sharp increases in minimum wages.

Indonesian labour in transition

TRADE AND DEVELOPMENT

A series of books on international economic relations and economic issues in development

Edited from the National Centre for Development Studies, The Australian National University

Academic editor
Ron Duncan, *National Centre for Development Studies, The Australian National University*

Advisory editors
Ross Garnaut, *The Australian National University*
Reuven Glick, *Federal Reserve Bank of San Francisco*
Enzo R. Grilli, *The World Bank*
Mario B. Lamberte, *Philippine Institute for Development Studies*

Executive editor
Maree Tait, *National Centre for Development Studies, The Australian National University*

Other titles in the series
Helen Hughes (ed.), *Achieving industrialization in East Asia*
Yun-Wing Sung, *The China–Hong Kong connection: The key to China's open door policy*
Kym Andersen (ed.), *New silk roads: East Asia and world textile markets*
Rod Tyers and Kym Anderson, *Disarray in world food markets: a quantitative assessment*
Enzo R. Grilli, *The European Community and developing countries*
Peter Warr (ed.), *The Thai economy in transition*
Ross Garnaut, Enzo Grilli and James Riedel (eds.), *Sustaining export-oriented development: ideas from East Asia*
Donald O. Mitchell, Merlinda D. Ingco and Ronald C. Duncan (eds.), *The world food outlook*
David C. Cole and Betty F. Slade, *Building a modern financial system: the Indonesian experience*
Ross Garnaut, Guo Shutian and Ma Guonan (eds.), *The third revolution in the Chinese countryside*
David Robertson (ed.), *East Asian trade after the Uruguay Round*
Yiping Huang, *Agricultural reform in China*

Indonesian labour in transition

An East Asian success story?

CHRIS MANNING

PUBLISHED BY THE PRESS SYNDICATE OF THE UNIVERSITY OF CAMBRIDGE
The Pitt Building, Trumpington Street, Cambridge CB2 1RP, United Kingdom

CAMBRIDGE UNIVERSITY PRESS
The Edinburgh Building, Cambridge, CB2 2RU, United Kingdom
40 West 20th Street, New York, NY 10011-4211, USA
10 Stamford Road, Oakleigh, Melbourne 3166, Australia

© Cambridge University Press 1998

This book is copyright. Subject to statutory exception and to the provisions of relevant collective licensing agreements, no reproduction of any part may take place without the written permission of Cambridge University Press

First published 1998

Printed in the United Kingdom at the University Press, Cambridge

Typeset in 10/12½ Palatino   [SE]

A catalogue record for this book is available from the British Library

Library of Congress Cataloguing in Publication data

Manning, Chris.
    Indonesian labour in transition: an East Asian success story? / Chris Manning.
        p.   cm. – (Trade and development)
    Includes bibliographical references (p.   ) and index.
    ISBN 0 521 59412 X
    1. Labor market – Indonesia.   I. Title.   II. Series: Trade and development (Cambridge, England)
HD5824.A6M239   1998
331.1'09598–dc21   97–6562   CIP

ISBN 0 521 59412 X hardback

Contents

List of figures	*page* x
List of tables	xii
Preface	xvii
Glossary	xxi

I Setting the scene

1 Labour market issues in Indonesian development — 3
  The Indonesian setting: key issues — 6
  Plan of the book — 10

2 Economic development and labour markets: international experience — 12
  The labour market challenge — 12
  The empirical record over 40 years — 15
  Contrasting patterns of economic development and labour market outcomes — 19
  A framework for analysing labour market transformation — 33
  Conclusions: economic growth, development strategies and labour market outcomes — 39

II Economic growth and labour market dynamics

3 Economic and social transformation: a remarkable record — 45
  Indonesia's low starting point — 45
  Economic growth and structural change — 59
  Economic policy — 67
  Population, human resources and labour force — 72
  Regional dimensions and international migration — 77
  Conclusions — 81

viii Contents

4 New jobs and rising productivity: the formal–informal sector divide   84
   Longer-term employment shifts (1971–90)   84
   Agricultural employment   88
   The M-sector   93
   The S-sector   95
   Urban and rural employment, and work status   95
   Labour productivity   98
   Episodes of employment change   100
   Economic slow-down and the non-oil export boom   106
   Conclusions   111

5 Wage growth in a labour surplus economy?   114
   Other empirical studies and the institutional context   114
   Trends in wage rates   117
   Trends in wage costs and competitiveness   129
   Conclusions   131

III Labour market structure and institutions

6 Segmented labour markets and regional integration: change and continuity   137
   The changing structure of work and wages   138
   Diversification of rural labour markets: the case of Java   141
   Urban labour markets and urban–rural links   148
   Regional labour market integration   155
   Conclusions   165

7 Unemployment and underemployment: pressing problems?   172
   Low unemployment and high underemployment in Indonesia?   174
   Youth unemployment and surplus labour in urban areas   176
   Changes in youth unemployment   185
   Underemployment   188
   Conclusions   193

8 Protecting and controlling workers in a labour surplus economy   199
   The foundations of labour policy   201
   The 'Panca Sila' approach to labour policy   204
   Labour policy and industrial relations in the 1990s   212
   Labour controls and state paternalism   226

9	**More women in the workforce: regress or progress?**	**231**
	Female labour force participation	233
	Changing patterns of employment	241
	Wages and earnings	257
	Occupational segregation	262
	Conclusions	264

IV Lessons from Indonesia

10	**Rapid economic growth and labour outcomes**	**275**
	Lessons from Indonesia	275
	The future	287

References	289
Index	315

Figures

2.1	The dynamics of labour market transformation in a labour surplus economy	page 37
3.1	Indices of relative labour productivity in major sectors, Indonesia and selected countries, 1965	58
3.2	Annual growth of non-oil GDP, 1971–1995	61
3.3	Share of GDP by major economic sector for selected East Asian economies, 1970 and 1993	65
3.4	Educational status of the population in Indonesia (level of completed schooling), 1971 and 1994	74
4.1	Agricultural and non-agricultural employment share: Indonesia, 1976–1993	87
4.2	Distribution of employment in Indonesia and selected East Asian countries, 1965 and 1990	90
4.3	Indices of relative labour productivity in A-, M- and S-sectors: Indonesia, South Korea and the Philippines, 1965 and 1990	100
4.4	Distribution of the increase in non-agricultural employment among wage and non-wage workers by gender: Indonesia, 1971–1980 and 1980–1990	110
4.5	Distribution of the increase in non-agricultural wage employment by major sectors: males only, Java and Outer Islands, 1971–1990	110
4.6	Agricultural employment: Indonesia, Java and Outer Islands, 1987–1993	111
5.1	Real wages in selected activities in Indonesia, 1971/2–1992/3	118
5.2	Real wages in selected activities, 1972/3–1992/3	119
5.3	Nominal and real civil service wages: Indonesia, 1971–1993	125
5.4	Real textile wages deflated by the Indonesia CPI and the KFM, Bandung and Indonesia, 1976–1993	128
5.5	Wage rates and average wage costs in textiles: Indonesia, 1976–1990	129
5.6	Real wage costs in Indonesian textiles (TFC) and all	

Figures xi

	manufacturing 1971–1993	130
6.1	Hourly wage differentials for males by activity: Indonesia, 1977 and 1992	139
6.2	Wage differentials by sector among less-educated employees: Java and Outer Islands, 1977 and 1992	140
6.3	Urban–rural wage differentials in selected sectors – less-educated male wage employees: Java and Outer Islands	150
6.4	Wages of production workers, large and medium manufacturing: Indonesia, 1980 and 1991	151
6.5	Ratio of annual wages in large- to small-scale firms: Indonesia, 1980 and 1991	153
6.6	Adjusted male earnings for less-educated employees per hour in construction, transport and services by major provincial groupings	166
7.1	Unemployment rates: urban Indonesia, 1976–1992	174
7.2a	Unemployment by age: urban and rural Indonesia, 1992	177
7.2b	Unemployment by level of schooling: urban and rural Indonesia, 1992	177
7.3	Open unemployment by age and education: urban Indonesia, 1992	178
7.4	Unemployment rates among people aged 15–29: urban Indonesia, 1976–1992	185
7.5	Open unemployment by age and education: urban Indonesia, 1992	186
9.1	Female participation rates by age: Indonesia, 1976–1993	235
9.2	Female participation rates by education: urban Indonesia, 1976–1993	237
9.3	Percentage distribution of female employment by sectors: Indonesia, 1971 and 1990	242
9.4	Sex ratio of employment among senior high graduates in urban Indonesia, 1971 and 1990	244
9.5	Real daily wages in rice (Java) and estate crops (Indonesia), by gender, 1976–1990	247
9.6	Gender gap in hourly earnings by major sector of activity in Indonesia, 1992	258

Tables

2.1	Population, GDP per capita and labour force growth in large countries, 1970–1993	*page* 14
2.2	GDP growth and changes in the distribution of employment by major sector: selected developing countries, 1960–90	18
2.3	Labour market change in some slow and rapidly growing economies, circa 1980–1992	19
2.4	GDP, employment and wage growth, selected East Asian countries, 1965–1990	21
3.1	Indicators of infrastructure and social development, selected East and South Asian countries, 1970	47
3.2	Employment by major sector, Java and Outer Islands, 1971	50
3.3	Selected characteristics of employed persons by major sector: Indonesia, 1971	53
3.4	Average hours worked per day in agricultural and non-agricultural activities in a central Java village, Kaliloro village, 1972–1973	55
3.5	Indicators of economic structure and change: Indonesia, 1965–1970 and 1993–1994	60
3.6	Key episodes of economic development and policy in Indonesia under the New Order, 1965–1995	68
3.7	Population size, distribution and growth: Indonesia, 1971–2000	73
3.8	Labour force growth rates by gender in rural and urban areas: Indonesia, 1971–1990	76
3.9	Gross and net recent migration between Java and Outer Island Provinces, 1975–1980, 1985–1990 and 1990–1995	80
3.1A	Labour force participation rates in Indonesia, 1971–1990	83
4.1	Employment, value-added, employment elasticities and labour productivity by major sector: Indonesia, 1971–1990	86
4.2	Distribution and growth of employment by major sector: Java and the Outer Islands, 1971–1995	87

4.3	Distribution and growth of agricultural employment, wage and non-wage employees: Indonesia, 1971–1990	90
4.4	Growth of employment by major sector: Java and the Outer Islands, 1971–1990	92
4.5	Distribution and growth of employment by sector: Indonesia, 1971–1995	93
4.6	Indices of labour productivity by major sector in Indonesia, 1971 and 1990	99
4.7	Rates of growth in employment of wage and non-wage workers, urban and rural areas: Indonesia 1971–1980 and 1980–1990	101
4.8	Estimated growth in manufacturing employment by major sub-sector, Indonesia 1975–1993	104
4.9	Share of employment by industry group in large and medium manufacturing, 1975–1993	105
4.10	Rate of growth in employment by major sector: Indonesia, males, 1971–1995	107
4.1A	Change in the structure of employment in Java and the Outer Islands, 1971–1990	113
5.1	Regression results from real wage equations with dummy variables for oil-boom and export-boom periods, selected sectors: Indonesia, 1971–1993	121
5.2	Correlation matrix of selected price deflators, first differences, 1976–1991	127
5.1A	Daily wages and wage growth in selected activities: Indonesia 1971–1993	133
6.1	Wage differentials between selected sectors among more educated employees: Indonesia, 1977 and 1992	140
6.2	Wage differentials and level of completed schooling and gender: Indonesia, 1982–1994	141
6.3	Real earnings per hour and share of labour inputs in off-farm activities: rural West Java, 1976 and 1983	144
6.4	Wages paid in domestic private, foreign and state-owned establishments in selected industries: Indonesia, 1980 and 1991	154
6.5	Population, economic structure and change by province: Indonesia, 1971 and 1990	157
6.6	Labour force characteristics and growth, migration and unemployment by province: Indonesia, 1971–1990	160
6.7	Urban and rural employment growth: Indonesia, 1971–1990	162

6.8	Gini coefficients of earnings among wage earners: Indonesia, 1977–1992	168
6.1A	Indices of wage income differentials by major sector, and completed schooling and gender: Indonesia, 1982–1994	169
6.2A	Employment and wages of production workers, large and medium manufacturing: Indonesia, 1980 and 1991	170
6.3A	Regression analysis of the determinants of manufacturing wages: Indonesia, 1991	171
7.1	Unemployment and underemployment by gender: urban and rural Indonesia, 1992	175
7.2	Duration of unemployment among job seekers by level of completed schooling: ages 15–29, Indonesia, 1992	180
7.3	Unemployment rates by education of the household head, all urban and young urban dependents: Indonesia, 1992	182
7.4	Unemployment and employment rates of upper secondary educated urban youth by education and income of household head	183
7.5	Persons working less than 35 hours available for more work by major sector, employment status and region, 1990	189
7.6	Mean number of hours worked and percentage of people working less than 35 hours: Indonesia, 1977 and 1990	191
7.7	Percentage of persons working less than 35 hours in main job by major sector and gender, 1980 and 1990	192
7.1A	Unemployment rates by age and education, 1992	196
7.2A	Unemployment rates by age and education: urban Indonesia, 1976–1992	197
8.1	Changes in labour policies and labour market developments during main periods of economic change: Indonesia, 1965–1995	205
8.2	Minimum wage, and minimum physical needs (kfm), 1982–1984	208
8.3	Union density in selected East Asian countries, circa 1990	210
8.4	Selected data on strikes: Indonesia, 1961–1994	212
8.5	Strikes in selected countries in Asia, 1961–1993	213
8.6	Causes of strikes: Indonesia, 1985–1991	215
8.7	Average annual growth of labour productivity, mean earnings in manufacturing, and minimum wages: Indonesia 1978–1992	217
8.8	Comparison of minimum wages and average wages in selected industries and regions: Indonesia, 1992	219

8.9	Characteristics of manufacturing employees in major regions, 1990	228
8.10	Monthly wages and per-capita incomes: selected East Asian economies, 1990	229
9.1	Labour force participation rates: selected East Asian countries, 1970/1 and 1900–1992	234
9.2	Female employment by major sector and work status, urban and rural Indonesia, 1971 and 1990	243
9.3	Female employment by major sector: Java and the Outer Islands, 1971–1990	246
9.4	Employment of female professional, managerial and technical workers: Indonesia, 1971 and 1990	249
9.5	Percentage of all non-agricultural employment absorbed in government, community and social services–educated, female workers: Indonesia, 1971–1990	250
9.6	Female participation in civil service employment: Indonesia, 1978–1992	251
9.7	Female employment in major industries: Indonesia, 1992	256
9.8	Decomposition of hourly earnings differentials: Indonesia, 1992	261
9.9	Ten major non-agricultural occupations by gender: Indonesia, 1985	263
9.10	Five major occupations by gender: Jakarta, 1980 and 1990	264
9.1A	Probit estimates of the determinants of female labour force participation: urban Indonesia, 1992	268
9.2A	Percentage share of females in total employment by sector: selected East Asian countries, 1970–1991/2	269
9.3A	Regression results of log earnings equations by gender: Indonesia, 1992	270

Preface

The book had its origins in my early experiences in Indonesia in the late 1960s. As a volunteer working for the Indonesian government – together with much more senior colleagues from the Bogor Agricultural University – I had the rare opportunity to stay for several months in two villages, and participate in field work on problems of agricultural and rural development in Karawang District, in northern West Java. That experience and subsequent long periods of work in Indonesia convinced me that Indonesia's fundamental development problem was rural poverty, a perspective which I have retained to the present

Although only superficially, I encountered the problems of poverty first hand – insecurity, dependence, infant mortality and a lack of self esteem associated with little education and choice in economic and social life. Many of these problems were associated with low labour earnings among landless households. My approach to the problem of labour markets developed on the basic premise that there would have to be a massive shift of workers out of agriculture in land-scarce Java, if some of these problems were to be overcome.

Subsequent involvement in a variety of research projects and institutions, working and living with Indonesians in Yogyakarta and Bogor, led to a more specific interest in labour problems – from the perspectives of rapid population growth and associated problems, the wage structure, the informal sector and unemployment. Increasingly I felt it necessary to try to understand the national dimensions of the labour problem from aggregate statistics, however imperfect. I developed an approach of trying to match the story implicit in aggregate figures with the not always consistent findings of micro studies.

At the same time, both the literature and my colleagues convinced me of the importance of the macroeconomic environment and of policies for a labour market transition which would contribute to poverty alleviation. The experience of other East Asian success stories loomed large in suggesting that many problems of rural deprivation could be overcome in a relatively short time frame – certainly in less than the life span of one generation. I remained sceptical, however, that this could be achieved on Java and in Indonesia more generally. For much of the 1970s and 1980s – as for much of the previous century – it seemed that the problems of rural poverty were endemic, and it would take a lifetime of several generations before they could be substantially overcome, even with the most favourable policies and considerable luck.

At the end of the project, I have had to admit that my colleagues were probably closer to the mark than I expected. The Indonesian story of labour market transformation is remarkable. However, my implicit message for the optimists is that Indonesia has still a long way to go before it can be described as successful in terms of levels of living rather than merely rates of change. Employment conditions and wages still have to undergo substantial improvements to guarantee sufficiently high living standards for the majority of the population – by almost any criteria which might be considered satisfactory in most industrial countries.

The book is an account of Indonesian economic development viewed from the perspective of labour market change. It covers a wide range of labour market experience, although some issues – such as child labour and education and training have only been dealt with summarily. The book has tended to concentrate more on processes on Java, primarily because much more is known of labour market change on this island compared with the Outer Islands of Indonesia.

The story of labour market change in this book has thus been long in the melting pot – and a considerable time stewing quite vigorously as well. I have laboured long in trying to make sense of the labour statistics and to reconcile the tale which they seemed to tell with both macroeconomic developments and the findings of community and firm-based micro studies. Ambitiously, the book has attempted to compare and contrast the Indonesian experience with those of other countries in the region. However, I believe it is only from such a comparative framework that we can gain some understanding of the significance of developments in Indonesia.

The book is written primarily for those interested in economic development and labour markets in Indonesia and the Asian region. Labour economics is not a fashionable field of specialisation in Indonesia and I hope that the book will stimulate more interest in this subject. I also hope that the book will be read by non-economists as well as economists. I suspect that many from disciplines other than economics might be sceptical of the 'success' implicit in the findings of much of the analysis – although the results by no means suggest that labour market processes have benefited all workers, or benefited them optimally at all times. In my view, a more fruitful dialogue is much needed between seemingly optimistic economists and other social scientists who hold less sanguine views on the processes of economic development, and their implications for social and political change. This book attempts to contribute to such a dialogue.

I am indebted to many individuals and institutions for their support and encouragement. Ross Garnaut, Professor and the Head of the Economics Division, and Hal Hill, Head of the Indonesian Project, both in the Research School of Pacific Studies, have given their full support to the project from the outset and gave valuable comments on the entire manuscript at various stages of writing. Peter McCawley read a first draft of the entire book (over Christmas in Manila as he was in the midst of moving!). His comments have made a major contribution to the clarity of the arguments. Several other colleagues in the Economics Department – Professors Jamie Mackie and Heinz Arndt, Premachandra Athukorala, Colin Barlow, George Fane, K. Kalirajan and Ross McLeod – gave helpful comments on various drafts of chapters or on the articles on which they are based. Professor Gavin Jones also contributed valuable comments. The stimulus which I received from joint research efforts with Gavin Jones, Sisira Jayasuriya and P. N. Junankar is also gratefully acknowledged.

Several institutions have had a hand both directly and indirectly in assisting the development of the book. Foremost, I wish to acknowledge the contribution of the Indonesian Project, the Department of Economics and the School of Pacific Studies at the Australian National for providing material support and a stimulating environment for research. I also developed some of the ideas for the book at Flinders University in South Australia, and while working at the Population Studies Center at Gadjah Mada University and later for the Agro-Economic Survey in Bogor in the early 1980s. I cannot mention individually all the many people from these and other institutions who helped me along the way, although I should especially thank Gunawan Wiradi, the late Yusuf Saefudin and Professor Dipak Mazumdar. I gratefully acknowledge the permission of the Central Bureau of Statistics in Jakarta for the right to use computer tapes on labour force and industry, and also the provision of materials by the Ministry of Manpower.

I owe thanks to several mentors for helping my understanding of Indonesia and development processes – Professor Peter Drysdale, Professor Masri Singarimbun, Dr Thee Kian Wie, the late David Penny and my late father, Alan Manning. The work has also been stimulated by the work of many researchers, both in and outside Indonesia, and who have assisted my learning of the intricacies of the Indonesian economy and labour market processes. Many Indonesian employers gave up their valuable time to provide information of wages and other matters. And, of course, I owe a great debt of thanks to many Indonesian workers – both in towns and villages – from whom I have gained insights, and about whom this book is primarily written.

Many people also helped in the production of the book. My inability to produce good tables meant that I depended on the support of Sonya Bodger, Iain Rowe and Jesmin Fernando at various times. Abrar Yusuf provided valuable assistance in computer programming and helped with the figures. Norma Chin applied her considerable keyboard skills, working long hours, and Maree Tait offered valuable advice and encouragement, to help me put together the final manuscript in a publishable form. I am extremely grateful for the cheerful and willing assistance of all these people – despite my grumpiness at times, disorganisation and sometimes outrageous requests.

Finally – although it sounds like a cliché which many male academics spout – I thank my generous and wonderful wife Tri for her patience and support. My two understandably sometimes miffed children – Ned and Karina – have also put up with long absences and lack of attention, and have also been kind enough not to drive their helpless Mum around the bend, to boot.

Glossary

Many Indonesian constructions are not acronym as such, but formed from the initial syllable or first few letters of the composite words, e.g., Pungli from *Pungutan Liar*. These are shown in lower case.

ASEAN	Association of South East Asian Nation
ASTEK	(Asuransi Sosial Tenaga Kerja) Government insurance fund
batik	Batik
becak	rickshaw
betawi	the original inhabitant of Jakarta
ceblokan and *tebasan*	traditional system of harvesting
CPI	Consumer Price Index
calo	jobbers, labour recruiters, middleman
FLPs	Female Labour Force Participation rates
FBSI	(Federasi Buruh Seluruh Indonesia) All-Indonesian Labour Federation
GDP	Gross Domestic Product
GOLKAR	(Golongan Karya) The ruling party
GSP	General System of Preferences
ILO	International Labour Organisation
INDOC	Indonesian Documentation Centre
INPRES	Presidential Instruction
ISI	Import Substitution Industrialisation
jamu	herbal medicines
kekeluargaan	principles of family cooperation
JABOTABEK	(Jakarta, Bogor, Tanggerang, Bekasi) planning region encompassing the city of Jakarta and districts of Bogor, Tanggerang and Bekasi
JAMSOSTEK	(Jaminan Social Tenaga Kerja) Worker Social Security
kampung	village
kadaluwarsa	outdated

kretek	clove cigarettes
keterbukaan	openness
Kompas	one of the biggest Indonesian Newspapers
LDC	Less Developed Country
M-Sector	manufacturing, construction, mining and utilities
MFN	Minimum Physical Needs or KFM (Kebutuhan Fisik Minimum)
MW	Minimum Wages
ngobjek and *ngompreng*	hiring out government vehicles, for private gain
NIEs	New Industrialised Economies
OPEC	Organization of Petroleum Exporter Countries
OPIC	The Overseas Private Investment Corporation
PERTAMINA	Perusahaan Pertambangan Minyak dan Gas Bumi (Indonesia's State Owned Oil Company)
Pancasila	(Five Principles) the state ideology
penghinaan	insult
pungli	(pungutan liar) illegal charge
PERTEKSI	Perserikatan Perusahaan Tekstil Seluruh Indonesia (All Indonesia Union of Textile Company)
PKI	(Partai Komunis Indonesia) Indonesian Communist Party
REPELITA	Rencana Pembanganun Lima Tahun (Five Year Development Plan)
RGDP	Regional Gross Domestic Product
SBM	(Serikat Buruh Merdeka) The Solidarity Independent Labour Union
SBSI	(Serikat Buruh Sejahtera Indonesia) The Prosperous Labour Union
SMA	(Sekolah Menengah Atas) Senior High School
SPSI	(Seriktat Pekerja Seluruh Indonesia) All Indonesia Workers Union
SOBSI	(Serikat Organisasi Buruh Seluruh Indonesia) All Indonesia Workers Organisation
S-Sector	the service sector (banking, government administration, petty trade, transport and personal services)
sawah	irrigated rice field
tahu and *tempe*	bean curd cakes
TFC	Textile, Footwear and Clothing
THR	(Tunjangan Hari Raya) Idul Fitri Allowance
unjuk rasa	strikes, stop work protests
tukang	artisan
warung	street stall

Setting the scene

1

Labour market issues in Indonesian development

Three decades of rapid economic growth under the New Order have fundamentally changed the Indonesian economy and society. Labour markets have also been transformed in a country much of which was a classic case of a labour surplus economy – demonstrably so in Java – in 1965–6. Despite these developments, many observers are disturbed by the low wages, poor working conditions and high rates of informalisation among Indonesian workers compared with those in more advanced East Asian economies. There is a general feeling that in the area of labour the Indonesian government has performed poorly, in contrast to other areas of social and economic life such as education, health and poverty alleviation. The implication is that Indonesia needs to rethink its development priorities and programmes, especially the recent phase of economic liberalisation since the mid 1980s.

This book focuses on issues raised in these debates. First, contrary to popular opinion, it argues that most ordinary workers have made substantial advances in wages, productivity and labour incomes – although the gains have not necessarily narrowed the absolute gap in living standards with higher-paid professionals and managers, or with unskilled workers in neighbouring countries. Second, it seeks to demonstrate why this finding is so different to public perceptions of labour processes. It shows why the benefits to wage workers have not been more visible or pronounced in terms of conventional indicators of labour market outcomes, and why labour outcomes have sometimes differed from those in neighbouring countries.

The book deals with this labour market transformation both in the context of national social and economic developments, and comparative labour market experience in other rapidly growing economies in East Asia. It examines aspects of initial economic circumstances and labour market conditions when Soeharto came to power, drawing attention to the extent to which Indonesia lagged behind many of its neighbours. And it looks at aspects of social and economic change which have influenced labour's gains, and

4 *Setting the scene*

losses. The body of the book deals with the labour market response: the movement of workers between jobs, sectors and regions; the delayed and then later accelerated response of agricultural wage rates to rapid economic growth; trends in unemployment and underemployment; industrial relations processes; and the changing role of women in the labour market.

The extent to which growth transforms labour markets has a major influence on both economic efficiency and equity. This is evidenced in markedly different labour market structures and outcomes between and within developing economies. Fluid, responsive and relatively undifferentiated employment and wage structures at one extreme contrast with fractured or segmented labour markets, in which there is a marked contrast in the wages and welfare of 'insiders' and 'outsiders', in terms of access to the prized modern sector jobs at the other.[1] These themes are emphasised in comparisons of labour market experience between regions and over time in Indonesia, and between Indonesia and other East Asian countries.

Labour market change has important implications for social and political structures. These include the extent of participation by vulnerable groups, discrimination by race, region and gender, and the representation of workers in political processes. While workers have been willfully suppressed in some countries, they have also been in the forefront of the democratic reform movement in some countries, such as South Korea during the 1980s.

The obvious point of comparison for a study of Indonesian labour is other rapidly developing countries in East Asia, in particular the NIEs and the larger ASEAN economies.[2] Rates of economic growth, episodes of economic liberalisation and the transition to export orientation have been similar to most of these other economies, notwithstanding some notable differences.

There have been surprisingly few major studies of the interaction between economic growth and labour market outcomes in the rapidly expanding East Asian economies. The mechanisms underlying development success – the roles of the market and the state, international economic integration, and technological change (Krugman's 'inspiration' rather than 'perspiration') – are well documented and have been widely debated in the literature.[3] Much less is known about the causes and

---

[1] Horton, Kanbur and Mazumdar (1994a), World Bank (1995a), ILO (1995).
[2] China is also an obvious country for comparison. However, owing to its size and complexity of labour market change in a previously centrally controlled economy, greater stress is placed on comparisons with other countries in the region.
[3] See especially Hughes (1988), Amsden (1989), Wade (1990), World Bank (1993) and Krugmann (1994).

consequences of differences in the impact of economic growth on labour markets.[4]

In part, mainstream economists working on East Asia have generally assumed that labour markets respond smoothly to sound economic management and 'getting prices right'. Yet we know this is not always true. Some well-integrated economies, such as Taiwan and Korea, followed quite similar growth paths and shared similarities in the nature of labour market response, such as in the speed of labour transfers from agriculture to manufacturing, and the subsequent wage rises. Nevertheless, even between these two countries, labour processes differed markedly in response to contrasting spatial (and size distribution) patterns of investment, government intervention in wage-setting mechanisms and human capital development. In a large and spatially dispersed economy like Indonesia, the contrasts in labour market processes and outcomes are likely to be even greater.

The analysis of labour institutions and policies in East Asia has largely been left to non-economists. These topics have been relegated to footnotes in mainstream economic analysis, or left to industrial relations specialists.[5] Many of these studies are rich in theory and detail on the political and dimensions of worker organisations and industrial relations. However, they frequently ignore the interaction between labour markets and economic change, which are fundamental to labour welfare and bargaining power as countries modernise.

The main topics of study were selected with Indonesia in mind. But they have much broader relevance. These issues include

- *different paths through which labour markets are transformed* – from initial conditions of extreme poverty and 'labour surplus' – in the process of structural change
- *the role of the labour mobility* (between jobs, sectors and regions) in productivity, wages and incomes growth
- *patterns of labour market adjustment* to changing economic circumstances, and to shifts in economic policy orientation – resource booms, import substitution and export-oriented industrialisation policies
- *the causes and consequences of labour market 'failure'* in the form of high levels of underemployment and urban unemployment, and labour market divisions (segmentation) by gender, region and type of investment

---

[4] The major references are Pang Eng Fong (1988a), Fields and Wan (1989), Deyo (1989), Ogawa, Williamson and Jones (1993) and Fields (1994).
[5] In recent years there has also been a spate of comparative studies of industrial relations and labour organisation in the region (See for example Frenkel 1993; Deery and Mitchell 1993).

6 *Setting the scene*

- *the role of changing labour market institutions and policies* in determining the efficiency and equity of labour markets, in traditional and modern settings – including adjustment of rural labour institutions and the role of trade unions.

Several developing East Asian economies have already undergone a turning point in which wages and labour incomes rose quickly. The NIEs (and, increasingly, Malaysia), are well along the path in a transition towards labour-scarce economies. This is indicated by rapidly rising unskilled real wages and the movement of labour to more skill and capital-intensive industries (Galenson 1992; World Bank 1995b). In contrast, it is debatable whether Indonesia was close to achieving a similar stage in labour market transition in the mid 1990s.

This raises several intriguing questions. For example, have macroeconomic processes and policies been less friendly to labour in Indonesia? Or were initial economic and labour market structures less prepared for rapid economic change? Such questions lead to an analysis of the nature of macroeconomic change and policies, and their interaction with microeconomic processes and structures.

The Indonesian setting: key issues

Indonesia is an engaging case for the study of labour market change in the process of economic development. The diverse sources of economic growth – abundant natural resources, excess labour supply (to the modern sector), high rates of domestic and foreign investment, and strong state support for agriculture and human resources – provide a rich foundation for examining labour market adjustment. Indonesia's unfavourable initial conditions yet sustained high growth rates provide fertile ground for investigating the nature of labour market transformation.

The Indonesian economy has been among the top ten achievers in the developing world since President Soeharto came to power in 1965. Some have labelled the country one of the miracle economic performers of recent decades. Others see it as a nascent New Industrialising Economy (NIE) of Asia – on the verge of becoming a middle tier, industrialised economy in the region.

Economic growth has been accompanied by substantial structural change. Relative to other sectors, the share of GDP produced in agriculture has fallen even quicker than in other fast-growing economies in East Asia.[6]

[6] In the book, the term 'rapidly growing' East Asian economies covers the NIEs of Asia (South Korea, Taiwan, Hong Kong and Singapore), Malaysia and Thailand. Comparisons are also made with the Philippines, but only fleetingly with China, the Indochinese states and Burma.

Much of the traditional manufacturing sector has been replaced by modern, large-scale industry. The latest technology is visible in the form of extensive communications and infrastructure networks, not only on Java but now extending into most Outer Island regions. Although Jakarta dominates, other major cities show unmistakeable signs of affluence – high-rise office buildings and hotels, supermarkets and widespread car ownership (with the concomitant, inevitable traffic jams!). More relevant to the living standards of the masses, the incidence of poverty is estimated to have declined at a rate almost unparalleled in the experience of the developing world (World Bank 1990).

Yet wage rates remain low, a small proportion of workers are employed in non-agricultural or skilled occupations and the ubiquitous informal sector abounds in major cities, just a few minutes walk from the modern centres of business. The contrast is stark if compared with the more advanced, neighbouring economies of East Asia, let alone with Japan or Western Europe. Per-capita incomes and wage rates were around one quarter of those in Malaysia and South Korea and closer to one-tenth of those in Taiwan, Singapore and Hong Kong in the mid 1990s.[7]

These issues are not just of academic significance. Indonesians themselves – particularly the industrial workers – have become increasingly frustrated with the slow rises in real wages and living standards. Recent substantial labour unrest reflects this concern.[8] In the political arena, criticism has been directed at the suppression of labour rights and of the relative standards of living in addition to absolute levels. Much attention has been given to the high incomes of the increasingly visible middle class and employees of wealthy business conglomerates, compared with the US$1–2 per day wages of ordinary workers.

Analysis highlights unique aspects of the historical and institutional framework in Indonesia over the past 30 years. Four aspects of Indonesia's labour market experience and its challenge distinguish it from several other neighbouring East Asian countries.

First, labour market change in Indonesia – by industry, occupation and region – can be expected to be closer to that in resource rich countries than in many of the countries of East Asia. Owing to an abundance of natural resources – especially oil – the country faces many of the same challenges as countries such as Brazil, Mexico or Nigeria, in areas of macroeconomic management, allocation of resources and the distribution of wealth. Surpluses generated from oil and natural resources enabled Indonesia to

---

[7] The differences were slightly smaller in purchasing power parity terms.
[8] Labour riots in the Sumatran city of Medan in April 1994 were a culmination of several years of increased labour action from 1991 onwards.

8 *Setting the scene*

remain less open to international markets than several of its neighbours. Manufacturing was heavily protected for a longer period, following the pattern of South Asian and Latin American countries. One might expect employment structures and growth – including a burgeoning informal sector – to resemble the less equitable patterns often observed in these countries.[9]

Second, with respect to the efficiency and flexibility of labour markets, integration of rural–urban and regional labour markets is an important topic in a far-flung archipelago. One view is that Indonesian labour markets work very well. Labour is regarded as highly mobile geographically and between sectors. An alternative view is that in Indonesia labour markets are imperfect: they are segmented by type of firm, industry and according to relationships between employers and employees.[10] One related issue is the change in labour market structures over time, especially during the period of deregulation since the mid 1980s. This is particularly relevant in the context of similar episodes of liberalisation which have occurred in East Asian economies.

The large size of the Indonesian population and workforce suggests that the labour market challenge might be qualitatively different than for smaller economies. With a population of almost 200 million and a workforce of over 80 million in the mid 1990s, Indonesia is the world's fourth most populous country. Some issues of labour absorption and their impact on welfare in poor countries are related to scale – the size of domestic and international markets, regional diversity and national integration.

It still has to be seen whether (and on what time scale) the larger countries of Asia – China, India, Indonesia, Pakistan and Bangladesh – can emulate the remarkable labour market transformation of the smaller East Asian NIEs. Indonesia has undergone sustained economic growth, and had a more liberalised economy over a longer time period than other large economies in Asia. Its experience should help provide a glimpse of possible outcomes for the other reforming and rapidly growing giants in the region.

A third important area of research deals with the impact of government policies on labour processes and outcomes. Like elsewhere in East Asia, some policies adopted by the New Order government have indirect effects

---

[9] Tokman (1984), Fields (1994), World Bank (1995b).
[10] Contrasting views regarding the efficiency of labour markets are put forward in two World Bank publications undertaken in the 1970s. The first (World Bank 1985) argued that unskilled labour markets were relatively open and efficient whereas the second (Lluch and Mazumdar 1985) argued that the labour market was highly segmented in both urban and rural areas.

on labour – such as general macroeconomic, stabilisation and investment policies (including allocation of resources to human capital). But other policies have been more directly focussed on labour market outcomes than in neighbouring countries. These include direct employment creation programmes, minimum wages and labour protection policies.

A controversial issue in Indonesia has been the extent to which labour policies (or their absence) have influenced labour outcomes. Some have argued that wage workers, especially females, have been exploited by monopsonistic employers, and that exploitation is due to government inaction and the stifling of independent trade unions. Extensive protection, minimum wages legislation and guarantees of labour freedoms are viewed as central to improving the situation.

Alternatively, it is asserted that greater government intervention in areas such as wage policy can harm nascent export-oriented industrialisation and discourage foreign investment (World Bank 1995a). Some observers of the NIE experience suggest that the absence of government labour market interventions contributes to rapid growth in jobs, and to equity (Fields and Wan 1989).[11] A *laissez-faire* approach in several countries encouraged investment and labour market adjustment to economic change.

A final set of issues relates to labour welfare and equity. The impact of rapid economic growth on the distribution of labour incomes is of interest, given that the initial allocation of assets was skewed and that there has not been any successful programme of land redistribution.[12] Key issues relate to the extent to which gains have been made by landowners and capitalists at the expense of labour, and the factors which have determined these outcomes.

One specific distributional issue in the Indonesian case is the low general education standards at all levels of schooling, and a paucity of skilled labour when economic growth began after 1965. Although school enrolments have grown very fast, it is questionable whether the increased supply of graduates has offset rising demand for skilled and professional labour.[13]

---

[11] Not all governments in the rapidly growing NIEs refrained from direct involvement in wage determination.
[12] The impact of an unequal distribution of land on employment opportunities and incomes has especially been a topic of debate in discussions on the impact of the green revolution in agriculture (see Hart 1986).
[13] On the demand side, it is likely that development has been more skill intensive in Indonesia than in the NIEs at a similar stage of development, particularly due to the greater importance of resource-based industries in Indonesia. One would thus expect a less equal distribution of wage incomes than in other East Asian countries.

Plan of the book

The book is divided into four parts.

Part I emphasises both connections with international labour market challenges and trends, and the importance of Indonesia's special historical and institutional environment. At the same time, particular attention is given to the remarkable demographic, social and economic transformation which has underpinned labour market change.

The main aspects of an emerging labour market transition are documented in part II. Not only has labour moved out of agriculture and into higher productivity sectors at an increasing rate, but wage rates began to rise quite steeply in the 1990s and labour markets became much more integrated across activities and regions. Not surprisingly, the process of labour market transformation has been anything but smooth. Thus I document how changing economic circumstances – the oil boom of the 1970s, the subsequent slowdown in economic growth and manufacturing-led export growth from the late 1980s – had quite contrasting effects on employment structure and wages.

Three key labour market challenges are discussed part III. It is argued that while urban unemployment is a pressing social and political problem, it is mainly related to segmented wage and employment structures rather than slow growth in labour demand relative to supply. Industrial relations are another area of controversy. Here the main issues are the impact of tight controls over the labour movement – mainly for political reasons – and attempts to guarantee worker welfare through other mechanisms, such as minimum-wage legislation. Finally, it is argued that Indonesia shares much in common with other East Asian countries in wage and job discrimination against women. Nevertheless relative to men, women have done remarkably well in capturing a larger share of new modern sector jobs, and play a much more influential role in the more skilled segments of the labour market than some commentators would have us believe.

Overall, I conclude that labour market transformation has made a major contribution to rising living standards in Indonesia over the past 30 years. Given economic fundamentals and policies in the mid 1990s, there are no longer grounds for pessimism – which even the most sanguine observers felt when Soeharto came to power – concerning better job prospects for most Indonesians as the country approaches the twenty-first century. Political reforms stalled in the mid 1990s and there are very genuine concerns about equity and the concentration of economic power and wealth in Jakarta among a small number of elite families. But the momentum of sustained economic growth has transformed the labour market, ridding it of many of the signs of classic labour surplus, all too obvious at the beginning of the New Order. It is also concluded that labour market adjustments resulting from internationalisation have contributed to a more – not a less – equitable society, contrary to the views of some sceptics regarding the distributional impact of the move towards a more open economy.

2

Economic development and labour markets: international experience

Economic development since World War II has been associated with profound changes in the structure of labour markets in most developing economies. These include the rapid increase in employment in industry and services, the rise in the share of educated, skilled and professional workers, and sustained wage growth in some countries. In addition to economic growth, a range of factors help explain labour market performance, including economic structure and labour market institutions and policies (Horton, Kanbur and Mazumdar 1994b; Freeman 1992a).

Nowhere has labour market transformation change been greater than in the rapidly growing economies of East Asia. However even in these countries, there are major questions regarding the labour market dimensions of their economic success: the human cost of flexible labour markets, the abuse of labour rights and the challenges increasingly faced in producing highly skilled manpower for new industries. These questions have been prominent in discussions of labour market processes in Indonesia.

In other developing economies, labour concerns have been related to disappointing economic performance. Concerns include slow employment growth in manufacturing, the overspill of surplus labour into low productivity sectors, high levels of unemployment and stagnant wages. They have often accompanied severe problems of labour market adjustment to economic shocks.

The labour market challenge

Simon Kuznets (1957) identified three characteristics of labour market change in industrial countries from the second half of the nineteenth century. These were the decline in the share of agricultural employment, a rapid rise in manufacturing employment and a faster increase in the proportion of service sector jobs. Changing patterns of demand as incomes rose, and differing rates of technical progress, were crucial to these changes, which were in turn associated with rising output per worker and rising levels of skill and wages. By the second half of the twentieth century, only a small proportion of the work force remained in agriculture – frequently less than 10 per cent – in most industrial economies. Labour productivity was initially low in agriculture. It rose relative to industry and services as labour shifted out and technical progress accelerated. Similarly, labour productivity in manufacturing was generally low relative to services in the early stages of development but rose much more rapidly than in services.

In his later work Kuznets contrasted the much more forbidding labour market conditions in most developing economies compared with the now industrial economies when the latter began to industrialise a century earlier.[1] The most important difference was much lower per-capita incomes. This was mainly the result of a greater concentration of employment and lower productivity and incomes in agriculture (Kuznets 1965: 178–86). The concentration of labour in traditional agriculture also meant that modern sectors had a limited capacity to absorb a significant share of the work force in the early stages of development.[2]

Developing economies also faced an additional challenge in unprecedented rapid rates of population and labour force growth in the post-war era. Not only were these markedly higher than the now industrial economies had ever experienced, but they are projected to remain so through into the next century in many countries. Table 2.1 indicates that they remain well above 2 per cent per annum in the poorer countries during the 1990s.

Given the initial challenge of shifting low productivity labour out of agriculture, high labour force growth rates raised the spectre of increasing rates of unemployment and underemployment – as much in East Asia as elsewhere in the developing world (Oshima 1971). Indeed, early studies suggested that as much as 20–40 per cent of the work force in most developing economies was underutilised (Myrdal 1968; Turnham 1971). This was especially threatening given the capital-intensive orientation of the early phases of manufacturing investment (Baer and Herve 1966; Morawetz 1974).

Thus the labour market challenge was viewed as formidable. Agriculture would have to continue to absorb more labour than most industrial economies a century earlier. Rates of non-agricultural sector

---

[1] Several factors – especially the availability of new technology – were favourable to rapid development in developing economies (Kuznets 1965).
[2] The share of agricultural employment was 75 per cent in developing countries in 1950 compared with a 56 per cent in the now industrial economies (including Eastern Europe) in 1880. The share was well below 50 per cent in most Western European countries in 1880 (Bairoch and Limbor 1968).

Table 2.1. *Population, GDP per capita and labour force growth in large countries, 1970–1993*

Country group	Population 1993	GDP per capita World Bank Atlas[a]	(US$) 1993 Purchasing power party	Labour force growth (% p.a.) 1970–80	1980–93	1993–2000[b]
Low income (excl. China and India)	1,016	300	n.d.	2.5	2.4	2.6
China	1,178	490	2,330	2.4	2.0	1.0
India	898	300	1,220	1.7	1.9	1.7
Pakistan	123	430	2,170	2.7	2.8	n.d.
Bangladesh	115	220	1,290	2.0	2.9	n.d.
Nigeria	105	300	1,900	3.1	2.7	2.9
Lower middle income	1,096	1,590	n.d.	n.d.	n.d.	n.d.
Indonesia[c]	187	740	3,150	2.1	2.3	n.d.
Philippines	65	850	2,670	2.4	2.5	2.4
Thailand	58	2,110	6,260	2.8	2.1	1.5
Upper middle income	501	4,370	n.d.	3.2	2.1	1.8
Brazil	156	2,930	5,370	3.4	2.2	2.1
Mexico	90	3,610	6,810	4.3	3.1	2.7
High income	812	23,090	24,740	2.3	1.0	0.8
USA	258	24,740	24,740	2.3	1.0	0.8
Japan	125	31,490	20,850	0.7	0.8	0.2
World	5,502	4,420	n.d.	n.d.	n.d.	n.d.

Notes: n.d. = no data.
[a] GDP converted at official exchange rates. [b] Projected. [c] Official Indonesia data estimate higher labour force growth rates (3.1 per cent per annum, 1971–90).
Source: World Bank, *World Development Report,* 1995 (Development Indicators), Oxford University Press, Washington.

growth would have to be higher than ever before to provide jobs for low-income workers and new work force entrants, let alone to raise labour productivity. Given the enormity of the problem, economists came up with the big push, or the achievement of a critical minimum effort, which used large labour surpluses for industrialisation to raise incomes and productivity.

None of the programmes based on these grand ideas fulfilled early expectations. But a significant number of developing countries made progress towards overcoming labour market challenges in less than half a century. In most developing economies, the growth of the non-agricultural employment sector was above that of the total labour force. The agricultural share of total employment declined markedly in response to shifts in the structure of GDP in favour of manufacturing and services. The story of how some countries achieved labour market transitions so rapidly, the problems they faced and why others were less successful, is one of the fascinating lessons of economic history in the post-war era.

The empirical record over 40 years

The international experience of development and labour market change provides a useful benchmark by which to judge Indonesia's achievements.

Unlike the Indonesian economy which stagnated until the late 1960s, economic growth was relatively buoyant in most developing economies in the early post-war period. Economic performance for 1950–80 was qualitatively different from the 1980s in many developing economies. In the former period, rapid economic growth in industrial countries supported development in the developing economies. Slower industrial country growth, in addition to special problems of adjustment and international indebtedness in the developing economies, constrained development in the 1980s. The different development experiences in the two periods was reflected in the change of employment, wages and labour productivity.

The 1950s to 1980

Per-capita output growth in the developing economies (excluding the two giants, China and India) was relatively stable at around 2 per cent during the 1950s and early 1960s. It rose close to 4 per cent and remained high through to the late 1970s before plummeting in the early to mid 1980s. For the entire period 1953–80 aggregate output rose by some 4 per cent and manufacturing output rose even faster (World Bank 1991: 15–18). Rapid agricultural growth, relatively favourable international markets, and sound macroeconomic policy in selected countries, all contributed to favourable economic performance.

Relatively rapid economic growth had a generally positive impact on labour demand in most developing economies during the period 1960–80. There were substantial shifts in employment out of agriculture, and labour productivity grew rapidly. Unemployment rates remained relatively stable despite high rates of urbanisation.

During the period 1960–80, growth of non-agricultural employment was well above that of the total labour force in most developing countries in contrast to the subsequent decade.[3] The agricultural share of total

---

[3] These data abstract from problems of international comparability of data (especially in the treatment of female and family workers). However, the orders of magnitude are generally invariant to the definition of labour force and employment (Kuznets 1982).

16 *Setting the scene*

employment declined markedly in response to shifts in the structure of GDP in favour of manufacturing and services (Gregory 1980).

Predictions that low-income service industries – the informal sector – would have to absorb the large bulk of surplus labour from agriculture were not confirmed by the general experience of developing economies. Although starting from a smaller base, industry employment creation (on average around 4 per cent growth per annum) was just as rapid as that of services in most developing economies. It was even more rapid than that in the services in several of the lowest income countries in the early post-war decades, although the base period share of manufacturing sector employment was very small (generally below 10 per cent).

Average labour productivity also rose substantially in developing economies. Squire (1981: 20) estimates that total value-added per worker rose by nearly 6 per cent per annum in the 1960s. This was compared with the earlier experience of closer to 3 per cent in industrial economies a century earlier.[4] Higher growth rates in productivity occurred not only in manufacturing but also in services and agriculture in developing economies.

Rates of urban unemployment rose to quite high levels in a range of countries, especially in Africa in the early post-war period (Frank 1968). This was mainly attributed to government wage and employment policies which encouraged rapid labour migration into urban areas (Harris and Todaro 1970; Weeks 1971). However, this experience of high and rising rates of urban unemployment was not general to developing economies in the 1960s. Despite high rates of growth in the labour force and urbanisation, unemployment rates showed no general tendency to rise or fall (Gregory 1980).

The 1980s

International circumstances changed dramatically as the world economy slowed in the 1980s. Many countries were forced to undertake drastic programmes of economic reform. While the world's most populous and largest developing economies, China and India, grew much faster than in previous decades, several countries in Latin America and Sub-Saharan Africa faced major problems of economic stagnation, internal and external balance and adjustment for much of the 1980s. Outside India and China, developing economy growth rates per capita fell back to 2 per cent or less, and many countries experienced negative growth rates. Under these

---

[4] Squire's data (table 6) are based on unweighted means for the period 1960–70 for developing economies (populations of 20 million or more) and for 1880–1900 in industrial economies.

conditions, labour market outcomes were much less favourable than in the previous two decades. Three patterns stand out from a comparison of faster and slower growing countries (table 2.2).

- There was a contrast between faster and slower growing countries in the 1980s.
- There was a marked slowdown in employment growth in industry among countries hit hard by the recession and forced to restructure in the 1980s. Whereas the manufacturing share of employment rose in all groups of countries in the period 1960–80, it hardly rose at all in the medium-growth group and actually declined in the slow-growth group in the 1980s. The percentage increase in the industry share was much greater in the more rapidly growing countries. Growth rates in manufacturing employment frequently exceeded 5 per cent per annum in these economies.[5]
- The relative role of services in employment growth was much greater in slower-growing economies in the 1980s.

Thus, the shift of labour out of agriculture continued at a rapid pace in the 1980s. However, the growth in industrial and manufacturing employment slowed, except in the minority of countries which made a successful transition to export-oriented industrialisation. The service sector bore the brunt of new job creation, despite substantial cutbacks in government sector employment in many countries (ILO 1992).

Labour productivity generally grew less rapidly in the 1980s, especially in countries where economic performance was poor (World Bank 1991a). Labour productivity almost doubled in manufacturing in faster-growing economies in the 1980s, compared with quite small increases in the slower-growing economies (table 2.3).

In the period 1960–80, the growth in industry value-added fuelled productivity growth, even in relatively slow-growing economies. It no longer played this role in the 1980s. Industrial growth fell below that of both agriculture and total GDP in the group of slow-growing economies (table 2.2). It barely exceeded growth in both sectors in the medium-level economic performers and average earnings growth was 3 per cent per annum in the more rapidly growing economies, compared with little increase in the medium group and negative growth in the poorly performing economies (table 2.3).[6]

---

[5] Increases in the industry share of employment were over 50 and 25 per cent in Brazil, Thailand, Korea and Egypt (1960–80), and Chile, Malaysia and South Korea in the 1980s, respectively.
[6] However, in only 13 out of 21 countries did trends in earnings move in the same direction as GDP (correlation coefficient of 0.56) or manufacturing value-added over the two decades.

Table 2.2. *GDP growth and changes in the distribution of employment by major sector: selected developing countries, 1960–1990*

GDP and employment Change/GDP growth group[a]	1960–80				1980–90			
	Agriculture	Industry	Services	Total	Agriculture	Industry	Services	Total
1 GDP growth (% p.a.)								
Country group: I High	3.6	9.2	8.4	7.3	3.6	7.1	6.7	6.3
II Medium	3.0	5.8	6.5	5.0	2.8	3.2	4.0	3.0
III Low	1.4	5.1	4.6	3.1	1.8	0.1	1.3	0.9
2 Share of employment in base year (%)								
Country group: I High	67	12	21	100	47	18	35	100
II Medium	61	14	10	100	43	21	36	100
III Low	76	10	14	100	34	24	42	100
3 Percentage change in employment share								
Country group: I High	–16	6	9	—	–9	4	5	—
II Medium	–15	3	6	—	–6	1	5	—
III Low	–9	3	6	—	–8	–3	8	—

Notes: Calculations for countries with a population of 5 million or more in 1990 and a plausible data on labour force distribution in 1960, 1980 and 1989–92 (for 1990, the data covered years 1989–92). [a]The growth rates of GDP and number of countries in each group are as follows: Group I (high GDP growth): 1960–80, >5.5% p.a.; 1980–90, >4.5% p.a. (7 countries). Group II (medium GDP growth): 1960–80, 3.5–5.5% p.a. (9 countries); 1980–90, 2–4.5% p.a. (5 countries). Group III (low GDP growth): 1960–80, <3.5% p.a. (8 countries); 1980–90, <2% p.a. (5 countries). Different countries are represented in each group for each period although several are in the high group for both (e.g. Pakistan, Indonesia, Thailand, Malaysia, Korea and Egypt).
Source: ILO, *Yearbook of Labour Statistics* various years, Geneva; World Bank, *World Development Report*, various years, Oxford University Press, Washington, DC; Horton, Kanbur and Mazumdar (1994a).

Table 2.3. *Labour market change in some slow and rapidly growing economies circa 1980–1992*

	Countries in which GDP growth was:		
	rapid (>4.5% p.a.)	medium (2.0–4.5% p.a.)	slow (<2% p.a.)
Number of countries	7	5	5
Mean rates of economic growth (p.a.)	6.3	3.0	0.9
Mean share of employment, 1990–2, % in			
Agriculture	38	37	29
Industry	22	22	21
Services	40	41	50
% change in share of employment (1980–90–92)[a]			
Agriculture	−21	−15	−18
Industry	25	8	−11
Services	19	15	16
Changes in manufacturing			
Earnings: % growth p.a. (1980–90/1)	3.0	0.7	−1.8
Labour productivity in 1990 (1980 = 100)	197	113	115
Mean rate of unemployment in the 1980s	5.5	5.9	7.6

Note: For all countries with a population of 5 million or above and a consistent series which at least covered the time period 1980–1989. [a]Relative change in share of employment (change in share 1980–90 divided by share in 1980, expressed in percentages).
Sources: ILO, *Yearbook of Labour Statistics*, various years, Geneva; World Bank, *World Development Report*, 1982, Oxford University Press, Washington, DC; Horton, Kanbur and Mazumdar (1994), various tables for selected countries and years.

Not unexpectedly, unemployment rose in many countries in the 1980s. In the highly indebted countries, unemployment rates oscillated and rose during episodes of structural adjustment. Rates also rose in most of Sub-Saharan Africa (ILO 1989, 1992).[7] Only the NIEs continued to register low open unemployment.

Contrasting patterns of economic development and labour market outcomes

Economic performance and labour market experience varied considerably across developing countries. It is useful to distinguish five patterns of

---

[7] Most countries in Sub-Saharan Africa registered substantial increases in unemployment during the 1980s: from 10–18 per cent on average from the mid 1970s to the mid 1980s (ILO 1992: 37). Structural adjustment and recession in the early 1980s had a negative impact on unemployment in debt-ridden Latin American economies, although employment improved in the late 1980s.

economic development and labour market change in developing economies. All have relevance to processes of economic growth experienced in Indonesia under Soeharto:

- export-oriented manufacturing development and labour market transformation under conditions of land scarcity (East Asian NIEs)
- more balanced agricultural and industrial development in environments of relative land surplus (parts of Southeast Asia)
- slow economic growth and delayed labour market transition in poor, densely populated rural economies (South Asia)
- import substitution manufacturing development associated with high levels of government intervention and considerable labour market segmentation (mainly in Latin America)
- economic growth and adjustment associated with natural resource booms and busts (oil exporters)

All have relevance to understanding the Indonesia case, especially given big changes in economic policy and performance since 1965, and considerable regional diversity in economic structure and performance.

Rapid economic growth, export orientation and labour market transformation: the NIEs

The NIEs of East Asia achieved the highest sustained economic growth rates among groups of developing countries in the post-war period.[8] This was achieved principally through a successful move to export manufactures in the late 1950s and early 1960s. It was supported by programmes of economic reform and maintenance of macroeconomic stability. Bearing in mind the relative land and resource scarcity in these countries and their vulnerable geo-political circumstances, penetration of international markets was pursued with a singlemindedness unique in the developing world (Abegglen 1994).

No less remarkable has been the transformation of labour markets in these countries, despite high labour force growth rates until very recently.[9] There was a rapid decline in the share of employment in agriculture in Taiwan and South Korea, and in low productivity service occupations in Hong Kong and Singapore. All countries recorded substantial productivity and real wage growth, and absorption of unemployed and underemployed labour into productive employment (Galenson 1992; Manning and Pang 1990).

[8] Riedel (1988), James, Naya and Meier (1989) and World Bank (1993).
[9] Labour force growth declined from over 2 per cent in the 1960s to 1.0–1.5 per cent in the 1990s; in Singapore it fell to below 1 per cent by the 1990s.

Table 2.4. *GDP, employment and wage growth, selected East Asian countries, 1965–1990*

	Taiwan	South Korea	Malaysia	Thailand	Philippines	Indonesia
1 GDP						
Per capita 1990 ($)	6,554	5,400	2,320	1,420	730	570
Growth 1965–90 (% p.a.)	9.3	9.8	6.3	7.5	3.7	6.2
2 Labour force growth 1965–91	3.3	2.8	3.2	2.7	2.5	2.7[2]
Sectoral share 1990 (%)[1]						
Agriculture	13	18	32	64	45	50
Industry	41	35	23	12	15	17
(Manufacturing)	n.d.	(26)	(16)	(9)	(10)	(12)
Services	46	47	45	24	40	33
	100	100	100	100	100	100
% Change in share 1965–87/90[1]						
Agriculture	−34	−37	−26	−18	−13	−23[2]
Industry	19	20	10	7	−1	9[2]
Services	15	17	16	11	14	14[2]
Growth in real earnings per worker in manufacturing (% p.a.)						
1970–80	6.2	8.4	1.8	1.9	−4.1	3.5[4]
1980–88/90	6.3	5.3	3.6	6.5	0.6[3]	5.6
1970–90	6.2	6.9	2.6	3.8	—	4.9[5]

Notes: [1] 1987 for Malaysia and Thailand. [2] 1961–90. [3] Real wages 1981–87 (from ILO, *Yearbook of Labour Statistics*). [4] 1975–80. [5] 1975–88.
Sources: [1] Except for Taiwan, GDP data from the World Bank, *Development Report*, 1992, Oxford University Press, Washington. Labour force growth rates for all countries except Indonesia from Galenson (1992), table 2.2.; [2] Employment distribution from ILO, *Yearbook of Labour Statistics* (for 1965, cited in Galenson (1992), table 2.4; for 1990 ILO, *Yearbook of Labour Statistics*, 1992); [3] Except for Indonesia and Taiwan, real earnings data in manufacturing from World Bank, *World Tables, 1989/90, 1991/92*; [4] Taiwan data from Taiwan, *Statistical Data Bank* and ILO, *Yearbook of Labour Statistics*, various years, cited in Galenson (1992, tables 2.2, 2.4 and 4.2), 1990. Employment data for Taiwan from US Department of Labour, *Foreign Labour Trends: Taiwan, 1990–91*; [5] For Indonesia, labour force and employment data from 1961 and 1990 Population Censuses; earnings data from *Annual Surveys of Large and Medium Establishments in Manufacturing*, 1975, 1980 and 1988).

Unique to the NIEs has been the extraordinarily rapid growth of manufacturing job creation (table 2.4). Rising labour productivity and wages in agriculture facilitated the process. Substantial growth in real wages accompanied labour market transformation. On average, real wage growth was over 6 per cent per annum in manufacturing in South Korea and Taiwan over the period 1965–88. Similarly rapid real wage growth was recorded

22 *Setting the scene*

in the island states of Singapore and Hong Kong in the 1970s and 1980s (ILO 1989: 25).

In all of the NIEs, unemployment declined from rates of around 5–10 per cent in the 1960s to 2–5 per cent by the late 1960s and early 1970s.[10] These low rates of unemployment were sustained, with minor variations, for two decades. Similar declines were recorded in rural underemployment in both South Korea and Taiwan (Kuo 1983; Kim 1986).

Labour-intensive growth

Favourable labour market outcomes were supported by policies which encouraged employment growth in labour-intensive sectors – principally small-scale, peasant agriculture and manufactured exports. Rapid increases in industrial employment were sustained in the NIEs by structural adjustment programmes undertaken in the 1960s. These paved the way for relatively labour-intensive manufacturing export growth.[11] Market-oriented reforms played an important part in the success of manufacturing exports. But government support policies were also of considerable significance, especially in the promotion of labour-intensive exports (Oshima 1988; Amsden 1991).

Emphasis has been placed on the role of manufacturing exports in employment creation in the NIEs. However, agricultural modernisation played a central role, especially in the early stages of development. This included increased productivity, and subsequent agricultural diversification – mainly into labour-intensive vegetable, fruit and livestock activities – in South Korea and Taiwan (Oshima 1988: chapters 2 and 3).[12]

Growth in higher value-added agriculture provided additional employment opportunities in food-processing industries (Kuo 1977: table 4). Increased farmer incomes in turn created a demand for non-farm goods and stimulated non-agricultural employment growth (Ho 1982). Finally, there was an increased demand for farm equipment, especially as labour shortages began to emerge in agriculture. In contrast to many other developing countries (including Indonesia) land reform after World War II was a key element. It encouraged agricultural modernisation, greater labour

[10] See papers in the 1976 edition of the *Philippines Economic Journal*. Middle-income Asian countries had the lowest unemployment rates (3.4 per cent) among groups of developing countries in 1980 (ILO 1987c: table 1.3).
[11] Kuo (1977: table 19) estimates that total employment due to manufacturing exports rose from 2–11 per cent of all employment in Taiwan in the period 1961–71, continued to rise in the 1970s.
[12] Increased productivity also occurred in the predominnntly smallholder rubber industry in Malaysia and Thailand (Barlow and Jayasuriya 1987).

utilisation and demand for labour-intensive, non-agricultural goods in both South Korea and Taiwan.

Human capital investment
The availability of a literate and increasingly educated work force has been identified as a major factor in the NIE success story. Early investments in primary schooling (stretching back to Japanese colonisation in South Korea and Taiwan) and increasingly in secondary and tertiary education, were key factors in the remarkable economic transition (Birdsall and Sabot 1993). With the exception of Hong Kong, enrolment rates have been consistently higher than might be expected from the level of GDP in these countries. The share of education in total expenditure was also higher than in most other developing countries in the 1970s and 1980s (Williamson 1993).

Declining young age dependency ratios – the percentage of young people supported by prime-age workers – enabled the NIEs to achieve high secondary and tertiary enrolment rates, and improvements in the quality of schooling by the 1970s. Economic growth additionally enabled rising shares of education in total government expenditure (especially in Taiwan) to be translated into substantial increases in the absolute value of educational expenditures.

Labour market institutions and policies
Institutional arrangements and labour market policies contributed to rapid labour market transition and improved living standards in the NIEs. It has been suggested that the absence both of direct government intervention in labour markets and effective trade union action were important for the labour market success. Fields and Wan (1989) argue that the absence of pressures to raise real wage rates above the supply price of labour helps explain the better employment experience of the NIEs when contrasted to several Latin American and Caribbean countries. The argument is compelling, although the negative impact of labour market intervention can be overstated (Freeman 1992a). In general, removal of distortions in product and capital markets were of far greater significance for better labour market outcomes in the NIEs than deregulated labour markets (Krueger 1981; Horton, Kanbur and Mazumdar 1994a).

NIE governments (with the exception of Singapore) avoided direct intervention in wage-setting mechanisms and generally undermined the potential influence of unions in political and economic affairs.[13] There were

---

[13] Intervention was aimed at maintaining high rates of investment and controlling wages in Singapore (Pang Eng Fong 1988b).

also attempts by governments to slow the rate of growth in wages through national guidelines and pressures on business, although such policies were not followed in all of the NIEs or pursued with vigour over long periods (Freeman 1992b).[14]

The absence of both labour market controls and constraints on flexible labour management at a national and enterprise level contributed to investment, economic and employment growth. An abundant supply of cheap, easily mobilised and relatively well-educated workers was a valuable source of comparative advantage in early years of rapid export-oriented growth.

Flexible labour markets also supported adjustment to international shocks. Labour markets adjusted quickly, and significant increases in unemployment were averted during the critical years of structural adjustment to oil price rises in the 1970s (Mazumdar 1993; World Bank 1993: chapter 3). These reforms, coupled with the absence of indexation and union-induced wage growth meant that international competitiveness was maintained through productivity increases which exceeded wage growth (Fields 1994).

Some writers have emphasised that the East Asian NIE economic success was achieved through exploitation and repression of unskilled labour (Deyo, Haggard and Koo 1987; Deyo 1989). According to this view, wage incomes and costs were kept below what they might have been if there had been greater direct government and trade union support for wage workers. Others have stressed the inequitable effects of relatively unfettered and flexible labour markets, particularly exploitation of low-wage workers by foreign investors and multinationals.

Market-determined labour conditions were harsh and job security was low for a large proportion of wage workers, compared with conditions in advanced economies. This was especially true in the early years of reform in the 1960s, and among certain groups of vulnerable wage workers. In addition to low wages and long hours of work, workers suffered a range of other problems: high rates of labour turnover, poor working conditions (threatening safety and health), lack of social security (except in Singapore) and frequent abuse of individual rights, especially in the case of labour activists.[15] Restrictions imposed on trade unions were an integral element of tight political controls (Lim 1978).

Young female workers, referred to by Deyo (1989) as the 'hyperproletariat', frequently bore the brunt of unstable jobs and abuse from employ-

---

[14] There were no direct government attempts to restrain wage outcomes in Taiwan and Hong-Kong, in contrast to South Korea and Singapore (Freeman 1992b).
[15] See Ogle (1990) for an account of abuse of individual and collective labour rights in South Korea.

ers (Lim 1993). It is noteworthy that large gender-based wage differentials in favour of males have been a feature of industrial labour markets in both South Korea and Taiwan (Gannicot 1987; Bauer and Shin 1986). These differentials remained, even if account is taken of the influence of different personal and employment characteristics between the sexes.

Two points should be emphasised regarding labour standards in the NIEs. First, low wages, long hours of work and low investment in worker health and safety were part of the development problem in all sectors of the economy in the early stage of development. All of the countries were very poor, with per-capita incomes of well below US$500 (1990 prices) in the 1950s (World Bank 1993). Low wages were more visible in the export-oriented industries and larger establishments. But they were at least on a par, and frequently better, in larger and foreign-owned firms than in domestic firms (Edgren 1984; Addison and Demery 1988).

Second, it is important to distinguish between wages, labour conditions and labour rights. While wages improved substantially in the 1970s and early 1980s, labour rights remained tightly controlled, as NIE governments sought to maintain centralised control over economic and political processes. In South Korea and Taiwan, progress was only made in the areas of trade union freedoms, worker rights and protection when severe labour shortages began to emerge in the labour market around the mid 1980s. At this juncture, demands for wide-ranging political reforms, including those involving labour protection and freedoms, could no longer be ignored (Pang Eng Fong 1988a; Park 1991; Freeman 1992b).

Economic growth, labour markets and welfare
Rapid economic growth and labour market transition were associated with substantial improvement in incomes, rapid poverty decline and relatively favourable patterns of income distribution in the NIEs (World Bank 1993: 4, 31). Three features of labour market change had a favourable effect on income distribution.

- The rapid growth of labour-intensive industries meant that the benefits of growth extended to large numbers of workers through inter-sectoral and intra-sectoral shifts in employment, rather than to a relatively small number of high-wage protected workers in modern sector jobs.
- The supply of educated manpower broadly kept pace with labour demand. These countries avoided substantial inequalities arising from excess demand for higher level professional and technical manpower (World Bank 1993).

- The absence of labour market policies which protected only a small proportion of modern sector workers.

Balanced development in land-surplus and labour-scarce economies (much of Southeast Asia)[16]

The ASEAN economies of Southeast Asia (outside Singapore) share much in common with the NIEs in terms of rapid economic change and transformation of labour markets, but there are important differences – less rapid economic growth, the more important role of agriculture in economic growth and exports and associated relative land abundance and labour scarcity during the early decades of development.

Hla Myint (1968) drew attention to relative land abundance and labour scarcity as an important distinguishing feature of most Southeast Asian rural labour markets in the early post-war period. In much of the region (Java and Luzon were notable exceptions) the labour supply of peasant farmers was relatively inelastic for the industrial sector and other forms of unskilled wage employment.[17] Unlike in much of East and South Asia, there was not a readily mobilisable source of underemployed labour on minuscule farms in much of Southeast Asia. Rather, farmers had for decades been engaged in successful export industries in both industrial and food crops – especially rubber and rice. Population growth had been accommodated by extending the land frontier. As the land frontier was taken up, intensification and diversification of production were a major source of income growth in the following decades (Barlow and Jayasuriya 1987).

Macroeconomic policy in turn was adapted to these different relative factor endowments. Early in the post-war years governments perceived a less urgent need to encourage manufacturing exports through economic reforms – a strategy which had been adopted earlier in the NIEs. Manufacturing exports did not begin to increase rapidly until the 1970s and 1980s when new policies were required to deal with emerging problems of employment and excess labour supply, and with rising demand for imports of raw materials and capital goods (Oshima 1976; Ariff and Hill 1985). However, while protected domestic industries developed (most extensively in the Philippines), import substitution in manufacturing only began in the post-war period. It was generally never as extensive as in the major Latin American countries (James, Naya and Meier 1989).

---

[16] Mainly Thailand and Malaysia, early development in the Philippines, and the islands of Sumatra and Kalimantan in Indonesia.
[17] During the colonial period, immigrants from China and India were brought in to work on the estates and in the tin mines of Malaysia and Indonesia.

Factor endowments provided a different context from which to view labour market changes in capitalist Southeast Asia compared with the NIEs. Three main differences are important.

- The labour shift from agriculture was much slower than in the NIEs (table 2.4). Employment in agriculture continued to rise absolutely in the 1980s, and the employment share in agriculture in Thailand, Indonesia and the Philippines was double that in South Korea and Taiwan in 1990.[18] Nevertheless, labour productivity continued to rise in this sector, especially in Malaysia (James, Naya and Meier 1989: 146).
- The manufacturing share of employment rose less quickly in the Southeast Asian countries. Despite sustained employment growth in the 1980s, the manufacturing share of total employment in 1990 was only about half of that in services in Malaysia, Thailand and Indonesia (and one-third of that in services in the Philippines) in 1990. In contrast, the percentage of total employment was almost the same in these two sectors in all of the NIEs to the mid 1980s, when service sector employment began to grow more rapidly.
- Growth in average earnings in manufacturing appears to have been almost as rapid in the Southeast Asian economies as in the NIEs (table 2.4). However, the growth in wage rates was not sustained in all sectors of the economy in any of the Southeast Asian economies during the 1970s and 1980s (Lim 1988; Pitayanon 1988). In contrast to the NIEs from the early 1970s, labour supply curves were relatively elastic in the Southeast Asian economies into the 1980s (Manning and Pang 1990).

Despite these differences with the NIEs, rapid economic growth rates were generally associated with impressive labour market outcomes in the rapidly growing Southeast Asian countries. Employment, productivity and labour incomes rose quickly. Unemployment rates remained relatively stable, although they fluctuated according to changes in economic circumstances. Macroeconomic management generally supported economic growth through cautious fiscal and monetary policy and quick response to economic crises.

Labour markets generally exhibited a similar level of flexibility to those in the NIEs. Private firms were given considerable freedom to hire and fire workers and to set wages according to market conditions. Even though

---

[18] The shift out of agriculture would have been even faster in Malaysia without large numbers of Indonesian immigrants in the estate sector.

minimum wages were introduced in several countries – in the Philippines in the 1950s, and Thailand and Indonesia in the 1970s – there was little attempt or capacity to implement them widely.

Slow economic growth in densely populated regions (especially in South Asia)

The experience of substantial changes in labour market structure in the East Asian economies contrasts with that of South Asia which experienced much slower economic growth. Except for Pakistan, growth rarely rose above 5 per cent per annum in any period from the 1960s compared with rates consistently well above 5 per cent in East Asia. Shifts in employment in South Asia were small and real wages generally stagnated. In part, the problem has been attributed to large, relatively low productivity in agricultural sectors, and associated low levels of income and human capital. It has been related to substantial government regulation of the economy which stifled private sector activity and kept savings and investment rates low (James, Naya and Meier 1989; Bhagwati 1993).[19]

More than any other region of the developing world, South Asia best fits the spirit of the Lewis model of surplus labour (Lewis 1954). Low levels of agricultural productivity and minuscule farms, coupled with a large, poor wage labouring class attached to agriculture, suggests a highly elastic supply of labour to the modern sector (Booth and Sundrum 1985; Bardhan 1984). There was extensive low-income off-farm employment and a visible informal sector in many South Asian cities. Absolutely low wage rates and long queues for any regular jobs were further evidence of a large residue of surplus labour. There is ample evidence of substantial numbers of persons available for work at going wage rates in the modern sector in many parts of South Asia.[20] The above conditions fit very well with conditions in rural Java when the Soeharto government came to power in 1965.

Four aspects of labour market operations and policy in various regions of India are of relevance to a study of Indonesia.

- The operation of rural labour markets was much more complex than suggested in the initial Lewis framework. They did not always adjust smoothly in accordance with competitive neo-classical processes through the operation of flexible wages and employment. Nevertheless, agricultural labour markets were much more respon-

---

[19] No presumption is made here to represent the voluminous literature on South Asian, and especially Indian, development, or the diversity of country and regional experience.
[20] The nature of this excess supply remains a matter of controversy.

sive to economic change than was implied by the labour surplus model. Wages responded to short-term fluctuations and regional variations in labour demand.[21]
- Response to labour demand and supply does not preclude the existence of wage differentials and unemployed and underemployed manpower – especially in periods of slack labour demand. Wage rates frequently did not adjust to absorb all unemployed and underemployed labour. The process of wage determination even within villages was often partly determined by social considerations rather than market forces.[22]
- Based on research in India, Bardhan (1984: 61–2) has suggested several factors which helped produce wage outcomes at variance with the competitive model. These included the monopsonistic power of landowners, tied labour and implicit contracts associated with landowner dependence on a ready supply of casual labour. Job segregation by caste remained one extreme form of discrimination in many parts of India (Banerjee and Knight 1991). Between villages, wage differentials persisted because of nominal wage rigidity, moral limits to the village economy and discrimination in employment against outsiders and migrant workers (see Bardhan and Rudra 1981; Bardhan 1984; Dreze and Mukerjee 1989).
- Labour market flexibility was adversely affected by the protection of workers in the public sector and in large private enterprises. This was the result of labour legislation and an active, relatively free trade-union movement. Like Indonesia, India had a large public enterprise sector, and employment was protected by complicated industrial relations legislation, which also applied to larger private establishments (Papola 1992: 39–40).

Protection and labour market intervention (especially in Latin America)

Given the relatively high levels of industrial protection which prevailed in Indonesia, the import substitution policies of some Latin American countries and their labour market effects are of some relevance. In the 1960s, protection of manufacturing was seriously considered by many countries as a viable pattern of industrialisation. The case for protection appeared persuasive in a world economy dominated by manufacturing exports from

---

[21] See especially Binswanger and Rosenzweig (1984); Bardhan (1984: chapter 3); Dréze and Mukerjee (1989) and Mazumdar (1989).
[22] The initial Lewis model was framed to explain transfers from peasant households to industry. It has also been applied to similar movements of farm wage labourers.

industrial economies, and given the declining terms of trade of some key primary exports.

The East Asian NIEs discarded this model earliest and stuck to export orientation doggedly, despite temporary set-backs (Riedel 1988).[23] In many other developing countries, industrial development was promoted through protection for a much longer period. However, the labour market effects of inward-looking industrialisation policies never matched the success of the East Asian NIEs, although there were short-term gains in some cases.

The impact of protected industrialisation on labour markets is exemplified in the early development experience of many countries in Latin America. High levels of protection were much more entrenched and widespread by 1960, prior to short episodes of liberalisation and a push towards export orientation in several countries in the 1960s and 1970s – in Brazil, Colombia and Chile in particular (Harberger 1988). Protection re-emerged in response to economic instability, partly induced by declines in output associated with the oil booms during the 1970s and inadequate policy responses to maintain internal and external balance (Lin 1988).

Modern and industrial sector employment growth was disappointing in many Latin American countries (Tokman 1984; ILO 1989). Employment growth was sometimes favourable, and real wage growth was substantial in several cases in the early years of protected development.[24] The rate of job growth in manufacturing slowed after the initial stimulus, however, and the contribution of industrial growth to labour market transformation was disappointing.

Many countries grappled with problems of macroeconomic balance and economic slowdown, but there was a major reversal of fortunes in the 1980s. High unemployment rates, rapid informal sector growth and wage stagnation plagued most of the relatively urbanised Latin American countries. ILO (1989: 31) data suggest that average real wages fell by over an average of 10 per cent in 17 Latin American countries in the 1980s, although a reversal of downward real wage trends occurred in Brazil and several other countries as a result of improved economic performance towards the end of the decade.[25] As in many African countries, public sector wages were particularly hard hit by economic reform packages.

Urban unemployment rates rose to high levels in most countries in Latin

---

[23] The NIEs did not discard protection entirely; the main thrust of economic policy was to ensure that labour-intensive manufacturing products were competitive in international markets.

[24] Economic reform supported employment growth in some cases, as during the 'miracle' period of economic growth in Brazil in the 1960s and 1970s (Morley 1982).

[25] Data cited in ILO (1989: 31).

America during the 1980s (ILO 1989: 28–30, 1992: 43–5). Although they peaked and declined in several countries which began economic restructuring programmes earlier – Chile, Uruguay, Colombia and Venezuela – they remained stubbornly high into the 1980s (World Bank 1995c). As attention has begun to focus on vulnerable groups – self-employed, casual, female and older workers in particular – research has challenged the notion that urban unemployment is a luxury and a rational choice on the part of rural–urban migrants and the more educated (Rodgers 1989; Berry 1975; Sabot 1977).

Three important features underlie the model of protected industrialisation experienced by many Latin American countries.

Policy. Problems of labour market adjustment were partly related to macroeconomic management and the capacity of governments to manage aggregate demand during periods of economic decline, such as occurred during the oil booms of the 1970s. Lin (1988: 184–90) argues that the failure of several Latin American oil-importing countries to cut demand and hold down costs was the main factor contributing to a return to high inflation and external imbalance during this period – in contrast to quicker responses and better economic management in the NIEs.[26]

Structure. In contrast to the rapid transfer of labour into wage employment in the NIEs, economic dualism appears to have been more entrenched during the period of import substitution in many Latin American cities. A small proportion of industrial workers earned high wages because of policies which favoured modern sector enterprises (Webb 1977).[27] A secondary labour market characterised by informal, casual and covert employment relationships played a role in labour absorption. The informal sector grew and was sustained in spite of economic decline. It included small-scale businesses unable to flourish because of regulations, as well as surplus labour displaced from (or unable to get into) the modern sector (De Soto 1989; Portes and Schauffler 1993). This occurred even during the years of relatively rapid economic growth during the 1960s and 1970s, and continued during the crisis years of the 1980s (Tokman 1984, Portes and Benton 1984; Horton, Kanbur and Mazumdar 1994b: 18).

---

[26] A study of labour market response in Asia and Latin America in the 1980s concluded that 'Most of the countries do show cyclical or trend increases in unemployment related to periods of recession and stabilisation' (Horton, Kanbur and Mazumdar 1994b: 14).

[27] Webb (1977: 246) argues that wages have often risen in large establishments in spite of repressive or neutral wage policies.

32 *Setting the scene*

Institutions. Both government and union intervention in labour markets were much more widespread in Latin America in the early post-war period than elsewhere in the developing world. The effects of these influences on economic efficiency and structure varied between countries: either through the impact of minimum wages, wage indexation and social security schemes, or as a result of strong unions. Although their impact has often been overstated (based on extreme cases such as Argentina), the effect of these institutions was two-fold. First, they tended to protect wages and working conditions of employees in the modern sector, and contributed to large wage differentials with unprotected sectors. Second, labour markets responded less quickly to shifts in labour demand and economic adjustment – both booms and busts.[28]

Resource booms, busts and the 'Dutch' disease

A final variant of labour market experience of relevance to Indonesia relates to the impact of resource booms in natural resource-abundant countries. The most far-reaching and widely discussed effects of such a boom were the outcomes of oil price rises managed by the OPEC cartel in the 1970s – in which Indonesia was an active participant (Corden 1984; Neary and van Wijnberg 1986; Gelb 1988).

There were two key features of the adjustment to the boom. The first was the shift in demand and relative prices in favour of non-tradable goods (the 'Dutch' disease). Depending on exchange rate policies and domestic demand management, this adversely affected both agricultural and manufacturing exports, both of which tend to be labour intensive. It occurred through the private and public spending effects of the boom.

Initial rises in public and private sector incomes during the oil boom provided a boost to consumption and investment. However, the price rise was temporary as oil prices began to slip back to their initial relative price levels from the early 1980s. The shift of resources out of labour intensive and agricultural exports created problems for labour absorption in the aftermath of the boom. Although some countries attempted to redress the problem through exchange rate depreciation, all the countries examined by Gelb experienced transition problems which had a negative effect on labour markets.[29]

The second important set of influences on the labour market largely depended on the government budgetary response, and on economic poli-

---

[28] Real wages did decline in most countries in the 1980s, despite minimum wages and indexation (World Bank 1995b).
[29] In four of the six countries (but not Indonesia) economic growth rates were negative after oil prices began to fall (1982–4) (Gelb *et al.* 1988: 126).

cies associated with the windfall gains.[30] As in other natural resource booms, the major beneficiary was the government through higher taxation receipts. In extreme cases such as Nigeria, the effects of government budgetary and macroeconomic policies were disastrous. Concentration of spending in urban areas raised real wage rates and drew labour out of agriculture. This caused a rapid rise in food prices and severe problems of inflation. Later, unemployment rose and real wages declined when the windfall effects of the boom dissipated (Pinto 1987).

Given supply constraints, a big challenge was to sterilise the effects of the boom (Corden and Warr 1981). But this was not easily achieved. Large capital-intensive projects, often aided by international loans, were rarely profitable. Many were poorly planned, lacked skilled manpower and saddled the countries with problems of repayment (Gelb et al. 1988). Some, including Indonesia, fared much better than most of the OPEC members because of more selective and decentralised expenditure on agriculture and rural public works.

One important lesson from the experience of the oil booms was that the impact on the economy and labour market depended critically on initial labour market conditions, for both unskilled and skilled labour (Garnaut 1977). Under conditions of relatively elastic, unskilled labour supply (the Lewis model), the spending effects of the boom translated into gains in employment. The effect on the prices of non-tradable goods was smaller, there was less real appreciation of the exchange rate and traditional exports fared better.

In the case of inelastic supplies of unskilled labour, however, wage rates and domestic prices of non-tradables rose steeply. The adverse impact on non-booming tradable sectors was greater. This was the case in Nigeria where food production fell partly in response to labour shortages.

Inelastic supplies of skilled manpower were more general among less-developed, oil-exporting economies. The response of prices during the boom depended on the extent to which skilled manpower could be imported to mann new projects. The effects of skill shortages affected income distribution particularly in the countries promoting capital- (and skill-) intensive investment most strongly.

A framework for analysing labour market transformation

Given the diversity of labour market experience discussed above, what framework might best characterise the interaction between economic growth

---

[30] The direct effects were typically small because of the capital-intensive nature of oil production.

and labour markets in Indonesia? One model of labour market change in poor, heavily populated economies of Asia is the celebrated Lewis–Fei–Ranis model of a labour surplus economy (Lewis 1954; Fei and Ranis 1964). This model hypothesises that labour supply to the modern sector is close to infinitely elastic prior to the achievement of a turning point. At this point the pool of low productivity workers becomes scarce in the traditional sector. Shortages of unskilled labour supply force real wages to rise swiftly.

There has been justified criticism of the original Lewis model, especially regarding the extent of disguised unemployment in traditional agriculture.[31] Nevertheless, several scholars have identified a specific period in economic development in East Asian developing economies when real wage growth accelerated and wage differentials narrowed in response to sustained economic growth (Minami 1973; Bai 1985). Labour market transformation according to the turning point theory is a discrete rather than continuous process, although it may be intertwined with stochastic shorter-term changes and longer-term rising, or falling, wage trends.

Indonesia is an apt case for the study of labour market transition. Rapid economic growth was sustained, beginning from a very low starting point according to most labour market indicators in the mid 1960s. For much of that period, there has been relatively little direct government intervention in wage-setting processes in the private sector. If the Lewis model ever applied to any Asian region, it might be expected to be relevant to Indonesia when Soeharto came to power in 1966.

Given the patterns of employment and wage change associated with development, how might one best conceptualise Lewis-type processes in a country like Indonesia. We start with the assumption of segmented or, more crudely, dualistic labour markets in the early stages of development.[32] These are related to sharp discontinuities in technology, as imported machinery is superimposed on a large traditional sector. In the labour market, the key characteristic is a substantial wage gap between modern and traditional sectors, and relatively elastic labour supply to the modern sector.

According to Lewis, wage differentials arise because labour is not paid according to marginal products in the traditional sector, either because of income-sharing arrangements (average product pricing of labour) or institutionally determined minimum wages. In the context of Indonesia

---

[31] The main criticisms challenged the idea that surplus labour could be withdrawn without any impact on production. See especially Schultz (1964), Eicher and Witt (1964), Sen (1966) and Hansen (1969).

[32] This is of course an oversimplification, as there is a range of technology in most industries (Little, Page and Mazumdar 1987).

and other East Asian countries, however, elastic labour supply to the modern sector can be explained by mechanisms which determine wages in the modern sector. This shifts the emphasis away from special wage-setting institutions in the traditional sector(s) to a more careful examination of how they are determined in the modern sector.

Thus, disguised unemployment or underemployment and wage-sharing mechanisms are not necessary for a highly elastic labour supply to the modern sector. The productivity gap between traditional and modern sectors – related to technology and the institutional context in which modern firms operate – contributes to the earnings gap and elastic labour supply. The process of wage determination in the modern sector is thus critical to the wage gap.

Wage determination in the modern sector(s)

According to this modified labour surplus model, higher than average market-clearing wages are related to higher (marginal) labour productivity in the modern sector. The latter is in turn associated with the characteristics of the enterprise and the market framework in which it operates. One important factor is the capital-intensive nature of technology, which leads to higher wages. These are based primarily on efficiency – wage considerations (see Akerlof and Yellen 1986). Modern sector firms pay workers above market-clearing rates in order to maintain high levels of productivity in the management of more expensive capital equipment. The objective is to encourage greater commitment, reliability and application among workers. In some countries, these firms have preferred to employ more stable, married workers whose reservation wage was above those of temporary and circular migrants (Mazumdar 1989).

Other factors can also play a role in supporting higher wages in the modern sector: foreign capital and management practices; excess profits (related to capital or product market imperfections; or other special forms of government protection) and government or trade union intervention in setting minimum wages and providing labour protection.[33]

Three points are important for later discussion of the Indonesian case. First, where large capital-intensive establishments are afforded special protection in product or capital markets, efficiency-wage explanations are not necessary to explain higher modern sector wages. High wages may merely represent redistribution of some of the extra-normal profits to

---

[33] In the case of Korea, Park (1980) argues that monopolistic product markets and imperfect capital markets contributed to high wages in large firms.

workers. Equity considerations are likely to be particularly prevalent in developing economies where the gap in wages between higher- and lower-level personnel is large.[34]

Second, the characteristics of enterprises, and the markets in which they operate, provide a persuasive explanation for high modern sector wages in developing economies, regardless of government wages policy, which was central to the Harris–Todaro model (see Harris and Todaro 1970; Todaro 1976). Finally, these differences in wages can be attributed to the different human capital characteristics of workers. High wages are frequently associated with a specific set of characteristics of workers in modern sector firms, in particular recruitment of more educated workers.[35]

Wage determination in traditional sector(s)

In the early stages of development, traditional sector wages are more likely to be responsive to shifts in both labour demand and labour supply (figure 2.1). This is unlike in the modern sector, where structure and shifts in labour demand largely determine equilibrium employment and wages.

Labour supply is likely to be less elastic to employers in the traditional sector, who may offer wages substantially below those in the modern sector. It is assumed, however, that there is a floor below which wages will not fall, depending on prevailing notions of wage justice.[36] In the bottom half of figure 2.1, this is denoted by WS ($= W_t^1$). Point W_t^1 in the traditional sector represents a socially determined minimum wage which sets a floor to wage rates, even in the presence of excess labour supply in the traditional sector. In practice, wages may fall below this level for self-employed workers unable to gain entry into wage jobs, especially in periods of slack labour demand in agriculture.[37]

It is assumed that traditional sector wages for similar kinds of work are likely to be more uniform than those in the modern sector. There may be significant variations between villages (depending on the extent of 'moral limits' to village labour markets), regions and seasons, depending on an individual's relationship to the employer (kin, neighbour, villager

---

[34] Establishments which receive government support are likely to be under greater pressure to pay high wages.
[35] The above discussion relates primarily to the private sector. A slightly different mix of factors mean that labour supply is also elastic to the public sector (lack of competition from outsiders, guaranteed employment and fringe benefits).
[36] Returns to more flexible, self-employed work may be lower than this floor. See Booth and Sundrum (1985) for a discussion of wage justice in Asian agriculture.
[37] For example, in low productivity home industries, or the Z-goods sector (Hymer and Resnick 1969).

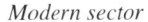

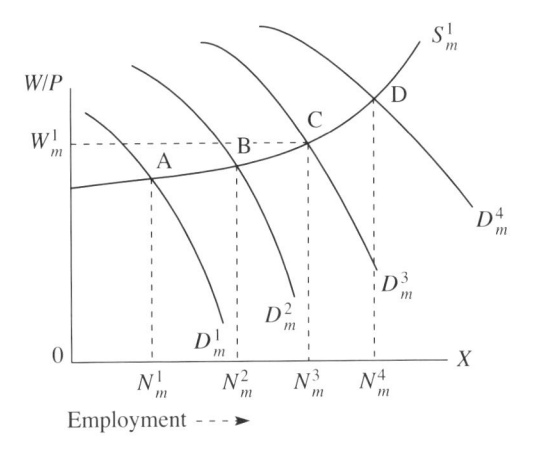

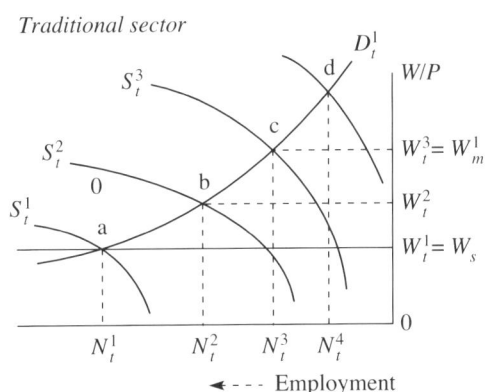

Figure 2.1 The dynamics of labour market transformation in a labour surplus economy

or outsider). Large, modern and traditional sector wage differentials can become institutionalised, as in the case of Japan, and persist for long periods even though wages have begun to rise in traditional sectors.

The turning point

The transition from a labour surplus to a labour scarcity situation has been termed the turning point.[38] Although not used here as an analytical tool for

---

[38] Fei and Ranis (1964) and Minami (1973). In practice, the timing of the turning point depends on a variety of factors: the rate and structure of economic labour market integration, institutions and the import of labour or export of capital.

empirical analysis, it is a useful concept for understanding labour market dynamics in densely populated agrarian societies like Indonesia. The turning point can be broadly defined as the period in development when unskilled wages rise on a sustained basis in real terms, in both modern and traditional sectors, in response to increased labour shortages in the traditional sector.

Indicators that a country has achieved the turning point are an absolute decline in the proportion of people engaged in agriculture, a fall in wage differentials between sectors, types of firm (large/small, foreign/domestic, etc.), unskilled and skilled labour, and equality between marginal product and wage rates in traditional sectors (Minami 1973).

In figure 2.1, the move towards the turning point is represented by a contraction in labour supply to the traditional sector from S_T^1 to S_T^2 and S_T^3, and an increase in traditional sector wages from W_T^1 to W_T^2 and W_T^3, as labour moves into the expanding modern sector (depicted by the outward movement of DM in the upper part of figure 2.1. At wage level W_T^3 in the traditional sector wages are equal to W_M^1 in the modern sector, thus signalling the disappearance of the wage gap between sectors (after accounting for cost of living differences and transport costs). Beyond point C in the modern sector and c in the traditional sector, real wages in both sectors increase together and conventional neo-classical rules of labour allocation apply. Shortages of unskilled labour in turn contribute to increasing real wage rates across industries and sectors. Both modern and traditional sector wage differentials and skill differentials begin to narrow.[39]

It should be noted that increases in average earnings – the indicator often used for analysing wage trends – is not an indication of countries having passed through the turning point. The transfer of labour to the modern sector inevitably involves rises in average real wages. This can be achieved, even though wage rates remain constant and differentials do not change between modern and traditional sectors. Rising average earnings merely represent a compositional change as the share of total employment in the former rises and in the latter falls.[40]

Thus, surplus labour is used to indicate elastic labour supply for jobs at going wage rates in the modern sector. Neither modern nor traditional sectors are defined here precisely but rather used as a heuristic device to interpret general patterns of labour market change. In practice, the struc-

---

[39] Wages in some segments of the modern sector, such as mining, will remain above those in the traditional sector.
[40] In practice, this also occurs within the modern sector: a rise in the share of capital-intensive output in the modern sector contributes to rising wage rates during the labour surplus period.

ture of labour markets is much more complex with wage and employment conditions varying along a continuum rather than strictly following a dualistic pattern.

Labour market transitions in other East Asian countries

The East Asian NIEs represent cases in which the transition to higher wages followed a relatively short and clearly defined turning point.[41] In these countries economic growth was rapid and its impact on labour demand substantial. Owing to the role of labour-intensive sectors, labour markets were well integrated spatially (urban–rural) and across sectors (agriculture and non-agriculture). There was relatively little government protection of workers through wage legislation and the like. South Korea and Taiwan were largely isolated from foreign immigrant labour until the mid 1980s. Both are remarkable in the low and declining level of wage differentials by skill (World Bank 1993).[42]

Alternatively, achievement of the turning point has been more difficult to identify in both Malaysia and Thailand. Wages outcomes fluctuated in the 1970s and 1980s in both countries (Lim 1988; Sussangkarn, 1993), although real wages first began to rise in agriculture in Malaysia from the mid 1970s (Barlow and Jayasuriya 1987). The relatively large size of the agricultural sector, fluctuating agricultural incomes and quite substantial in-migration of labour from neighbouring countries – first in Malaysia and more recently in Thailand – are factors common to both countries.

Conclusions: economic growth, development strategies and labour market outcomes

Overall gains in terms of employment shifts and productivity growth have been substantial in most developing economies since 1960. They were much more marked in 1960–80 than in the 1980s. However, there is now reason to doubt the early optimism regarding the dynamic role of manufacturing in labour market transition. This contrasts with Kuznets' findings for the industrial countries. Low and unstable earnings and employment, the rapid growth in informal sector employment was one of the disappointing aspects of the employment record in many developing economies, especially in the 1980s.

---

[41] In Korea, Bai (1985) identifies 1975 as a critical year when wage differentials narrowed significantly, a decade after economic reforms were initiated.
[42] Real wages of unskilled labour also rose in Singapore and Hong Kong, despite inflow of international labour migrants (Pang Eng Fong 1994).

40 *Setting the scene*

The slow growth in modern sector employment in many countries was frequently of their own making, although lower rates in world economic growth made policy formulation more difficult. Policies favoured capital-intensive investments and adversely affected economic growth, competitiveness and employment growth – especially in manufacturing. In contrast, a handful of countries, particularly in East Asia, negotiated difficult problems of macroeconomic management and resisted pressures to limit competition. They registered different labour market outcomes to many other countries in the developing world.

Several general conclusions emerge from the survey of empirical data and the literature on developments in different groups of developing countries.

- *Economic growth and economic structure are critical to labour market outcomes.*
  High rates of economic growth are a necessary but not a sufficient condition for rapid generation of employment and rising labour incomes. In economies with a relatively elastic supply of labour, a labour-intensive pattern of economic growth is critical to an early achievement of a turning point. Protected, import-substitution industrialisation, frequently associated with relatively capital-intensive investment, is generally linked to disappointing labour market outcomes in the medium to longer term. This is equally true of large economies (such as India) and relatively small economies. It applies to both employment generation and income distribution.
- *Countries with rich natural resource endowments often find it difficult to develop policies favourable to employment generation.*
  Relative prices tend to discriminate against labour-intensive exports and these countries face the additional challenge of maintaining economic stability during alternative periods of increasing and declining natural resource prices.
- *Macroeconomic management plays a critical role in contributing to favourable labour market outcomes*
  Macroeconomic policy is critical to the favourable impact of economic growth and adjustment on labour markets. Fiscal and monetary policies need to be flexible and capable of responding to changing economic conditions. Management of exchange rates, control of the money supply and the capacity to cut expenditure in periods of economic downturn are essential for maintaining the rate of employment growth. Macroeconomic management in boom conditions (especially the shocks posed by large, natural resource price increases) can be just

as important as management in slumps, especially to ensure that relative price shifts do not discriminate against labour-intensive products.
- *Labour markets mostly work well, even in the face of restrictive institutional arrangements*
  Labour markets generally adjust quickly to fluctuations in economic growth and economic structure. This is despite the prevalence of traditional, and more recent, labour market institutions which have the effect of restricting labour mobility and wage adjustments. Labour tends to be relatively mobile in response to new job opportunities and wage increases (or declines). Wages and employment have adjusted to changes in economic conditions, often despite government and trade union intervention and labour legislation. However, as in industrial countries, wage discrimination against females is one specific area where labour markets do not work efficiently or promote equity.
- *Careful sequencing of human capital investments is critical for labour productivity and equity*
  Investment in human resources, especially education, has a major impact on the labour market through its influence on the quality of labour inputs and the supply of labour available to perform specialised tasks. The sequencing of investment in education, beginning with emphasis on literacy and primary education, is particularly important for ensuring that increases in productivity are widely enjoyed in the early stages of growth. Such investments also contribute to equity, in concert with labour-intensive strategies for growth. In contrast, too much early emphasis on educating higher-level labour (often associated with high-tech and capital-intensive strategies) contributes to unequal income distribution.
- *Rapid labour market transitions involve substantial hardship and frequent neglect of worker rights*
  The longer-term gains to labour as a class from rapid and sustained export-led growth are unambiguous. However, there are substantial transitional costs, borne especially by unskilled workers in general, certain vulnerable groups and individuals. Flexible labour markets and intensive utilisation of capital equipment demand sacrifices in terms of job security, hours of work and working conditions at early stages of development, compared with those made by workers in industrial countries. Given an absence of state-supported social security networks and labour protection, the costs are especially great for young females and older, less mobile workers. Costs are exacerbated

where organised labour is tightly – and sometimes repressively – controlled by the state.
- *Changes in casual and informal employment play a major role in labour market adjustments*
  Changes in wages and unemployment rates are important indicators of labour market adjustment. However, they may only capture a small part of the change in aggregate demand and supply of labour in developing economies. Changes in the size and composition of rural farm and non-farm employment and work in the informal sector are critical indicators of labour market change. In economies without state support for the unemployed, unemployment rates tend to reflect excess supply of educated labour and labour market segmentation, rather than problems of labour market imbalance.

There are limits to the potential insights from comparative research on the interaction between labour markets and economic development. The interconnections are sufficiently complex as to require detailed case studies (Freeman 1992a). In the following chapters, I examine the validity of the six propositions, derived from our comparative survey of labour market developments, in the Indonesian case.

Economic growth and labour market dynamics

3

Economic and social transformation: a remarkable record

The accession of the military and Soeharto to power in 1965–6 marked a watershed in Indonesia's economic affairs. Economic stability and growth received primacy in national affairs. Markets and encouragement of private enterprise were affirmed as the major channels for the achievement of economic goals.[1] Foreign investment was encouraged, and foreign aid played a key role in supporting economic stability and development programmes.

The change in policies contributed to rapid economic growth and transformation in the structure of the economy in favour of more productive, non-agricultural sectors. During this period of structural change, the economy adjusted to several international and domestic developments which required shifts in policy emphasis. Most important was coping with the marked fluctuations in international oil prices. Labour market adaptation was affected by sharp policy adjustments, and also depended partly on social and demographic conditions which influenced the supply and quality of manpower.

I begin with the starting point and labour market challenge, and then highlight the extent of economic and social transformation under Soeharto. Later sections draw attention to how labour growth still plays a central role in the national and regional employment equation.

Indonesia's low starting point

When Soeharto took control in 1965–6, the Indonesian economy was in dire straits. Declining economic growth, food shortages and spiralling inflation, and a general breakdown in communications and infrastructure all contributed to what Higgins referred to as a 'basket case'. Others agreed.[2]

---

[1] See Woo, Glassburner and Nasution (1994) and Hill (1995) for a detailed treatment of economic developments and policy under Soeharto. Other general surveys include Dapice (1980), Booth and McCawley (1981), Booth (ed.) (1992) and Hill (1994).
[2] Higgins is quoted in Hill (1994: 54). See Tan (1967) and Arndt (1971).

These unfortunate economic conditions were only partly the product of rapid economic decline during the final years of the Soekarno era. Japanese occupation during the war, and a period of political instability and armed conflict during the revolution, meant that civilian administration and economic management were interrupted for almost a decade through to 1949. Even in 1939, Indonesia was little prepared for modern economic growth. Heavy dependence on primary product exports, an extremely small modern sector and low levels of literacy all made rapid economic development a daunting task (Furnivall 1939; Paauw 1963). Building an elementary physical, human and institutional framework for development was a major challenge, given the effects of colonial rule and a troubled 20-year period after Independence. Inevitably, it was to be a big component of early economic performance in the era of growth after 1965.

Four dimensions of development which placed Indonesia well behind other East Asian countries and much closer to those in South Asia in the 1960s are of particular importance for our discussion of labour market change.

- High levels of landlessness. Landlessness in Java amounted to around 30–40 per cent of all rural households in the 1960s and 1970s, and minuscule farms used traditional technology in much of Indonesia. In terms of the size distribution of holdings and extent of landlessness, densely populated rural Java – where over half of the total population lived – had much more in common with Bangladesh than with Thailand, the Philippines or Malaysia (Booth and Sundrum 1985).[3] The majority of households in Java owned less than half a hectare (slightly more than an acre) in 1973. Average holdings were only just above this mark.
- Poor infrastructure and communications were a feature especially in the Outer Islands where over one-third of the population lived. In terms of a range of indicators – kilometres of paved road, low electricity and power consumption – Indonesia was less developed than Thailand and the Philippines, and much less developed than Malaysia or South Korea in the 1960s and 1970s (table 3.1).
- Low levels of development in terms of a range of social indicators compared with neighbouring countries. These included high infant mortality (141 in 1970), low life expectancy (47 in 1970) and little access to safe water or sanitation for the majority of the population

---

[3] In the early 1970s, Java had by far the largest number of farmers (82 per cent) and the highest proportion of total land area (49 per cent) in farms of less than one hectare of any Asian country, including Bangladesh.

Table 3.1. *Indicators of infrastructure and social development, selected East and South Asian countries, 1970*

				Infrastructure				Social indicators			
Country	Population (M.) (1970) (1)	Land area (000 sq.km) (2)	Paved roads (3)	Electricity consumption (kilowatts/hr '000 pop.) (4)	Per capita energy consumption (kva)[a] (5)	Telephone main lines (7)	Urban population (%)[b] (6)	Life expectancy (yrs) (8)	Infant mortality[c] (9)	Safe drinking water (10)	Sanitation (11)
South Korea	32	99	4	86	654	n.a.	41	59	53	58	n.a.
Malaysia	5	330	15	187	558	194	27	64	39	29	57
Thailand	36	513	10	21	183	237	13	58	75	17	n.a.
Philippines	37	300	16	59	267	304	32	56	60	36	58
China	839	9,561	n.a.	29	374	3,262	17	61	69	n.a.	n.a.
India	548	3,288	325	30	138	1,465	20	47	139	17	18
Indonesia	116	1,905	21	8	115	219	17	47	141	3	13

Notes: [a] Kva (coal equivalent); [b] 1975; [c] Per 1,000 births.
Sources: World Bank, *World Development Report, 1994* (Appendix: Infrastructure data); Asian Development Bank, *Key Indicators of Development in Developing Asian and Pacific Countries*, 1991.

48 *Economic growth and labour market dynamics*

(table 3.1). According to most of these indicators, Indonesia was closer to India than to any neighbouring country, outside the Indochina countries and Burma, and was well behind China on a range of social and infrastructure indicators. Partly as a legacy of the colonial period, Indonesians suffered from extremely limited educational opportunities, despite improvements during the 1950s.

The daunting labour market challenge

Geertz's classic book painted a moving picture of lost opportunities in the colonial past in Java – in contrast to Japanese modern economic history – making the task in raising labour incomes much more difficult after Independence.

> [In Java, there was] no significant expansion [of employment] outside traditional agricultural pursuits, but a rapid expansion within them made possible by the perfection of labor absorbing productive techniques which raised land but not labor productivity. Peasants provided unskilled, occasional labor for…plantations, but at a price well below the marginal productivity. (Geertz 1963: 137–8)

By 1970, commentators such as Heinz Arndt were optimistic regarding macroeconomic improvement but were gloomy on prospects for employment especially in light of enormous structural problems faced by Java in particular.

> The crucial problem is no longer food but employment…the need for new employment opportunities, both for the unskilled urban unemployed and rural under-employed and for graduates of high schools and universities, is growing every year more desperate. Only a further acceleration of economic development, including large-scale industrialisation, offers any hope of coping with the problem. (Arndt 1971: 37)

Optimism was undoubtedly warranted from a macroeconomic stand point. Economic stability had been achieved, substantial deregulation was in process and new foreign investment had begun to flow into Indonesia by 1970. Nevertheless, given the size, density and growth of the population, meaningful improvements in labour welfare appeared a long way off. In the mid 1960s, only Japan among the Asian countries had demonstrated the capacity to develop into a modern economy.

It was understandable that even those who saw some prospect for relatively rapid economic growth doubted whether it would impact widely enough to improve living conditions of Indonesian workers and peasants. Many observers believed at the time that importation of modern technology in industry and agriculture would be disastrous for the poor in Java.[4]

These problems were reflected in the structure of employment and earnings, and in the labour force growth rates which confronted the new government in the late 1960s. Three key characteristics of the labour market were indicative of more general problems of underdevelopment:

- a high proportion of employment in low productivity agriculture in which landlessness was a key feature in Java
- a large, traditional and mainly rural non-agricultural sector in which family and micro-enterprises dominated, and returns were commonly much lower than daily wages in agriculture
- a tiny modern sector, especially outside government (and military) employment, epitomised by a very small proportion of professionals and other white-collar and educated workers.

Several of these features of the labour market reflected the situation in Java, where problems of rural poverty and land scarcity were most entrenched. With hindsight, and as the results of more research became available, it is clear that problems of overpopulation and land scarcity were not limited to Java. Nevertheless, poverty and surplus labour were characterised by different labour market conditions in many regions outside Java. A high proportion of workers were employed on subsistence and semi-subsistence family farms, and the share of urban and non-agricultural employment was very small.

Agricultural employment

In 1971 agricultural employment comprised a relatively small proportion of total employment for a country at Indonesia's stage of development. Just under two-thirds of the employed population was engaged in agriculture, mostly as self-employed and family workers (table 3.2). While still high compared with Latin America and some other parts of East Asia, this share was low in comparison to shares of well over 70 per cent in many poorer countries in Asia and Africa.

In Java, where around two-thirds of the population worked, the proportion of agricultural employment was lower and the share of wage employees – mainly casual workers – was much higher than in the Outer Islands. This reflected relatively high levels of landlessness, even by South Asian

---

[4] Books like *The Showcase State* (Mortimer 1973) reflected this view.

Table 3.2. *Employment by major sector, Java and Outer Islands, 1971*

Sector	Java N (000)	Java %	Outer Islands N (000)	Outer Islands %	Indonesia N (000)	Indonesia %
Agriculture	15,107	61.0	10,679	74.2	25,786	65.8
Non-agriculture	9,655	39.0	3,722	25.8	13,377	34.2
Urban						
Manufacturing	507	2.0	185	1.3	692	1.8
Trade	1,043	4.2	483	3.4	1,526	3.9
Services	1,363	5.5	564	3.9	1,927	4.9
Other[a]	666	2.8	321	2.2	986	2.5
Sub-total	3,579	(14.5)	1,553	(10.8)	5,131	(13.1)
Rural						
Manufacturing	1,778	7.2	599	4.2	2,377	6.1
Trade	2,243	9.0	536	3.7	2,779	7.1
Services	1,449	5.8	697	4.8	2,146	5.5
Other[a]	606	2.5	337	2.3	944	2.4
Sub-total	6,076	(24.5)	2,169	(15.0)	8,246	(21.1)
All Sectors	24,762		14,401		39,163	100

Note: [a] Includes mining, public utilities, construction, transport and financial services.
Source: CBS, Population Census, 1971 (Series C).

standards, among rural people in Java in the early 1970s.[5] It also reflected labour demand patterns in irrigated rice cultivation, the dominant agricultural activity. Even well before the green revolution, irrigated rice cultivation in Java was characterised by intensive and seasonal use of casual, wage labour (White 1979, Barker and Herdt and Rose 1985).

Despite the smaller share of agricultural workers than in some other countries, most rural households had some involvement in agriculture, if only as agricultural labourers participating in the harvest for a few days a season. Wage work in rice farming was distinctly preferred to many other lower-paying activities. However, income from agriculture no longer provided sufficient support, even for subsistence needs, for a high proportion of households. The process of agricultural involution – following Geertz's controversial description of the adaptation of agriculture to extreme population pressure during the colonial period – had well and truly broken down.

[5] Depending on how the denominator and numerators are defined, estimates of landlessness were around 30–40 per cent of the rural population on Java in the early 1970s, similar to 30 per cent recorded for Bangladesh, but was much higher than elsewhere in Southeast Asia (Booth and Sundrum 1985: 146–54; Manning 1988a: 16–18; see also Horstmann and Rutz 1980).

The structure of land holdings underpinned the operation of rural labour markets on Java. Although the average size of holdings was very small, one-half of all land was owned by farmers owning one hectare or more. Although by no means rich by international standards, this group employed most hired labour – especially in harvest work usually open to most villagers in wet rice (*sawah*) – and acted as patrons to the poor in hard times.

In general, returns to labour in agriculture were low by regional standards. International comparisons suggest that daily wage rates in agriculture in Java were on par with those in Bangladesh and the poorer regions of India, and well below those in most of Southeast Asia (Barker, Herdt and Rose 1985; Penny and Singarimbun 1973: 45). In contrast, generally more extensive land use in many Outer Island regions meant a much greater involvement in agriculture and higher output per worker in key crops such as rice and rubber (Booth 1988). Penny and Singarimbun (1973: 26) contrasted the situation in one Java village (Sriharjo) with that in new villages in North Sumatra in the 1960s.

In the new villages in Sumatra each family can get work for 97 days in the land preparation phase. The Sriharjo average of 18 days gives some indication of the wastage of the 'capacity to produce. . . . During the rice growing season in the new villages farmers do little work other than rice work. . . . In Sriharjo on the other hand the shortage of land forces people to seek other employment, even in the main rice season.'

Agricultural production was conducted with virtually no assistance from purchased inputs, except in the small pockets of plantation agriculture. Returns to labour (and other factors) in small-holder cash crops were highly dependent on variable international prices (Pelzer 1963).

The traditional sector dominance of non-agriculture

Historically, cottage industries had been an important source of employment throughout Indonesia up to the 1960s. Especially in Java, petty trade – the ubiquitous small food stalls or *warung*, market sellers and hawkers – was widespread at the turn of the century. Trading provided an important source of employment for poorer women in an already widely monetised rural economy (White 1991). *Batik*, hand-loom weaving, food processing, *kretek* cigarettes and agro-processing had become increasingly important sources of employment after Independence. This was especially the case during the period of economic decline, foreign exchange shortages and heavy import controls from the late 1950s (Hawkins 1963).

It is not surprising, therefore, even after a period of steady economic growth in the 1950s, that over 60 per cent of all non-agricultural employment was located in rural areas in 1971. Most non-agricultural employment was either in trade or services (including in government) or in manufacturing (table 3.2). Whereas nearly half of the service sector employment was located in urban areas, both trade and manufacturing jobs were heavily concentrated in rural areas. Female self-employed and family workers dominated employment in both, especially in Java.

The structure of manufacturing employment provides a vivid reminder of the relatively underdeveloped structure of the economy at this juncture. Manufacturing employment still accounted for less than 10 per cent of all jobs recorded in the 1971 Census. Rural work – heavily concentrated in cottage industry – accounted for 80 per cent of the total. Only about 40 per cent of rural manufacturing workers were wage employees, many of these in micro-enterprises, and the majority of employees were women (table 3.3).

McCawley (1981: 70) estimates that cottage industries accounted for close to 80 per cent of all manufacturing employment in 1963 and again in 1974/5.[6] The large majority of jobs were not in the conventional export-oriented textile, footwear and clothing industries, which had taken off in the NIEs by the early 1970s. Rather, they were in traditional agro-processing industries, often selling to final consumers in local markets and almost entirely oriented to the domestic market. Thus, bamboo processing (baskets, mats and string), rattan, coconut sugar manufacture and bean curd cakes (*tahu* and *tempe*), accounted for just under two-thirds of all cottage industry employment and over half of all manufacturing jobs in 1974/5.

Low earnings
Extremely low earnings per hour worked in these industries is one indicator of the extent of labour supply pressures which dominated labour markets in the early 1970s in Java. Returns per hour were lowest in bamboo basket weaving and coconut sugar processing, according to two village studies conducted around this time (Penny and Singarimbun 1973; White 1976). Earnings per hour worked were one-half to less than one-third of those in rice. This is remarkably low, even if account is taken of potential differences in the intensity of labour inputs.[7]

Drawing on these and other village studies conducted around this time, Lluch and Mazumdar (1985) proposed an earnings ladder to describe the

---

[6] According to the 1974/5 industrial census, cottage industries were defined as all establishments with less than five workers (paid and unpaid); in 1963, it referred to all establishments with no paid workers.
[7] Many of those employed in bamboo weaving were women and children who combined the work with household tasks.

Table 3.3. *Selected characteristics of employed persons by major sector: Indonesia, 1971 (per cent)*

Sector		Female	Wage employees[a]	Completed schooling < Primary	Completed schooling Secondary +	White-collar workers[b]
Agriculture		33	22	79	(0.3)	(0.3)
Non-agriculture		34	51	56	8	15
Urban	Manufacturing	32	75	48	8	10
	Trade	37	21	53	7	4
	Services	32	81	32	22	39
	Other[c]	4	81	40	13	15
	Subtotal	30	62	42	14	20
Rural	Manufacturing	54	43	77	1	2
	Trade	48	9	74	(0.1)	(0.6)
	Services	24	77	42	12	48
	Other[c]	2	72	66	3	4
	Subtotal	38	44	65	4	13
All sectors		33	32	71	3	6

Notes: [a] Includes both casual and more permanent (no distinction made in official statistics);
[b] Professional, managerial and clerical workers, some professionals (i.e., traditional healers) are not strictly 'white' collar; [c] All other non-agricultural sectors.
Source: CBS, Population Census, 1971 (Series C and D).

returns to labour in various rural jobs (table 3.3). Wage employment in rice and construction were close to the top of the ladder, petty trading activities (depending on the amount of capital required) were somewhere in the middle, and home industries were at the bottom.

Another labour market feature was the segmentation of rural employment opportunities according to class. Access to higher-wage (or exchange labour) jobs in agriculture was more difficult for poorer landless labourers in periods of slack demand. These groups also gained less-favourable employment contracts than their better-off neighbours and were forced to depend on lower-paying activities outside the rice sector.

Several factors explain why there was such a wide range in earnings, even within the same village. First, the need to minimise recruitment costs, the importance of timeliness in particular operations and the need for more concentrated effort in rice. Second a preference for low-paying but more secure employment in activities such as coconut sugar. Third the maximisation of joint household (rather than individual) income in home industries and other activities.[8]

---

[8] See especially the work of Gunawan *et al.* (1977; 1979), White (1979), Hüsken (1979) and Hart (1986).

Labour utilisation

One final characteristic of employment in rural Java was relatively *high* levels of labour utilisation as part of a survival strategy. Children played a major role in the household economy, especially among the poor (White 1976; Hart 1986). In some households, gathering and scavenging of waste or surplus agricultural products were common: collection of feed for farm animals, fishing in irrigated rice fields and collection of leftover rice from harvested paddy fields (*ngasak*). Earnings from migrant labour were important, but mainly in rural areas and in locations close to the individual's village of residence.[9]

Importantly, rural non-farm activities were often undertaken independent of seasonal changes in labour demand in agriculture. Many households had access to employment in rice for a very limited period, even in busy times in the agricultural cycle. Low earnings and variable earnings across activities were not merely seasonal responses to excess labour supply in slack periods in agriculture, as in some other countries (Hansen 1969; Bertrand and Squire 1980). In the case of the two industries investigated by White (1976), and Penny and Singarimbun (1972) basket weaving was interrupted for only very short periods when workers were engaged in rice harvesting and coconut sugar production was conducted throughout the year.

White's (1976) village study of the early 1970s showed that labour time allocated to non-agricultural activities accounted for the bulk of hours worked, even during the busy season in agriculture (table 3.4). There was not a major fluctuation in average hours worked during the busy and slack seasons, although the type of work changed, especially among women.[10]

Thus open underemployment was not a general feature of rural labour markets in Java. There was considerable surplus labour at going wage rates in agriculture. *Ex-ante*, labour markets did not clear. But *ex-poste* they did because poorer households had to find some activity to survive.

There is much less information on the operation of rural labour markets outside Java. Anthropological and sociological studies indicate a wide range of employment situations (Pelzer 1963). Despite this diversity, the macro data suggest two important differences compared with Java. First, non-agricultural employment was much less important than in Java, particularly in rural areas (table 3.2 above). Government, and other services dominated non-agricultural employment. Plantation workers in agricul-

---

[9] The one major exception seems to have been harvesting in monoculture rice regions where migrant workers moved from village to village (Budhisantoso 1975).

[10] See also Edmundson (1976) and Gunawan *et al.* (1977; 1979). Seasonality in employment and real wages were greater in the lowland rice monoculture regions.

Table 3.4. *Average hours worked per day in agricultural and non-agricultural activities in a central Java village, Kaliloro village, 1972–1973*

	Adult male		Adult female	
	Average hours	(%)	Average hours	(%)
'Busy' months[a]				
Agriculture	3.9	48	2.3	36
Non-agriculture	4.2	52	4.1	64
Total	8.1	100	6.4	100
(Slack) months[a]				
Agriculture	2.3	29	0.7	11
Non-agriculture	5.6	71	5.5	89
Total	7.9	100	6.2	100

Note: [a] Five busy months (in agriculture) and seven slack months were reported.
Source: White (1976: 214); data for Kaliloro village (Kulon Progo, Yogyakarta, Special Region).

ture, government officials and school teachers probably accounted for around 70–80 per cent of all wage employment outside Java in the early 1970s. The balance was widely dispersed – in small mining and oil industries, logging companies and small urban manufacturing enterprises oriented to meet the needs of relatively isolated local markets.

Second, self-employment and family work made up a higher share of work in key non-agricultural sectors outside Java, especially in manufacturing. The domination of rural micro enterprises in manufacturing employment was even more evident in the Outer Islands: over 80 per cent of rural manufacturing jobs were held by non-wage workers outside Java. Poor communications and isolation, which worsened in the later years of the Soekarno period contributed to the survival of these activities.

Modern sector employment and earnings

Another feature of the labour market in Indonesia in the late 1960s was the small size of the modern sector. Although the precise quantification is difficult, workers in medium- and larger-scale establishments and in government service probably accounted for around 10 per cent of a total workforce of 39 million and one-quarter of the non-agricultural workforce.

Civil servants, including teachers, health personnel and the military, accounted for around half of the total. The balance was made up of around 750,000 employees in large- and medium-scale manufacturing, 200,000 permanent or semi-permanent employees on estates, and as many as 750,000 persons in established public and private firms in mining and services – in hotels, restaurants, construction and public utilities.

The domination of modern sector employment by civil servants was not unusual in developing economies where fledgling modern private sectors were only beginning to become established in the early post-colonial era. In Indonesia, as in many other countries, the modern private sector was not a significant employer of labour prior to Independence. Employment was limited to a handful of mining, public utilities, manufacturing and transport, trade and communications firms set up under the Dutch (Furnivall 1939, Soehoed 1967).

Within large-and medium-scale manufacturing, the large majority of workers were concentrated in what can only be termed traditional jobs from an international perspective. The largest share of workers were in weaving (employing close to 20 per cent). Around half of these employees were in non-mechanised hand-loom industries, and a further 20 per cent were in smaller mechanised establishments using labour-intensive equipment (Hill 1980). The second largest industry *kretek* (clove cigarettes) employed around 15 per cent of the total, the majority in large non-mechanised establishments. A further two-thirds worked in a range of other industries which were either non-mechanised or used labour-intensive technology (rice, rubber, tea and tobacco processing, sawmills and batik).[11]

Much of the private sector which was still under foreign control after Independence was nationalised from around the mid 1950s. Nationalisation extended the web of public sector employment conditions and remuneration in all sectors (Mackie 1967). This process only began to be reversed after 1965 when many enterprises were returned to their previous owners, although significant segments of the modern sector remained under state control. State enterprises accounted for around 20 per cent of total employment in large and medium firms in non-oil manufacturing in 1974–5. This is a high ratio given that some large sectors such as *kretek* cigarettes were almost entirely privately owned. State enterprises were prominent in textiles, cement, paper, machine goods and fertiliser (Soehoed 1967).

Occupation, education and earnings

The limited size of the modern sector is further reflected in the small share of professional and other white-collar and educated workers in total

---

[11] In these sectors, value-added per worker was frequently much less than half of that in sectors such as spinning, chemicals, paper and metals (World Bank 1981).

employment. White-collar workers – professionals, managers and clerical employees – accounted for 15 per cent and high school graduates less than 10 per cent of total non-agricultural employment in 1971. If services are excluded, the share of white-collar workers and secondary educated drops to 5 per cent. The proportion of white-collar and more educated workers was below 10 per cent even in urban areas (table 3.3).

Of course, this was not surprising for a country at Indonesia's stage of development. The share of white-collar workers was not much higher in the more developed, East Asian countries (Galenson 1992: 37). However, in light of later developments, it is important to emphasise how thin the human capital basis was for the development of a modern economy.

Associated with the labour-intensive structure of many manufacturing industries, average earnings were low, except for a very small segment of modern sector enterprises. There was a large gap between average monthly earnings in the small capital-intensive segments of manufacturing and the agro-processing, food and textile industries in 1974/5 (Manning 1979). Average earnings in manufacturing were close to four times higher than in the low-wage sectors.

One other feature of modern sector employment and earnings, rapid inflation eroded the real value of wages from the late 1950s (Papanek 1980: 85). Whereas Indonesian labour in the small modern sector and in the civil service occupied relatively high-wage positions during the Dutch period, this was no longer the case in 1965–6 (Furnivall 1939). Prestige and job security remained important attributes of jobs in the bureaucracy, even though official earnings from government jobs were probably lower than earnings in many self-employed occupations in the later Soekarno years.

One consequence of this development was the wide wage differential between the small number of foreign firms, on the one hand, and state and domestic private firms, on the other. In the former, wages for both skilled and unskilled labour were much higher even than in the relatively capital-intensive state enterprises (Manning 1979: 117).[12]

The practice of moonlighting (*ngobjek*, and *ngompreng* – hiring out government vehicles for private gain) became widespread in this period and remained a feature of civil service administration throughout the 1960s and 1970s. Petty corruption spread as civil servants at all levels sought to maintain, or restore, their real earnings (Arndt and Sundrum 1975; Gray 1979).

Two features of economic and employment structure sets Indonesia

---

[12] Although a range of fringe benefits were offered to many public sector and government workers.

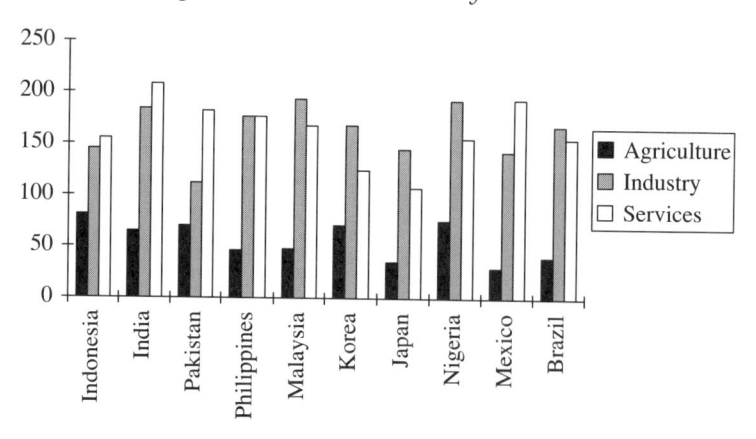

Figure 3.1 Indices of relative labour productivity in major sectors, Indonesia and selected countries, 1965 (all sectors=100)
Source: World Bank, *World Tables* and *World Development Report*, various years.

apart from a selection of other countries, with the partial exception of Nigeria. First, the industrial sector was smaller, contributing only 13 per cent of GDP and 8 per cent of total employment. These figures contrast with around 20–5 per cent of GDP and 10–15 per cent of employment deriving from this sector in the other countries in 1965 (appendix table 3.1).[13]

Second, there was a much less marked spread in the index of average labour productivity across sectors in Indonesia (figure 3.1). In most other Asian countries, agricultural labour productivity was much lower relative to productivity in both industry and services than in Indonesia (an index of 77). While the index of labour productivity in both industry and services was above the national average, the gap was less than in other countries, especially in industry.

Because the modern sector was so small, average non-agricultural productivity remained low, in contrast to some higher-income developing countries such as Brazil. In these countries, average productivity, and presumably incomes also, was much lower in agriculture than in other sectors of the economy (Morely 1982). In part, these patterns might be attributed to severe economic hardship experienced in Indonesia in the mid 1960s. But they were also a legacy of the long period of colonial rule during which the industrial sector was minuscule.

---

[13] Thailand is the exception (5 per cent of the workforce employed in this industry), partly related to differences in definitions.

Economic growth and structural change

Together with several of the East Asian NIEs, Indonesia has been one of the most rapidly growing economies in the world since 1965. More than any other factor this helps to explain the substantial transformation of Indonesia's labour market. Total economic growth rates averaged a remarkable 6–7 per cent over the entire 20-year period 1971–95, resulting in average per-capita income growth of around 4–5 per cent per annum (figure 3.2). This was only rivalled on a sustained basis by several neighbours in East Asia.

These changes included a dramatic fall in agriculture's share of GDP and the concomitant rise in industry. There was a large increase in rice and textiles production per capita, in the share of gross domestic investment to GDP and in the value of foreign investment (table 3.5). These were all features of economic growth shared by other rapidly expanding East Asian economies. By the mid 1990s, Indonesia's economy probably had more in common with its neighbours Thailand and Malaysia than the South Asian economies which it had so much resembled several decades earlier.

One important characteristic of economic growth in Indonesia over this period – despite some major challenges – was that it lacked extreme troughs and peaks experienced by some other countries in the region.

Only in 1976 did real non-oil GDP growth fall below 4 per cent, and only in several did it reach double digits (figure 3.2). Economic management was generally conservative – guided by President Soeharto's (and advisor 'technocrats') careful attention to balancing economic, social and political development. Thus it was not as rapid on a sustained basis as in South Korea or Taiwan, or as rapid as in China, Thailand and Malaysia since the mid 1980s. In the light of the difficult starting point, the failure of the Indonesian economy to grow more rapidly is one factor which helps explain why labour transformation has not been as extensive as in some of the other East Asian economies.

Nevertheless, there were important differences in economic performance and policy in several sub-periods. Four major periods of economic growth can be distinguished since the Soeharto government came to power (Sundrum 1986, 1988; and Hill 1996):

- the period of stabilisation and rehabilitation (1967–73)
- the oil boom period (1973–81)
- the period of slower economic growth (1981–7)
- the final period of internationally oriented industrialisation when GDP growth rose again (1987–94).

Table 3.5. *Indicators of economic structure and change: Indonesia, 1965–1970 and 1993–1994*

	1965–67[a]	1992–93[a]
1 GDP per capita (US$)	190[b]	740
2 Structure of production		
% of GDP: Agriculture	53	18
Industry	11	40
Production per capita		
Rice (index)	100[c]	146[c]
Textiles (metres)	4	28
Exports (% GDP)		
Total	12	27
Non-oil	8	21
3 Investment/savings		
GDI/GDP (%)	5	35
Foreign investment approved		
($, 1985 prices)	157[d]	1,370[d]
4 Inflation rate (% p.a.)	110	9
5 Government expenditure/revenue		
Total expenditure/GDP (%)	9	22
Development expenditure (% total)	20	42
Revenue: % oil-gas	11	26
non-oil	60	55
aid	29	18
6 Poverty (% very poor)[e]		
Java	61	10
Outer Islands	52	7

Notes: [a] Earliest and latest year data available; [b] 1991 prices; [c] For years 1969–71 and 1992–3 (two-year average); [d] For years 1969–70 and 1990–2 (two-year average); [e] For years 1976 and 1990.
Source: CBS, Statistical Yearbook, various years. The author is indebted to Hal Hill for permission to use some of the data from table 1.2 in Hill (1996).

Average growth rates of non-oil GDP were much higher during the periods of rehabilitation and oil boom.[14] Rates were much lower in the third period and then bounced back in the final period.

---

[14] Nevertheless, statistically significant results were obtained for a time trend equation (including dummy variables for each of the time periods) $g = a + b^2D^2 + b^3D^3 + b^4D^4 + u$ (where g = annual rates of non-oil growth, D^2 = early oil boom period dummy, D^3 = the later oil boom dummy, and D^4 = the export boom period dummy). The equation results were: $g = 5.46\,(0.41) + 1.95D^2\,(0.72) + 5.06D^3\,(0.71) + 1.90D^4\,(0.74)$ (Durbin–Watson = 2.08; $R^2 = 0.70$). All coefficients were significant at 5 per cent and the constant and later oil boom period at a 1 per cent level.

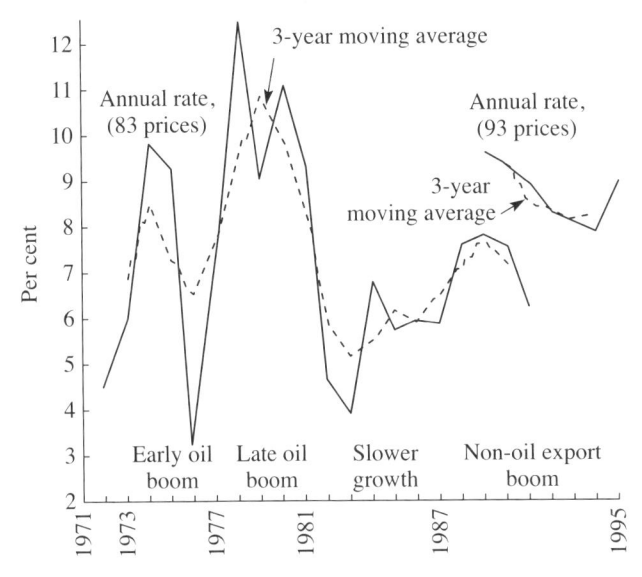

Figure 3.2 Annual growth of non-oil GDP, 1971–1995 (per cent)
Source: CBS, National Accounts, various years.

Sectoral growth patterns

All sectors grew rapidly from the 1970s. Average growth in industry fluctuated considerably, falling dramatically in the early 1980s and then rising again. The average growth of other sectors was more stable (Hill 1996).

Agriculture

Agricultural growth rates have been quite rapid by international and even regional standards. They were most rapid during the late 1970s and early 1980s when growth rates averaged 6 per cent, the only extended period of very rapid agricultural sector growth during the New Order.

Foodcrops continued to account for over half of total value-added in agriculture in the late 1980s (Tabor 1992). The dominant rice sector was the leading sector in agricultural development through to the mid 1980s, accounting for most of the large variations in growth rates since the mid 1960s. Despite the very high levels of landlessness and the small average size of rice holdings in Java, rice production growth contributed to increased rural incomes and consumption, and to poverty alleviation (Timmer 1993).

In contrast to rice, the performance of other agricultural commodities was much less impressive. Despite considerable rhetoric concerning diversification of the food crop sector, productivity had only risen significantly in corn to the late 1980s (Tabor 1992). Partly because of poor project management and unfavourable commodity prices especially in the 1980s, smallholder commercial crops production grew less rapidly than in Thailand and Malaysia where productivity in cash crops such as rubber and sugar rose substantially in the 1970–80s (Booth 1988; Bautista 1993). The failure of smallholder production to modernise has important implications for employment and incomes in many Outer Island communities. The estate sector also stagnated, partly because of government controls on private sector entry until the 1980s, although private investments in sugar, cocoa and oil palm have proliferated particularly in Sumatra and Sulawesi in recent years (Barlow and Tomich 1991).

Fisheries and forestry grew more rapidly. Fisheries are a major sector of employment for many of the poor in Java and in the Outer Islands. This sub-sector expanded with the introduction of new technology in trawling and deep sea fishing. Shrimps became a major export commodity in the 1980s, growing faster than any other agricultural export. Forestry also expanded rapidly with the opening up of large areas of the Outer Islands to foreign and domestic investors after 1965 (Manning 1971), although log and rattan exports were badly hit by the bans on exports in the 1980s. Both employment and incomes were adversely affected in several regions such as Central Sulawesi and in Kalimantan, and the export bans – which were replaced by prohibitively high tariffs in 1993 – have been costly, especially to the Outer Island economies.

Industry
Industry was the *prima donna* sector from the late 1960s, starting from a very small base share of GDP (11 per cent in the mid 1960s). From the late 1980s, manufacturing alone contributed to close to 30 per cent of total GDP growth, in contrast to around a 10 per cent contribution to growth in the late 1960s (Hill 1990, 1996). Only South Korea among developing economies achieved higher rates of sustained growth in manufacturing than Indonesia in the period 1970–90.[15] Indonesia was blessed with a potentially strong labour-intensive sector fed by abundant labour supply, and a range of primary products (timber, rubber and petroleum products) in which value-added could be achieved through domestic processing. Manufacturing investment thus responded quickly to a stable economic

---

[15] Growth of manufacturing in China from 1980–93 rivalled that of Indonesia. In both countries the sector grew at slightly over 11 per cent per annum.

environment, growing consumer demand and government support and protection in the 1970s.

Greater incentives in turn led to the speed-up in growth of manufacturing exports which rose to over half of all exports by 1993 from a minuscule share a decade earlier. Slower growth of some key commodities in the early 1990s – especially garments and the highly regulated plywood industry – raised question marks regarding the sustainability of growth (James 1995). Nevertheless, there has also been diversification into a wide range of labour-intensive products – footwear and toys, chemicals, electronics and machine goods.

Part of the growth in the industrial sector can be attributed to rapid expansion of the construction industry, in both urban and rural areas. Considerable government emphasis on infrastructure development helped this growth, especially during the oil boom years when construction sector value-added grew by around 13 per cent per annum. The wide geographical dispersion of public works programmes in turn made a major contribution to regional development (Hill 1996).

Services

The share of services in GDP remained relatively stable, although the sector grew steadily since the late 1960s. Transport, financial services and government administration all grew at around 10 per cent per annum over the period 1970–90. Growth was particularly rapid during the period of rehabilitation and oil boom when government administration and services expanded widely, although expansion of the service sector slowed down in the 1980s. Improvements in infrastructure supported the growth of both trade and transport throughout the archipelago. Even the most isolated villages in Java had been connected through public transport routes to towns and major cities by the mid 1980s.

Income growth, poverty and welfare

Rapid economic growth since 1967 has contributed to a significant improvement in per-capita incomes and a sharp decline in the incidence of poverty. Sustained economic growth together with falling population growth rates meant a near tripling of per-capita income through to 1992. Even more eye-catching was the decline in the incidence of poverty from well over 50 per cent in 1976 to around 20 per cent in 1987 and 14 per cent in 1993 (World Bank 1990; Hill 1996: table 10.2). Other indicators support the picture of a sustained improvement in the welfare of the population. These include large increases in per-capita rice and food consumption, declining fertility and mortality and a dramatic increase in the consumption of basic consumer durables – radios, bicycles and the like.[16]

At the same time, caution needs to be taken in drawing comparisons between Indonesia with the East Asian miracle economies, or even with Thailand or Malaysia. Per-capita income in purchasing power parity terms was only one-half of that in Thailand and around one-third of that in Malaysia in the mid 1990s. In per-capita income terms, Indonesia was still closer to India and Pakistan than to either of these two countries, let alone the more industrialised economies of East Asia.

Similarly, while poverty decline has been impressive, the cut-off point was very low – less than US$20 per capita per month in the early 1990s, even in urban areas. Average per-capita expenditure in the late 1980s was close to US$25 per capita per month, and at a cut-off point of US$50 per month around half the Indonesian population would have been below the poverty line. Thirty years is not enough time for the majority of the population to enjoy living standards which could be judged acceptable by even semi-industrialised economy standards.

Aggregate data suggest that income has remained relatively evenly distributed by developing country standards. The gini ratio for consumption expenditure was around 0.30–0.35 throughout the 1970s and 1980s. This is much lower than figures of closer to 0.5 or above reported for incomes in both Thailand and Malaysia, and common in many Latin American countries (Booth 1992b; Krongkaew 1994).[17]

For many, such trends are surprising in light of the conspicuous consumption of a small minority of relatively rich Indonesians. Few would disagree that the distribution of wealth, at least the share of the top 1 per cent or less, probably worsened, especially during the more recent period of deregulation, consistent with a general perception of a worsening in the distribution of non-wage incomes from rent and capital assets.

Comparisons with neighbouring countries

General improvements in living standards have been common to all rapidly growing economies in the region. Like many of the other East Asian economies, high savings and investment rates, and recent rapid growth in exports underpin economic performance in Indonesia. Indonesian development has shared much in common with Malaysia and

---

[16] See village-level developments reported by Keyfitz (1985), Singarimbun (1993) and Edmundson (1994).
[17] Direct comparisons from expenditure data cannot be made with distributional measures based on income – gini ratios are generally lower for expenditure than for income.

Economic and social transformation 65

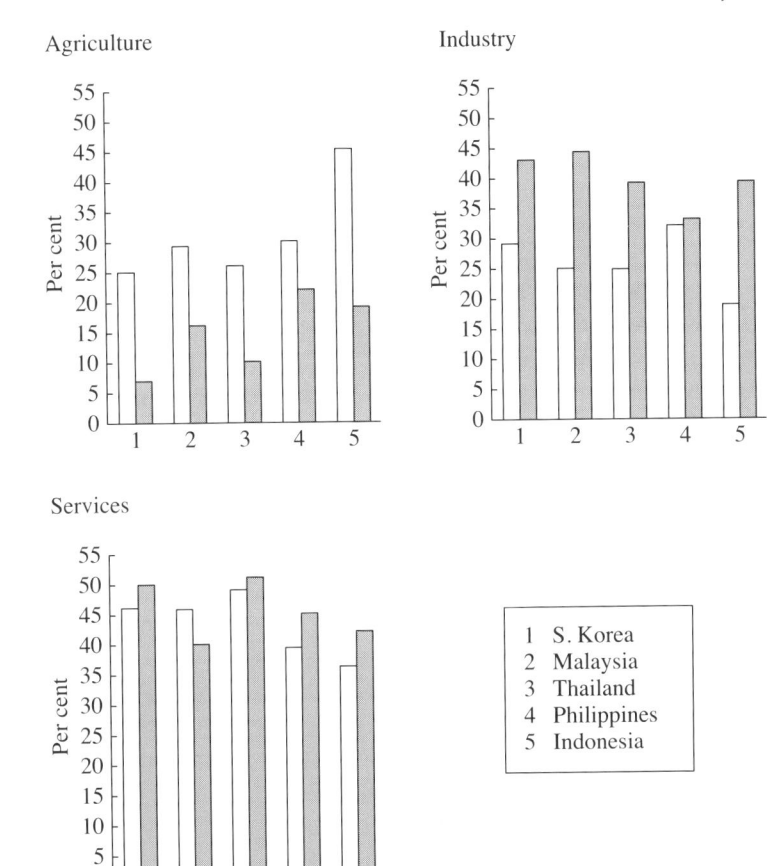

Agriculture

Industry

Services

1	S. Korea
2	Malaysia
3	Thailand
4	Philippines
5	Indonesia

☐ 1970   ■ 1993

Figure 3.3 Share of GDP by major economic sector for selected East Asian economies, 1970 and 1993 (per cent)
Notes: 1 South Korea, 2 Malaysia, 3 Thailand, 4 Philippines, 5 Indonesia
Sources: World Bank, *World Development Report*, 1985 (World Development Indicators, various tables); Asian Development Bank, Key Indicators, 1994 (data for Malaysia 1993).

Thailand, including the declining share of agriculture, the dramatic increase in the share of industry in GDP and steady growth in the service sector share (figure 3.3).[18]

---

[18] The manufacturing share grew more rapidly in Malaysia, where the share of services actually declined as a share of GDP over the period 1970–93.

Aside from a low starting point, five important differences help explain why labour market changes varied from several of Indonesia's rapidly growing neighbours

- The rice sector accounted for around half of all food crop value-added in Indonesia in the late 1980s (Booth 1988). In contrast, agricultural development was much more diversified in the early years of development in South Korea and especially in Taiwan, and later in Malaysia and Thailand.[19] Real wage incomes were protected through an increasingly abundant supply of the staple foods in Indonesia. However, the dominance of rice in agriculture growth meant that there was limited potential for production linkages to agro-processing and light industry based on agriculture.
- Investment was largely generated through foreign capital inflow (public and private) and taxes on oil production rather than higher rates of household saving in the early years. Agricultural producers were not squeezed, nor for the most part were household savings mobilised to generate capital for industrialisation to the same extent as occurred in some other countries.
- The public sector played a major role in the growth in domestic demand and capital formation, rising from less than 10 per cent of GDP in the 1960s to over 20 per cent in the 1990s. While domestic private investment became more important in the 1980s, the public sector has been central to development performance.
- A significant share of growth was in heavily protected industries. Several of these (such as steel, fertiliser, oil refining and aircraft manufacture) were dominated by government direct investment (Hill 1990). It was only in the second half of the 1980s that private, export-oriented manufacturing growth began to become a powerful force in Indonesian development – 10–20 years later than in the NIEs, Malaysia and Thailand.
- Although the share of exports to GDP rose steeply in Indonesia, the manufacturing share was much lower than in all other rapidly growing East Asian economies until the 1990s. Even then, the manufacturing export share of GDP (around 10–15 per cent) was less than half that of South Korea and much lower than that of Thailand and Malaysia. Whereas labour-intensive agricultural products remained important sources of foreign exchange in Thailand and Malaysia in the early 1990s, these commodities accounted for less than 15 per cent of total exports in Indonesia. The bulk of primary exports consisted of

[19] Oshima (1988), Barlow and Jayasuriya (1987) and Siamwalla (1993).

oil, gas and other mineral exports. Thus, on balance, although Indonesia is a relatively open economy, its exports were less concentrated in rapidly growing manufacturing or in agriculture, where employment effects of output growth were likely to be substantial.

Economic policy

There have also been many similarities in the overall economic policy framework adopted by the Soeharto government and that of other rapidly growing East Asian governments. Economic stability was pursued through conservative fiscal and monetary policies (by developing country standards) and swift response to potential economic crises. Economic growth was supported through a deft combination of deregulatory reforms, on the one hand, and substantial government intervention in economic affairs, on the other.

The overall mix of these policies adopted by the government has had important implications for labour market outcomes (table 3.6).[20]

Stabilisation policies

Economic stabilisation was understandably a key objective of policy for a government that had inherited a legacy of runaway inflation, a foreign exchange crisis and food supply uncertainty (Arndt 1971). A tradition of quasi-balanced budgets, control over the money supply and the courting of aid donors for foreign exchange, became important elements of stabilisation policy under Soeharto.[21] In general, the policies were remarkably successful. Although still high by regional standards, rates of inflation were held at below 20 per cent during the oil boom period and below 10 per cent from the mid 1980s (Hill 1994: 88–90). Despite fears of capital flight, the government boldly devalued the rupiah substantially on three occasions. It contained subsequent domestic demand pressures after the last two devaluations, in a successful attempt to ensure maintenance of international competitiveness in key export industries (Garnaut 1980; Warr 1984a, 1992).

Domestic sources of revenue were pursued vigorously in the 1980s, following an initial period of dependence on foreign aid and oil revenues.

---

[20] The most detailed treatment of economic policy formulation can be found in Woo, Glassburner and Nasution (1994: chapters 6–10).
[21] In a technical sense the budget was never balanced, since aid and foreign borrowings are recorded as revenue to meet the gap between government domestic revenues and outlays (Booth 1992a).

Table 3.6. *Key episodes of economic development and policy in Indonesia under the New Order, 1965–1995*

Years/episodes	1965–73 Stabilisation and rehabilitation	1973–81 The oil boom
1 Major challenges/problems	Economic stabilisation (control of inflation, balance budget and reduce current account deficit); restore international confidence. Problems of stagnant agricultural and industrial output, and breakdown in communications and inter-regional transport linkages.	Manage the substantial increase in the current account surplus and government revenue associated with the oil boom. Avoid overvaluation of the exchange rate and use the oil boom to directly support and help stimulate economic and social development. Control extra-budgetary expenditures (the PERTAMINA oil company crisis in 1975) and considerable nationalist criticism of dependence on foreign aid and investment.
2 Macro-economic policies and reforms	Introduce balanced budget, control money supply, deregulate foreign account and encourage foreign aid.	Sterilisation of the windfall oil gains, faced with problems of inflation and an overvalued exchange rate. Considerable budgetary discipline, despite temptations, and tightening of management after PERTAMINA crisis. Increasing recourse to protection mainly through quantitative restrictions.
3 Development programmes and investment	Support for rice sector and rehabilitate infrastructure and communications. Policies adopted to attract foreign investment and encourage domestic investment. First five-year development plan with a heavy influence on agriculture. Beginnings of a national family planning programme.	Large investments in irrigation, rural and regional infrastructure and social sectors (education and health) through expanded development budget and regional grants. Expansion of transmigration and state investment in capital-intensive industries. Restriction of foreign investment. Greater emphasis on poverty alleviation and equity.
4 Economic performance leading sectors	Stabilisation achieved in 1967–68. Rapid output growth in all three major sectors (agriculture, industry and services). Substantial growth in manufacturing and significant inflows of foreign investment.	Oil and gas are the leading sectors. Continued rapid and relatively balanced economic growth across sectors and regions. Rapid manufacturing growth oriented to domestic market. A steep decline in rural poverty, especially on Java.

| Years/episodes | 1982–7
Slower economic growth | 1987–95
The non-oil boom |
|---|---|---|
| 1 Major challenges/ problems | Slowdown in economic growth in 1982 with decline in oil prices and world recession. Major budgetary crisis in 1986 with plummeting of oil prices and fall-off in revenues. Following the yen revaluation in 1985, a sharp rise in Indonesia's foreign debt. | Economic reform to support non-oil export growth and private investment. Maintain economic stability as the economy began to grow rapidly again. Raise domestic revenue to replace stagnant oil revenues, and maintain government spending, despite heavy debt repayments. |
| 2 Macro-economic policies and reforms | Rescheduling of major high-tech and resource-based projects. First deregulation of banking, and taxation reforms (including a value added tax). Beginnings of liberalisation of trade regime and foreign investment regulations. Major devaluations in 1983 and 1986 lowering the real exchange rate. Cut-backs in budget expenditures to accommodate increased debt repayments and the fall in oil revenues in 1986. Freeze in public sector salaries and bans on exports of logs and rattan. | Reforms in both the financial and real sectors. Liberalisation of foreign investment controls, reduction in effective rates of protection and replacement of non-trade barriers with tariffs. Control of inflation and 'shock therapy' taken to avoid possible currency crises. Banking reforms (1988) allow competition from foreign banks. An active programme of labour market intervention through minimum wages and worker social security legislation. |
| 3 Development programmes and investment | Early emphasis on regional and rural development programmes in years of slower economic growth and then a reversal of these policies with the second oil price 'shock' in 1986. Substantial cut-backs in development expenditures and attempts to bolster investment through increased incentives to foreign and domestic investors. | Maintenance of major development programmes owing to success in raising tax revenues. Major investments in high-tech projects such as aircraft. Substantial increase in foreign investment inflows. Replacement of economic 'technocrats' and greater influence of Minister Habibie in economic decision-making. |
| 4 Economic performance/ leading sectors | Slower economic growth. Major role of rice sector in economic growth in the early 1980s. Non-oil exports begin to emerge as a leading sector. Despite economic difficulties, poverty continues to decline, especially on Java. | Return to high rates of economic growth (6–8 per cent per annum). Substantial growth in non-oil exports in manufacturing as the leading sector. Domestic inflation high but below double digit levels. Rapid manufacturing employment growth, continued poverty decline and stable income distribution. |

Foreign and domestic investors gained confidence from relative economic stability and growth in investment contributed to rapid expansion of the private sector.

Liberalisation versus government controls

The Indonesian economy was heavily regulated when Soeharto came to power. Three periods of changing regulation occurred through to the mid 1990s: an initial period of liberalisation (1967–73), a period of increased regulation (1974–83) and a second period of liberalisation (1983–95).

In the initial period prior to the oil boom, freeing of the Indonesian economy to capital flows, the lifting of restrictions on foreign investment and the abolition of multiple exchange rates all contributed to investment and trade. Less pressure on the balance of payments and the necessity to court foreign investment during the oil boom led to a reversal of the liberalisation process. This period was marked by the introduction of various controls over foreign investment, a mushrooming of both tariff and non-tariff barriers to trade and involvement of the government in investment in heavy industry (Booth and McCawley 1981). Although the economy grew rapidly, there were strong pressures to restrict competition.

From 1983 to 1988, and especially after a major oil price slump in 1986, the government introduced a series of deregulation measures. The main goal was to stimulate private investment and manufacturing exports.[22] Oil could no longer play the leading sector role it had done in the 1970s, and overall economic growth and stability were jeopardised.

The reforms, concentrated in the period 1983–8 covered three major areas

- the removal of controls over banking and interest rates
- reduction in tariffs, removal of non-tariff barriers
- the dismantling of the plethora of restrictions and bureaucratic obstacles which hampered foreign and domestic investment (table 3.6).

The reforms were remarkably successful, attracting new investment and stimulating non-oil exports. Economic growth was not only higher, but there was also expansion of labour-intensive manufacturing output, in contrast to more capital-intensive investments in the1980s.

---

[22] See especially Arndt and Hill (1988), Woo, Glassburner and Nasution (1994: chapter 9) and James (1995).

Development programmes

From early in the New Order, the government introduced a separate development budget as part of its longer-term development planning effort.[23] Investments in the development budget were especially targeted to agriculture, infrastructure, education and regional development, much of which was dispersed to the far-flung regions of Indonesia, in both urban and rural areas.[24] From the second Five-Year Plan (REPELITA II) beginning in 1974/5, employment creation was included as one of the main objectives of the development plan.

The development budget grew rapidly in real terms to slightly over half of total expenditure during the oil boom years, before falling back to closer to 40 per cent in the years of slower economic growth in the 1980s. The introduction of a special programme of public works (INPRES) in the early 1970s was especially important for regional development and employment (de Witt 1973).

Adjustment to oil boom and slump

The most dramatic macroeconomic development during the period 1970–90 was the oil boom, marked by the 1973 and 1979 increases in international oil prices. The boom offered the Indonesian government a unique opportunity to raise domestic capital formation substantially. It also reduced pressing foreign exchange and budgetary constraints. The challenge was to raise public spending without causing substantial inflation and economic instability, jeopardising growth in output and incomes.

Indonesia was one of the most successful oil exporters in managing the oil boom (Gelb *et al.* 1988; Warr 1986, 1992a). Three aspects of this management were particularly relevant to labour markets

- One of the major objectives of government policy through the oil boom period was to achieve rice self-sufficiency. After some early setbacks, this policy was spectacularly successful. Investments in irrigation and subsidies for production inputs made a major contribution to output growth (Booth 1988; Tabor 1992). A relative surplus of foreign exchange provided the government with the opportunity to import large quantities of rice prior to the achievement of self-sufficiency. This was achieved with minor disturbance to existing development

---

[23] Plans extended over a five-year period beginning with the first five-year plan in 1969/70.
[24] In 1992 these allocations accounted for approximately 60 per cent of the total development budget (Hill 1996: table 4.4).

programmes. Indonesia's most important wage good remained cheap, short periods of rising prices due to poor seasons notwithstanding, and in abundant supply throughout the 1970s.
- The oil boom facilitated a major expansion in investment on infrastructure through the INPRES and other government programmes. These developments had a major impact on labour mobility and access to new local and interprovincial employment opportunities. Indonesia made a quantum leap in investment in human capital, in particular in primary schooling and primary health care.
- The oil boom was not entirely a blessing, although it was not the curse that it had been in many other developing economies. The boom enabled an extension of government into many areas of economic policy. It also produced 'Dutch disease' effects which discouraged the growth of traditional and new manufacturing exports. East Asia oil importers made major adjustments which facilitated export and employment growth at this time. Indonesia delayed the transition to a more open economy, with important implications for the labour market.

The government's adjustment to the slump in oil prices was swift, confirming the saying that good times frequently make for bad policies and *vice versa*. The pace of reform slackened after economic growth rates picked up in the late 1980s. However, despite pessimism regarding increasing vested and first family interests in business affairs, trade reform continued unabated. There was a substantial decline in estimated effective protection in almost all sectors from 1987–94 (Fane and Condon 1996).

Population, human resources and labour force

This period of rapid and episodic economic change occurred in an environment in which labour supply was growing rapidly. Four aspects of Indonesia's population are relevant to the discussion of labour markets: its size, rates of growth, age structure and educational composition.

Population

Like many developing economies, Indonesia faced major problems of high levels of population density and rapid population growth when economic development began to be pursued in earnest after 1965. When Soeharto came to power in 1965, Indonesia's population was a little over 100 million, nearly half was aged less than 15, over 80 per cent lived in rural areas and

Table 3.7. *Population size, distribution and growth: Indonesia, 1971–2000*

	1971	1980	1990	1995[a]	2000[a]
Total population (m.)	119	147	179	195	210
% on Java	65	62	60	59	n.a.
% Urban	17	22	31	n.a.	n.a.
% <15 years	44	41	37	33	31
15–64	53	56	59	63	64
65+	3	3	4	4	5
Population density (persons/km^2)					
Indonesia	62	77	93	–	–
Java	576	690	814	–	–
Growth of population[b]					
Total	2.3	2.0	1.7	1.5	
Age 15–64	2.9	2.7	2.6	2.3	
Urban	5.2	6.4	n.a.	n.a.	
Rural	1.7	0.8	n.a.	n.a.	
Java: Total	2.0	1.6	1.3	1.1	
Rural	1.0	0.1	n.a.	n.a.	
Outer Islands: Total	3.0	2.4	2.2	2.0	
Rural	2.8	1.7	n.a.	n.a.	

Notes: [a] Projected; [b] 1971–80 excluding East Timor.
Source: CBS, Population Censuses, 1971, 1980 and 1990; Population Projections by Province, 1990–2000, Jakarta, 1993.

nearly 70 per cent lived in Java (table 3.7). A very small proportion (less than 10 per cent) of the population aged 15 and above had completed lower secondary school (figure 3.4).

This profile of the population is not much different from that of many developing countries at that time, except that the numbers were much larger in Indonesia. Inevitably the small modern sector would have to grow very rapidly to absorb a significant proportion of the working population, let alone provide jobs for new job entrants.

Thirty years later, the population had nearly doubled to just under 200 million. The younger age group in the population was absolutely larger at around 65 million. The urban population share had increased to over 30 per cent. The largest, rapidly growing urban regions were the industrialising centres close to Jakarta. However, unlike the situation in countries such as Thailand and South Korea, urban population growth has continued to be widely spread throughout the archipelago.

In 1990, Indonesia had the lowest level of capital city primacy (16 per cent of the population living in Jakarta) of all the major countries of Southeast Asia, compared with Bangkok (57 per cent) at one extreme and Kuala Lumpur (22 per cent) at the other (Pernia 1993a).

74 *Economic growth and labour market dynamics*

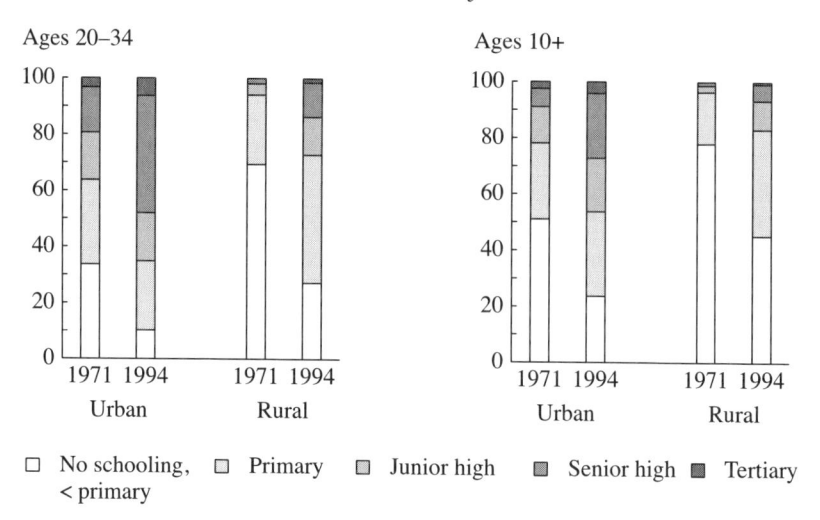

Ages 20–34

Ages 10+

☐ No schooling, < primary   ☐ Primary   ☐ Junior high   ■ Senior high   ■ Tertiary

Figure 3.4 Educational status of the population in Indonesia (level of completed schooling), 1971 and 1994
Source: CBS, Population Census, 1971 (Series D) and National Labour Force Survey, 1994.

Population increased quite rapidly, over 2 per cent per annum in the 1970s, and the working age population (15–64) grew even more rapidly due to the young age structure.

However, Indonesia is among a handful of countries in which a fall in population growth rates has been dramatic, both because of rapid economic changes and government policy. By the late 1980s population growth had begun to decline quite markedly. It fell below 2 per cent for the decade, and is expected to record around 1.5 per cent per annum for the period 1995–2000. A substantial decline in fertility (especially during the 1980s) was the major factor contributing to lower rates of population growth.[25]

Population growth rates were much higher in the Outer Islands. Rates of natural increase were around one-third higher than in Java during the 1970s and 1980s, principally because of higher birth rates. Inter-regional migration has also been significant and has had a more immediate impact on labour markets, especially during the peak years of the transmigration programme.

Looking to the future, lower fertility will in turn translate into a fall in working age population growth rates from the mid 1990s when it is pro-

[25] Hugo, *et al.* (1987) and Hull (1991). Total fertility rates are estimated to have fallen from 6 in the late 1960s to 4.7 in the late 1970s and 3.3 in the late 1980s among women aged 15–49. They more than halved in Jakarta, East Java and Bali.

jected that the number of young labour force entrants (aged 15–19) will hardly grow at all. These effects will be felt first in Java, where fertility decline preceded that in the Outer Islands, and where net out-migration still predominates.

Education

Indonesia recorded one of the fastest expansions in primary and secondary schooling enrolments in the following two decades of any country in the developing world. The proportion of persons with lower and upper secondary and tertiary schooling more than tripled (figure 3.4). Greater education achievement was associated with relatively rapid urban population growth, supported by movement of persons from less-favourably placed rural areas. It also represented substantial improvement in the schooling of urban residents.

A second key aspect of this educational expansion was the relative rise of female enrolment and educational status. At all levels of schooling the gap between male and female levels of schooling narrowed, as in several other East Asian economies (Jones 1988), with important implications for female labour force participation.

Nevertheless, the extraordinary expansion of education at all levels could only be achieved at some cost in terms of quality and was reflected in quantitative indicators such as dropout rates and teacher–pupil ratios.[26] There is also a wide range in the quality of schooling across institutions and regions with important implications for labour market behaviour of young job seekers.

Labour force growth

In addition to an unfavourable starting point in the late 1960s, relatively rapid labour supply was a major challenge faced by the New Order government. Along with other East Asian countries, Indonesia has faced the forbidding task of absorbing rapidly increasing numbers of young people into the workforce. Not only has labour supply been elastic at prevailing wage rates in the modern sector, but the labour supply curves have moved out continuously.

Labour force growth rates accelerated from just under 3 per cent in the 1970s to 3.4 per cent in the 1980s and then began to slow to slightly below 3 per cent in the 1990s. These growth rates were not particularly high by

---

[26] Godfrey (1992); McMahon and Boediono (1991) and Hill (1992).

Table 3.8. *Labour force growth rates by gender in rural and urban areas: Indonesia, 1971–1990*

	Urban	Rural	Total
Java			
Male	6.3	1.6	2.7
Female	7.4	1.9	3.1
Both sexes	6.6	1.7	2.9
Outer Islands			
Male	5.1	2.9	3.3
Female	7.7	3.9	4.4
Both sexes	5.8	3.3	3.7
Indonesia			
Male	5.9	2.1	2.9
Female	7.5	2.7	3.6
Both sexes	6.4	2.3	3.2

Sources: CBS, Population Census, 1971 (Series C), 1990 (Series S2).

developing economy or East Asian standards in the post-war period – although they were higher than when industrial economies first began to industrialise.[27] Labour force growth meant a near doubling of the total labour force in less than 25 years, increasing to 80 million in the mid 1990s. This growth, combined with the large population base, adds a further dimension to the labour market problem as annual increases in numbers of job seekers grew to over two million in the mid 1990s.

Associated with urbanisation, the urban labour force grew at almost triple the rate of growth of the rural labour force – at just over 6 per cent per annum compared with slightly over 2 per cent per annum for the rural population (table 3.8). Consequently the share of the urban workforce almost doubled from 15 per cent of the labour force in 1971. Urban areas accounted for just over 40 per cent of the increment in the labour force during the same period.[28]

The 1970s and 1980s were decades when absorption of relatively uneducated workers was top of the policy agenda. As Jones (1994: 172–3) notes, a major challenge for the rest of the 1990s will be to cope with the dramatic increase in growth in numbers of secondary educated.

> The 1990s will remain a problem period for employment...attention will shift to the issues of 'age dualism' in the labour force (a rapidly growing older and

---

[27] Labour force growth rates were around three times those in Japan, and the difference was even greater compared with most countries in Europe when they began to industrialise.
[28] The rate of urban growth is overstated, owing to both reclassification and changing definitions of rural and urban areas between 1971 and 1980. See especially Hugo *et al.* (1987).

poorly-educated segment and a slowly growing and well-educated, younger segment) and the problem of altering the structure of employment quickly enough to provide 'acceptable' jobs for the growing number of educated young labour force entrants.

Increased female participation rates contributed to around half the growth of the female labour force in the 1980s and just under 40 per cent of the growth in the period 1971–90. These increases were also a significant contributor to higher total labour force growth: higher activity rates among women contributed to around 20 per cent of the total labour force growth in the 1980s.[29]

Regional dimensions and international migration

The focus on national patterns is justified on the grounds that the concentration of political power in Jakarta has meant much less regional political and economic autonomy than in other large countries, notably India and China. Provinces in Indonesia have little control over regional finance, there is remarkable similarity in development programmes initiated throughout the country, and there are virtually no formal barriers to population movement throughout the country. Nevertheless, in a country as physically dispersed as Indonesia, it is impossible to ignore the large differences in economic structure and growth between various regions of the country.

Traditionally a dichotomy has been drawn between Java and Bali, and the Outer Islands of Indonesia in terms of a range of demographic, economic and ecological factors. Java (which contained just under 60 per cent of the population and 7 per cent of the land area in 1995) is characterised by a range of problems associated with high levels of population density. At the same time, it has benefited from the concentration of population, political and administrative power since colonial times.

While there are good grounds for this dualistic characterisation of Indonesian social and economic life, it has become less relevant as the demographic and economic structure has changed. New patterns of regional differences have emerged.[30] While most of Indonesia's population still resides in Java, several Outer Island provinces have high levels of population density and much higher levels of poverty than in Java. The regions to the west and east of Java stand out in particular – Lampung and

[29] Appendix table 3.2 shows data on participation rate changes, 1971–90.
[30] See especially Pelzer (1963) for a discussion of regional contrasts circa 1960. Hill (1989) is the standard reference on the subject of regional economic structure and change through to the mid 1980s.

the two Nusa Tenggara provinces. Agriculture continues to dominate the economies in the poorer regions of Indonesia. In many of these regions rural populations have continued to grow rapidly, despite low agricultural productivity and limited job opportunities.

On the other hand, the development advantage held by Java increased in some respects. Java was always more urbanised, although at a low level until the 1980s. The contrast with many other parts of Indonesia has grown as Java's rural population growth slowed, and people increasingly became absorbed into non-agricultural employment in major cities. Manufacturing production continues to be heavily concentrated in Java. While rural poverty in Java was unquestionably Indonesia's major development challenge in the late 1960s, this was much less the case in the 1990s. Attention increasingly turned to the worrying human resource development profile and the development prospects of Eastern Indonesia.

Finally, uneven rates of economic development across provinces have contributed to a wider range of economic structures, even if measured inequalities across provinces do not appear to have worsened significantly (Akita and Lukman 1995). The concentration of new mining, gas and oil activities in several provinces in Sumatra and Kalimantan, the growth of manufacturing employment in timber-based industries in Kalimantan, and the expansion of estate cash crops in southern Sumatra are all developments which point to much more varied rural economies than two decades ago.

Regional labour force growth and migration

While labour force growth rates had begun to fall sharply in Java (and Bali), rates remain high in the Outer Islands. Like population, labour force growth rates have been more rapid in the Outer Islands than in Java. There was a tendency for these differences to widen in the 1980s. Higher growth in the Outer Islands' labour force was primarily reflected in a more rapid increase in rural areas, partly a legacy of the transmigration programme.

Labour mobility between regions has long been an important feature of Indonesia's labour market. Mobility increased greatly after economic growth accelerated (Hugo 1978). Three types of flows have dominated interprovincial migration

- government-assisted family transmigration, principally to rural Sumatra, which peaked in the period of the late 1970s and early 1980s
- spontaneous movement of individual workers especially to the resource-rich provinces

- the movement of Outer Islanders to urban Java, primarily to the Greater Jakarta region.

The net movement of recent migrants – those moving in the five-year period prior to the census – was strongly in favour of the Outer Islands in 1975–80 and 1985–90 (table 3.9). Aggregate net flows from Java principally to rural areas in the Outer Islands were largest during the heyday of the transmigration programme during the oil boom period. The impact on total population growth in Java was quite small. During this period it probably lowered population growth by around 5 per cent below that which would have resulted from natural increase alone.[31]

The impact was much greater in receiving areas in Sumatra. Transmigration had the effect of raising total population growth by about 10–15 per cent above the rate which could have been produced by natural increase alone. The net impact declined in importance, however, during the 1980s as migration to rural Sumatra slowed and the counter flows to urban Java increased. Counter flows to urban Java point to Java's growing attraction for more mobile and educated workers from the Outer Islands, as job opportunities expanded during the liberalisation period. By 1990–5, probably for the first time in the New Order period, net migration was in favour of Java, as rural flows to Sumatra and other Outer Islands fell dramatically.

The impact of transmigration and labour migration on labour force growth rates was quite uneven among Outer Island provinces. By far the largest flows were to rural Sumatra, especially to the southernmost province of Lampung. Lampung had been the prime destination area for transmigration up till the late 1970s. The flow of migrants from Java to resource-rich provinces was much smaller and directed to urban as well as rural areas. The impact of transmigration was nevertheless quite large in sparsely populated regions, such as East Kalimantan, where net migration increased population growth by around one-third.

While there was in-migration to the resource-abundant provinces (Sumatra, Kalimantan and Irian Jaya) several other land-scarce and poorer provinces (West Sumatra, West and East Nusatenggara, South and North Sulawesi) experienced out-migration. During the 1970s and increasingly in the 1980s the principal flows were to Java, to other resource-rich provinces and abroad.

---

[31] These rough orders of magnitude do not take into account the indirect effects of migration on age structure, birth rates and mortality patterns in sending and receiving areas. See World Bank (1984: annex 2, part II, table 2.9) for calculations for the 1970s.

Table 3.9. Gross and net recent migration between Java and Outer Island provinces, 1975–1980, 1985–1990 and 1980–1995[a]

	1975–80 Currently residing			1985–90 Currently residing			1990–95 Currently residing		
	Urban areas	Rural areas	Both urban & rural	Urban areas	Rural areas	Both urban & rural	Urban areas	Rural areas	Both urban & rural
Migration flows (000)									
Java to Outer Islands	239	870	1109	393	707	1100	323	292	615
(Java to Sumatra)	(111)	(699)	(810)	(154)	(465)	(619)	(129)	(159)	(188)
Outer Islands to Java	304	114	418	449	256	705	465	292	757
(Sumatra to Java)	(196)	(65)	(260)	(280)	(179)	(459)	(282)	(175)	(457)
Net Migration (000)									
Java with the Outer Islands	+65	−756	−691	+56	−451	−395	+142	0	+142

Note: [a] Recent migrants are defined as all persons aged five years and above resident in a province, who lived in a different province up to five years earlier.
Source: CBS, Population Censuses, 1980 and 1990, and Intercensal Survey, 1995.

International labour migration

Compared with the neighbouring Philippines and Malaysia, the volume of international migration flows have quite small in comparison with total population and labour force growth. Owing to substantial illegal migration to Malaysia, it is difficult to provide an estimate of net flows.[32] Three patterns are clear:[33]

- Out-migration remains small in relation to total population and labour force growth: rarely exceeding 50,000 per annum for most years from 1965–90, and probably between 50,000 and 100,000, stabilising around the mid 1990s.
- Net out-migration exceeded in-migration by a considerable margin, probably by a factor of around 3–5:1. The registered foreign workers – around 18,000 in the mid 1980s, rising to just under 60,000 in 1995 – were mainly professional and managerial personnel.
- Both out- and in-migration streams increased in the 1990s; out-migration to Malaysia became increasingly attractive after Malaysia's real wage rates began to increase substantially in the second half of the 1980s (Guinness 1990; Hugo 1993).[34] Whereas migrants to Saudi Arabia (as in Hong Kong and Singapore) were mainly female domestic servants, in Malaysia they were involved in a wider range of sectors (services, construction, estate agriculture and timber). Out-migrants mainly consisted of Sumatrans, Javanese and Sasak from Lombok to West Malaysia, and the migration of workers from Flores and South Sulawesi to East Malaysia. Local labour market effects appear to have been especially intense in the poorer and smaller islands of Lombok and Flores.

Conclusion

It is sometimes difficult to recall the labour problems which Indonesia faced in 1965, based on a perspective of Indonesia from Jakarta or other major cities in the mid 1990s. The fundamental problems posed by low

---

[32] Estimates are based on Hugo (1993a, 1993b). Department of Manpower (1993: 117–27) and reports in Indonesian and Malaysian media and other official publications (see especially *Dewan Masyarakat* [Kuala Lumpur] June 1995, p. 9; *New States Times*, 3 June and 18 May 1995; *Kompas 19* June 1995, 23 and 27 September and 16 December 1993). The author thanks Sidney Jones for drawing attention to the Malaysian sources.

[33] Based on Hugo (1993a, 1993b), Department of Manpower (1993: 117–27) and media reports in Indonesia and Malaysia.

[34] The number of illegal TKI working in Malaysia rose from half a million around 1990–1 to closer to between 750,000 and one million by 1995 (*Dewan Masyarakat* June 1995, *Kompas 19* June 1995).

levels of rural productivity and incomes dominated discussions of employment in the early period of the New Order, and are often forgotten given the current focus on issues of industrial unrest and human resource development.

Enormous changes have occurred in economic life since the mid 1960s. These have permeated all sections of society and affected all regions of Indonesia, albeit unevenly. The overall picture is one of extraordinary economic gains compared with initial conditions. These were for the most part supported by astute stabilisation and development policies.

Rapid economic growth has had a major impact on employment and wages through its influence on labour demand, as in other East Asian countries. At the same time, several special features of economic growth in Indonesia had distinct labour market effects. These include big improvements in physical and human capital from a slender base, the effect of the oil boom on economic performance and the delayed introduction of liberalisation measures until the 1980s.

The tendency to ignore the problem of labour conditions in rural Indonesia today can be traced to a failure to appreciate the fundamentally rural origins of the employment problem in the 1960s. Labour activists see the desperate plight of workers in factories as a product of employer exploitation. Technologists led by the dynamic Minister Habibie often view investment in know-how as the principal means for achieving economic progress. The pursuit of comparative advantage based on the reality of low wages is often derided as revisionist and callous.

Both groups underestimate the challenge posed by continuing rural deprivation, partly related to the underdeveloped nature of the economy in 1965. Even in the mid 1990s, after 30 years of sustained growth, the major problem is to provide better jobs for well over half the population which resides in poor villages or in urban slums.

Appendix table 3.1. *Labour force participation rates in Indonesia, 1971–1990*

	1971	1980	1990	% increase 1971–90
Male				
Urban	61.2	59.1	64.0	5
Rural	70.4	71.2	74.4	6
Total	68.7	68.5	71.1	3[a]
Female				
Urban	22.5	24..2	31.6	40
Rural	34.2	35.2	42.2	23
Total	32.1	32.7	38.8	21[a]
Both sexes	49.9	50.2	54.7	10
Age standardised[b]				
Male	70.0	68.5	71.4	2
Female	31.9	32.7	38.6	21

Notes: [a] The total is *less* than the percentage increase for urban and rural areas because of changing composition of work force.
[b] Age distribution in 1971 as standard.
Source: CBS, Population Censuses, 1980 and 1990.

4

New jobs and rising productivity: the formal–informal sector divide

> The shift from agriculture to other sectors means urbanisation and the numerous corollaries which this change in mode of life implies; it means a shift from small, individually managed enterprises, to large-scale productive units, often organised in even larger economic management units – with all the implications that follow for economic status of human beings and the division of society into economic and social classes. (Simon Kuznets 1957: 56)

Two shifts in the structure of employment have been associated with economic change in rapidly growing East Asian economies (see chapter 2)

- a decline in the share of employment in low productivity sectors (especially agriculture)
- rapid expansion of wage employment much of which has typically been concentrated in manufacturing.

This pattern of employment growth contrasted with parts of Latin America and South Asia, which experienced various combinations of stunted labour absorption in manufacturing, and the greater role for service industries in labour absorption.

Indonesia has experienced a mix of both favourable and less-favourable employment outcomes. This result can be attributed to the different starting point, the economic structure, external economic shocks and economic policy. Following the experience of other countries described by Simon Kuznets, the fall in the share of employment in agriculture has meant greater wage employment in larger units, both in the private and public sectors. At the same time this has also been accompanied by growth in non-wage employment, chiefly in informal activities in towns and cities throughout Indonesia.

Longer-term employment shifts

Employment growth was rapid from the 1970s,[1] mirroring that of the labour force. Aggregate unemployment rates remained remarkably stable

---

[1] More recent data are available from national labour force surveys (SAKERNAS). Because of substantial year-to-year fluctuations, these data have to be interpreted with care, and are

over this period – fluctuating at around 2 per cent until the mid 1990s when it rose perceptively.[2] Thus aggregate employment grew at just over 3 per cent per annum, slightly slower than the total labour force.

The change in the structure of employment differed in several important respects from the changing structure of value-added (see chapter 3). Three patterns stand out. First, the share of agricultural employment fell from around 65 to 50 per cent. Non-agricultural employment grew at over 5 per cent per annum during the period 1971–90 (table 4.1).

This declining trend of agricultural employment was most pronounced in the 1970s when both M- and S-sector shares rose appreciably, and then again from the late 1980s (figure 4.1).[3] Nevertheless, agricultural employment continued to grow absolutely (at just under 2 per cent per annum). The important role which agricultural employment has played is one important characteristic of Indonesia's development over this period.[4]

The agricultural employment share declined slowly compared with that in South Korea, Taiwan or Malaysia, and non-wage employment remained a major feature of employment outside agriculture, both in urban and rural areas (table 4.2). Indeed, the change in the structure of the workforce was closer to the Philippines where economic growth has been much less impressive than these other countries.[5]

Second, the M-sector (chiefly manufacturing and construction) played a significant role in this change. Compared with its low share of total employment (10 per cent), the M-sector recorded a much larger proportionate gain in employment than services. But, relative to growth in value-added in the M-sector (11 per cent per annum), employment growth was

unreliable for detailed examination of longer-term trends. These fluctuations are related to both sampling and non-sampling errors, associated with the small sample fraction covered in the SAKERNAS and changing coverage of specific groups of workers, in particular family workers. See Jones and Manning (1992).

[2] Unemployment rates are generally a poor indicator of labour market imbalance (Turnham 1993). However, the structure of urban unemployment, and how this has changed over time, is an important indicator of the behaviour of urban labour markets (chapter 7).

[3] Indonesia follows international practice in identifying nine one-digit sectors according to the International Standard Industrial Classification (ISIC) Codes, grouped into the three super-sectors as follows: A (agriculture), M (mining, manufacturing, public utilities and construction) and S (trade, transport, banking and other services – government, community and personal services).

[4] In contrast, absolute numbers of persons employed in agriculture had begun to decline by approximately 1980 in both South Korea and Taiwan (Manning 1995).

[5] Nevertheless, Indonesia does differ from the Philippines in one respect: all the decline in the agricultural sector share of employment was associated with a growing S-sector share in the Philippines. The larger gain in the percentage share of employment in the S-sector was experienced by Indonesia, Thailand and the Philippines in contrast to South Korea, Taiwan and Malaysia.

Table 4.1. *Employment, value-added, employment elasticities and labour productivity by major sector: Indonesia, 1971–1990*

		Agriculture	Industry Total	Industry Excluding oil and mining	Services	All sectors Total	All sectors Excluding oil and mining
Employment[a]							
Total (000)	1990	36,113	12,048	11,330	23,409	71,570	70,852
% distribution	1971	66.0	10.0	9.9	24.0	100	100
	1990	50.5	16.8	15.8	32.7	100	100
% growth (p.a.)	1971–80	1.2	6.0	5.6	5.7	2.9	2.9
	1980–90	2.2	5.7	5.6	4.0	3.3	3.2
	1971–90	1.7	5.8	5.6	4.7	3.1	3.1
Distribution of	1971–80	24.2	23.8	21.9	52.0	100	
increment (%)	1980–90	35.2	26.2	24.9	38.6	100	
	1971–90	31.1	25.3	24.0	43.6	100	
Value added and productivity							
Growth of value added[b]	1971–80	4.2	9.4	14.2	7.4	7.3	7.5
(% p.a.)	1980–90	3.2	4.1	8.4	8.0	5.3	6.8
	1971–90	3.6	6.6	11.1	7.7	6.2	7.1
Employment elasticity[c]	1971–80	0.3	0.6	0.4	0.8	0.4	0.4
	1980–90	0.7	1.4	0.7	0.5	0.6	0.5
	1971–90	0.5	0.9	0.5	0.6	0.5	0.4
Labour productivity indices[d]	1971	77	74	46	86	67	66
(1983 prices, 1983 = 100)	1980	100	100	100	100	100	100
	1990	110	85	131	150	122	142
% increase p.a.	1971–90	1.9	0.7	5.5	2.9	3.2	4.0

Notes: [a] All employment data adjusted for exclusion of rural Irian Jaya and East Timor from the 1971 Census. Due to lack of data on hours worked in 1971, no adjustments are made for underemployment in different sectors in the data on employment trends over time; [b] Constant 1983 prices; [c] Percentage change in employment resulting from a 1 per cent change in output; [d] Productivity measured by value-added per employed worker per year.
Sources: CBS, Population Census, 1971 (Series C); 1980 and 1990 (Series S2); National Accounts, various years.

Table 4.2. *Distribution and growth of employment by major sector: Java and the Outer Islands, 1971–1995*

	Share of employment (per cent)			Increment 1971–90[a]	Growth of employment (per cent per annum)	
	1971	1990	1995		1971–90	1990–5
Java						
A	61	43	35	19	1.1	−2.4
M	12	20	23	32	6.0	4.1
S	27	37	42	49	4.6	4.4
Total	100	100	100	100	3.0	1.8
N (000)	(24,762)	(43,795)	(47,834)	(19,033)		
Outer Islands[b]						
A	74	62	57	48	2.4	1.3
M	8	12	12	16	5.5	3.9
S	18	26	31	36	5.2	6.4
Total	100	100	100	100	3.3	3.0
N (000)	(14,401)	(26,813)	(32,276)	(12,412)		

Notes: [a] Share of total employment growth absorbed in each sector; [b] Growth rates for 1971–90 exclude Irian Jaya and East Timor.
Source: CBS, Population Censuses, 1971 (Series C) and 1990.

(a) Agricultural employment share

(b) M- and S-sector employment share

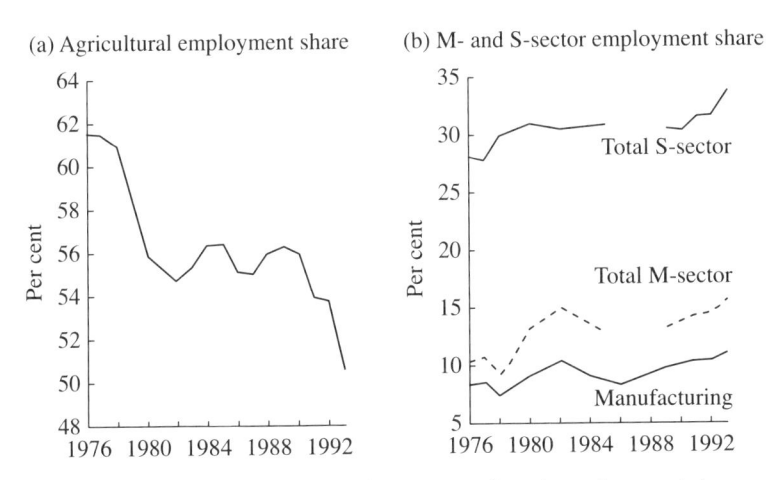

Figure 4.1 Agricultural and non-agricultural employment share: Indonesia, 1976–1993 (per cent)
Note: No data available on the M- and S-sector shares in 1986–8. Total and agricultural employment interpolated for 1979, 1981 and 1983–4.
Sources: CBS, National Labour Force Surveys, 1976–93; Intercensal Survey, 1985; Population Census, 1980.

slow;[6] as a result value-added per worker rose by 5 per cent per annum. Growth rates in value-added per worker were similar to that recorded in the NIEs, but growth of employment in manufacturing was much slower (Galenson 1992; World Bank 1993).

Third, the S-sector also played a major role in employment creation. Growth in value-added was more than double that in agriculture. However, growth in value-added per worker was slow – only slightly above half of that recorded in the M-sector. Consistent with the characteristically dualistic structure of service employment in developing economies (Berry 1978) many of these new jobs in services were relatively labour-intensive. Especially in the early years, they were taken up in response to the relatively limited job opportunities in both agriculture and manufacturing.

Agricultural employment

As in other densely populated Asian countries, trends in agricultural employment are an important indicator of labour welfare. A substantial decline in the share of agricultural workers in total employment, and a fall in the number of people engaged in agriculture, are indicators that a country is close to the turning point (see chapter 2).

Agriculture recorded an overall growth rate of employment of slightly under 2 per cent per annum similar to that recorded by many low-income countries in the period 1960–80 (see table 4.1). The absolute number of people engaged in agriculture continued to rise from just over 25 million in 1971 to just under 40 million in 1990, when the number of agricultural workers began to decline.[7] However, the decline in the share of agricultural employment (65–51 per cent for 1971–90) was considerably slower than the fall in the agricultural sector's share of GDP, which was rapid by developing economy standards over the period 1971–90.

This does not mean, however, that agricultural performance was poor and workers were crowded into a depressed agricultural sector (Warr 1992b). Given growth in agricultural output (above 3.5 per cent per annum), the increase in agricultural employment was partly in response to rapid growth in output. There was a 50 per cent increase

---

[6] Fluctuations in international oil prices have a major impact on trends in production and value-added in the M-sector. Since this sub-sector is negligible in terms of employment, it is useful to refer to non-oil and mining value-added and productivity.

[7] This fall was principally related to a quite steep decline on Java – from a peak of 22 million in 1989–90 to 20 million in 1993–4.

in real value-added per worker in agriculture in the period 1971–90.[8]

The difference between the rapid decline in the agricultural share of GDP, and the slower decline of the labour force share, has been one important structural characteristic of development in Indonesia over the past 20 years. The difference is reflected in a more rapid increase in labour productivity in non-agricultural sectors relative to that in agriculture compared with other developing economies. Whereas the ratio of labour productivity in agriculture to that in the economy as a whole more than halved in Indonesia for 1971–90, it fell only by around one-third in all developing economies over a similar time period. The ratio of labour productivity in non-agriculture to labour productivity in all sectors increased by 25 per cent compared with little change in all other developing economies.[9] Labour productivity was low in non-agricultural sectors initially, and non-agricultural value-added rose more quickly in Indonesia.

The contrast in the labour absorption of wage employees versus non-wage workers has been more marked in agriculture than in other sectors. On the one hand, wage employment in agriculture declined absolutely for Indonesia as a whole in 1971–90. Agriculture's share of all wage work fell dramatically from close to one-half to one-quarter. Alternatively, employment in the non-wage jobs – mainly consisting of self-employed and family workers on small farms – grew by over 2 per cent per annum and accounted for around one-third of all new jobs created (table 4.3).

Java

Two aspects of employment growth have been important in agriculture in Java. Despite many predictions to the contrary, the absolute number of workers continued to increase for two decades. Second, the number of wage workers declined and their share in total employment fell substantially. The share of agriculture in total employment first declined quite sharply during the oil boom, then remained constant in the 1980s, and a sharp decline became evident in the 1990s (figure 4.2).[10]

---

[8] It was the very rapid increase in value-added in both the M- and S-sectors, rather than poor performance in agriculture, which contributed to the steep fall in agriculture's share of GDP. Output growth averaged less than 3 per cent per annum in agriculture in both low-income and middle-income countries (outside China) in the 1980s, and in low-income countries in the 1970s (World Bank, *World Development Report*, 1992).

[9] See ILO (1995: 29) for data for all developing countries.

[10] Writing before the 1985 Intercensal Population Survey results were known, Booth (1988: 187–8) speculated (based on a comparison of data from labour force surveys for 1976 and 1982) that there had been substantial decline in male but not female agricultural employment in Java during the oil boom years. All the national surveys find, however, that this trend was not sustained from around the mid 1980s.

90 *Economic growth and labour market dynamics*

Table 4.3. *Distribution and growth of agricultural employment, wage and non-wage employees: Indonesia, 1971–1990*

	Wage workers	Non-wage workers	All workers
Agricultural employment as a share of total employment (%)			
1971	46	75	66
1990	24	65	50
The increment in agricultural employment as a share of the increment in total employment (%) 1971–90[a]	−2	51	31
Growth rate of agricultural employment (% p.a.)	−0.3	2.1	1.7

Note: [a] Share of total employment growth absorbed in agriculture.
Source: CBS, Population Censuses, 1971 (Series C) and 1990.

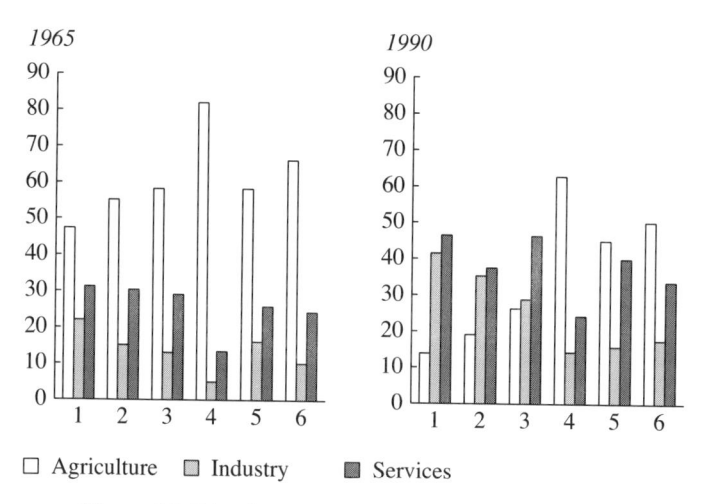

Figure 4.2 Distribution of employment in Indonesia and selected East Asian countries, 1965 and 1990

Notes: 1 Taiwan, 2 South Korea, 3 Malaysia, 4 Thailand, 5 Philippines, 6 Indonesia

Sources: World Bank, *World Development Report*, 1988; ILO, *Yearbook of Labour Statistics*, various years; US Department of Labor, *Foreign Labor Trends*, various years.

The employment record in agriculture in Java is remarkable, despite the common belief that the densely populated island had long reached a stage when surplus labour needed to be directed elsewhere – and given the widely held gloomy predictions for agricultural employment during the green revolution.[11] Several authors drew attention to the labour-displacing potential of new technology and institutions accompanying the introduction of high-yielding rice varieties in the early 1970s.[12] Major displacements of labour did occur, particularly in highly commercialised villages close to major cities (Collier et al. 1982). However, with the benefit of hindsight, predictions based on earlier research were overly pessimistic.

In addition, continued employment growth in Javanese agriculture is related to increased output of products oriented to growing consumer demand. These included upland vegetable farming, cultivation of fruit such as citrus fruits and apples, and animal husbandry, including labour-intensive dairy farming and chicken farming.[13]

The second major development – the decline in the proportion of wage employment in agriculture in Java – has probably been the most important structural change in the Indonesian labour market (table 4.4). Wage employment in agriculture in Java, which accounted for approximately one-third of agricultural jobs in 1971, declined absolutely by just under 1 per cent per annum over the period 1971–90.

What has happened to people previously employed as agricultural wage labourers in Java, or people who would have been absorbed into this sector in previous periods? Three patterns predominated

- a high proportion of people found jobs in informal sector work in urban areas, especially during the oil boom period when agricultural employment registered its most rapid decline
- many existing and potential wage workers found non-agricultural employment in rural areas, especially in service activities such as trade, transport and construction during the oil boom period
- younger people from rural areas increasingly found jobs in manufacturing.

---

[11] Geertz (1963) and Penny and Singarimbun (1973). The intensity of employment in agriculture was not high – indeed official data suggest that a large proportion of persons (53 per cent) employed in agriculture worked fewer than 35 hours in 1990.
[12] See especially Collier et al. (1974), White (1979) and Collier (1981).
[13] Two examples are vegetable and dairy farming in the upland regions of West and Central Java respectively (Manning, Hill and Saefuddin 1988; Effendi 1991).

Table 4.4. *Growth of employment by major sector: Java and the Outer Islands 1971–1990[a] (per cent per annum)*

	Java		Outer Islands	
	Wage workers	Non-wage workers	Wage workers	Non-wage workers
Agriculture	−0.8	1.8	1.8	2.4
	(48)	(70)	(36)	(83)
Non-agriculture	5.2	4.8	6.4	4.2
	(52)	(30)	(64)	(17)
Urban M-Sector	8.7	9.0	7.5	3.9
S-Sector	5.3	6.9	6.1	5.0
Sub-total	6.4	7.1	6.4	4.8
Rural M-Sector	5.2	3.4	8.9	1.8
S-Sector	2.5	3.7	4.4	4.8
Sub-total	3.9	3.7	6.3	3.8
All sectors	3.1	2.9	5.1	2.8
N (000) 1971	9,926	14,836	2,592	11,809
1990	17,914	25,881	6,870	19,943

Note: [a] Figures in parentheses refer to percentage distribution in 1971.
Source: CBS, Population Censuses, 1971 (Series C) and 1990.

The Outer Islands

Growth in agricultural employment was much more rapid in the relatively land-abundant regions of the Outer Islands than in Java. Non-wage work on family farms rose by 2.6 per cent per annum outside Java and made a significant contribution to total employment growth in the Outer Islands in the period 1971–90.

No one activity dominated output and employment like rice in Java. Several factors encouraged growth in agricultural job opportunities such as the expansion of irrigated rice farming, the transmigration programme, and the expansion of relatively large-scale estates producing products such as oil palm, cocoa and sugar (Booth 1988).

Booth (1988: 27–8) notes, however, that probably the largest share of new jobs came with the cultivation of smallholder cash crops, largely unassisted by government programmes. Relative isolation and land availability in many places outside Java ensured a large expansion in agricultural employment. This contrasts with Java, where new jobs in nearby cities offered alternatives to agricultural employment, and where work in agriculture was limited because of land shortage.

Table 4.5. *Distribution and growth of employment by sector: Indonesia, 1971–1995*

	Share of employment (%)			Growth of employment (% p.a.)
Sector	1971	1995	Increment[a] 1971–95	
Agriculture	65.8	44.0	23.1	1.2
M-sector				
Manufacturing	7.8	12.6	17.2	5.0
Construction	1.9	4.7	7.4	6.7
Mining	0.3	0.9	1.7	10.3
Public utilities	0.1	0.2	0.2	6.5
Sub-total	10.1	18.4	26.3	5.5
S-sector				
Trade, restaurants & hotels	11.0	17.3	23.4	4.9
Govt, comm. & personal services	10.4	15.1	19.7	4.3
Transport & communications	2.4	4.3	6.1	5.4
Financial services	0.3	0.9	1.4	7.9
Sub-total	24.1	37.6	50.6	4.8
All sectors	100	100	100	2.9
N (m.)	39.2	80.1	41.0	

Note: [a] Share of total employment growth absorbed in each sector.
Source: CBS, Population Censuses, 1971 (Series C) and 1990.

The M-sector

M-sector employment growth in Indonesia has also been high by developing economy standards.[14] This was largely the result of substantial job growth in the small sub-sectors of industry – construction, mining and public utilities – over the period 1971–95 (table 4.5).

Manufacturing

Employment growth in manufacturing in Indonesia was comparable with that achieved in some more rapidly industrialising economies. But it was well below that achieved in the rapidly growing export-oriented economies such as South Korea or Taiwan, where annual rates

---

[14] The share of industrial sector employment increased more rapidly in Indonesia than in lower-income developing economies and lower-middle-income developing economies (7–11 and 11–16 per cent respectively, 1960–80). Data taken from Bloom and Freeman (1986: 399).

of employment growth of 10 per cent per annum were common in the 1970s and 1980s (Kuo 1983; Kim 1986). Given the growth of value-added in manufacturing, the overall employment elasticity was probably not much higher than in agriculture in Indonesia. Both the relatively capital-intensive investments made in the 1970s, and backwash effects on the large, low-productivity manufacturing sector help explain these developments (Hill 1990).

Two points should be noted regarding the dynamics of manufacturing development. First, manufacturing output and employment growth was not only rapid in large-scale firms. Small-scale enterprises continued to account for the lion's share of employment in the sector. Hill (1990) estimates that output increased by close to 9 per cent per annum in small firms from the mid 1970s to the mid 1980s. Both value-added and employment growth made major contributions to growth in small-scale enterprises. Much of the new job creation in these smaller establishments was in much higher value-added goods than produced by the small and cottage industries which had previously dominated manufacturing. Second, a high proportion of all manufacturing development and employment was still concentrated in Java, related to the more developed infrastructure and the need for abundant unskilled and skilled labour.

Construction

Indonesia's major effort in developing infrastructure had a large spin-off in terms of unskilled and semi-skilled jobs created in construction. Aside from the small mining, public utilities and banking sectors, employment in this sector grew more rapidly than in any of the other sectors. Construction accounted for close to 15 per cent of all non-agricultural jobs created among males in Indonesia over the period 1971–95.

Two points are noteworthy regarding this development. A substantial proportion of construction work was in self-employed jobs, among semi-skilled and skilled *tukang* involved in construction of private dwellings. This was a direct spin-off from increased incomes among middle-class and poorer families, especially in rural Java.

Second, spending on government INPRES construction projects probably made a major contribution to jobs in this sector. The effects of this programme are difficult to quantify. Patten *et al.* (1980: 169–72) estimated that around half a million jobs were created by INPRES projects shortly after they were introduced in the 1970s. By the early 1990s, INPRES accounted for around five million part-time jobs – almost double the number for construction in 1990.[15] Importantly, many of these projects were located in rural areas and spread throughout the country, although skilled labour has often been recruited in towns and cities.

The S-sector

Like manufacturing, the service sector is highly differentiated. It includes high valued-added sectors (banking and government administration), and also low-productivity activities (petty trade and personal services, household help). Two larger sub-sectors, trade and other services (government, community and personal services), accounted for the lion's share of new jobs created. Employment growth was more rapid in the smaller transport and especially financial services segments of the S-sector. Employment in financial services grew from 10 per cent per annum as banks and financial institutions spread rapidly throughout the country in the 1990s.

Employment growth in other services, including government administration, can be linked to expansion of government spending. This was not the case in trade. Most of the jobs in this sector were taken up by females in self-employed and family work. In rural areas, unlike other non-agricultural jobs which tended to be mainly located in towns and cities. Petty trade dominated occupations in the service sector. Self-employed and family workers in petty trade (including stalls, market traders and hawkers) alone were estimated to account for approximately 40 per cent of all employment in services in the mid 1980s (Manning 1992).

In contrast to manufacturing, service sector employment was not heavily concentrated in Java. Government, community and personal services contributed a significant share of total employment and employment growth in the Outer Islands. This contrasts with the plethora of labour-intensive services which were more common and likely to be located in low-wage Java.

Urban and rural employment, and work status

A rise in the share of non-agricultural employment has been associated with a rise in both the shares of wage and urban workers in total employment. These processes have been less marked in Indonesia than might have been expected. Non-wage employment has played a major role in

---

[15] Employment of 100 days per annum is assumed arbitrarily. The 1990 calculation is based on the conservative estimate that 30 per cent of the total 1.5 million rupiah devoted to INPRES in 1990 was allocated to labour (bearing in mind that there is considerable leakage of funds at various levels of government). See Manning (1993: 71).

total employment growth in both urban and rural areas. Rural non-agricultural jobs continued to grow quite rapidly during the 1970s and 1980s.

Although urban–rural divisions in employment structure are not always clear-cut – especially in Java and some of the more densely populated islands – urban growth rates were quite different from those in rural areas. As in other countries, employment growth has been most rapid in urban areas in Indonesia – on average at over 6 per cent per annum. This was over twice the growth in rural employment over the period 1971–90 (table 4.4 above).[16]

This urban–rural difference in the rate of labour absorption can be attributed to the slower rate of agricultural employment growth. However, both M- and S-sector job creation was more rapid in towns and cities than in rural areas. The M-sector grew at over 8 per cent per annum and the initially much larger S-sector at just under 6 per cent in urban Indonesia 1971–90.

Nevertheless, Indonesia has not experienced extreme patterns of urban bias in economic structure common to many other developing economies. Non-agricultural employment grew at just over 4 per cent per annum in rural areas.

In contrast to the successful NIE economies, wage employment grew only slightly more rapidly than non-wage employment outside agriculture in Indonesia from 1971–90. Non-wage employment growth was especially rapid in the S-sector (in petty trade and transport in particular). This suggests similar processes of employment redistribution to parts of Latin America, where the urban informal sector was dominant in job expansion from the 1960s (Portes and Benton 1984, Tokman 1984).[17] This similarity with patterns in Latin America was related to the high proportion of rural landless in Java which sought employment in Indonesia's towns and cities as the economy expanded during the 1970s and 1980s.

One feature of employment growth has been the relatively even spread of new non-agricultural jobs across regions. Agricultural employment expansion was understandably more rapid in the land-abundant Outer Islands (see table 4.2). Nevertheless, M-sector and especially S-sector employment increased rapidly outside Java, although it did so from a smaller base share. In both regions, urban employment grew more rapidly than in the countryside, and wage employment grew quickly in urban areas.

[16] These high growth rates are partly related to changes in definitions and urban boundaries.
[17] However in contrast to some areas of Latin America, rural, non-agricultural employment also grew strongly in Indonesia.

There were, however, some important contrasts between Java and the Outer Islands. The most noteworthy feature of employment in Java has been the rapid growth in urban non-wage jobs.[18] The absorption of urban self-employed persons especially in trade, transport and services accounted for just under 40 per cent of total urban employment growth in Java in 1971–90.

Alternatively, growth in wage jobs was more rapid in the Outer Islands, both in urban and rural areas (see table 4.4). In rural areas, this has been associated with the expansion of employment in new construction, mining and resource-based industries (and related manufacturing processes) as well as with the spread of services from a low base. The pressure for jobs, or the opportunities for informal sector activities, has not been as great as in Java. In part the government has played a key role in the direct promotion of employment in Outer Island cities and villages through the spread of public administration, education and health (Hill 1989).

Which segments of the labour market (wage or non-wage, urban or rural) have benefited from the shift of employment away from agriculture? Non-agricultural employment growth can be separated into two components by a simple decomposition procedure

- that which would have occurred given initial shares of employment and the rate of labour force expansion (supply effects)
- that which could be attributed to the changing composition of employment between agriculture and non-agriculture (demand effects).

The actual expansion in employment in non-agriculture 1971–90 (a) is compared with that which would have obtained if the same expansion of total employment had occurred but the non-agricultural share had remained the same (b). The difference between these two figures (a − b) shows the amount of non-agricultural employment growth which might be attributed to structural change (demand effects). The balance in non-agricultural employment growth can be attributed to labour force and employment growth (supply effects) (appendix table 4.1).

Two of the earlier patterns are confirmed from this exercise. First the increased urban share of non-agricultural work constituted the largest shift in the structure of employment, most of this through the increase in the share of urban employees. The two other relative gains associated with

---

[18] Details of the changing distribution of non-agricultural employment are shown in appendix table 4.1. The increasing share of urban and wage workers in manufacturing was especially marked in Java. In the large trade sector, by contrast, employment remains heavily dominated by non-wage workers and concentrated in rural areas in both Java and the Outer Islands.

the declining agricultural share were not so obvious. There was a big rise in the share of urban informal sector workers in total non-agricultural employment in Java. Finally, a substantial increase occurred among non-agricultural employees working in rural areas outside Java – especially in construction, transport and services.

Labour productivity

Labour productivity growth has been particularly rapid outside agriculture (see table 4.1). The rapid growth in manufacturing value-added in particular made a major contribution to productivity growth. In contrast, the increase in value-added per worker in services was much slower.

Regardless of shifts in employment between sectors, increased productivity in each of the major sectors made a major contribution to total growth in value-added per worker. National trends suggest that around 70 per cent of total productivity growth can be attributed to increases in labour productivity within major sectors and only 30 per cent to shifts in the share of total employment between sectors.[19]

Factors underlying the very rapid growth in value-added per worker in industry requires some elaboration. Relative to the national total, the index of labour productivity in industry rose by just under 50 per cent over the entire period 1971–90. This increase was greater than that recorded for all low- and low-middle-income countries in the period 1960–80 (table 4.6).[20]

Labour productivity in industry quickly caught up with services. Whereas labour productivity in services is estimated to have exceeded that in manufacturing by approximately 15 per cent in 1971, it fell (relatively) to around 25 per cent below manufacturing in 1990. While manufacturing shed a considerable amount of low-productivity labour, the opposite was true in the case of services: many workers have moved into low-income segments of this sector.

One might expect a substantial share of surplus labour in agriculture and traditional activities to flow into low-wage manufacturing employment in the early stages of industrialisation. This did not happen to this

---

[19] These figures are based on a calculation of labour productivity in 1990 (assuming no change in the share of employment by major sector, 1971–90), and comparing the result with recorded increases in labour productivity. The sectors are highly aggregated. Considerable gains in productivity would have been made through shifts in labour between activities and occupations in various sub-sectors (and even between low- and high-technology segments in the same industry, such as moving from hand-loom to mechanised textile weaving).

[20] The index is reported to have increased from 133 to 155 in low-income countries (outside India and China) and from 200 to 219 in lower-middle-income countries over this period (Bloom and Freeman 1986: 401).

Table 4.6. *Indices of labour productivity by major sector in Indonesia, 1971 and 1990 (current prices)*

	Index of labour productivity[a] (excluding oil and mining)			1990 (Rp.000) Adjusted
Major sectors	1971 Unadjusted	1990 Unadjusted	1990 Adjusted	
Agriculture	74	49	53	1,497
Industry[c]	<u>136</u>	<u>195</u>	<u>181</u>	<u>5,093</u>
	(219)[b]	(234)[b]	(217)[b]	(7,143)[b]
Manufacturing	117	206	194	5,477
Construction	193	155	129	3,874
Services[c]	<u>158</u>	<u>140</u>	<u>131</u>	<u>3,702</u>
Trade	160	135	129	3,637
Transport	197	177	158	4,457
Other services[d]	136	108	102	2,863
All sectors[c]	100	100	100	2,819
				(3,289)[b]

Notes: [a] 1990 data are adjusted based on full-time person equivalents (35 hours worked per week). For 1971, no adjustment could be made for underemployment because of lack of data; [b] Figures in parentheses include oil and mining in the calculation; [c] Includes smaller sectors in the total (public utilities in industry and banking and insurance in services); [d] Excludes banking and insurance.
Sources: As for table 4.1.

extent in other East Asian countries, although employment in more labour-intensive industries began to increase quickly when non-oil export growth took off in the 1980s. The highly capital-intensive nature of resource-based industries and several large, highly protected manufacturing activities (such as steel), had a substantial impact on average value-added in manufacturing.

A comparison of trends in Indonesia, the Philippines and South Korea, illustrates the economic significance of labour productivity changes across major sectors. In three respects, the changes in Indonesia were closer to those in the Philippines than in South Korea. Whereas Indonesia started off with quite high labour productivity in agriculture relative to other sectors, this plummeted from the mid 1960s, partly due to the rapid growth in labour productivity in manufacturing (see figure 4.3). Also important was the rapid growth in employment in agriculture in the Outer Islands.

Second, the rise in labour productivity in industry was similar to the Philippines, even though employment growth in this sector was much

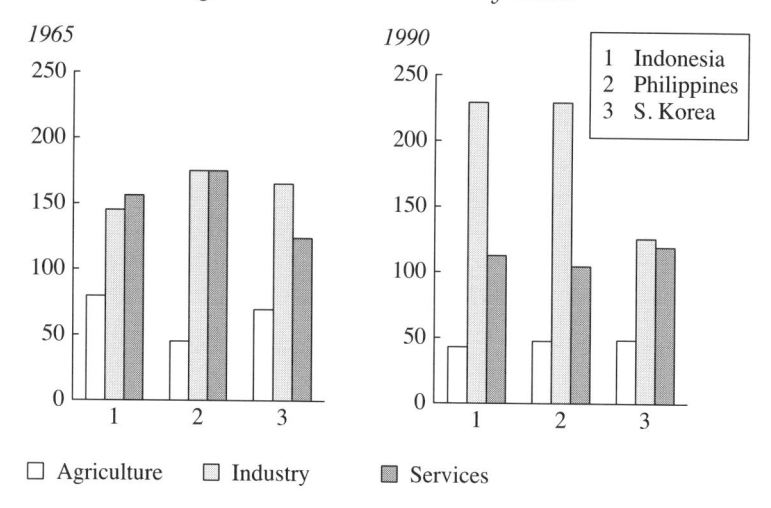

100 *Economic growth and labour market dynamics*

Figure 4.3 Indices of relative labour productivity in A-, M- and S-sectors: Indonesia, South Korea and the Philippines, 1965 and 1990
Notes: 1 Indonesia, 2 Philippines, 3 South Korea. Value added per worker in all sectors=100.
Sources: World Bank, *World Development Report*, various years; ILO, *Yearbook of Labour Statistics*, 1992 and 1993; and CBS Indonesia, Population Census, 1990.

faster in Indonesia. Alternatively, productivity in industry actually fell relative to other sectors in South Korea, mainly due to expansion of employment in labour-intensive industries.

Finally, in Indonesia and the Philippines, labour productivity in services fell precipitously compared with that in other sectors. Workers who were unable to find jobs in agriculture or manufacturing crowded into service activities. In South Korea, relative productivity in services remained largely constant – growth in value-added was matched by modest expansion in employment as the economy diversified.

Episodes of employment change

Varying economic fortunes during different periods of economic policy have been reflected in discontinuities in labour market change: recovery and the oil boom (1971–80); slow down in economic growth in the early 1980s (1980–5); and subsequent economic liberalisation (1985–90).[21]

Rapid non-agricultural urban employment growth, and low levels of

---

[21] These trends are based on data from the national censuses and intercensal surveys. From 1986–94 the CBS, National Labour Force Surveys enable a continuous (although not entirely reliable) series on employment.

Table 4.7. *Rates of growth in employment of wage and non-wage workers, urban and rural areas: Indonesia 1971–1980 and 1980–1990 (per cent per annum)*

	Wage 1971–80	Wage 1980–90	Non-wage 1971–80	Non-wage 1980–90	All workers 1971–80	All workers 1980–90
Java						
Agriculture	−2.5	0.7	2.5	1.2	1.0	1.1
Non-agriculture	3.7	6.5	7.8	2.2	5.8	4.3
All sectors	1.2	4.9	4.4	1.6	3.2	2.6
Outer Islands						
Agriculture	−0.2	3.6	1.5	3.2	1.3	3.3
Non-agriculture	4.3	7.8	6.2	2.4	5.6	5.0
All sectors	3.2	6.9	2.4	3.0	2.6	3.9
Indonesia						
Agriculture	−2.1	1.4	2.0	2.2	1.2	2.1
Non-agriculture	4.0	6.9	7.3	2.2	5.8	4.5
Urban	4.7	8.0	7.8	5.1	6.0	6.8
Rural	3.3	5.7	7.1	0.6	5.6	2.7
All sectors	1.6	5.4	3.6	2.2	3.0	3.2

Source: CBS, Population Censuses, 1971 (Series C), 1980 and 1990.

recorded unemployment, were common to each of the periods. There were several differences, however, associated with changes in economic performance and policy: slow growth in agricultural employment and robust growth in self-employed work in urban areas during the oil-boom period; then first agricultural sector employment expansion in the period of slower economic growth, followed by the take-off in manufacturing and construction job creation into the 1990s.

The oil boom period

Increased rice production, the huge growth in public expenditure (especially on infrastructure and human resources), and the expansion of a largely protected manufacturing sector were key features of economic growth. Agricultural employment rose slowly during the oil boom period, despite substantial increases in agricultural output. Total agricultural employment grew at just over 1 per cent per annum (table 4.7). Two developments were important: the decline in wage employment in Java and slow growth in employment in all agricultural work in the Outer Islands.

In the 1970s wage employment in agriculture in Java declined, at a rate of 2.5 per cent per annum. Fortunately, growth in non-wage employment on family farms of just under 2 per cent offset the decline in wage employment. Wage labour moved out of agriculture and there was substitution of wage workers in favour of family labour.[22]

Unlike in several other OPEC countries, the slow growth of jobs in agriculture was not principally related either to a relative neglect of agriculture, or to unfavourable shifts in relative prices in favour of urban, non-traded goods during the boom. Rather, it was the result of the introduction of new technology and institutions (especially the sickle and contract *tebasan* system in harvesting) which contributed to the decline in wage employment in Javanese agriculture. The spread of this relatively simple technology, and of new institutions, under the banner of the green revolution was concentrated in the decade of the oil boom (Manning 1988a). The new technology largely affected wage workers, many of them landless labourers, rather than owner-operators and family workers, and hence the income distribution effects were probably adverse (Hart 1986; White and Wiradi 1989).

Nevertheless, the oil boom did stimulate substantial growth in non-agricultural employment in both urban and rural areas, and contributed to real wage growth outside agriculture. Rural non-agricultural employment in particular grew strongly during the 1970s. Emphasis on rural public works and agriculture paid off in terms of job growth. In many other developing economies about half of new jobs created outside agriculture have been attributed to urbanisation. In contrast, in Java, around 70 per cent of non-agricultural employment growth can be attributed to the expansion of rural jobs, and only around 30 per cent to urbanisation.[23]

Agricultural employment growth was considerably slower outside Java in the oil boom period than in the subsequent decade when the terms of trade shifted against several major export crops (Tabor 1992: 169–70). Both food and non-food output growth was relatively rapid in the Outer Islands during the 1970s (Booth 1988: 33–6, 195–200). Growth in non-food output was supported by improvements in the terms of trade for major commodities. Output rose quickly especially among smallholders who dominated commercial agriculture in several of the land abundant regions.[24]

---

[22] Squires and Tabor (1994) found that these two forms of labour were close substitutes. However they find, surprisingly (p. 182), that family labour has tended to be replaced by wage labour (based on agricultural survey data).

[23] These figures are based on a decomposition of total non-agricultural employment growth into three components: urban and rural employment structure and urbanisation. See Manning (1988b: 61–2) and United Nations (1980: 70).

[24] The main products were rubber, coconuts, coffee, tea and sugar (oil palm production only began to grow rapidly from the mid 1980s), mainly concentrated on Sumatra with the major exceptions of coconuts (Sulawesi) and sugar (Java).

The main explanation for slow agricultural employment growth in the Outer Islands probably lies in the opening up of a wide range of non-agricultural employment opportunities. This was associated with rapid urban growth and improvement in rural communications and services. Most important was the absorption of considerable amounts of labour in both wage and self-employed non-farm jobs in services associated with widely dispersed spending during the boom period.

Rapid services and informal sector job growth

Indonesia avoided some of the problems associated with extreme urban bias which occurred in some oil-exporting countries. Trade and service activities among non-wage workers in urban areas were most prominent in the mix of new jobs taken up during the oil boom period. The S-sector – which comprised 30 per cent of total employment in 1971 – accounted for over half of the increase in all jobs in the 1970s. Its expansion can be thought of as comprising two main elements – new jobs created directly as a result of the expanded public sector budget and opportunities created indirectly as incomes rose among civil servants and other direct beneficiaries of the boom.

Increased public expenditures created wage jobs in the government sector and social services, especially among educated persons. Government sector employment growth was very rapid in the second half of the 1970s and the early 1980s rising by just under 7 per cent per annum in the period 1975–83. It was supported by the expansion of schools and health facilities in Java and of government administration outside Java. Employment growth among senior high and tertiary graduates in government administration and social services grew by almost 14 per cent in the same period.

Nevertheless, this expansion was dwarfed by informalisation of the urban economy which had been dominated by wage employment in the early 1970s. Whereas urban and rural employment in wage jobs in services rose by approximately 5 and 3 per cent per annum, non-wage employment growth was twice as fast in both. The largest contributor to growth (around 60 per cent) came from increased non-wage jobs in petty trade and other services, including household servants, barbers, service repair shops, tailors and the like. Growth in employment among females was particularly rapid among self-employed and family workers.

Table 4.8. *Estimated growth in manufacturing employment by major subsector, 1975–1993*

	N (000)		%		Growth rates (% p.a.)		
	1975	1993	1975	1993	1975–86	1986–93	1975–93
Large and medium	1,026	3,498	26	40	5.4	9.0	6.8
Small cottage	443	952	12	11	5.8	1.8	4.2
Reported[a]	*	(3,888)	–	–	*	(4.4)	*
Residual[b]	2,311	4,334	62	49	2.1	5.8	3.5
Total Industry statistics	*	8,338	–	–	*	5.8	*
Labour force statistics	3,780	8,784	100	100	3.6	6.4	4.7

Notes: [a] Based on periodic surveys/censuses of cottage industries; [b] The difference between total manufacturing employment reported in the National Labour Force Surveys and the sum of total employment estimated in large, medium and small industries in each year; * 1975 cottage industry figures were implausibly too high and are not consistent with any other data on the cottage industry sector.

Sources: Employment data for large and medium establishments are based on the estimates of Hal Hill (1996: table 8.6) from the industry and economic censuses in 1975 and 1986, and reported figures from industrial sector surveys in 1993 (CBS, Statistical Yearbook 1994). The residual for cottage industries is based on National Labour Force Surveys 1976, 1986 and 1993 (adjusted for 1975 by applying annual growth rate of manufacturing employment in 1971–80). National Labour Force Survey data are preferred to the Intercensal Survey Data (1976 and 1986) because they provide a more plausible estimate of employment trends in the 1970s. The National Labour Force Surveys suggest a significantly slower growth in cottage industry from 1976 to 1986, than the Intercensal Surveys.

Slow manufacturing employment growth

Manufacturing sector employment growth was disappointing compared with growth in value-added during the 1970s. Despite incomplete data,[25] several patterns are clear. Overall, total manufacturing employment rose at just under 4 per cent (table 4.8). Large and medium industry, and small industry sub-sectors grew at around 5–6 per cent per annum. Investment in light manufacturing during the early 1970s contributed to relatively rapid growth in manufacturing employment, whereas later there was a shift towards more capital-intensive investment.

The trend towards more capital-intensive investment is clearly visible from the composition of employment in large- and medium-scale man-

---

[25] Unfortunately, reliable estimates can only be made for all sub-sectors for the period 1975–86, which covers both the oil boom period and the later years of recession. Cottage industry data are at best guesstimates based on data from the National Labour Force Surveys beginning in 1976. See Hill (1990, 1996) for a fuller discussion of data sources (Indonesia: CBS various years).

Table 4.9. *Share of employment by industry group in large and medium manufacturing, 1975–1993 (shares in per cent)*

Industry[a]	1975 %	1980 %	1986 %	1993 %
I Relatively labour intensive	<u>70.3</u>	<u>60.5</u>	<u>54.2</u>	<u>53.4</u>
1. Food processing (31)	37.5	33.2	30.8	21.1
2. TFC industries and other (32 & 39)[b]	32.8	27.3	23.4	32.3
II Wood and paper products (33 & 34)	8.5	10.0	14.2	17.6
III Relatively capital intensive	<u>21.2</u>	<u>29.5</u>	<u>31.6</u>	<u>29.0</u>
1. Heavy processing (35 & 36)	12.7	16.12	20.0	17.6
2. Metals and machinery (37 & 38)	8.5	13.4	11.6	11.4
Total	100	100	100	100
N (000)	1,026	?	1,869	3,498

Notes: [a] The numbers in parentheses refer to International Standard Industrial Classification (ISIC) Codes; [b] Textiles, footwear and clothing, and mainly toys included in ISIC Code 39.
Sources: CBS, Large and Medium Manufacturing Survey, 1993 and Industrial Censuses 1975 and 1986. Distributions for 1975 and 1980 derived from adjusted figures estimated by Hill (1996: table 8.2).

ufacturing (table 4.9). The share of relatively labour-intensive employment fell in food processing and the TFC (textiles, footwear and clothing) industries in both periods. The share of both value-added and employment expanded in wood and paper, heavy processing and metals and machinery. The government was intent on investing some of the oil proceeds of the oil boom in capital-intensive industries, such as Krakatau Steel and petrochemicals. The overvalued exchange rate during the later oil boom years, and the plethora of controls over investment which discriminated against small industry discouraged any move towards more labour-intensive export industries (World Bank 1981).

Trends in cottage industry employment are less clear.[26] Cottage industry employment probably grew at around 2 per cent per annum during 1975–86.[27] Although quite low, this is consistent with relatively little increase in rural employment in manufacturing during the 1970s and early 1980s. Slow growth in cottage industry jobs inevitably had a substantial

---

[26] Estimates are calculated as a residual from employment figures from the 1976 and 1986 National Labour Force Surveys.
[27] Data from The National Labour Force Survey (SAKERNAS) are preferred to the Intercensal Survey (SUPAS) data owing to the implausibly high level of employment recorded in agriculture in SUPAS (see Indonesia, CBS various years, 1978).

impact on total employment growth. Cottage industries still provided over half of all jobs in manufacturing industry.

Thus, in contrast to several of the East Asian countries, macroeconomic reform was not associated with liberalisation and rapid growth in employment in manufacturing in Indonesia during the oil boom.[28] Resources provided by the oil-boom enabled a postponement of liberalisation for over a decade.

Informal sector work, much of it located in Java and motivated by labour supply pressures and changes in labour demand, was the main avenue through which families sought new income opportunities outside agriculture. The service sector rather than manufacturing was the main source of new jobs, many of them in rural Indonesia.

Economic slow-down and the non-oil export boom

The 1980s saw a major change in the pattern of employment growth. Wage employment in manufacturing grew more rapidly, especially towards the end of the decade. At the same time, agricultural employment first picked up in the years of slow growth, and then slowed markedly as non-agricultural sectors expanded quickly from the second half of the 1980s. Both these sources of employment obviated pressures for growth of the informal sector at the extraordinarily rapid rates recorded in the 1970s.

Employment trends, 1980–5: after the boom

The period of slower economic growth in the early 1980s coincided fortunately with impressive growth in rice production. Labour absorption in agriculture was much better than in the previous decade, especially in Java. It was fortunate, because in the wake of slower growth in government expenditures and private investment the growth of non-agricultural employment fell steeply in both urban and rural areas. Not only did manufacturing employment increase slowly (as it had done in the previous decade) but so did employment in services. For males, only trade and transport among the major sectors recorded higher growth rates in employment than in the previous decade (table 4.10).[29] Non-agricultural employment growth was particularly slow in rural areas.

---

[28] In South Korea, for example, total employment in manufacturing grew at over 10 per cent per annum and wage employment by close to 12 per cent per annum during the decade 1963–73 (Kim 1986: 62).

[29] This discussion focusses on trends in male employment. The 1985 intercensal survey showed an implausibly high rate of employment growth among females, largely due to more extensive enumeration of family workers.

Table 4.10. *Rate of growth in employment by major sector: Indonesia, males, 1971–1995 (per cent per annum)*

	1971–80	1980–85	1985–95
Agriculture	1.4	2.1	0.5 (−0.4)[a]
Non-agriculture	5.8	3.7	4.9 (4.8)[a]
Urban: Manufacturing	7.3	7.0	8.5 (6.7)[a]
Construction	6.7	6.6	7.3
Trade	4.4	8.1	6.2
Transport	3.6	5.4	6.4
Other services	6.0	4.4	4.6
Rural: Manufacturing	4.9	2.1	4.0 (3.2)[a]
Construction	9.6	3.5	5.0
Trade	4.0	3.1	2.5
Transport	6.5	6.0	4.9
Other services	5.6	−0.4	2.4
Total M-sector	7.1	4.0	6.0
Total S-sector	5.2	3.6	4.3
All sectors	3.0	2.8	2.7 (2.3)[a]

Note: [a] Figures in brackets for 1990–95.
Source: CBS, Population Census, 1971 (Series C), and 1980 and National Intercensal Survey, 1985 and 1995.

Rapid rice sector growth was not associated with the same labour-displacing impact of new technology which characterised the early years of the green revolution. The 'second stage' of induced technology did not diffuse at the same rate in Java as in some neighbouring countries. And expansion of irrigated areas and multiple cropping offset the backwash effects of new technology and institutions on employment of wage labour.[30]

Agricultural employment increased relatively rapidly in the Outer Islands, and almost entirely involved self-employed and family workers on family farms. This development is puzzling, in light of relatively depressed prices of commercial crops which were the backbone of the agricultural economy in many regions outside Java (Tabor 1992). Several explanations can be offered

- less opportunities for non-agricultural jobs in many of the Outer Islands regions in the post oil boom period

[30] See Jayasuriya and Shand (1986). Even wage employment seems to have grown again in Java in the early 1980s, albeit at a slow rate of just over 1 per cent per annum among males.

- economic policies which mitigated the effects of declining terms of trade, and improvements in infrastructure which extended to relatively isolated Outer Island regions (Tabor 1992: 169–71).
- substantial expansion of transmigration programmes based on land settlement in the first half of the 1980s. The number of transmigrant families moved during this plan period (1979–84) was estimated at just over 300,000 (approximately 1.5 million persons), more than twice the number settled during the preceding 80 years since the programme was begun in 1905. The largest annual transfers ever recorded under the programme occurred in this period (World Bank 1986: 1–11).[31]

The non-oil export boom

The situation changed dramatically in the latter half of the decade and into the 1990s. Employment in manufacturing took off and, for the first time in the New Order period, began to grow more rapidly than in all other major sectors. Growth in jobs approached rates recorded in South Korea, Taiwan and Malaysia during their early periods of rapid industrialisation. From absorbing only around 15–20 per cent of additional non-agricultural jobs, this sector provided jobs for close on half of all males – and probably as many if not more females – who found employment outside agriculture.

This expansion was spearheaded by growth in jobs in large- and medium-scale manufacturing which expanded at 9 per cent per annum in the period 1986–93 (table 4.10). Rapid growth in manufacturing employment occurred in both Java and the Outer Islands, and was particularly strong in urban areas.

The changed composition of output in favour of labour-intensive, export-oriented industries, was the major factor contributing to this new growth in manufacturing employment. The decline in share of TFC industries in total large- and medium-scale manufacturing employment was dramatically reversed, rising almost 10 percentage points to just under one-third in 1993 (table 4.9).

The share of wood products in employment, led by plywood and furniture, continued to climb, providing jobs outside Java. This industry, together with the TFC sector, accounted for just under two-thirds of all employment growth in large- and medium-scale manufacturing in the period 1986–93. Their rise was counter-balanced by a fall in the share of

---

[31] Net migration was much smaller than these figures imply. Nevertheless, it favoured large net shifts of Javanese to the Outer Islands (see chapter 3).

employment in heavy processing industries which had risen during the oil boom years. The share of employment in food processing also continued to decline.

More rapid employment growth was not limited to larger establishments. The big cottage industry sector also appears to have registered a substantial increase in new jobs – the rate of increase is estimated at 6 per cent per annum (compared with around 2 per cent during the oil boom and slower growth periods). Interestingly, this expansion was also primarily in the two largest export-oriented sectors: the TFC and wood industries. Small furniture and garments businesses in particular were able to thrive in the much more competitive environment. This occurred despite the general perception among many that it has only been the large establishments and conglomerates which have gained from liberalisation.[32]

The increasing role of manufacturing in total employment underpinned another important trend – the increasing share of wage employees in total employment in both urban and rural areas. Strong growth of informal sector activities in urban Indonesia was not maintained during the 1980s, especially during the second half of the decade, or among females.[33] Whereas non-wage employees mainly in services accounted for approximately two-thirds of the total growth in non-agricultural employment in the 1970s, they accounted for only 25 per cent of additional non-agricultural jobs in the 1980s (see figures 4.4 and 4.5). Manufacturing wage labour accounted for less than 10 per cent of the total increment in non-agricultural employment among females in the former period but just under one-third in the 1980s.[34]

By the 1990s, employment in Javanese agriculture began to decline, and it rose only slightly outside Java. The share of agricultural employment in Java began to dip sharply, after a period in which the share flattened out during the 1980s (Figure 4.6). Ironically this trend seems to be related more to expansion of employment opportunities in non-agricultural sectors, rather than to the overcrowding associated with land scarcity that has played such an historically important role in Javanese agriculture.

Wage employment also began to grow quite rapidly in agriculture towards the end of the decade. Large estates had begun to spread widely

---

[32] See Van Diermen (1995) for a discussion on how many of these small industries thrived in Jakarta through copying brand-name designs, quickly adapting to new demand and utilising a pool of rural-based workers.

[33] Although the data on female employment trends from the 1985 SUPAS are not directly comparable with the census data for 1980 or 1990, the shifts in the structure are so marked as to warrant mention.

[34] The increase in female employment in manufacturing was dominated by employment of young, new entrants to the work force in the 1980s and early 1990s (chapter 9).

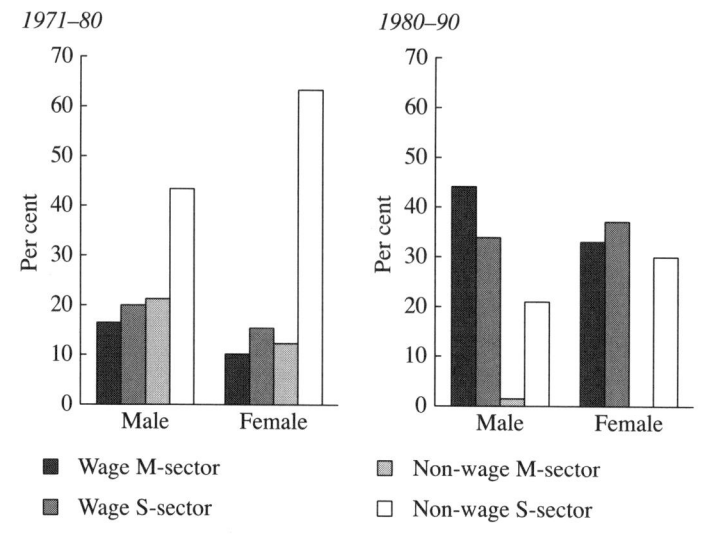

110 Economic growth and labour market dynamics

Figure 4.4 Distribution of the increase in non-agricultural employment among wage and non-wage workers by gender: Indonesia, 1971–1980 and 1980–1990
Sources: CBS, Population Census, 1971 (Series C), 1980 and 1990 and National Intercensal Survey, 1985.

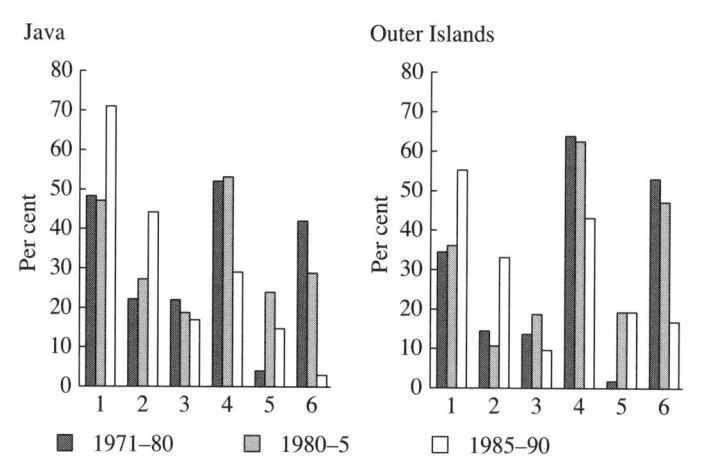

Figure 4.5 Distribution of the increase in non-agricultural wage employment by major sectors: males only, Java and Outer Islands, 1971–1990 (per cent)
Notes: 1 M-sector, 2 manufacturing, 3 construction, 4 S-sector, 5 trade and transport, 6 other services.
Sources: CBS, Population Census, 1971 (Series C), 1980 and 1990 and National Intercensal Survey, 1985.

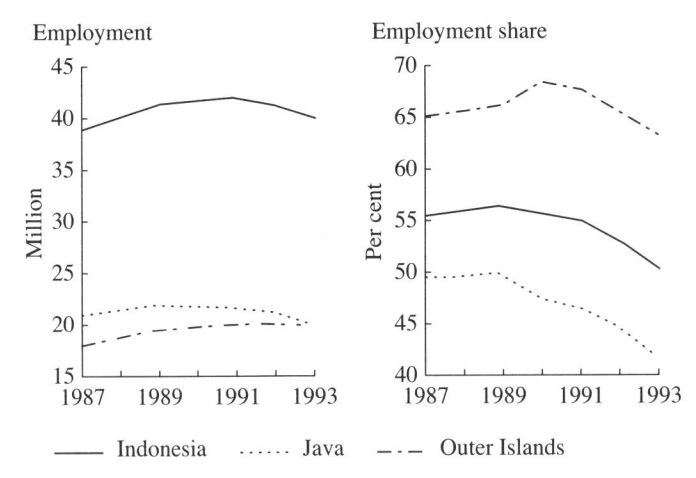

Figure 4.6 Agricultural employment: Indonesia, Java and Outer Islands, 1987–1993 (millions, three-year moving averages)
Source: CBS, National Labour Force Surveys (SAKERNAS), 1986–94.

in Sumatra in particular during the 1980s – in palm oil, sugar and cocoa and other cash crops. Some were established as part of the nucleus estate and transmigration programmes, and some through investment by large, private companies (Tabor 1992). Wage labour even in smallholder crops became more common, especially as some of the Javanese sought to supplement their sometimes meagre incomes from farming for the new transmigration settlements (World Bank 1986: 24–7).

While the slow-down in agricultural employment growth augers well for productivity growth in that sector, patterns of employment growth in manufacturing were disquieting in the first half of the 1990s. Whereas new wage jobs in manufacturing played a key part in employment expansion 1985–90, non-wage jobs in rural areas and in the informal sector played a greater role in the 1990s. This development raises questions regarding the sustainability of labour market transformation during the recent reform period. Pressures for greater government intervention to support high-tech industries and for direct intervention in labour markets through minimum wages appear to have dampened job growth prospects in manufacturing.

Conclusions

Four patterns of intersectoral interspatial employment change were key features of the Indonesian labour market transformation from the 1970s:

- increasing shares of non-agricultural, urban and wage workers in total employment
- continued rapid growth in agricultural employment (especially in the Outer Islands) accompanied by substantial absolute decline in the number of agricultural wage workers in Java
- slower growth in the M-sector than in several other rapidly industrialising countries
- a substantial increase in the number of non-wage (informal sector) workers in urban areas, particularly in trade and service activities.

Economic policy facilitated labour market change. This included agricultural development programmes, rural and regional construction and the extension of social services. Indonesia averted two extreme outcomes experienced by some developing countries. Indonesia did not experience economic stagnation and continued concentration of persons in low-productivity employment. Neither was there rapid urbanisation and non-agricultural employment growth which contributed substantially to widening urban–rural income gaps.

Nevertheless, formal sector employment in Indonesia lagged in response to economic change. The latter did not bring about as rapid a shift towards labour market transition as experienced in other East Asian NIEs – the agricultural sector continued to absorb workers, informal sector work was widespread and continued to grow in the cities through to the late 1980s, and rural self-employed and family work still contributed a major share of total employment. It was only after the liberalisation measures of recent years that employment growth began to resemble that of the NIEs.

Of course, slower movement of labour out of agriculture and manufacturing employment growth could still be associated with real wage growth under conditions of rising labour productivity in all sectors and relatively tight labour markets. In the next chapter, we see that real wage rates did increase, during the oil boom period. That growth was not sustained, however, and only picked up again from around 1990.

Appendix table 4.1. *Change in the structure of employment in Java and the Outer Islands, 1971–1990*

	Change in employment due to change in the structure of jobs (000)[a]			Share of total change in employment due to structural shifts (%)[b]			Share of each sector/status group's employment change due to structural shifts (%)		
	Java (1)	Outer Islands (2)	Indonesia (3)	Java (4)	Outer Islands (5)	Indonesia (6)	Java (7)	Outer Islands (8)	Indonesia (9)
Agriculture									
Employees	−4,361	−420	−4,781	−54	−13	−43			
Non-employees	−3,694	−2,763	−6,456	−46	−87	−57			
	−8,055	−3,183	−11,238	100	100	100			
Non-agriculture									
Urban: Employees	2,835	1,234	5,069	48	39	45	68	64	66
Non-employees	2,510	479	2,989	31	15	27	73	54	66
Rural: Employees	879	1,229	2,108	11	38	19	18	63	43
Non-employees	831	241	1,072	10	8	9	14	17	22
Total change due to structural shifts	8,055	3,183	11,238	100	100	100	42	24	36
Total change in employment 1971–90	19,033	13,412	313,445	n.a.	n.a.	n.a.	n.a.	n.a.	n.a.

Notes: [a] Defined on the actual level of employment recorded minus the level which would have obtained if the structure of employment had been the same in 1990 as in 1971 (given the same total growth rate in employment); [b] Column percentage distribution of data included in columns 1–3.
Source: CBS, Population Censuses, 1971 (Series C) and 1990.

5

Wage growth in a labour surplus economy?[1]

How did the changes in labour demand and supply impact on wages, and what can this tell us about Indonesia's progress towards the type of labour market transition that occurred in the NIEs in the 1970s? To what extent was wage expansion in the modern sectors constrained by elastic labour supply – despite outward movements in the labour demand, as portrayed in the adapted Lewis model (figure 2.1)?

Employment trends observed in previous chapters showed that, on the one hand, growth in non-agricultural wage employment was rapid. On the other, continued expansion of agricultural employment and of jobs among self-employed and family workers suggested excess labour supply to the modern sector remained a driving force in the determination of labour market outcomes.

Wage trends emerged as an increasingly important issue in the national economic and political scene in Indonesia in the 1990s. Deregulation and subsequent growth in non-oil exports brought wage costs and trends into focus, particularly in comparison with developments amongst Indonesia's neighbours. In addition, several factors drew attention to wage costs and trends in the early 1990s: the increasing concentration of workers in the capital city, the spate of strikes and labour action and more comprehensive minimum wage legislation.[2]

Other empirical studies and the institutional context

Growth in real wages accompanying growth in labour productivity has been a key dimension of labour market transitions in the NIEs of East Asia. In all these countries, real wages rose rapidly from the 1970s and growth was sustained throughout the 1980s (see Fields 1994; Galenson 1992). Rapid structural change discussed in earlier chapters accompanied by upgrading of skills and education have been identified as the

---

[1] This chapter expands on Manning (1994a).
[2] See chapter 8 for details.

major factors contributing to rapid wage growth (World Bank 1993, 1995).

Given Indonesia's starting point and its failure to move into the club of manufacturing exporters earlier, wage growth could be expected to be less favourable than in the NIEs or neighbouring Malaysia and Thailand. The perception of some senior government spokespersons and critics of the government's development record, that real wages did not keep up with other indicators of development, seems plausible.[3] This view has frequently been linked to arguments regarding wage repression, especially through denial of trade union freedoms.

A more favourable perspective has emphasised the link between rapid economic growth, labour productivity and real wage increases. World Bank data put Indonesia in the same league as South Korea and Taiwan, in terms of growth of average earnings over the period 1970–90, ahead of both Malaysia and Singapore (World Bank 1993: 263).

It is puzzling that authoritative sources can come up with such different prognoses.[4] Neither tell the entire story. While there has been real wage growth, it has not been sustained over the 20-year period. Researchers have come to different conclusions partly because they have focussed on different indicators and different periods: the sceptics have focussed on wage rates in the second half of the 1980s; the optimists on average earnings throughout. More fundamentally, discussion of wage trends has sometimes failed to take account of the impact of substantial swings in economic performance and policy on the labour market over the past two decades.

The institutional context

As in other rapidly industrialising countries, contracts vary enormously depending on sector and activity in Indonesia. At one extreme, casual wage rates are often negotiated on an individual basis in rice agriculture and construction. They may vary from person to person, depending on the relationship between the employer and employee.[5] Wage agreements for just one activity in the rice sector often involve commitments to work on other tasks in the agricultural cycle (such as in *kedokan* contracts). In many construction activities, exact wages paid to each individual are difficult to

---

[3] At a seminar in 1994 the State Minister for Bappenas, Ginanjar Kartasasmita, argued that real wages had declined or stagnated in manufacturing, agriculture (rice) and estates during the period 1982–91 (Ginanjar 1994).
[4] Other studies also suggest different and sometimes surprising wage outcomes. See Papanek (1980), Mazumdar and Sawit (1985), Naylor (1990) and Godfrey (1992).
[5] Stoler (1977), Tjondronegoro (1977) and Hart (1986).

determine because the amount paid is at the discretion of the foreman (Sjahrir 1993).

At the other extreme, government wage structures are rigid. They are determined by educational level, years of service and position. Here, non-basic wage emoluments (both official and unofficial) play an important role in determining total labour incomes (Gray 1979). Less rigid are permanent and semi-permanent wage contracts in manufacturing. Sometimes these can be based on formulae such as those applied to civil servants. Among more skilled persons they may vary considerably according to skill, experience and relationship to the employer. Unskilled workers tend to have a wide range of employment contracts, depending on the type and size of firm.[6] Workers may have informal and casual, or more formal contracts. The latter usually provide for a semi-permanent or permanent employment relationship, often in accordance with the requirements of labour legislation.

The calculation of wage rates is further complicated by the variety of emoluments offered in kind to workers during years of high inflation, and more recently in and around major cities. The provision of food, housing and accommodation by employers has complicated the calculation of absolute wage levels. Their changing weight relative to basic wage payments can influence trends over time. Payments in kind are also a key feature of agricultural wage systems. Subtle differences and changes in in-kind components – the quantity and quality of food, provision of cigarettes and other small inducements – have an impact on labour welfare and wage costs in different regions.

As in other developing economies, the low level of wages and the high demand for income has meant that workers frequently work long hours. Overtime payments are often a major component of labour earnings. Piece-work systems of remuneration are widespread in labour-intensive industries. Thus, wage rates are likely to be a less reliable and stable indicator of labour earnings than in more industrialised countries. This is particularly true among smaller firms.

When the Soeharto government came to power, the public sector played a dominant role in modern sector employment. At the time, public sector salary adjustments had an important influence on those in the private sector (Arndt and Sundrum 1975). As the private sector grew during the 1970s, wages were increasingly left to market forces, unions were tightly controlled and minimum wages introduced largely for cosmetic reasons.

---

[6] See Manning (1979) for a discussion of variations in wage contracts.

From around 1990 onwards the institutional framework changed significantly for modern sector firms. Increasing attention was paid by the government to the implementation of provincial minimum wage legislation in establishments with 25 workers, especially those close to the major cities.

These complications necessarily make evaluation of wage trends difficult. The interpretation of wage trends in this chapter is based on three assumptions.

> Market forces were the main factors which determined wage outcomes for most of the period covered by this survey, despite important contrasts in wage setting mechanisms between various segments of the labour market (Lluch and Mazumdar 1985).
> There were no major imperfections in the labour supply response of unskilled labour which might distort wage trends over time.
> There was no large, systematic change in the basic composition of regular wage payments to bias the trend in wages in a particular direction.

Trends in wage rates

A clear distinction in the analysis is made between wage rates and average earnings and wage costs of unskilled labour.[7] Trends in wage rates are most relevant for an assessment regarding changes in general labour market conditions, especially for unskilled labour.

The analysis of wage rate trends focusses on five selected activities

- hoeing in rice (Java)
- all activities on estates (national)
- unskilled labour in construction (Jakarta)
- minimum negotiated wages in textiles (Bandung)
- lower echelon civil servant salary levels (national).[8]

Of these five series, the rice wage best approximates traditional sector wages. Almost entirely, it relates to casual labour employed on a daily basis. The other agricultural series, daily wages on estates, is influenced by government wage policies because many plantations are partly or wholly

---

[7] Labour earnings refer to the total income of labour from employment, including overtime and fringe benefits paid in cash (and also payments in kind, valued in terms of their money equivalents). Wage rates usually refer only to basic wage payments per unit of time (daily, weekly or monthly).
[8] Although several of the series are not national, in all cases the regional indices are for major industries on a national scale.

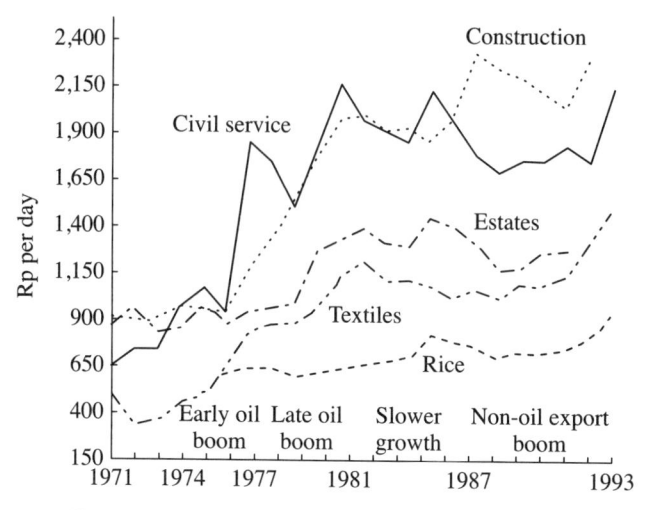

118 *Economic growth and labour market dynamics*

Figure 5.1 Real wages in selected activities in Indonesia, 1971/2–1992/3 (Rp/day, 1983 prices)
Notes: Rice for males in Java; textiles for both sexes in Bandung; civil service for both sexes in Indonesia; estates for both sexes in Indonesia, construction for males in Jakarta.
Sources: CBS, Unpublished data and Average Wages on Estates, various years; PERTEKSI, Annual Agreements on Wages, various years; Department of Finance, unpublished data.

government owned. The construction wage series involves casual, unskilled workers. This series might be considered quasi modern as it covers many workers on government projects in the capital city. The textile wage series most closely approximates modern sector wage rates. It applies to workers in mechanised weaving establishments and is nominally negotiated annually by representatives of producers and the government union. The outcome of these negotiations reflects employer judgements of labour market conditions.

Data on trends in real wages in each of these segments of the labour market are presented in figures 5.1 and 5.2.[9] They indicate real wage growth of the order of 2–6 per cent per annum for the entire period depending on the series, although the growth appears to have been concentrated in the oil boom years of around 1974–81, and in the 1990s.

Growth rates differed substantially between sectors. They were much

---

[9] See also appendix table 5.2. In each case, the nominal wage series is deflated by the most relevant cost of living index. The impact of different deflators on the results are discussed below. Since 1983, CBS has collected data on the consumer price index in rural areas as part of the farmers' terms of trade; this is closely correlated with the rural cost of living index (Naylor 1990).

Wage growth in a labour surplus economy 119

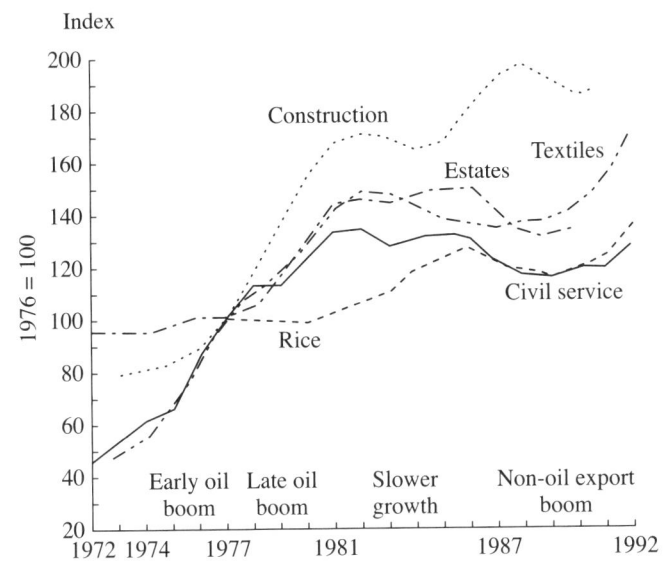

Figure 5.2 Real wages in selected activities in Indonesia, 1972/3–1992/3 (1976=100, 3 year moving averages)
Sources: CBS, Unpublished data and Average Wages on Estates, various years; PERTEKSI, Annual Agreements on Wages, various years; Department of Finance, unpublished data.

higher in the modern sector and in non-agricultural activities than in agriculture. Textile and public sector wages grew most rapidly, at annual rates of around 5 per cent per annum over the entire period. On the other hand, agricultural wages rose only 1–2 per cent per annum. Wages of casual labour on construction sites increased by 3 per cent per annum.[10] These differences in trends between non-agricultural and agricultural wages were quite marked for almost all time periods examined.

Clearly the patterns of wage changes do not fit with a pattern of orderly wage increases in the traditional rice sector. Nor are they consistent with an elastic supply of labour to the modern sector, as suggested by a modified Lewis model. Non-agricultural wage rates rose steeply especially during the 1970s, despite the apparent surplus of labour in the agricultural sector. To explain these findings, wage growth during various time periods since the early 1970s are examined.

Movements in wage rates were more uniform by region, sector and gender than might have expected (see chapters 6 and 9). Such movements

---

[10] It should be noted that the data on civil service salaries which relate to basic salaries only tend to overstate the rate of wage growth.

lend support to the notion of the emergence of an integrated, national labour market. In one example of wage changes in agriculture by gender, there was considerable similarity in wage adjustments. Although female wages were lower than those earned by males and appear to have grown more rapidly in the 1970s, they nevertheless rose at roughly the same rate in both sectors.

Fluctuations in wage growth

In the following discussion of real GDP growth and structural change, four periods are distinguished

- the early oil boom period (1974–7)
- the later oil boom period of accelerated growth (1977–81)
- the period of slower economic growth (1982–7)
- a final period when GDP growth rose again and non-oil exports began to play a significant role in economic growth (1987–93) (see Sundrum 1988; Hill 1994).

A common pattern of wage growth in all non-agricultural sectors during the oil boom years and the second half of the 1980s was rapid growth in the former period and stagnation in the latter (figure 5.2). In the estates, textiles, construction and government sectors, real unskilled/semi-skilled wages rose from the early to the mid 1970s to 1981/2. Rates of growth were much lower during the years of slower economic growth, and fluctuated around a constant or even slightly declining trend until the end of the 1980s. From around 1990 this trend is reversed in several sectors, most notably in the tradable (with qualifications) rice and textile sectors.

In contrast, real wage rates in rice stagnated in the 1970s. Subsequently, they rose during the recession years of the early 1980s, levelled off and then rose strongly again in the early 1990s. Only in this last period did all series move unequivocally in the same direction.

The trends were confirmed by statistical analysis, although there was not a close relationship between non-oil GDP growth and various measures of wage increases for any one series.[11] Equations which regressed wages on a time trend, and dummy variables representing the late oil boom and export boom, yielded several statistically significant results. The dummy variable for the late oil boom period was significant for both

---

[11] Various specifications of the wage variables (including the log of real wages, real wage change, lagged real wages and nominal wages) for each of the non-agricultural series did not yield consistent results when regressed with various measures of GDP and sectoral value-added growth.

Table 5.1. *Regression results from real wage equations with dummy variables for oil-boom and export-boom periods, selected sectors: Indonesia 1971–1993*[a]

	Agriculture wages		Non-agriculture wages	
	Rice (Java) 1976–93 (18)	Estates (Indonesia) 1971–91 (21)	Construction (Jakarta) 1972–92 (21)	Textiles (Bandung) 1971–93 (23)
C (Constant)	6.20 (0.080)	6.68 (0.047)	6.59 (0.064)	5.87 (0.754)
T (Years)	0.028 (0.056)	0.036 (0.004)	0.060 (0.006)	0.076 (0.007)
DT_1 (Late oil boom – 1977–81)	−0.016 (0.043)	−0.011 (0.047)	0.137** (0.057)	0.280** (0.077)
DT_2 (Export boom – 1987–93)	−0.114 (0.053)	−0.277** (0.069)	−0.268 (0.081)	−0.356 (0.108)
R^2	0.81	0.81	0.92	0.90
DW	1.06	1.29	0.72	1.32

Note: [a] The regressions were estimated in log linear form to indicate average growth rates associated with unit (single year) changes in the explanatory variables (Thus $LW = C + b_1 T + b_2 DT_1 + b_3 DT_2 + u$). Bracketed figures are standard errors. Stars denote significant at a one and 5 per cent level (*,** respectively). All constants and T variables (years) were significant at one per cent (not shown).
Sources: CBS, Unpublished data and Average Wages on Estates, various years; PERTEKSI, Annual Agreements on wages, various years; Department of Finance, unpublished data.

construction and textile wages but not for the agricultural wage series (table 5.1). Surprisingly, the non-oil export boom period (1987–93) dummy variable was not significant in the equations for any of the wage series. It was negative and statistically significant for both the non-agricultural series.

The early period of rehabilitation and growth

Textile, estates, construction and government wages rose in real terms from the early 1970s. These trends may seem surprising, given widespread reports of surplus labour in agriculture and difficulties in the rice sector in the early years of the New Order. Nevertheless, they are consistent with Papanek's (1980) findings of significant real wage growth in the early years of the New Order. The previous period of economic decline and inflation had led to a marked narrowing of wage rates between the then tiny modern sector and traditional sectors (Hawkins 1963).

Rapid growth in modern sector wages during the early 1970s can partly be interpreted as attempts by firms to restore wages to levels which would guarantee a regular supply of labour, and raise labour productivity which declined steeply in the previous decade. The differential between textile and civil service wages, on the one hand, and the wages of the largely casual agricultural and construction workers, on the other, had narrowed substantially by 1976/77 (appendix table 5.1). They had been strongly in favour of agriculture and construction in the early 1970s.[12]

The oil boom period

Why did real wage rates rise in the non-agricultural sectors yet remain unchanged in the rice sector during the oil boom? The later phase of the oil boom – coming after several years of sustained economic growth – appears to have spilt over to a general excess demand for wage labour in non-agricultural sectors. Large government salary increases during this period also appear to have contributed to rapid modern sector wage growth.

But it is clear that this did not signal a general tightening of labour markets, as evidenced by trends in rice sector wages. While non-agricultural wages and employment rose rapidly in urban areas, the impact was not sufficient to bring about an increase in rice wages in relatively poor rural Java. As in the modified Lewis model, wage determination in the modern sector was only indirectly linked to labour market conditions in the countryside.

Three explanations can be offered as to why rice wages failed to respond to rapid economic growth during the oil boom period. Rice output only began to take off from well into the oil boom period, and hence the direct impact on labour demand was lagged (Manning 1988b). Second, there were signs of considerable slack in rural labour markets when sustained growth began. There had been several seasons when the harvest was disrupted because of major pest problems – specifically the infamous *wereng* or brown plant hopper in the mid 1970s. Poor harvests and labour displacement associated with new technology contributed to elastic labour supply curves at the time of accelerated growth from around 1978.

Finally, the structure of employment and earnings in rural Java in the early 1970s meant that employment growth did not immediately affect wages in the rice sector. The nominal rice wages were set according to pre-

---

[12] It is worth reiterating that the absolute differences in these wage rates may not mean very much given quite different wage systems (including emoluments) which prevailed in each sector.

vailing regional notions of wage justice.[13] As urban labour demand began to expand rapidly, people employed in marginal activities were drawn into higher paying jobs, a process which did not directly influence rice wages (Jayasuriya and Manning 1990). It was not until the end of the oil boom period that expanding labour demand both within and outside agriculture began to affect wage rates in the rice sector in Java.

Wage stagnation during the 1980s

The substantial impact of the oil boom on labour demand can be considered a one-off effect. Real modern sector wages rose largely because of a sharp and substantial outward shift in labour demand brought about by exogenous circumstances. From early to mid 1980s when economic growth slowed, though by no means stagnated, slower nominal and real wage growth can partly be attributed to relative stagnation of domestic demand, which had grown so rapidly during the previous decade. Slow wage growth was also influenced by a more competitive environment affecting both employment and wages, as deregulation measures were introduced to promote greater efficiency and investment in the private sector.

It is of some interest that real wage rates remained constant through to the end of the decade. This was despite the revival of Indonesia's economic fortunes associated with economic reform after 1986. Macroeconomic policy had an important influence on this. Exchange rate policy, marked by two major devaluations in 1983 and 1986 and a subsequent steady depreciation of the rupiah, was accompanied by a mild deflationary policy aimed at maintaining Indonesia's international competitiveness (Hill 1995). Indonesia successfully averted an appreciation of the rupiah due to inflation of the real exchange rate, as experienced in the earlier oil boom period (Warr 1992a). Such a policy could only be achieved by maintaining pressure on domestic costs, including wages, to ensure that they remained in line with those of Indonesia's major trading partners.

Paradoxically, rice wages rose during the years of slower economic growth. As in the oil boom, rapid expansion of labour demand in rice did not spill over to a general tightening of labour markets in the cities. Labour markets were not well integrated, at least in the short to medium term.

One other point should be mentioned regarding the different trend in rice wages compared with non-agricultural wages during the early 1980s. Real wage growth was double digit in only two years over the 20-year

---

[13] In some regions, the floor to agricultural wages was based on rice equivalents (for example, the rupiah equivalent of one kilogram or litre of rice).

period, 1985 and 1993, when rice prices and the rural cost of living in Java both declined absolutely. Rice self-sufficiency was achieved in 1984 and a bumper harvest was experienced in 1993. In neither case did surplus rice stocks spill over in significant amounts to exports, and rural rice prices were depressed. This decline in rice prices contributed to an unprecedented annual increase (16–17 per cent) in real rice wages in each year. These movements in rice prices show the importance of price movements of basic consumption goods for real wages and labour welfare.

Favourable trends in food production can have a significant, positive influence on rural welfare through their short-run effect on prices. Conversely, of course, unexpected food shortages such as those experienced in the 1960s and early 1970s can adversely affect wage incomes as a result of sudden price hikes. Avoidance of such crises was one of the important achievements of the Soeharto government since the late 1970s.

Tightening labour markets in the 1990s

By the early 1990s, real wages had begun to grow in all sectors for the first time in the New Order period. Casual wages in rice increased sharply after 1991. So too did wages in construction, textiles and government administration. Rapid growth in non-oil exports had finally begun to have an influence on the general price of unskilled labour. Institutional change probably also influenced wage increases in the modern sector. Substantial increases in minimum wages began in 1992 and accelerated in 1994 and 1995.[14] Minimum wages aside, these wage increases appear to have been largely stimulated by increases in private rather than public sector labour demand.

Government pay and employment policies

Government pay policy had major implications for wages in the modern private sector until the late 1980s when deregulation began to give the private sector a more independent role in economic activity. Civil service salary revisions were adopted in public enterprises, which were important in almost all major sectors. The impact was also related to expectations created by highly publicised government salary increases, especially revisions in larger foreign- and domestic-owned establishments.

Two major periods of significant changes in government salaries can be

---

[14] In the latter two years minimum wages were raised by one-third and 21 per cent, respectively, nationally, and by more in the industrial regions near Jakarta (see chapter 8).

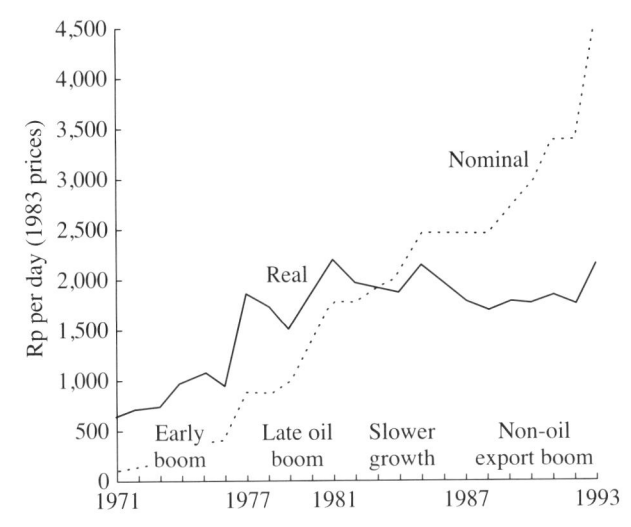

Figure 5.3 Nominal and real civil service wages: Indonesia, 1971–1993 (Rp/day, 1983 prices)
Sources: CBS, Unpublished data and Average Wages on Estates, various years; PERTEKSI, Annual Agreements on Wages, various years; Department of Finance, unpublished data.

clearly identified. The first was the late 1970s and early 1980s. The oil boom offered an opportunity for the government to raise salaries to improve the welfare and performance of a discouraged and overstaffed civil service. It did this from the early 1970s with a dramatic doubling of nominal wages in 1977 and substantial increases again in 1980 and 1981. From 1976 to 1981 basic salaries of lower-level civil servants were increased by more than fourfold and real basic wages rose by over 100 per cent (figure 5.3).[15]

The second period, in the second half of the 1980s, was one of slower economic growth. Nominal civil service wages remained constant and real wages declined by about 25 per cent in the period 1985–8. This effect was felt more intensely at lower levels where basic salaries were a larger component of employee incomes.[16]

What was the effect of these government salary revisions on wages in other sectors? Annual increases were positively correlated with increases

---

[15] In the early 1970s payments in kind – chiefly the rice allowance – accounted for slightly over one-third of total incomes of civil servants, and probably more at lower levels (Arndt and Sundrum 1975). This share had fallen to less than 10 per cent for lower level civil servants by the late 1970s.

[16] In the 1970s, the government introduced special functional (job related) and structural (position related) allowances which increasingly became a major part of total pay packages for upper echelon civil servants (Manning 1992).

126 *Economic growth and labour market dynamics*

in wage rates in the Bandung textile sector and to a lesser extent with construction, estate and even rice wages over the period 1972–91.[17] Regression equations fitted real wage rates (in logs) in each of these sectors to a time trend, and the log of government real wage rates. Except for rice, the exercise produced significant coefficients for government wages for each of the wage series over the same time period.[18] The lack of a correlation with rice wages is understandable, given that the latter are largely casual rates paid to farm labourers in an atomised small-scale sector.

The close relationship between government sector wages and the other series (excluding rice) can be seen clearly from figure 5.2. Textile wages rose steeply in two periods (1975–7 and 1979–81), estate wages rose steeply in 1979–81 and both stagnated from 1983 to 1988. Construction wages rose fastest over the period 1976–81, and fluctuated at other times.

A further point related to the impact of government wages is the apparent decline in the influence of changes in civil service salaries on those in textiles, from around the mid 1980s. Textile wage growth was of a similar magnitude to civil servant salary increases in earlier periods. Nevertheless, real wages in textiles began to rise quite rapidly in the late 1980s, despite slow growth in real civil service salaries until the 1990s.[19] The rapid increase in the size of the private sector during the deregulation period, and the more internationally competitive nature of new export industries, resulted in a greater role of market demand in wage determination.

Price deflators and trends in labour costs

These trends appear relatively robust irrespective of which measure of wages is used. Nevertheless, the application of different price deflators and use of earnings rather than wage rate data does influence the conclusions regarding the magnitude and timing of real wage change.

First, with regard to the choice of deflators. The most relevant price index has been used to deflate each of the wage series. During the second

---

[17] Correlation coefficients were 0.79, 0.44, 0.39 and 0.35.
[18] The equation was log $RWt = a + b1T + b2LogRWg + u$ where log RWt = the log of real wages (textiles, etc.), $b1T$ = the time trend and $b2LogRWg$ = the log of real government wages. For example, in the case of textiles the resulting coefficients were log $RWt = -0.141$ (-0.66) + 0.020T (0.004) + 0.890 LogRWg (0.095) (DW = 1.99; R2 = 0.94). This implies that after taking account of the time trend in real wages, a 1 per cent increase in government salaries raised textile wages by close to 0.9 per cent. The coefficients were much lower (0.2–0.3) for estate and construction wages.
[19] The latter were increased in 1993; this restored real wages to levels achieved in the early 1980s.

Table 5.2. *Correlation matrix of selected price deflators, first differences: Indonesia 1976–1991*

	Indonesia CPI	Jakarta 9 Comm. Index	Java Rural 9 Comm. Index	Jakarta KFM
Indonesia CPI	1.00	0.79	0.58	0.32
Jakarta 9 Comm. Index	–	1.00	0.61	0.27
Java Rural 9 Comm. Index	–	–	1.00	0.20
KFM, Jakarta				1.00

Sources: CBS, various sources.

half of the 1980s, trends in the various price deflators diverged.[20] A correlation matrix linking annual changes (first differences) in the four series – the Indonesia CPI, the Jakarta nine–commodity index, the Java rural price index and the Jakarta minimum physical needs index (MFN) (table 5.2). The MFN index was not closely correlated with all the other price indices, even the Jakarta nine–commodity index.

How much does the application of different deflators influence trends in real wage rates? Use of different deflators did not significantly influence trends for the total 20-year period. But real wage trends were sensitive to the choice of the deflator during specific time periods (Manning 1994). For example, textile wage rates deflated by the MFN declined more steeply during the 1980s than when the CPI was used as the deflator (figure 5.4).

The extent of wage declines implied by the MFN series in the 1980s are doubtful compared with the other series, and they represent an upper band with regard to non-agricultural wage change. They do suggest, nevertheless, that a cost of living index which is more realistically weighted in line with consumption patterns of lower-income wage workers, produced a wage outcome less favourable to workers than implied by data deflated by the CPI.

Second, how do these changes in wage rates compare with trends in labour wage costs in particular activities?[21] Average costs in manufacturing

---

[20] The basically urban indices – the Indonesia CPI, Jakarta and Bandung nine-commodity price indices – rose less rapidly than the rural cost of living index on Java, in particular, and the MFN index for Jakarta and Bandung. One other index of labour incomes which is commonly used is the consumer goods component of the farmers' terms of trade. This index rose less rapidly than the rural nine-commodity index in the late 1980s but more rapidly than the Indonesia CPI. Because the index was revised in 1983, it is not appropriate however to use it for earlier periods.

[21] Two sources of data provide information on this subject: wage costs as a proxy for average earnings in large and medium manufacturing and average wage incomes collected in the National Labour Force Surveys (SAKERNAS).

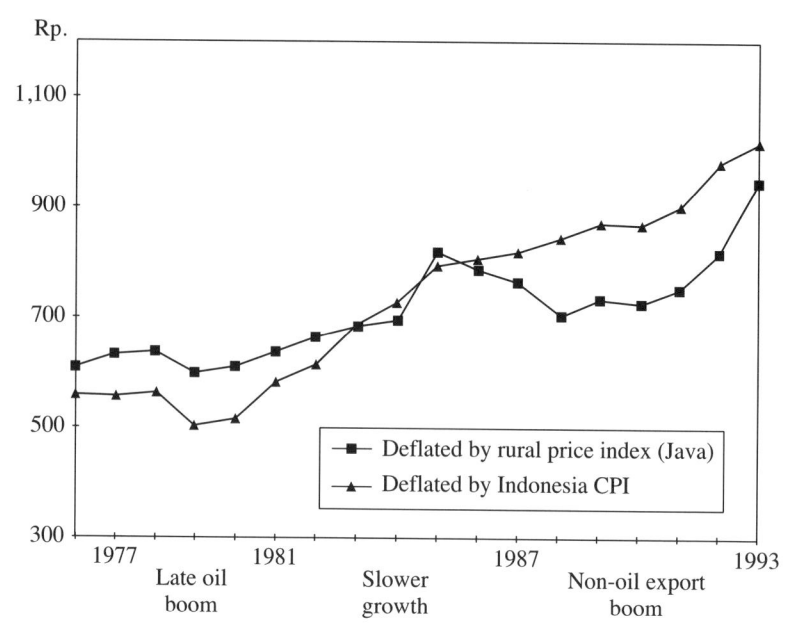

Figure 5.4 Real textile wages deflated by the Indonesia CPI and the KFM, Bandung and Indonesia, 1976–1993
Sources: CBS, Unpublished data and Average Wages on Estates, various years; PERTEKSI, Annual Agreements on Wages, various years; Department of Finance, unpublished data.

grew more rapidly than wage rates, especially in the 1980s. For example, growth in real manufacturing costs in textiles was sustained over the entire period, and has continued up to recent years (figure 5.5).

Why have average costs increased more rapidly than wage rates? First, modernisation of industry and the growth of capital-intensive manufacturing imply greater application of skilled manpower and capacity utilisation. The shift away from labour-intensive to more capital-intensive production implies a higher share of employment in more stable and skilled occupations (Hill 1990).[22] A second explanation is that workers are increasingly absorbed into larger establishments with more stable operations, and they receive more overtime payments and annual bonuses.[23]

---

[22] See Manning (1979) for a discussion of the link between capital-intensity and earnings in the textile industry. Hill (1990b: 96) finds substantial real wage growth in labour-intensive industries such as food processing, tobacco, textiles and garments in the intercensal period 1975–86.

[23] Evidence from surveys of manufacturing in the mid 1970s and late 1980s indicate that overtime earnings were a major component of worker incomes in larger establishments (Manning 1979; White *et al.* 1992).

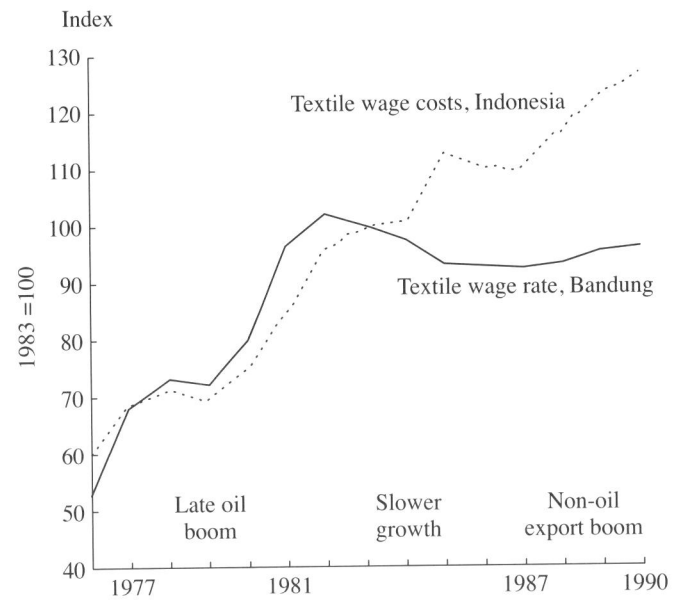

Figure 5.5 Wage rates and average wage costs in textiles: Indonesia 1976–1990 (1983=100)
Sources: CBS, Annual Survey of Large and Medium Manufacturing Establishments, various years; PERTEKSI, Annual Agreements on Wages, various years; Department of Finance, unpublished data.

Trends in wage costs and competitiveness

Finally, wage cost trends throw some light on developments in Indonesian competitiveness during this period (figure 5.6). Trends in real rupiah wage costs are compared with real wage costs expressed in US$ values.[24]

Like wage rates and earnings, real rupiah wage costs show an upward trend from the early 1970s. This was true of the oil boom period and again in the early 1990s. Expressed in US$ terms, we find a slightly different picture. During the period of rehabilitation and the oil boom, dollar wage costs rose steeply. A pegged nominal exchange rate (Rp. 415) from 1971 to 1978, accompanied by relatively high rates of domestic inflation, was associated with a large appreciation of Indonesia's real exchange rate.

The US$ value of wage costs fell briefly and then rose again after the first major devaluation in 1978. The first devaluation was only partially successful in improving international competitiveness. Domestic inflation

---

[24] Nominal wage data are deflated by Indonesian produced prices (the wholesale price index). Trends in this series are compared with the real US dollar value of wages converted at nominal exchange rates and deflated by the US producer price index.

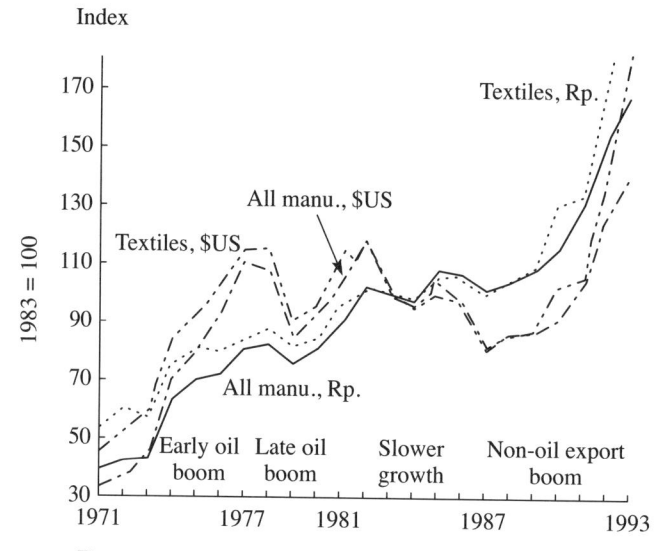

130 *Economic growth and labour market dynamics*

Figure 5.6 Real wage costs in Indonesian textiles (TFC) and all manufacturing, 1971–1993 (1983=100)
Notes: Wages in Rupiah: nominal wages costs deflated by Indonesia wholesale price index. Wages in dollars: nominal wage costs converted to US dollars at nominal exchange rate deflated by US producer price index.
Source: CBS and IMF, *Yearbook of International Financial Statistics*, 1994.

eroded real exchange rate gains, and labour demand expansion put strong pressure on modern sector wage rates in the late oil boom period. However, following the second devaluation in 1983, they fell and then remained relatively constant until 1991 when there was another sharp acceleration.

The US$ wage comparisons are illustrative only.[25] They point to the importance of managed depreciation of the exchange rate following the two major devaluations in the 1980s. This helped contain growth in wage costs. Stabilisation policy seems to have played an important role in supporting the non-oil export drive, accompanied by reforms which boosted labour productivity.

These trends also sound a warning. Real wage costs began to rise steeply in both rupiah and US$ values in the 1990s, especially in the critical textile industry. It seems that labour markets may have begun to tighten around this period. At the same time, modern sector wages in labour-intensive industries were probably influenced by substantial

[25] Expressed in terms of yen (South Korean won or Taiwanese dollars), for example, Indonesian wages would have fallen quite sharply after 1985 given the revaluations which occurred in all these currencies following the Plaza accord.

increases in minimum wages and the introduction of comprehensive worker social security legislation in 1992 – since more than half of the contributions are levied on employers. Both help to account for the sharp rise in wage costs in 1993.

Conclusions

The story of wage trends does not neatly fit either with the modified Lewis model hypothesized in Chapter 2 or with a neoclassical interpretation of sharply rising wage rates associated with rapid economic growth. Unskilled wages rose more steeply in the modern sector than might have been expected if the supply of labour was highly elastic. At the same time, wage growth was not sustained in the modern sector over the 20-year period. Real wages remained relatively flat for an extended period in the 1980s, including a period of slower economic expansion and then recovery in the middle of the decade. Indonesia did not experience a period of relatively unhindered real wage growth which was a feature of economic development in the NIEs for several decades from the 1960s.

The Indonesian experience suggests four major conclusions regarding the relationship between economic growth and wage outcomes. First, trends in real wage rates can diverge for extended time periods across major sectors of activity in the early stages of economic development. The outcome depends on initial conditions, the source and intensity of growth and the way in which these factors affect labour demand in various sectors. This especially applies to a large and relatively fragmented economy such as Indonesia, where the transmission of economic stimuli occurs with lags. Thus wages in the rice sector were largely unaffected by the expansion of labour demand during the oil boom for a period of close to a decade. Later, rapid expansion of this sector contributed to real wage growth in rice agriculture for a period when modern sector growth faltered.

As low-wage and underemployed workers are transferred out of low-productivity sectors, and these sectors themselves begin to modernise, one would expect labour market changes to spread more quickly and widely across sectors. Indonesia – at least Java and the more developed Outer Island regions – began to enter this stage of economic development in the early 1990s.

Second, it is difficult to separate out the effects of short-term shifts in the balance of labour demand and supply from longer-term trends. Although economic growth in Indonesia has been relatively stable for over 25 years, the leading sectors in economic growth have differed at various time periods. The oil boom had its greatest impact on the modern sector and urban labour markets, even though the Indonesian government paid special attention to rural and regional development. Later, rapid growth in the rice sector and then non-oil export growth became the leading sectors.

Third, macroeconomic policy has had a powerful impact on wage outcomes. Following the experience of rising costs in the modern sector during the period of fixed exchange rates in the 1970s, the government followed a more careful policy of containing domestic costs. This was achieved through a more flexible exchange rate policy and mild domestic deflation. Such policies encouraged structural change and employment growth in non-oil export sectors. At the same time the policies contributed to slower real wage growth.

Finally, contrary to popular opinion in Indonesia, labour-intensive growth is not inimical to wage increases. Rice sector growth in the early 1980s was accompanied by real wage increases which had a widespread impact on the welfare of many labourers. The non-oil export boom did not initially have similar effects on wage rates in manufacturing, although average earnings rose from the mid 1980s. But real wages rose substantially in manufacturing in the 1990s, even prior to the revamped minimum wage policy.

Increases in the unit value of wages – most commonly shown in hourly rates – result from relative shortages of labour at going wage rates. Even if account is taken of differences in the quality of labour and jobs, rises in average earnings can reflect much more: the changing skill and educational composition of the workforce and the new structure of industry. Such rises also result from increases in the intensity of work and payment of special productivity-related emoluments (incentive allowances and bonuses).[26]

The growth in average earnings in manufacturing in Indonesia have been much closer to that recorded in South Korea, than they have been to increases which occurred in slower-growing economies such as the Philippines in the 1970s and 1980s. But longer-term growth in wage rates were much slower in Indonesia than in South Korea and also Malaysia, where agricultural and urban traditional and construction wages rose steeply from around the mid-1970s (Bai 1985: 132–5; Mazumdar 1993). Indonesia only began to reach this stage in labour transition when the agricultural work force began to decline in the 1990s.

---

[26] The latter are likely to be associated with changes in employment, especially related to movement out of casual employment in sectors like agriculture to more permanent contracts in manufacturing.

Appendix table 5.1. *Daily wages and wage growth in selected activities: Indonesia, 1971–1993[a]*

	1971/2 Early oil boom	1976/7	Late oil boom 1980/1	Slower growth 1986/7	Non-oil export boom 1992/3
(A) Nominal wages (Rp)					
Rice	–	250	432	1,056	2,011
Estates	142	362	905	1,792	–
Textiles	70	305	775	1,343	2,750
Construction	300[b]	573	1,490	2,417	4,200[c]
Civil service	110	692	1,590	2,439	3,944
Index (textiles = 100)					
Rice	–	82	56	79	73
Estates	200	119	117	133	–
Textiles	100	100	100	100	100
Construction	429	188	192	180	153
Civil service	157	227	205	182	143
(B) Real wages (Rp, 1983 prices)					
Rice	–	618	625	675	885
Estates	923	914	1,312	1,359	–
Textiles	410	734	1,051	1,049	1,424
Construction	896	1,064	1,889	2,184	2,194
Civil service	695	1,401	2,022	1,880	1,961
Growth (% p.a.)					
Rice	–	–	0.3	1.6	4.6
Estates	–	−0.2	7.5	0.7	–
Textiles	–	12.3	12.6	0	5.2
Construction	–	3.5	15.4	2.9	0.1
Civil service	–	15.1	9.5	−1.4	0.7

Notes: [a] All data two year averages; [b] 1972; [c] 1991/92
Notes on sources: Rice: From Central Bureau of Statistics (CBS); average of monthly data collected 1976 onwards; unweighted mean of daily wage rates in hoeing (males) for West, Central and East Java (to October 1993). Estates: From CBS, average of half yearly data for permanent production workers (both sexes, Indonesia; 1971–92). Construction: Unpublished data from Department of Public Works (Jakarta). Average of monthly data unskilled workers, Jakarta (1972–Nov. 1992). Textiles: Minimum wage for unskilled labour based on annual agreements between the association of textile producers (PERTEKSI) and the labour unions (SPSI); Bandung, 1971–93. Civil Service: Basic salary only; generally included in the budget beginning in April (1971–93). Grade 1b/Level 9, covering primary and lower secondary graduates.
Sources: CBS, Unpublished data and Average Wages on Estates, various years; PERTEKSI, Annual Agreements on wages, various years; Department of Finance, unpublished data.

III

Labour market structure and institutions

6

Segmented labour markets and regional integration: change and continuity

One key theme underpins the discussion of changing earnings structure – greater integration of labour markets across industries, regions and between rural and urban areas. Earnings differentials have narrowed as labour has been drawn out of low-wage activities.

Labour markets tend to be poorly integrated at early stages of development (see Turner 1965; Berg 1969; Mazumdar 1989, 1996). We have seen that this was true in Indonesia. Rudimentary communications and uncertain transport contributed to imperfect labour market information, high costs of movement and low levels of labour mobility. Wages varied widely across industries and labour market areas, and occupational differentials were large. Labour contracts differed widely in local labour markets, especially in Java where tied labour, land and capital markets were common. Wages respond slowly to changing patterns of labour supply and demand. These factors contributed to the inefficient allocation of labour and high levels of inequality among wage earners.

Typically, labour markets are heterogeneous according to enterprise characteristics in developing economies. This was especially the case in Indonesia where foreign investment, imported technology and natural resource industries were important from the early years of the New Order. Larger, more capital-intensive establishments adopted more formalised rules regarding recruitment, pay and labour organisation. They coexisted with large numbers of small establishments in which labour contracts were less formal, and employment and hours of work variable. Wages and labour contracts also varied considerably across market segments: between the public sector with rigid recruitment and wage systems, the urban informal sector and the large agricultural and rural non-farm sectors in which casual wage workers, self employed and family labour dominated (Mazumdar 1989).

In chapter 2 we presented a stylised dualistic labour market to illustrate the process of labour allocation and wage determination in labour surplus economies. High modern sector wages were attributed to efficiency wage considerations, monopolistic structures and labour policies of foreign and state-owned companies. In reality, a strictly dualistic structure rarely exists (Ohkawa 1972), but rather a range of employment systems depending on the technology, size and type of ownership of firms, and the skill composition of the workforce. Some of these contrasts, and how they have changed over time, are examined in this chapter.

Two opposing forces have influenced the wage structure: integrating forces such as improvements in communications, labour mobility and information flows, were to some extent countered by the influence on the wage structure of new technologies and a wider range of products. In addition, changing economic policies have influenced the wage structure differently at various stages in the past 30 years.

The changing structure of work and wages

The discussion begins with an examination of an earnings hierarchy among less-educated wage earners. There was considerable narrowing of wage differentials from the late 1970s.[1] Relative gains made by government employees during the oil-boom period were not maintained during the 1980s (figure 6.1). Growth in manufacturing employment contributed to improvements in wages relative to other sectors, especially in the export-oriented textiles sector in Java. Although wages remained relatively low in textiles, differentials with less-educated male government officials had fallen considerably by 1992.

The changes were most marked in rural areas and in Java where the growth of labour-intensive manufacturing had been faster. Workers in the relatively low-wage agricultural sector also gained relatively to most non-agricultural sectors, with the exception of the rapidly growing textile sector in Java (figure 6.2). The index of labour earnings in agriculture rose from 59 in 1977 to 76 in 1992 relative to all other sectors in Java.

This latter development seems puzzling, given the much faster growth of non-agricultural wage rates noted in the previous chapter. The explanation lies partly in the diversification of employment activities among farmers. Many farmers gained access to higher-income jobs both within and outside their home villages in the 1980s.

Despite these changes, differentials between sectors remained large and

---

[1] The starting year, 1977, can be considered early to middle in the oil-boom period, whereas by 1992 the economic liberalisation programme and non-oil export boom was well under way. Unfortunately there are no comparable data for the early 1980s and the National Labour Force Survey only collected data on a limited number of sectors during the late 1980s.

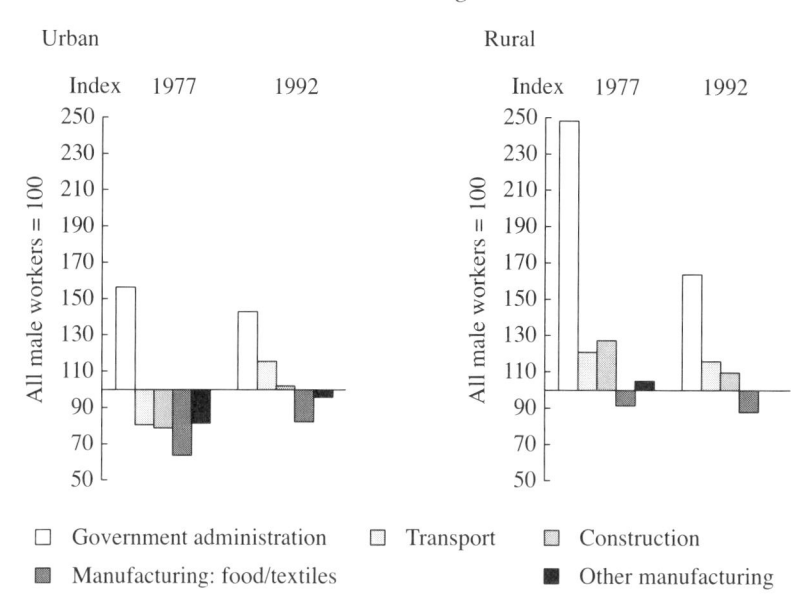

Figure 6.1 Hourly wage differentials for males by activity: Indonesia, 1977 and 1992 (all male workers=100)
Note: Data are based on total earnings of employees by major sector of employment working a minimum of 25 hours in their main job. All male employees with a completed junior high education or below.
Source: CBS, National Labour Force Surveys, 1977 and 1992, Jakarta.

surprisingly stable over time. Segmentation remained a feature of the Indonesian labour market in the 1990s. Wages of less-educated employees were highest in the government and small enclave mining sectors and lowest in agriculture at both points in time. Even in 1992 after a period of slower income growth in the 1980s, earnings reported by the government exceeded those in all other sectors by a considerable margin. Manufacturing wages for the less-educated workers were relatively low, especially in the labour-intensive food-based industries, among the eight major non-agricultural sectors.

Changes in wage differentials were smaller among more educated workers. They widened between the rapidly growing private sectors (banking, manufacturing) but narrowed in government administration (table 6.1). Senior high graduates (academic stream) who worked as government officials earned relatively high salaries in both years. Among tertiary graduates, earnings of government officials fell relative to the private sector by 1992. Although employing a high proportion of graduates, the government was less able to compete with private sector employers for higher quality workers.

140 *Labour market structure and institutions*

Table 6.1. *Wage differentials between selected sectors among more educated employees: Indonesia, 1977 and 1992[a] (all sectors=100)*

	Senior high (academic stream) 1977	Senior high (academic stream) 1992	Tertiary 1977	Tertiary 1992
Public utilities/banking	73 (3)	122 (8)	118 (6)	139 (9)
Government administration	122 (30)	110 (30)	86 (44)	84 (48)
Other services	104 (39)	99 (12)	76 (29)	93 (17)
Manufacturing	63 (6)	82 (20)	70 (5)	121 (9)
Other	70 (22)	94 (30)	90 (16)	113 (17)
All sectors	100 (Rp.145)	100 (Rp.898)	100 (Rp.392)	100 (Rp.1656)

Note: [a] Figures in parentheses represent shares in total employment.
Source: CBS, National Labour Force Survey, 1977 and 1992, Jakarta.

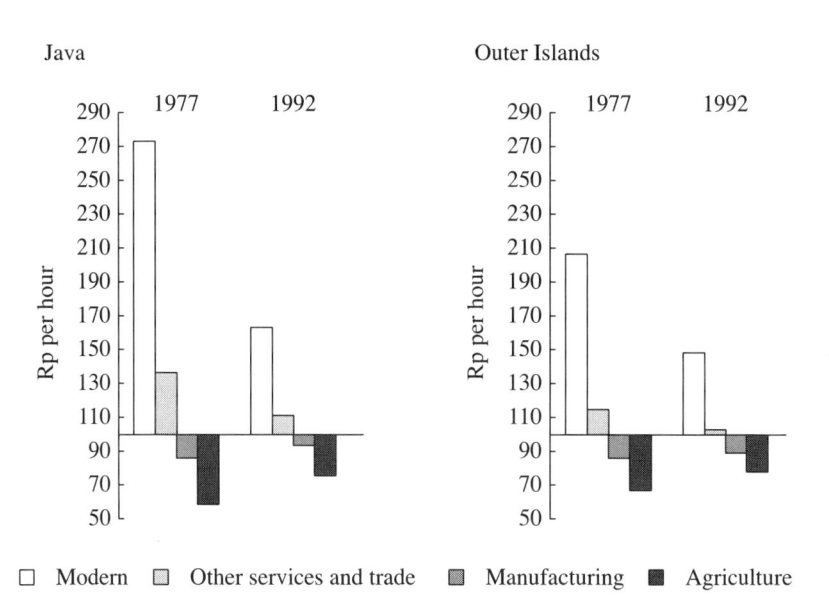

Figure 6.2 Wage differentials by sector among less-educated employees, Java and Outer Islands, 1977 and 1992 (Rp/hour, all sector=100)
Source: CBS, National Labour Force Surveys, 1977 and 1992, Jakarta.

Table 6.2. *Wage differentials and level of completed schooling and gender: Indonesia, 1982–1994 (primary schooling=100)*

	Male				Female			
	1982	1987	1990	1994	1982	1987	1990	1994
<Primary	70	78	82	82	66	78	79	81
Primary	100	100	100	100	100	100	100	100
Lower secondary	143	133	130	126	192	176	161	147
Upper secondary								
General	175	166	175	167	243	238	228	237
Vocational	185	167	171	176	248	272	253	270
Tertiary	289	291	300	322	385	430	401	424

Sources: CBS, National Labour Force Surveys, 1977, 1987, 1990, Jakarta and CBS, National Social Economic Survey, 1982 (computer tapes).

In all sectors, the earnings of upper secondary relative to primary graduates were constant over the period 1982–94 (table 6.2). The widening of differentials was partly related to the increasing proportion of educated employees in manufacturing: the wage gap between the more- and less-educated workers was much greater than in services (appendix table 6.1). However Indonesia had not yet reached the stage where the supply of upper secondary and tertiary graduates was sufficiently large to compress earnings across the entire spectrum of educational achievement. Rising wage rates among less-educated workers were counterbalanced by the rapid growth in demand and increased salaries of educated workers. Nevertheless, rapid increase in supply of the educated workers prevented a substantial widening of wage differentials by education, as occurred in several Latin American countries (Webb 1977).

Diversification of rural labour markets: the case of Java

Three interrelated aspects of rural labour market change in Java are examined

- integration of rural labour markets across activities,
- more intense urban and rural labour market linkages,
- corresponding changes in wage institutions and contracts.

There were profound labour market changes in rural Java accompanying the expansion of non-agricultural employment and wage growth. Shifts in work patterns in many Outer Island regions were also far-reaching. Rural–urban labour markets became more closely integrated, and the distinction blurred as links intensified into the 1980s and 1990s in rural Java (McGee 1987).

The most important development in income growth and poverty reduction was the disappearance of many subsistence income activities in Java. Integration of rural labour markets meant the compression of an attenuated earnings ladder, in which rice wages were formerly close to the apex, among poorer households in rural Java. There was also adaptation – sometimes disappearance – of labour contracts which spread in the earlier periods as rationing and wage adjustment mechanisms.

It is useful to distinguish three phases of transformation: the early years of the rehabilitation and green revolution, the oil-boom period, and the move to non-oil export expansion, after an uncertain period of slower economic growth.[2]

Labour market stress in the 1970s

During the first phase of economic stabilisation and rehabilitation, excess labour supply pressures were painfully evident in Java, despite renewed rice production growth, improved transport, and the beginnings of rapid modern sector and urban growth. Two patterns of adaptation occurred. First, rural wage rates stagnated, and labour was displaced in the harvesting and processing of rice.[3] New rice harvesting technology and increased commercialisation of rice production saw the spread of special labour contracts, hiring arrangements and systems of payment. These had the effect of reducing wages and job access among the poor.[4] Another sign of rural labour market strain was the increase in inter-regional migration of landless workers in some regions (Budhisantoso 1975). Rural hardship was exacerbated by two periods of crisis in rice production in the early and mid 1970s.

The second major form of adaptation was rural–urban migration. Significant numbers of villagers sought a tenuous foothold in the fledgling but growing urban economies. Employment growth was primarily in non-wage jobs taken up by many rural–urban migrants.

Hugo's (1978) seminal study of West Java describes the intensive migration flows primarily to the informal sector from a range of villages of

---

[2] The focus is in Java partly because changes have been much more widely researched than in the Outer Islands.
[3] See especially Collier *et al.* (1974), Collier (1981), Hart (1986) and Manning (1988a) for surveys of the literature and empirical data.
[4] Hayami and Kikuchi (1981) argue that rural wages fell through changing forms of contracts, and Hart (1986: 189–90) noted that exclusionary labour arrangements spread because of weakening of rural labour's political position after 1965.

varying distances from Jakarta and Bandung.[5] Many of the informal sector workers were commuters and circular migrants, retaining links with their villages. Improved transport networks encouraged out-migration from more remote villages. This out-migration was primarily motivated by higher-earning employment opportunities in the cities and difficulties in finding rural jobs.

However, this first phase of involvement in urban employment had relatively little impact on the structure of earnings in villages, although remittances benefited households and villages where out-migration was intense. Most villagers, especially those with little access to land, were little affected by urban growth. They continued to depend on low-paying jobs outside farming but close to their village. Hart (1986) provides a graphic picture of survival strategies adopted by poor households in 1975. Most allocated a substantial amount of their time for low returns in farm labour, fishing and gathering in surrounding villages. The poorest households were pushed into less desirable marginal work, often outside the village.[6]

The late oil-boom and rice sector growth period

The situation began to change as the oil-boom intensified in the late 1970s. Many traditional labour-intensive industries found it more difficult to compete with new industries in urban and peri-urban locations. Activities such as non-mechanised weaving of cloth, and basket and mat weaving from bamboo were increasingly replaced as the cheaper goods produced in factories spread to rural markets.[7] At the same time, there was growth in job opportunities associated with greater spending on rural public works programmes, and with sustained rice production growth.

For most observers, these developments were unexpected. Collier *et al.* (1982) documented the changes. An article written by Collier (1981), published one year earlier, was deeply pessimistic about employment and income distribution trends in Java. New research findings pointed to two developments: widespread reports of labour shortages in the rice sector and the increasing pull of young people into higher earnings activities located outside villages adjacent to urban areas.[8]

Why the sudden turnabout? As a result of increased public and private

---

[5] See Steele (1980) for a discussion of similar processes in Surabaya.
[6] See Stoler (1977) and several Agro-Economic Survey (Bogor) reports on rural labour markets conducted in 1976–1978 (Gunawan *et al.* 1977; Gunawan, Nurmanaf and Sawit, 1979).   [7] Hill (1980), Sawit (1980) Dick and White (1986).
[8] Collier *et al.* (1982) mentions 1979–82 as the years when rural labour shortages began to be reported by villages in Java, although informants reported that such problems applied in less than half of the 26 villages studied.

Table 6.3. *Real earnings per hour and share of labour inputs in off-farm activities: rural West Java, 1976 and 1983 (rp. hour, per cent)*[a]

Activity	Landless/marginal farmers[b] 1976	1983	Small farmers[b] 1976	1983
Farm labouring	169 (40)	166 (30)	178 (18)	178 (15)
Non-agriculture				
Home industry	38 (15)	74 (7)	45 (34)	32 (19)
Wage labour[c]	196 (12)	256 (26)	230 (10)	236 (17)
Petty trade	129 (18)	272 (15)	210 (10)	349 (14)
All off-farm	161 (85)	235 (78)	109 (72)	187 (65)

Notes: [a] Data for six paddy villages, expressed in 1983 prices. Figures in parentheses are the proportion of *total* hours worked outside self-employed and family labour in agriculture; [b] Marginal farmers operate <0.1 ha. of paddy land, small farmers operate 0.5 ha. of paddy land; [c] Includes trishaw (*becak*) drivers, other transport workers, construction workers and casual labour.
Source: Manning, 1987, 'Rural economic change and labour mobility: A case study from West Java', *Bulletin of Indonesian Economic Studies*, 23(3): table 3.

spending during the oil boom, workers also moved into newer rural activities within the village where labour earnings were higher. Many more found jobs in urban areas. Labour reallocation outside agriculture drove some of these changes in West Java villages in the period 1976–83 (table 6.3). There was a shift in total labour allocation and returns per hour in favour of higher-earning activities among households who owned little or no land. Work in wage labour activities increased, especially in construction. Less household time was now devoted to work in low-wage cottage industries, which were increasingly undertaken by older men and women, or younger children (Sawit, Saefudin and Sri Hartoyo 1985). Developments within the rice sector which played a major role in the tightening of rural labour markets were

- a substantial increase in production per crop
- a large increase in cropping intensity in favourably located rice villages
- the failure of mechanization to spread as quickly as earlier feared (Manning 1988a).

These developments countered the backwash effects from the introduction of new technology in the early period of the green revolution. Besides real wage growth, total household hours worked in rice farming rose in some areas while in others, they remained stable or declined slightly (World Bank 1985: 128; Collier *et al.* 1982; Manning 1988a: 33–5).

Many landowning households began to derive most of their earnings from non-agricultural sources by the early 1980s (Mintoro 1984; Rietveld 1986). Earnings patterns in Java were beginning to follow what White (1986: 36–9) has termed the 'East Asia' pattern. The landless and those with little land now earned incomes outside agriculture comparable with those of larger landowners.[9] As government funding of rural services increased, the number of teachers, health care providers and government officials proliferated, contributing to an increase in the demand for goods and services.

Another development was greater involvement of rural households in the informal sector in the urban economies in Java, through commuting and circular migration. Collier *et al.* (1982) stress the importance of increased urban employment among villagers living adjacent to cities. In some surveys of more distant West Java villages the process was more widespread. There was a significant increase in workers in petty trade and transport (*becak* driving) in towns and cities in Java (Colter 1984; Manning 1987). The transport revolution, which saw the penetration of small minibuses to outlying villages, played a key role in increased urban–rural linkages.

Most villagers engaged in urban employment were still involved in agriculture in the rice growing villages surveyed – few families had moved out of agriculture altogether.[10] The main movement was of less-educated, temporary migrants and commuters, in contrast to smaller permanent migration flows, favouring better-educated villagers going into formal sector jobs (Manning 1987: 63).[11]

While urban population and labour force growth remained high throughout the 1980s, growth in the rural workforce slowed (1.5 per cent per annum among males in the early 1980s compared with 2 per cent in the previous decade). Declining birth rates, rural–urban migration and the

---

[9] This is with the exception of the largest landowning class in most villages which continued to earn much higher incomes from investments outside agriculture. See Shand (1986) for comparative trends with several other countries in the region.

[10] Although migrants from very poor, upland agricultural regions in Central Java shifted out of agriculture around this time (Hetler 1989).

[11] Hugo (1978) for example found that temporary migration flows far outweighed permanent movement in rural West Java in the early 1970s. See Akilu and Harris (1980) on the educational composition of permanent migrants.

146 *Labour market structure and institutions*

movement of rural population to the Outer Islands as part of the transmigration programme contributed to this trend (see chapter 3).

The non-oil export boom

By the early 1990s, there had been a shift in the forces contributing to rural change. Rural labour markets were now, increasingly, influenced by the growth of factory employment. New jobs in industry contributed to agricultural labour shortages, wage growth and the elimination of labour-tying and employment-sharing arrangements. One study indicates a significant numbers of persons (50 or more) in just under half of the 25 villages throughout Java were working mainly in city factories by the early 1990s (Collier et al. 1993).

This new phase of rural labour market change had the greatest impact on labour markets in villages close to cities. Collier *et al.* noted that a high proportion of workers in villages within a radius of 60 kilometres from cities and industrial centres had moved out of agriculture altogether by 1993. Labour shortages were widely reported in many of these now peri-urban villages, and real wage rates had increased substantially in rice equivalents since 1980.

Rural young people educated beyond primary school no longer opted to work in agriculture. At the same time, opportunities for agricultural work were more limited, owing to the spread of mechanisation and the reduction of labour inputs through the widespread use of herbicides.[12] Agricultural labourers increasingly came from outside, many from locations where schooling was less widespread.

New rural–urban linkages involved villagers from more distant places. Long distance migration became more common, especially for work in factories in the formal sector. Many of the less-exposed villages had become more closely linked to the largest urban labour market centred on Jakarta. Younger, new entrants to the workforce, especially females, sought work – or were recruited for work by agents – in cities far from their home villages. Even for East Java villagers residing closer to the big city of Surabaya, Jakarta and environs (JABOTABEK) was the major destination area.

Perceptions of distance within Java had changed radically by the 1990s, aided by intensified transport linkages. Singarimbun (1993: 267–8) summarises the key change in attitudes which had taken place in the village of Sriharjo, south of Jogjakarta:

---

[12] Rice cultivation was distinguished by a relatively low level of mechanisation by regional standards, until the late 1980s (Manning 1988a).

Improvements in transportation and information media changed peoples perception of distance. An informant's remark that big cities like Jakarta, Surabaya and Bandung are 'almost like your neighbours' represents this change of perception. In the past, these cities were seen by villagers as extremely distant places.

The above cities, where a substantial proportion of young people from Sriharjo now worked, were 200 kilometres or more from Jogjakarta. Fifty people were also employed in Saudi Arabia. This was a village where, in 1969, the majority of people had never been to Jogjakarta – just 18 kilometres to the north!

Long hours of work and continuous production in larger-scale manufacturing plants meant the new generation severed links with the rural labour market. Improved educational status of young people, their rejection of agriculture as a source of work and desire for urban jobs contributed to the change.

One development related to long-distance migration was the increase in rural residents working abroad in Malaysia and the Middle East, a rare occurrence a decade earlier. The phenomenon was widespread, although it had a significant labour market effect only in a minority of villages.[13]

The changing structure of rural wages

How did these changes influence wages and earnings structure in rural areas? Whereas real wages had not improved in isolated locations during the 1970s, they did rise in terms of rice equivalents in most areas in the 1980s. Regression analysis of monthly data for the period 1986–92 carried out by Collier *et al.* (1993: appendix B) indicated that increases were statistically significant in both agricultural and non-agricultural activities in most villages.

Labour contracts adapted to the changing balance of labour supply and demand in rural areas. There had been a shift away from tied contracts giving some villagers preferential access to scarce jobs in rice in the 1970s (see Mintoro 1984; Collier *et al.* 1993; Naylor 1994). Naylor's (1991) study of rural labour markets in several regions of Java and Sulawesi in the late 1980s indicates the trend towards a more integrated structure of earnings in more exposed villages. In Kediri (lowland East Java) – the location of the giant *kretek* factory Gudang Garam – unskilled non-agricultural wages were close to rice wages in most activities. They were higher in some areas,

---

[13] In only four of the 24 villages surveyed by Collier *et al.* in 1992/3 did 30 or more persons work abroad. But half of the villages had at least a few workers employed in Saudi Arabia or Malaysia.

such as Klaten in Central Java where small metallurgy workshops proliferated, and in Majalaya (West Java) where rural households found work in mechanised textile factories (Hardjono 1993).

In contrast, earnings were lower than in rice in a range of traditional industries – tiles, bricks, collecting sand, and labouring in sugar mills – in more isolated Majalengka, in West Java. Here, even with considerable out-migration, many households remained dependent on low-earnings activities, especially in off-peak periods in agriculture. In these less-exposed communities, rural economic change was slower. Some upland regions had benefited from agricultural diversification, producing vegetables, fruit and milk for the growing urban markets (Manning, Hill and Saefudin 1988). New activities provided employment opportunities – motor cycle and bicycle repairs, hairdressing, tailoring and trade stalls (Effendi and Manning 1993). But, the majority of households still depended on rural wage employment, and on work in small farms for their main source of income.

As in South Korea, rural economic change was influenced by the participation of workers in urban factory work (Ho 1982). But unlike in South Korea by the mid 1970s, or Malaysia in the 1980s, the impact of industrial employment growth had only begun to affect rural labour markets in less-exposed regions in Java, let alone in Outer Island regions.

Urban labour markets and urban–rural links

Three developments in labour markets contributed to a different pattern of earnings within urban areas, and between urban and rural areas in the 1990s

- the reallocation of less-educated workers away from relatively low wage rural occupations
- the fall in the share of less-educated wage workers in more protected public sector employment
- the rise in the share of better paid, more-educated workers in all sectors.

Two processes influenced income growth within urban areas, and between urban and rural areas. The first was the reversal in declining modern sector wages and the expansion of employment in the protected government sector, social services and larger-scale enterprises in manufacturing. The second was the growth in informal sector employment.

Returns were often much higher in the urban informal sector than in rural Java in the early 1970s (Papanek 1974). Hugo (1978: 237–40) found that mainly male migrants from a range of villages in West Java employed in petty trade, *becak* driving and casual wage labour earned around Rp. 2000 per week (net) in Jakarta compared with daily wages of Rp. 100–200 in their home villages in West Java in 1972–4.[14]

In 1977, urban–rural wage differentials remained substantial, after several years of unsteady rice sector growth. On average, urban earnings per hour were close to twice those in rural areas. This was principally influenced by high earnings among less-educated government employees (Rp. 190 per hour) in towns and cities, compared with low earnings among agricultural wage labourers (Rp. 45 per hour). In other sectors, differentials among male employees were also high, although much more in line with what might be expected: a 40–60 per cent wage differential between urban and rural areas (figure 6.3).[15]

With rapid economic growth and changing employment, these differentials narrowed amongst less-educated workers in Java. Urban wages in construction, transport and manufacturing were only 20–30 per cent above those in rural areas in Java by 1992. Differentials were smaller in the Outer Islands, although the situation is complicated by greater diversity of employment.

By 1992, the composition of urban and rural employment had changed dramatically. High-wage government employment now accounted for 10 per cent of the total among both males and females. Manufacturing and construction were the major sectors of employment for unskilled male wage workers. Construction now provided jobs for around 16 per cent of less-educated males in both urban and rural areas.

Within urban areas, there was a substantial differential in earnings among unskilled workers by sector in the mid 1970s (figure 6.1). Government employees, together with mining and banking sector workers, formed a high-wage segment of the labour market. The big increases in government salaries during the oil-boom period had clearly restored public sector wages compared with other low-wage urban workers.

Lower-level civil servants constantly faced everyday problems of meeting daily consumption and basic health and education needs of their

---

[14] These data overstate the differentials in wage rates, since food was often provided to agricultural workers and they generally worked fewer hours a day. Nevertheless, nominal earnings per hour were probably 50–75 per cent higher in Jakarta than in agriculture in villages in West Java.
[15] We have reported data for males only, partly to standardise for confounding effects of gender composition on wage differentials, and partly because wage employment in several sectors (most notably construction and transport) was heavily dominated by males (see chapter 9).

150 *Labour market structure and institutions*

Figure 6.3

Index (Rural wages = 100), bars for 1977 and 1992, Java and Outer Islands.

☐ Construction ☐ Transport ☐ Manufacturing: food/textiles ■ Other

Figure 6.3 Urban–rural wage differentials in selected sectors – less-educated male wage employees: Java and Outer Islands (rural wages=100)
Note: Based on hourly earnings data. All male employees with a completed junior high education or below.
Source: CBS, National Labour Force Surveys, 1977 and 1992, Jakarta.

families. Incomes and the quality of life of officials were still low by regional standards. They were, nevertheless, better off than unskilled workers in many other sectors.[16]

The wage advantage held by less-educated civil servants persisted into the 1990s, even after the three-year wage freeze in the mid 1980s. The perception that government employees are considerably better off than employees elsewhere in the economy is confirmed by these data – especially if stability of employment, hours worked and opportunities for moonlighting and other informal sources of income are taken into account.[17] Higher earnings help explain the enduring strong preference for work in the public sector.

Nevertheless, civil servant earnings among less-educated workers had fallen relative to other sectors by 1992. They were around 20–30 per cent

[16] See Singarimbun (1992: 219–22) for comparisons in the mid 1980s.
[17] This has important implications for processes of job search and unemployment among young people (Gray 1979: chapter 7).

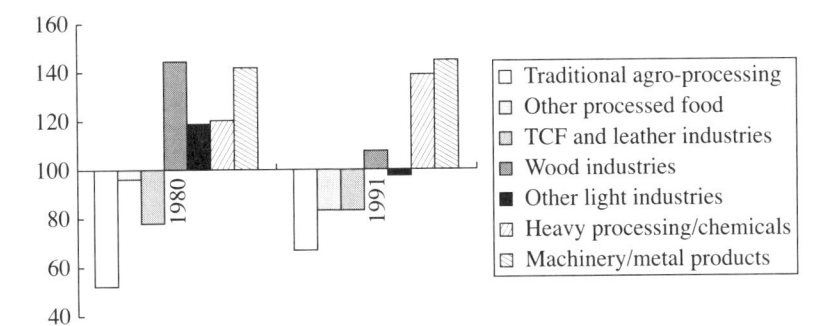

Figure 6.4 Wages of production workers, large and medium manufacturing: Indonesia, 1980 and 1991 (Indonesia=100)
Notes: See appendix table 6.2 for details.
Sources: CBS, Annual Survey of Large and Medium Establishments, 1980 and 1991 data tapes, Jakarta.

higher than in other urban sectors, compared with 40–50 per cent 15 years earlier.

Continuing public–private sector differentials were probably partly related to the different migrant status of employees in government, and in other high-wage modern sectors, compared with less-educated construction, transport and manufacturing workers. The latter included a high proportion of younger people (both male and female) who were either unmarried or whose families remained in their villages of origin.[18] Conversely, the public sector had a much higher proportion of older employees with dependents, many of whom probably resided in cities and towns. The reservation wage within urban areas was likely to be higher for government employees supporting their families in more costly urban environments (Mazumdar 1989).

Manufacturing

Why have manufacturing earnings remained low despite rapid industrial growth? The structure of manufacturing employment changed in favour of lower wage, labour-intensive industries as deregulation took hold in the 1980s (figure 6.4).[19] The share of employment in low-wage industries – garments and footwear in particular – expanded more rapidly in the 1980s.

---

[18] According to the National Labour Force Survey, approximately 40 per cent of urban construction workers and half of all transport sector wage workers were aged less than 30 in 1992. This contrasts with around 20 per cent of all less-educated government employees.

[19] See also appendix table 6.2. The data are based on average wage costs paid to production workers in manufacturing. They are a relatively good measure of total labour income earned by wage workers in large and medium manufacturing (Hill 1990).

152 *Labour market structure and institutions*

Growing segments of manufacturing were no longer relatively high wage, with the exception of plywood.[20] Average wages of production workers in the garment and footwear sector were a little over half of those in more capital-intensive branches of manufacturing in the early 1990s.

These trends contrasted with developments during the previous decade. During the oil-boom, more rapid growth of relatively capital- and resource-intensive industries contributed to a widening of differentials between the small, high-wage segment of manufacturing and the rest of the sector. Wages in the chemical, heavy processing and machinery industries which provided most new jobs in large- and medium-scale manufacturing, were more than twice those in traditional agro-processing industries. Wages were 50–100 per cent higher than those in other food processing and TFC industries (figure 6.4). The share of better-paid workers rose during this period of sluggish employment growth in the factory sector.

Many larger-scale new investors, especially foreign enterprises, offered high wages to attract a stable and committed workforce in the 1970s (Manning 1979). The value of real wages was not only restored in state enterprises but was substantially above those in small- and medium-scale private enterprises (table 6.4). High wages among unskilled workers in the weaving and cigarette industries were positively related to technology and ownership (foreign, state and private), and to a lesser extent, firm size. At the same time, the more capital-intensive and foreign firms recruited better educated workers, even for unskilled jobs. They reaped the benefits from higher wages in the form of low rates of labour turnover and absenteeism. Higher labour productivity was thus partly reflected in higher wages, even under conditions of elastic labour supply to the small modern sector.[21]

In contrast, wages were not always high among new foreign firms in the 1990s (Manning 1993). Hourly earnings (although not necessarily total earnings) were lower in some of the South Korean and Taiwanese firms than in small, local establishments in footwear and garments.[22] Unlike the investors of the 1970s (Japanese, American and European) low wages rather than market access was a prime consideration for NIE investors who faced steeply rising wage costs at home and went off-shore to maintain their export markets (Thee 1991).

---

[20] There was a secular decline in low-wage, traditional agro-processing and other food industries.
[21] Although wages were not always higher in large or even some foreign firms, especially among those located in rural areas (Mather 1983).
[22] This was before the government began a concerted effort to raise minimum wages from 1993 onwards. See especially White (1993), Thamrin (1993) and Van Diermen (1995).

Segmented labour market structure 153

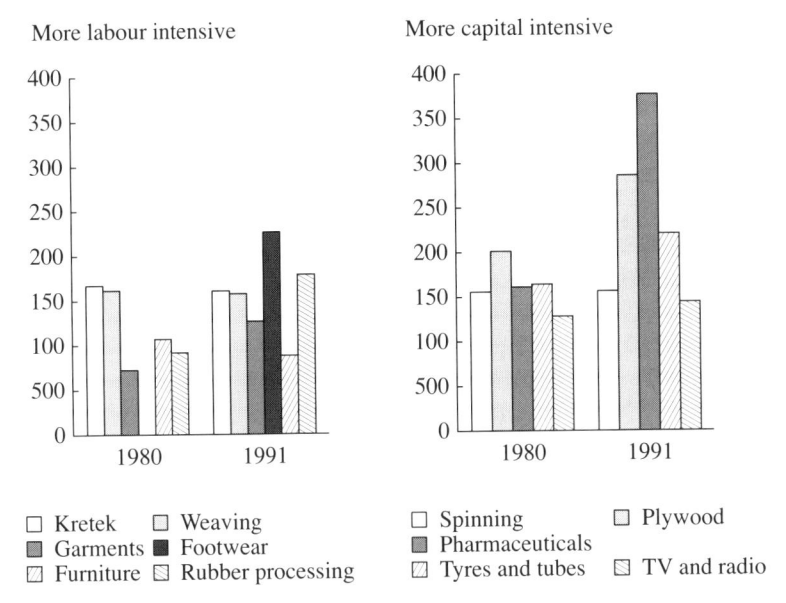

Figure 6.5 Ratio of annual wages in large- to small-scale firms: Indonesia, 1980 and 1991
Note: For production workers in domestic private establishments. Small firms are defined as 20–49 workers, larger firms defined as 1,000 workers and above. Exceptions include spinning, plywood and TV/radio (small=59–99 workers) and pharmaceuticals, rubber processing and tyres and tubes (large=500 workers and above).
Source: CBS, Survey of Large and Medium Manufacturing, 1991 data tape, Jakarta.

Thus, there was not a substantial difference in average wages paid to production workers in larger, privately owned establishments in garments and furniture compared with smaller establishments in 1980 and 1991 (figure 6.5). Nor were average wages higher on average in foreign-, government-, and domestic-owned firms in these industries or in other light industries in 1991 (table 6.4). Although similar comparisons could only be made in two industries (spinning and weaving) for 1980, wage differentials between domestic private establishments, and both foreign and government firms narrowed considerably.

In contrast, interfirm wage differentials were much larger in the more capital-intensive (pharmaceuticals, tyres and tubes and plywood) manufacturing industries in the 1990s and widened in the 1980s. Similarly wages remained high relative to the overall industry average among foreign firms in the more capital-intensive industries. The coefficient of variation in

Table 6.4. *Wages paid in domestic private, foreign and state-owned establishments in selected industries: Indonesia, 1980 and 1991 (production workers only)*[a]

	All establishments			Larger establishments[b]		
Year/industry	Domestic private	Foreign	Government	Domestic private	Foreign	Government
Index of mean wages (industry total=100)						
1991						
More labour intensive						
Weaving	93	229	162	123	239	158
Garments	100	109	95	124	118	–
Footwear	97	126	86	143	129	–
Furniture	94	106	108	84	99	–
Rubber processing	89	123	123	120	128	133
More capital intensive						
Sugar	91	–	103	104	–	99
Spinning	79	160	127	92	125	144
Plywood	92	159	82	96	159	82
Pharmaceuticals	66	216	107	149	420?	–
Steel products	80	200	122	63	224	–
1980						
Spinning	73	115	168	86	110	180
Weaving	97	200	157	95	242	243

Notes: [a] Mean wages in each ownership group as an index of total mean wages in each industry; [b] Establishments with 500 employees or more. Foreign firms include both fully owned foreign firms, and those engaged in joint ventures with private capital. Government firms are defined as all firms with some government equity.
Source: CBS, Survey of Large and Medium Establishments (Data Tape, 1991), Jakarta.

average production worker wages widened in the 1980s, both overall and within major industry groupings (appendix table 6.2).[23]

Regression analysis confirms that wage differentials within manufacturing were closely associated with firm characteristics in the early 1990s. The log of average earnings of production workers was positively related to firm size, capital intensity (non-wage value-added) and foreign and government ownership (appendix table 6.3). Coefficients for non-production worker wages as a share of total wages were also significant.

Thus, Indonesia's peculiar blend of capital, resource-intensive and labour-intensive industries exerted a powerful influence on its wages

---

[23] The exceptions were traditional agro-processing, food processing and the group of other light industries.

structure. On the one hand, the growth of labour-intensive industries contributed to slower growth in average wages in manufacturing in the 1980s than might have otherwise occurred. In two of the most rapidly growing industries – garments and furniture – wages were quite uniform by firm size. In contrast, differentiation of medium- and large-scale manufacturing by technology and product type, and the rising average size of establishments, contributed to a greater dispersion of wages. This occurred despite the growth of labour-intensive, export-oriented industries.

Regional labour market integration

A final aspect of changing labour market structure relates to the changing structure of wages and earnings across Indonesia. The Outer Islands are a heterogeneous group, including both resource and land abundant provinces in Sumatra and Kalimantan, as well as several which are densely populated and share some of the labour market characteristics of Java.

According to a range of economic and social indicators, the sharp contrast between densely populated Java and many of the land surplus Outer Island regions was no longer evident by the 1990s.[24] The labour market response to these changes was remarkably swift. With the exception of several poorer Eastern islands, the share of the workforce working outside agriculture and in urban areas grew rapidly throughout Indonesia. There has also been inter-regional migration from land-scarce provinces of Java, Sulawesi and Nusa Tenggara to land-abundant and to more rapidly growing resource-rich regions, as well as a reverse flow to Java – especially of educated people.

The oil-boom was not only a bonus to the national economy in terms of infrastructure and human capital, it also stimulated non-agricultural employment growth across Indonesia, directly in services and indirectly in other sectors, aided by the diversified natural resource base. This sets Indonesia apart from several neighbouring countries such as Thailand, where economic development has been concentrated in a few regions (Krongkaew 1994). The regional labour market landscape might also have been different had liberalisation and non-oil export growth been the pillar of economic growth from the early years of the New Order, as it has been in the past decade.

At the same time, patterns of inter-regional economic change contributed to several clearly identified contrasts in provincial and sub-provincial

[24] For a survey of developments in the regional economies of Indonesia during the New Order see Hill (1989, 1992).

156 *Labour market structure and institutions*

labour market structures, especially in the Outer Island regions. The contrasts have been principally related to differing agricultural potential and natural resource availability, although recent patterns of manufacturing development and legacies of educational achievement have also played a part.

To assist analysis of labour market change, the Outer Island provinces (excluding Bali) have been divided into five groups, based on factors relevant to both labour supply and labour demand trends[25]

- resource-abundant provinces in Sumatra, Kalimantan and eastern Indonesia (Aceh, Riau, East and Central Kalimantan, Irian Jaya and Maluku)
- major transmigration destination areas in southern Sumatra (South Sumatra, Jambi, Bengkulu and Lampung)
- other land-abundant, mainly agricultural-dependant provinces (West and South Kalimantan, Central and Southeast Sulawesi)
- the out-migration provinces of North and West Sumatra
- densely populated and/or relatively poor Outer Island provinces (North and South Sulawesi, West and East Nusa Tenggara and East Timor).[26]

The following sections compare labour developments in these five Outer Island groups with those in Jakarta and the Java provinces and Bali, over the period 1971–90.

Population, economic structure and growth

The economy of densely populated Java-Bali was more diversified than the economies of the Outer Island regions when rapid growth began in the late 1960s (table 6.5). The share of agriculture in regional gross domestic product (RGDP) was above 50 per cent in most Outer Island regions. According to a range of other development indicators – literacy, electricity consumption, vehicles and length of roads per land area and even per capita – the Outer Islands lagged behind the Java provinces and Bali (Hill 1989).

Several Outer Island provinces, especially the large province of North Sumatra, stood out according to a range of indicators – the share of RGDP

---

[25] The grouping of provinces is to some extent arbitrary. The characteristics of several provinces overlap across these groups – or any grouping one might attempt. See Hill (1989).
[26] East Timor is included in this group but is not covered for most variables due to lack of data in 1971 and 1980.

Table 6.5. *Population, economic structure and change by province: Indonesia, 1971 and 1990*

	Province group/Province							
	Resource abundant	Southern Sumatra	Other land abundant	Sumatran outmigration	Densely populated/poorer	Java & Bali	Jakarta	Total
Population 1990[a]								
Million	13.5	15.6	8.9	14.3	16.8	102.1	8.3	179.4
% Urban	24	21	21	31	19	30	100	31
RGDP per capita 1990[b]								
Index (Indonesia=100)	123	85	78	99	51	87	260	100 (Rp.956)[c]
Real RGDP growth 1971–90								
% p.a.	9.1	8.2	8.1	8.3	7.3	7.5	9.2	7.3
Index (Indonesia=100)	125	112[d]	111	114	99	103	126	100
% of RGDP in selected sectors (Indonesia=100)								
Agriculture								
1971	118	115	126	102	132	110	10	100 (43)
1990	125	132	134	134	216	114	4	100 (25)
Manufacturing								
1971	51	50	39	85	37	112	74	100 (11)
1990	59	68	64	79	26	81	139	100 (19)
Government administration								
1971	97	88	108	126	101	108	156	100 (5)
1990	116	124	152	98	226	118	51	100 (5)
Trade								
1971	96	91	70	86	74	74	197	100 (23)
1990	110	95	91	92	87	97	99	100 (23)

Notes: Data on RGDP shares are approximate only; data quality does not permit meaningful analysis of growth rates over time. Non-oil RGDP in oil-producing regions and for Indonesia as a whole. All sub-totals except for rows 1 and 2 are unweighted means. These are preferred because of different sizes of provinces within groups and our emphasis on spatial contrasts.[a] Sub-totals refer to total population in each group; [b] Calculated at constant 1983 prices. Based on RGDP growth rates per capita calculated by Hill (1996: table 11.1) and intercensal population growth rates 1971–90; [c] Rp.000 per annum; [d] Index of unweighted means=95 if the small province of Bengkulu (index 163) is excluded.
Sources: CBS, National Accounts, various years and Statistical Year Book, various years; Hill, 1996.

158 *Labour market structure and institutions*

produced outside agriculture, the proportion of educated workers and the level of RGDP per capita. Other exceptions were the resource-abundant provinces of Riau and East Kalimantan, the larger provinces of West and South Sumatra, and North Sulawesi. The latter group of provinces were more urbanised, in contrast to many of the less-developed provinces where the share of urban population was below 10 per cent in 1971.

The period 1970–90 saw convergence in these indicators in most Outer Island provinces compared with Java. With the exception of Lampung (the main destination of inter-island migrants from Java), the average rate of per-capita income growth did not fall below 3 per cent (outside oil and mining in the resource-dependent provinces). Total RGDP growth was over 5 per cent per annum, and in most it was slightly above 7 per cent per annum (table 6.5). It was generally highest in the resource-rich provinces and lower in the densely populated regions of eastern Indonesia and Java. But, even in the latter, average (unweighted) aggregate RGDP growth rates were above 7 per cent per annum. Compensating natural population growth rates and net-migration meant smaller differences in per-capita RGDP between these two groups: population (and labour supply) grew much less rapidly in the more densely populated provinces.

Several patterns stand out regarding the sectoral share of RGDP.[27] The agricultural share of RGDP fell in all province groups and provinces. There were large increases in the share of government administration to RGDP in most Outer Island provinces.[28] These gains underpin one of the major achievements of the New Order government: the wide regional diffusion of services and infrastructure.

Nevertheless, there are important differences in economic performance between the five groups of Outer Island regions. The greatest contrast is between the first group of resource-rich provinces and fifth group of the poorer, more densely populated regions. Not only did total RGDP rise faster in the former, but the growth in RGDP per capita was also more rapid, despite considerable in-migration. The index of agriculture's share of RGDP (Indonesia = 100) rose substantially in the poor provinces whereas that of manufacturing rose more quickly in the resource-rich group share.[29]

---

[27] There are large and implausible differences in the shares in 1971, and change in 1971–90, in some provinces, reflecting the weak data base which existed when the series began.
[28] This can be partly attributed to the centralised distribution of grants to provinces (based on per-capita income and land area), and the spread of government services and related infrastructure.
[29] This was especially the case in West and East Nusatenggara where the agricultural share of RGDP was still 58 and 68 per cent in 1990, per-capita income the lowest and the incidence of poverty among the highest.

The index of manufacturing in RGDP actually fell to only one-quarter of the Indonesian share in the group of densely populated/poorer provinces of Eastern Indonesia. Conversely, the share of government administration rose most rapidly. This reflected special government attention, but it was also related to stagnation of other sectors such as manufacturing.[30]

Between these two extremes there was considerable diversity. The index of agriculture's share of RGDP rose quite rapidly in Southern Sumatra. New land was opened up for cultivation by transmigrants, and private investment also expanded in agriculture. In the other land-abundant regions of Sulawesi and Kalimantan, the agricultural share rose from an already high level compared with the rest of Indonesia. Expansion of manufacturing from a tiny base was the major new development, especially related to the growth of the timber industry. Perhaps surprisingly, the index of the main non-agricultural sector shares in RGDP rose relatively little in the two more developed, out-migration provinces of Sumatra. Not only relatively well-educated labour tended to move elsewhere, but businesses tended to invest outside their home province.

Labour supply trends and unemployment

Labour supply growth was much higher in all Outer Island groups than in Java-Bali from 1971 (table 6.6). Higher birth rates characterised most of the regions outside Java, and inter-regional migration affected labour force growth. Migration flows mainly from Java to Lampung in Southern Sumatra gave way to a more diversified pattern by the end of the 1970s. New areas of Sumatra and the land-abundant regions of Kalimantan and Sulawesi became destination areas for the transmigrants (Hugo et al. 1987: 179–85).[31] The resource-rich provinces, transmigration recipient areas and relatively small, hitherto underdeveloped provinces such as Bengkulu in Sumatra, recorded high rates of net in-migration (relative to their population in 1971).

Thus, labour force growth rates were generally above 4 per cent per annum in Southern Sumatra and the resource-abundant provinces, and were slowest in the Sumatran out-migration provinces, and in the poorer,

---

[30] See Barlow and Hardjono (1996) and Azis (1996) for a discussion of slow economic growth in several regions of Eastern Indonesia.

[31] The peak period of government-assisted transmigration was in the Third Five-Year Plan period (1979–84). The largest destination areas were the provinces of South Sumatra, Lampung, Jambi and Riau; the former province replaced Lampung as the largest province of origin in the mid 1970s. The share of transmigrants going to Kalimantan, Central and Southeast Sulawesi and Irian Jaya also rose steeply (30–40 per cent of all transmigrants).

Table 6.6. *Labour force characteristics and growth, migration and unemployment by province: Indonesia, 1971–1990*

	Province group/Province							
	Resource abundant	Southern Sumatra	Other land abundant	Sumatran outmigration	Densely populated/ poorer	Java & Bali	Jakarta	Total
Labour force growth 1971–90								
% p.a.	3.9	4.6	3.4	2.7	3.0	2.7	4.5	3.1
Index (Indonesia=100)	126	149	112	88	97	88	146	100
Net lifetime migration[a]								
Rate 1971	3.6	13.4	−0.2	−1.7	−1.0	−4.2	36.8	–
Change 1971–90 (000)	1,239	1,416	548	−801	−375	−2,503	430	–
% Population 1971	17.5	23.9	13.4	−8.0	−2.8	−3.2	9.4	–
Urban female labour force								
Participation rate (%) 1971	17	17	17	16	21	30	20	23
Increase 1971–90 (%)								
Index (Indonesia=100)	144	176	168	201	125	82	136	100
Urban unemployment rate								
1990 (%)	8.2	6.1	7.7	7.3	7.0	4.7	7.2	7.0
Index (Indonesia=100)	135	99	126	118	116	78	117	100
Education of the workforce								
% of total junior high+ 1971	8.1	5.8	5.2	10.7	8.9	5.9	28.8	9.1
% increase 1971–90[b]	167	178	183	137	96	178	82	100
% of urban senior high+ 1971	11.0	8.1	9.0	13.9	11.0	11.2	10.8	12.7
% increase 1971–90[b]	243	240	227	123	148	103	199	100

Notes: [a] Net migration rate=in-migrants minus out-migrants divided by total population (expressed as a %). Change in net lifetime migration is one crude estimate of interprovincial population mobility. Lifetime migrant defined as a person living more than six months in a province, other than their province of birth at the time of the census. Sub-total equals total number of net migrants (000) in each group; [b] Index Indonesia = 100. [c] If Bali is excluded, the index falls to 96.
Sources: CBS, Population Census, 1971 (Series D) and 1990 (Series S2), and National Labour Survey 1990, Jakarta.

densely populated group; the latter experienced net out-migration over the period 1971–90.[32]

Rapid labour force growth can be partly attributed to rising female participation rates in most Outer Island provinces: by 50–100 per cent in urban areas in most provinces. However, there was relative uniformity in urban unemployment rates between province groups in 1990. Rates ranged from 6–8 per cent (unweighted mean) between province groups outside Java-Bali, compared with a lower 4.7 per cent in the latter. Rates of urban unemployment were higher in the resource-rich provinces, however, owing to rapid expansion of non-agricultural employment opportunities and higher wages which attracted in-migrants from poorer regions.

Finally, the educational status of the workforce became more uniform across Outer Island regions (table 6.6). Although improvements in rural educational levels lagged in the poorer provinces, the level of those who had completed their education among the workforce in urban areas rose rapidly. In contrast, there has been considerable out-migration of more educated people from North and West Sumatra. Java-Bali, East Java and Bali also began to catch up with the rest of the Java in terms of educated people in urban and rural areas.

The changing structure of employment

Contrasts in employment between Java and most Outer Island provinces were initially greatest in agriculture and M-sector activities than in trade and services. Consistent with the structure of RGDP, employment was heavily concentrated in agriculture in all Outer Island groups in 1971 and resembled more closely African or South Asian rather than East Asian countries in the early 1970s. Conversely, the M-sector provided a tiny fraction of jobs, frequently below 10 per cent in most Outer Island groups.

Thus, agricultural employment growth was most rapid in the southern Sumatran 'transmigration' provinces, which implies high elasticity of employment with respect to output growth. In addition to absorbing workers from the region, the southern Sumatran provinces have also helped ease problems of land scarcity in parts of Java, principally Central Java where most of the transmigrants originated. There were new commercial agricultural opportunities in cocoa, sugar and oil palm, many of them led by large investments in plantations rather than smallholder

---

[32] Within groups, rates of urban labour force growth were more variable than rural growth, depending on the initial size of urban populations, development of new administrative centres and, in some cases, reclassification of urban boundaries.

expansion (Barlow and Tomich 1991). However, transmigration was not always successful in raising incomes of new settlers, in contrast to the substantial income gains made by 'spontaneous' migrants (World Bank 1986; Sobary 1987). Lampung had the highest index of poverty of any province by 1990.

Surprisingly, agricultural employment growth was also rapid in the resource-rich provinces as well as in the densely populated and poorer provinces. The growth of resource industries did not draw labour out of agriculture at a rate faster than elsewhere in Indonesia. Several of these provinces also became a focus of the transmigration programme for a short period.

Patterns of M-sector and manufacturing employment were more varied. Both the resource-rich and southern Sumatran provinces recorded relatively rapid growth in manufacturing employment – in both cases exceeding that among the Java-Bali provinces. Among some of the resource-rich provinces, the growth of the timber, especially plywood, played a central role in jobs growth. In contrast, both M-sector and manufacturing employment growth was slowest in the group of densely populated/poorer provinces. This was consistent with the low rate of RGDP growth in provinces which lacked natural resources, and had not developed an environment which stimulated labour-intensive industrial growth.

In individual provinces, the increasingly diversified North Sumatran economy is reflected in rapid growth in manufacturing employment. Jobs grew quickly, for less-obvious reasons in Lampung than in southern Sumatra and East Nusa Tenggara. The low share of M-sector activities (covering manufacturing, construction, mining and public utilities) in employment and RGDP in 1971 meant any growth of medium- and small-scale industry would have a major impact in several regions.[33]

On Java-Bali, there was a contrast between Central Java and Jogjakarta and other provinces. There was concentration of cottage industry in these two provinces, in contrast to the rapid expansion of larger, export-oriented establishments in the west and in the east of Java (Jones 1984; Hill 1990). Compared with their initially low shares, East Java and Bali recorded high rates of growth in manufacturing employment relative to other sectors and Indonesia as a whole. Export-oriented manufacturing industries developed in a range of industries, including food processing, garments and wood industries, especially in the Greater Surabaya region of East Java, and in garments and handicrafts on Bali (Dick 1993).

---

[33] New agro-processing industries such as rubber, oil palm and sugar (especially in Lampung), in addition to the uneven distribution of large fertiliser and cement factories (in the tiny city of Kupang, East Nusa Tenggara and in various locations in Sumatra), contributed to the increase (Hill 1989).

Two different patterns were apparent in S-sector employment growth. There was rapid growth in employment in trade in all Outer Island province groups, through expansion of rural trade networks and the urban informal sector. Employment growth was less even in other services. It was slow compared with other sectors in the rapidly growing resource-abundant and southern Sumatran groups, but rapid in the other land-abundant and Java provinces.

Expansion of services was associated with big increases in jobs in government administration and services in the less rapidly growing Outer Islands (table 6.7).[34] In contrast, trade employment expansion was more rapid in the faster growing southern Sumatran regions and resource-rich provinces, especially in rural areas.

The third change has been concentrated in Java, especially around Jakarta, involving the expansion of jobs in labour-intensive manufacturing. Service sector employment is now less dominant in Java's cities and in some Outer Island regions. Educated persons are turning to higher-paid jobs in manufacturing and private services as an alternative to civil service employment, which has been paramount since colonial times. Even among the tertiary educated, many opportunities have come about in the rapidly growing export-oriented sector, especially if links with banking and other service industries are taken into account.

One pattern which stands out in rural–urban comparisons is the higher ratio of urban employment growth relative to that in rural areas in all sectors in the Java-Bali provinces, compared with almost all Outer Island provinces. Partly this was because more of Java-Bali was increasingly classified as urban. Yet employment in both formal and informal sectors has also been concentrated in the towns and cities of Java. This was especially true in Central Java and Jogjakarta, where rural employment growth in agricultural and non-agricultural sectors was slow in the 1980s. High rates of out-migration from poor rural areas presumably played an important role, as did the slow growth of cottage industry employment. Trade and services also grew slowly in rural compared with urban areas.

Inter-regional wage differentials

Inter-regional wage differentials were large in the 1970s but had declined substantially by the 1990s. Both nominal and real wages (after adjusting

---

[34] Higher growth rates in labour force and employment growth in many of the Outer Island regions were reflected in more rapid growth in jobs in all sectors than in Java. But significant contrasts emerge after the rates of growth are standardised according to rates of expansion in total employment in each province.

Table 6.7. *Urban and rural employment growth: Indonesia, 1971–1990*

	Province group/Province						
	Resource abundant	Southern Sumatra	Other land abundant	Sumatran out-migration	Densely populated/poorer	Java & Bali	Jakarta	Total
Urban employment growth 1971–90								
% p.a.	6.9	5.3	6.7	5.5	4.9	7.9	4.7	6.3
Index (Indonesia=100)	109	85	106	88	78	124	74	100
Rural employment growth 1971–90								
% p.a.	4.0	4.4	3.0	1.8	2.5	1.7	n.a.	2.3
Index (Indonesia=100)	176	195	130	81	112	75	-	100
Ratio of urban to rural employment growth 1971–90								
Manufacturing	104	63	89	225	101	260	-	231
Trade	79	73	106	137	130	282	-	170
Services	109	103	162	175	149	202	-	168

Notes: Different urban rates of growth across provinces are partly related to changing urban boundaries in certain major cities. Urban population growth rates are overstated for this reason and also the change in definition of urban areas in the 1980 and 1990 Censuses.
Source: CBS, Population Censuses, 1971 and 1990, Jakarta.

for cost of living differences) in construction, transport and other services were higher in the Outer Island provinces in 1977.[35] In the resource-rich provinces they were close to double those in Java in nominal terms and nearly 50 per cent higher in real terms. Jakarta was the other high-wage province – in the capital, average wages even exceeded those in the resource-based provinces in 1977.

Real wage differentials between groups of provinces were smaller by 1992, with the exception of Jakarta, the Sumatran out-migration provinces (North and West Sumatra) and the densely populated, poorer regions of Eastern Indonesia. In Eastern Indonesia, relative wages were already below the national average in 1977, and fell below those in the Java provinces in 1992.

By 1992, the index of wages (adjusted for cost of living across provinces) in the Java-Bali provinces had risen (figure 6.6). Conversely, relative wages declined in the resource-abundant provinces. The spread between the highest- and lowest-wage provinces (Aceh and Riau, on the one hand, and Central Java and Jogjakarta, on the other) fell, as did the ratio of wages of the five highest to the five lowest wage provinces.[36]

However, these changes were not as great as expected. The index remained close to the national average in the land-abundant regions, despite large in-migration. Demand for labour in non-agricultural activities appears to have kept abreast of labour supply in these provinces, aided by government spending on infrastructure and services.[37]

Conclusions

The national labour market has undergone remarkable changes under the New Order. Change occurred from the beginnings of a fragmented labour market – across and within industries, between urban and rural areas, and across regions.

Various dimensions of labour market structure underwent rapid change, especially during Indonesia's oil-boom in the 1970s.

- Inter-industry wage dispersion declined, reducing the relative advantage of the public sector for less-skilled workers.

---

[35] Agricultural wages collected from the National Labour Force Survey show unpredictable shifts over time, as do the rice wage series collected by CBS on a monthly basis from a selection of provinces since 1980.
[36] The ratio of the highest- to lowest-wage province was 240 in 1977 and 219 in 1992. The decline was smaller among the five high- and low-wage provinces: from 192 in 1977 to 185 in 1992.
[37] There were, however, quite large differences in trends in wages between provinces within the groups.

Index

□ Resource abundant □ Southern Sumatra
▨ Other land abundant ▓ Sumatran out-migration
■ Densely populated/poorer ▥ Java-Bail (excl. Jakarta)
▧ Jakarta

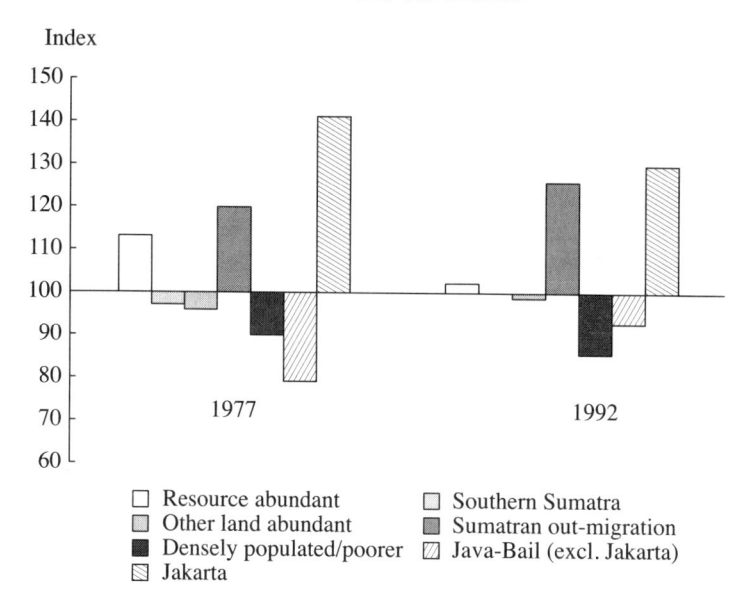

Figure 6.6 Adjusted male earnings for less-educated employees per hour in construction, transport and services by major provincial groupings (Indonesia=100)
Notes: Totals are unweighted provincial means, adjusted for differences in cost of living across provinces according to the KFM (Minimum Physical Needs) index earliest year, and 1992. For lower secondary graduates or below, exclude public sector employees.
Sources: CBS, National Labour Force Surveys, 1977 and 1992 data tapes, Jakarta.

- Urban–rural gaps both in employment structure narrowed, principally in Java but also in several Outer Island regions.
- The national labour market consolidated; growth and diversification in fledgling and isolated Outer Island provinces and labour mobility contributed to labour market integration.

Two aspects of change have been slow and the subsequent benefits from new job growth less apparent. Most important has been employment in the poorer, densely populated regions of eastern Indonesia where the shift of workers out of agriculture has been slow and earnings have fallen relative to the rest of Indonesia. This has to some extent been compensated for by out-migration (both within Indonesia and abroad), but the level of poverty remains high compared with other regions.

Second, much industrial growth was in relatively capital-intensive industries where wages are high but employment gains have been small. A small segment of the labour market, of both unskilled and skilled workers, benefited from the protection afforded to foreign investors, state enterprises and government-backed companies in relatively capital-intensive and heavy industries.

High wages in these industries are related to higher levels of skill and industry protection. The high wages enjoyed in these industries and in mining and natural resource industries, bring important welfare benefits to perhaps 5–10 per cent of the unskilled industrial work force. They also provide a demonstration effect regarding the appropriate level of wages in labour-intensive manufacturing industries. However, the latter could not remain competitive if they offered a similar level of wages and benefits – at least given current levels of productivity.

In addition, the effects of sustained economic growth has been a big rise in the number of middle-income workers. A growing lower-middle-income and middle-income group of wage earners and self-employed probably now rivals, in absolute numbers, the mass of poorer workers which dominated employment when Soeharto came to power. New patterns of rural diversification have contributed to improvements in the economic status of previously very poor and highly vulnerable villagers.

As employment structure has diversified, the private sector now plays a significant role in the employment of educated people, integrating professionals and managers more closely with international and regional labour markets. The group of higher-income earners is probably larger in Indonesia, in relative terms, than in other rapidly growing East Asian countries (outside China) at similar stages of development. This can be attributed to

- capital-intensive patterns of growth (and incomes earned directly and indirectly through rent-seeking behaviour) associated with the intensified exploitation of Indonesia's abundant natural resources
- the greater role of foreign and state capital which has often afforded considerable numbers of workers better working conditions than labour market conditions might have dictated
- the greater and longer period of domestic industry protection which has enabled workers to capture a share of the rents from excess profits.

Gini indices of labour earnings among employees suggest that wage income was less-favourably distributed than expenditure. The ratio was 0.37 in 1992 for all employees, and 0.38 for manufacturing employees compared with a gini ratio of expenditure of closer to 0.33–0.34 for all Indonesia in the late 1980s (Booth 1992b; Hill 1996). But Gini ratios were lower than those for total income found in other Southeast Asian countries, and even lower than in much of Northeast Asia where gini ratios ranged from 0.35 to 0.45 in the early 1990s (Krongkaew 1994).

Table 6.8. *Gini coefficients of earnings among wage earners: Indonesia, 1977–1992*

	1977	1982	1987	1992
Agriculture	38	35	34	33
Non-agriculture				
Urban	46	39	36	37
Rural	46	41	35	32
Java	46	42	39	38
Outer Islands	46	39	33	33
Manufacturing				
Urban	48	40	37	39
Rural	43	44	34	31
Total	48	45	38	38
All sectors				
Male	45	39	35	36
Female	49	44	43	38
Total	48	42	38	37

Sources: CBS, National Labour Force Surveys, 1977, 1987 and 1992; National Social Economic Survey, 1982, Jakarta.

However, it is important to bear in mind that the distribution of earnings narrowed considerably, like in several Northeast Asian countries. In Indonesia, the gini index fell from a higher level (48) for all wage earners and for manufacturing wage earners to 34 and 38 respectively over the period 1977–92 (table 6.8).[38] Declines occurred mainly during the late oil-boom period when unskilled wages rose steeply, and the slower growth period in the 1980s, when the rice sector boomed and government salaries were tightly controlled.

In the 1990s, there was widespread dissatisfaction in Indonesia with the income distribution in society, especially the concentration of business wealth among conglomerates and the first family. Nevertheless, the process of job creation and wage growth among wage earners contributed to an improvement in the distribution of labour earnings. Three sets of changes, in particular, appear to have contributed to this result. Most far-reaching have been changes in rural Java, where labour markets diversified, away from dependence on agriculture and home industry. Out-migration was substantial, and intensive rural–urban linkages have blurred the distinction between town and city.

---

[38] In South Korea, the gini ratio of earnings fell from 0.40 to 0.31 from 1972 to 1988, and other indicators of earnings distribution show a similar decline (Lee 1990: 4–5).

The second major change was in the hitherto underdeveloped but growing Outer Island regions. New jobs were provided for populations initially highly dependent on agriculture through the spread of services and infrastructure, growth in resource-based industries and associated expansion of small-scale and some modern manufacturing.

Appendix table 6.1. *Indices of wage income differentials by major sector, and level of completed schooling and gender: Indonesia, 1982–1994 (Primary schooling=100)*

	Male				Female			
	1982	1987	1990	1994	1982	1987	1990	1994
Manufacturing								
<Primary	82	78	88	94	68	83	87	86
Primary	100	100	100	100	100	100	100	100
Lower Secondary	129	121	122	120	132[b]	143	136	135
Upper Secondary								
General	205	174	167	161	210[b]	248[b]	197	188
Vocational	251	164	171	160	192[b]	226[b]	196	163
Tertiary	472	340	447	400	*	520[b]	439[b]	471
Services[a]								
<Primary	68	85	87	79	88	97	96	89
Primary	100	100	100	100	100	100	100	100
Lower Secondary	130	124	119	124	182	182	178	156
Upper Secondary								
General	141	144	157	151	227	227	222	263
Vocational	146	152	158	163	257	257	265	327
Tertiary	230	248	236	244	373	373	368	427
All sectors								
<Primary	70	78	82	82	66	78	79	81
Primary	100	100	100	100	100	100	100	100
Lower Secondary	143	133	130	126	192	176	161	147
Upper Secondary								
General	175	166	175	167	243	238	228	237
Vocational	185	167	171	176	248	272	253	270
Tertiary	289	291	300	322	385	430	401	424
Mean wages (Rp.'000/month)								
Agriculture	23	41	60	97	12	21	29	54
Manufacturing	49	77	105	169	21	37	55	97
Services	66	92	120	214	40	63	82	145
All sectors	50	81	113	177	27	47	68	113

Notes: [a] Government, community and personal services.
[b] 10–99 cases in category.
* Less than 10 cases in category.
Sources: CBS, National Labour Force Survey, 1987, 1990 and 1994, and National Social Economic Survey, 1982 (computer tapes).

Appendix table 6.2. *Employment and wages of production workers, large and medium manufacturing: Indonesia, 1980 and 1991*

Industry group	Number of firms 1980	Number of firms 1991	Percentage of all employees 1980	Percentage of all employees 1991	Mean no. of workers per firm 1980	Mean no. of workers per firm 1991	Non-wage value added per firm 1980	Non-wage value added per firm 1991	Mean production worker wages per firm 1980	Mean production worker wages per firm 1991	Coefficient of variation of production worker wages (per firm) 1980	Coefficient of variation of production worker wages (per firm) 1991
1 Traditional agro-processing[a]	<u>701</u>	<u>1,045</u>	<u>19.7</u>	<u>10.6</u>	<u>239</u>	<u>270</u>	<u>102</u>	<u>75</u>	<u>52</u>	<u>67</u>	137	136
Kretek Cigarettes	144	100	12.9	4.4	762	1,172	89	77	45	52		
2 Other processed foods	1,192	2,602	17.4	12.9	124	131	101	115	97	83	131	108
3 TFC and leather industries	<u>1,279</u>	<u>2,496</u>	<u>24.1</u>	<u>29.7</u>	<u>160</u>	<u>315</u>	<u>48</u>	<u>54</u>	<u>78</u>	<u>83</u>	64	96
Garments	644	939	1.3	8.3	181	235	42	43	95	85		
Weaving	61	405	11.7	6.8	154	444	37	53	77	77		
Footwear	n.a.	247	n.a.	4.6	n.a.	492	n.a.	43	n.a.	81		
4 Wood industries	<u>469</u>	<u>1,590</u>	<u>7.0</u>	<u>15.8</u>	<u>127</u>	<u>263</u>	<u>115</u>	<u>72</u>	<u>144</u>	<u>107</u>	93	104
Plywood	36	125	2.4	7.5	577	1,590	321?	181	127	170		
Furniture	88	540	0.5	3.5	49	171	34	44	122	103		
5 Other light industries[b]	425	1,207	4.3	6.6	87	144	74	65	119	98	96	94
6 Heavy processing/chemicals[c]	<u>917</u>	<u>1,878</u>	<u>14.8</u>	<u>13.8</u>	<u>137</u>	<u>194</u>	<u>138</u>	<u>188</u>	<u>120</u>	<u>139</u>	116	127
Fertiliser, cement, pulp	n.a.	21	n.a.	1.3	n.a.	1,634	n.a.	947	n.a.	514		
Pharmaceuticals	114	165	1.9	1.1	139	175	270	319	188	230		
Steel products	20	64	1.0	1.0	413	410	70	409	175	237		
7 Machinery/metal products	<u>587</u>	<u>1,313</u>	<u>11.9</u>	<u>10.1</u>	<u>172</u>	<u>203</u>	<u>181</u>	<u>142</u>	<u>142</u>	<u>145</u>	86	100
Radio/TV assembly	34	56	1.7	0.9	427	431	293	78	152	107		
Car and car components	14	67	0.4	0.4	216	1,514	818	664	215	319		
Aircraft	n.a.	1	n.a.	0.6	n.a.	14,830	n.a.	n.a.	n.a.	266		
All sectors	5,724	12,495	99.2[d]	99.5[d]	149	212	100	100	100	100		
N (100)	850	2,562										

Notes: The distribution of firms and workers is slightly different to that shown in table 5.13, owing to a slightly different classification of industries (see notes below). [a] Includes tea, coffee peeling, rice, tobacco and rubber processing. [b] Includes printing, plastics and toys. [c] Includes paper products and all other chemical and metal industries except rubber processing and clay products (tiles, bricks and ceramics). [d] Excludes clay products and other industries (ISIC 39) except toys.

Source: CBS, Annual Survey of Large and Medium Establishments, 1980 and 1991 data tapes.

Appendix table 6.3. *Regression analysis of the determinants of manufacturing wages (LOGW): Indonesia, 1991 (Production workers, large and medium establishments)*

Variable[a]		Beta coefficient	T-ratio
INTERCEPT LOGW= dependent variable	Log of average production worker wages	2.724	162.21
OWN1*	100% private domestic		
OWN2	>50% foreign	0.258	17.07
OWN3	>50% government	0.212	14.55
OWN4	Other ownership groups	0.241	13.48
CAPINT	Capital intensity indicator[b]	0.000	0.27**
SIZE1	100–499 workers	−0.095	−14.85
SIZE2*	500–999 workers		
SIZE3	1000 workers +	0.059	5.61
HCAP1*	Human capital index <15[c]		
HCAP2	Human capital index 15–<20	0.181	9.77
HCAP3	Human capital index 20–<30	0.334	10.21
HCAP4	Human capital index 30–50	0.337	5.61
HCAP5	Human capital index >50	0.412	12.38
YEAR1*	<5 years operation		
YEAR2	5–9 years operation	0.046	6.21
YEAR3	10–19 years operation	0.050	6.92
YEAR4	20 years + operation	0.026	3.08
IND1*	Traditional agro-processing		
IND2	Kretek cigarettes	0.205	6.22
IND3	Other food/beverages	0.297	21.61
IND4	Weaving/batik	0.291	14.68
IND5	Garments	0.311	18.94
IND6	Other textiles	0.339	20.58
IND7	Plywood	0.455	13.98
IND8	Other wood industries	0.384	25.24**
IND9	Paper & chemicals	0.427	30.08
IND10	Non-metallic minerals/basic industries	0.352	22.85
IND11	Metals & machinery	0.504	33.13
IND12	Other industries	0.283	11.63
PROV1*	DKI Jakarta		
PROV2	W. Java	−0.121	−13.43
PROV3	C. Java and Yogyakarta	−0.293	−28.52
PROV4	E. Java	−0.245	−25.50
PROV5	Bali	−0.075	−3.22
PROV6	N. Sumatra	−0.065	−4.95
PROV7	Other Sumatra	−0.036	−2.75
PROV8	Kalimantan	−0.031	−1.68
PROV9	Other	−0.155	−9.21

Notes:
* Reference category.
** Coefficients not statistically significant at 5 per cent level or better.

R^2 : 0.31   DF
S.E. : 0.31   Regression : 32
F-test : 186.9   Residual : 13257
DW-test : 1.60   N : 13290

[a] The equation was estimated with intercept dummies except for the capital-intensity indicator.
[b] Value of electricity consumption per unit of output.
[c] Ratio of non-production wages to all wages.

Source: CBS, Annual Survey of Large and Medium Establishments, 1991.

7

Unemployment and underemployment: pressing problems?[1]

Since the early years of the New Order government, there has been concern regarding Indonesia's 'unemployment problem'. Brand was pessimistic just after the new government had begun to re-establish economic stability.

> The manpower situation is likely to become worse before there will be a turn for the better. . . . Even if the maximum economic growth that can be reasonably hoped for were to be achieved over the next Plan period, it could not possibly absorb new growth of the labour force and at the same time make any substantial inroads on the appallingly high rate of underemployment . . . and on the present unknown, but probably high, rate of unemployment (1968: 69–70).

Twenty-five years later the Minister of Manpower in the fifth cabinet, Abdul Latief, made headline news highlighting the severity of high underemployment and unemployment.[2] 'Global' unemployment, a term coined to cover both unemployment and underemployment, was estimated to affect just under 40 per cent of the workforce in the early 1990s. The problem would seem to have changed little since Brand examined the situation 30 years earlier. The majority of unemployed according to the Ministry's definition were working few hours; a smaller proportion experienced open unemployment according to more conventional definitions of labour force status.[3]

Stubbornly high rates of underemployment do not fit with the picture of rapid growth in jobs and rising wages. High rates of economic growth

---

[1] Much of the analysis for this chapter is based on Manning and Junankar (1994). The author wishes to thank P.N. Junankar for his contribution to several of the ideas developed here, although the normal disclaimers apply.
[2] See ministerial statements entitled 'National Manpower Strategy' and 'Seven Policy Priorities' (Jakarta, October 1993).
[3] All those working less than 35 hours a week – regardless of job search activity or availability for work – were regarded as unemployed. Similar figures were quoted two years later when the Minister reflected on results from the 1994 National Labour Force Survey. In this latter statement, he also drew attention to an unemployment rate of 13 per cent defined as all people working less than 15 hours a week or not working and looking for work.

suggest that unemployment and underemployment should have fallen, as they did in other East Asian countries during the 1960s and 1970s. However, relatively slow growth in manufacturing employment and the segmented structure of earnings could be expected to result in high rates of urban unemployment,[4] given the increase of secondary and tertiary educated workers entering the labour market – groups which have frequently experienced high unemployment in other countries (Blaug 1974; Turnham 1993).

To place Indonesian unemployment in a broader perspective, it is useful to highlight two contrasting views regarding the economic and social significance of unemployment in developing economies.[5] The neoclassical view stresses labour market efficiency. It questions pessimism regarding the capacity of labour markets to accommodate either rapid growth in the supply of labour or unexpected shifts in labour demand, and argues that unemployment is an indicator of distortions introduced by government policies than evidence of market failure. Unemployment is seen as a rational response of people who endeavour to gain access to high-wage jobs in segmented labour markets, rather than a symptom of labour market failure. Similarly, underemployment is attributed to seasonal fluctuations in labour demand, and the prevalence of part-time work among females and children in rural and agricultural work (Bertrand and Squire 1980).

The alternative view emphasises inadequate labour market response to increases in the workforce, and structural and cyclical change. Turnham (1993: 54–6) points to high unemployment rates in urban areas of many developing economies, high even by industrialised economy standards where unemployment is a key indicator of labour market imbalance.[6] He further suggests the luxury unemployment hypothesis – which stresses unemployment as a bourgeois problem in developing economies – has little empirical basis.[7]

Evidence to support the structuralist view includes a high incidence of long-term unemployment in many developing economies, and limitations on the choices available to new job seekers for supposedly 'easy-entry', informal sector work. It is also argued that older workers from less-affluent

---

[4] High rates of urban unemployment have been especially associated with large urban–rural wage differentials and migration to urban areas (Todaro 1976).
[5] For a discussion of some of these issues see especially Turnham (1993: chapter 2), and also Berry and Sabot (1978), Squire (1981) and Horton, Kanbur and Mazumdar (1994b).
[6] Turnham (1971: 56) found the average rate of unemployment was 10 per cent for 36 developing countries in the mid to late 1980s. In some cases, rates were endemically high whereas in others they were quite variable according to economic circumstances.
[7] Myrdal emphasised disguised unemployment but dismissed unemployment as a 'bourgeois' problem (1968: 1231) experienced mainly by better-off households.

174 *Labour market structure and institutions*

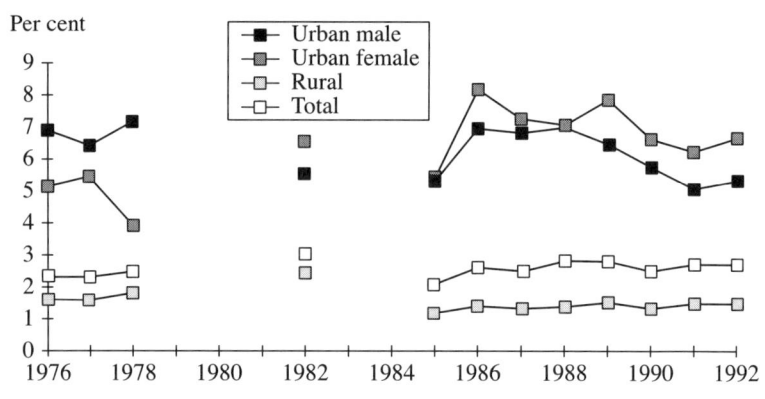

Figure 7.1 Unemployment rates: urban Indonesia, 1976–1992
Sources: CBS, National Labour Force Survey, all years except 1982, National Social and Economic Survey, 1982 data.

families are beginning to dominate unemployment queues as developing economies become more industrialised and urbanised (Rodgers 1989).

Although the narrow interpretation of disguised unemployment has largely been discredited, many countries record a significant proportion of employees working less than normal working hours (Squire 1981: 72). Even if occasional or seasonal, structuralists argue, underemployment presents a problem, in terms of utilisation of the existing workforce and the low incomes among participants.

Low unemployment and high underemployment in Indonesia?

As in some other developing economies, unemployment figures imply mixed signals regarding labour market outcomes in Indonesia. Low national figures (1.5–2.5 per cent nationally and a higher 5–7 per cent in urban areas, figure 7.1)[8] have emerged consistently over the past two decades, implying little cause for alarm.[9] They are low compared with rates in other Southeast Asian countries in the late 1980s (6–8 per cent in Malaysia, 4–7 per cent in Thailand and around 10 per cent in Philippines).

Although youth and educated unemployment rates in Indonesia have

---

[8] Aggregate unemployment rates rose in the late 1980s in particular compared with the previous decade but fell again slightly in the early 1990s, and then rose again in the middle of the decade.

[9] The most recent 1994 National Labour Force Survey results available at the time of writing suggested a rise in overall unemployment rates to over 4 per cent, but did not include any time reference period on the period of job search, in contrast to the one week period adopted in earlier surveys.

Table 7.1. *Unemployment and underemployment by gender: urban and rural Indonesia, 1992*

	Urban Male	Urban Female	Rural Male	Rural Female	Total
Number (000)					
Unemployed[a]	771	533	494	388	2,186
Underemployed: involuntary[b]	676	534	4,152	3,138	8,500
voluntary[c]	1,375	1,678	8,193	10,614	21,859
Total labour force	14,462	8,093	34,970	23,179	80,704
Rate (column %)					
Unemployed[a]	5.3	6.6	1.4	1.6	2.7
Underemployed: involuntary[b]	4.7	6.6	11.9	13.5	10.5
voluntary[c]	9.5	20.7	23.4	45.8	27.1
Distribution (row %)					
Unemployed[a]	35	24	23	18	100
Underemployed: involuntary[b]	8	6	49	37	100
voluntary[c]	6	8	37	49	100
Total labour force	18	10	43	29	100

Notes: [a] Working <1 hour; [b] Working <35 hours and looking or available for work; [c] Working <35 hours and not looking/available for work.
Source: CBS, National Labour Force Survey, 1992, Jakarta.

been high (frequently above 10 per cent), involuntary underemployment accounted for 10.5 per cent of the total labour force (table 7.1). In all, just on 13 per cent of the labour force could be categorised as underutilised, including those who did not have a job and were looking for one, who were working less than normal hours and looking for more work and those who reported that they were willing to extend their hours of work (or seek a new job).

Why is this level of underutilisation so much smaller than most estimates of surplus labour in Indonesia? To some extent low unemployment rates are a statistical anomaly, related to the structure of work – the large size of agriculture and the small share of wage employment – where active job search is rare. For example, the rate of unemployment jumps to three times the official rate when it is calculated for wage workers only (8.7 per cent overall, and over 10 per cent in urban areas).[10] Unemployment was only slightly lower than involuntary under-employment in 1992 when this definition is used.

Second, low overall unemployment is related to the extraordinarily low

---

[10] Specifically, unemployment rates are calculated as follows: $(U/[W+U]) \times 100$ where U represents the number of unemployed and W the number of wage workers.

recorded unemployment among less-educated people and those aged 35 or above. People who had not completed primary school (40 per cent of the workforce) and those aged 35 or above recorded unemployment rates around half a percentage point in the early 1990s. These figures imply a ratio of around 20:1 in unemployment rates among the younger and the more educated, on the one hand, compared with older people, on the other, much higher than in a sample of countries surveyed by Turnham (1993).[11]

Why were rates among older people are so low in Indonesia? Part of the explanation is the predominance of non-wage employment. Low unemployment at older ages also points to the existence of institutional rigidity which discourages people from moving between employers, especially in the government sector. Upper secondary and tertiary graduates aged 35 and above recorded very low unemployment rates. Either they move very quickly between jobs or, more likely, once getting into modern sector jobs, older, educated people tend to stay there.

Youth unemployment and surplus labour in urban areas

Unemployment rates among young and educated people in the 1990s were as high if not higher in Indonesia than in many other developing economies, in contrast to rates in aggregate and for older people. In urban areas they were 15–20 per cent among people aged 15–24 and among upper secondary graduates, peaking at 20–30 per cent among female senior high graduates from academic streams. Data for 1992 are shown in figure 7.2. These rates were surpassed only in Sri Lanka, among ten Asian countries in the mid to late 1980s (Turnham 1993: 80). Disturbingly, youth unemployment rates seem to have risen in the mid 1990s, especially among females and tertiary graduates.[12]

Which age–education cohorts were most affected by unemployment? In the early 1990s, unemployment rates were very high (20–30 per cent) among two age–education cohorts: upper secondary graduates (from both academic and vocational streams) in their early twenties and tertiary graduates in their late twenties (figure 7.3) (appendix table 7.1). Graduates from upper secondary schools in their early twenties alone accounted for nearly one-third of all urban unemployed in 1992, whereas they accounted for 7 per cent of the urban labour force.

[11] The data reported by Turnham (1993: 80) are for ages 15–24 and 25 and above. The ratio in Indonesia was slightly over 10:1 compared with the next highest ratio of approximately 6:1 in India and closer to 3–4:1 in most of the other Asian countries.
[12] According to the 1995 intercensal survey (SUPAS), unemployment rates were 30 per cent among women aged 15–24 and 20 per cent among female tertiary graduates, although these data cannot be directly compared with National Labour Force Survey data (no time limit was specified for job search activities in the SUPAS).

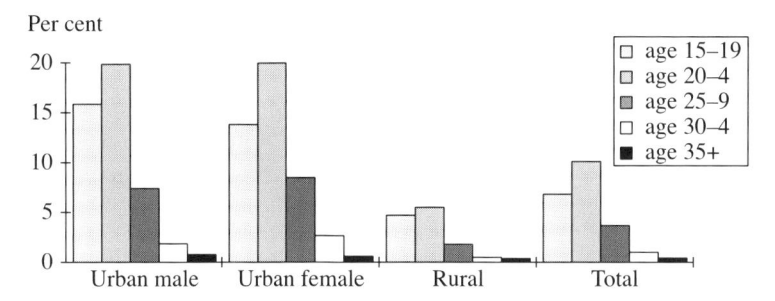

Figure 7.2a Unemployment by age: urban and rural Indonesia, 1992
Source: CBS, National Labour Force Survey, 1992.

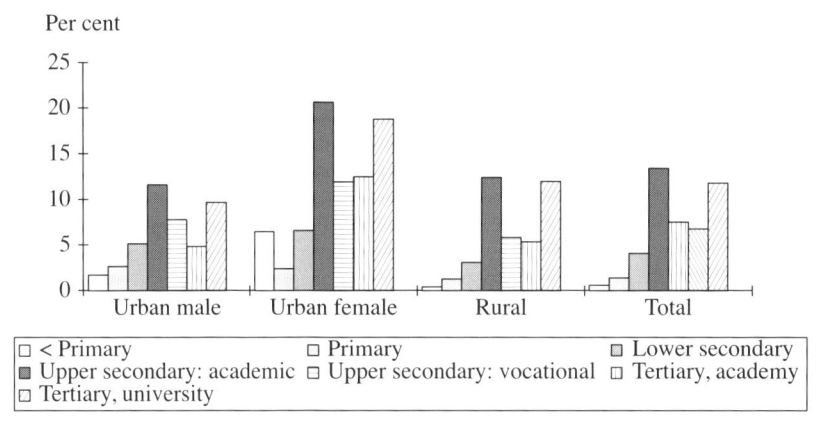

Figure 7.2b Unemployment by level of schooling: urban and rural Indonesia, 1992
Source: CBS, National Labour Force Survey, 1992.

These high rates suggest a major wastage of human resources – many of the unemployed experience long periods searching for work – yet the steep fall-off in unemployment rates among subsequent cohorts implies that young graduates are quite quickly absorbed into gainful employment. Before examining these apparent contradictions, I turn to two additional problems: low participation in any activity among urban youth, and long-term unemployment.

Underutilisation of urban youth

Based on labour force concepts, utilisation of labour can be defined in several ways. The most commonly used measures are unemployment rates and participation rates which measure the unemployed as a percentage of the labour force (employed plus unemployed), and the labour force

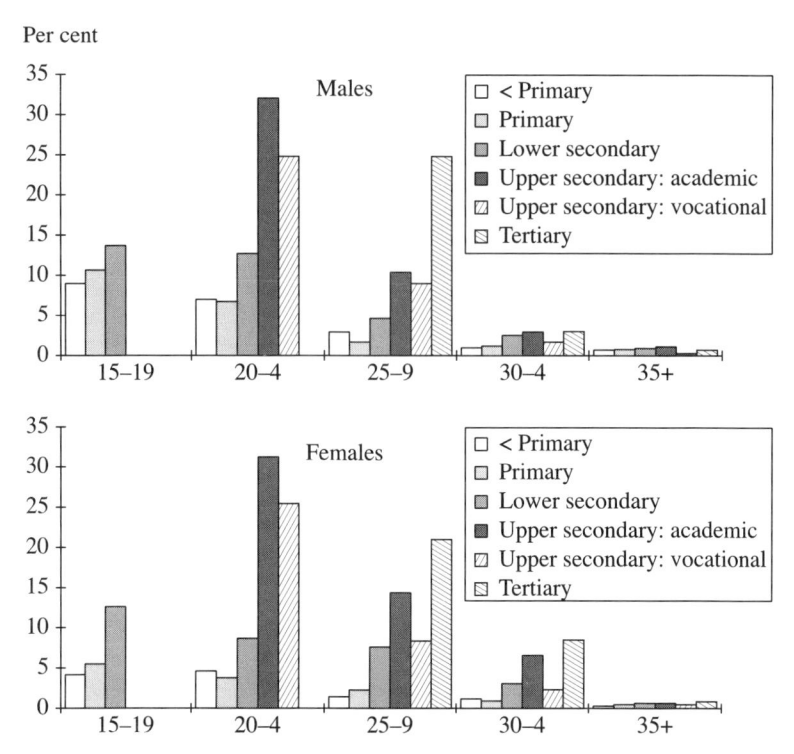

Figure 7.3 Open unemployment by age and education: urban Indonesia, 1992
Source; CBS, National Labour Force Survey, 1992.

as a percentage of the working age population respectively. Labour market specialists have also begun to focus on the structure of employment rates as a more useful summary measure of total labour utilisation and participation (Gregory 1991). These measure the employed as a percentage of the working age population.

Differences in employment rates among population sub-groups reflect both variations in unemployment and participation rates, which may offset one another. Employment rates help identify the extent of hidden or disguised unemployment which affects people who are outside or have withdrawn from the labour market.

Employment rates have been quite low among young people in urban Indonesia: less than 50 per cent among young males and less than one-third for young females in 1992. Low employment rates were related to several factors additional to unemployment: rising levels of schooling participation and a significant share of people not employed, and not at school or involved in housework as a principal activity. Besides one half of all young males in work, a further one-third were in school, 8 per cent were unemployed and 9 per cent were classified as 'other'.[13] Approximately two-thirds of young males and half of young females who reported no activity outside the workforce, said they were available for work in urban Indonesia in 1992. If this group of 'hidden' unemployed is added to the 'open' unemployed, then overall rates of youth underutilisation rise to over 30 per cent for upper secondary and tertiary graduates.[14]

If the group of people at school and performing housework who report that they are available for work is also included, then the proportion of young people who might be considered as hidden unemployed rises to 27 per cent for young males and as high as 37 per cent among females.[15]

One can only speculate on what activities this 'other' group are engaged in. Most are likely to live at home supported by parents. Some were probably engaged in informal work in family businesses, or in self-employed activities, which they did not consider as work. In a technical sense they should not be considered as unemployed. But in terms of job expectations, they were unemployed since they were involuntarily without a formal sector job.

The long-term unemployed

One important dimension of the unemployment problem is the extent of long-term unemployment. Recorded unemployment averaged 10 months for males and under one year for females in 1992. Close to one-third of both males and females reported looking for work for 12 months or more. A relatively high percentage (approximately 15 per cent) reported searching for work for two years or more (table 7.2).[16] This aspect of the unemployment problem appears to be more severe in Indonesia than in several other Asian countries,[17] and although it has fallen slightly over time, durations have remained stubbornly high from the late 1970s (Dhanani 1994a).

---

[13] A quite high proportion – between 6–10 per cent – of young people enumerated as 'other' (unclassified) and outside the work force has also been consistently recorded since the early National Labour Force Surveys in 1976–7. See especially Jones (1974, 1981) and Cremer (1990).

[14] The hidden unemployed are defined as young people who were not employed and not looking for a job, but were available for work.

[15] Caution must be taken, of course, in assuming that those available for work but outside the work force can be considered unemployed, in the same sense that those looking for work are defined as such. For example, those whose principal activity is school (and to a lesser extent housework) may be only available for part-time work.

[16] See Clark (1983) for data in the late 1970s. Of course, many of the unemployed may contribute to economic activity in self-employed work or family businesses while searching for modern sector jobs.

[17] Durations of more than 48 weeks unemployment were only recorded by a significant proportion of the work force in Malaysia among several Asian countries (Philippines, Thailand, Sri Lanka and India) for which data were available around 1970 (Mazumdar 1981: 281).

Table 7.2. *Duration of unemployment among young first job seekers and previously unemployed by level of completed schooling – ages 15–29: Indonesia, 1992*

Gender and education	First job seekers					Previously employed				
	Mean duration (months)	N (000)	Percentage searching			Mean duration (months)	N (000)	Percentage searching		
			<6 months	12 months+	24 months+			<6 months	12 months+	24 months+
Male										
Primary	8	(61)	53	27	9	5	(38)	75	12	6
Junior High	9	(76)	42	30	10	7	(37)	62	26	5
Senior High	10	(329)	38	37	13	9	(82)	47	29	10
Tertiary	9	(43)	48	32	11	7	(7)	46	24	7
All levels	10	509	42	34	12	7	164	57	24	7
Female										
Primary	9	(36)	43	35	14	6	(19)	62	17	15
Junior High	9	(52)	47	28	7	12	(10)	55	32	13
Senior High	11	(322)	37	36	16	9	(43)	51	24	9
Tertiary	7	(44)	51	24	3	7	(7)	38	26	0
All levels	10	(454)	40	34	13	8	(79)	52	23	7

Source: CBS, National Labour Force Survey, 1992, computer tape, Jakarta.

Young secondary school leavers in Indonesia are prepared to endure open unemployment in search of better-paid modern sector jobs. Long durations of unemployment are not inconsistent with substantially lower unemployment rates among older compared with younger people. There is strong evidence since the 1970s that the young unemployed are eventually absorbed into the labour force and a long period of job search has paid off for the educated in terms of higher earnings in modern sector jobs (Clark 1983; Budiono and McMahon 1991). The fall off in unemployment rates with age has been a feature of the Indonesian labour market for some time.[18]

This is not the entire story, however. Unemployment is not only experienced by young people from better-off families. Often poorer households, or those from regions with less resources to fund quality schools, find themselves in low-quality educational institutions from which it is more difficult to move into wage employment.

Is unemployment a luxury among the better off?

The absence of unemployment benefits in most developing economies means that the unemployed have to find a means of earning a living, unless they can be supported by their family. It is often argued that only the rich have access to such support and hence can afford to be unemployed (the 'luxury unemployment' hypothesis, Myrdal 1968). Since poorer job seekers have to support themselves, they are forced to take informal sector or casual, less well-paid jobs compared to better-off households.

The luxury hypothesis is indirectly supported by data showing that most of the unemployed have higher levels of education and are not heads of household (Turnham 1993). However, considerable evidence points to barriers to entry even to informal sector jobs among the poor, and they frequently suffer quite high rates of unemployment (Breman 1980; World Bank 1995; Visaria 1981; Rodgers 1989).

To test the luxury unemployment hypothesis, I examined unemployment rates among dependents according to the socioeconomic status of the household head.[19] Some data tend to confirm the luxury unemployment hypothesis. Unemployment rates were lower among job-seekers in which the household heads were primary educated or below, both for both females and males among all household members and young members aged 15–29 (table 7.3).

---

[18] There is sharp decline in the unemployment rates among upper secondary school graduates aged 25–9 in 1982, 1986 and 1992 compared with those aged 20–4 in 1976, 1982 and 1986 respectively (Manning and Junankar 1994).
[19] Data problems precluded analysis of the link between unemployment and the socioeconomic status of all the household.

182 Labour market structure and institutions

Table 7.3. *Unemployment rates by education of the household head, all urban and young urban dependents: Indonesia 1992[a]*

Education of household head	All dependents		Youth[b]	
	Male	Female	Male	Female
<Primary	12.5	6.5	14.7	12.8
Lower secondary	21.0	10.2	24.3	18.8
Upper secondary	21.6	8.3	28.0	14.8
Tertiary	21.1	6.5	24.8	11.4
All levels	15.3	7.4	18.0	14.1

Notes: [a] Household members excludes household head; [b] Ages 15–29.
Source: CBS, National Labour Force Survey, 1992, Jakarta.

However, the luxury unemployment hypothesis was not generally confirmed by data from Indonesia. There was little difference in unemployment rates among members from households in which the head was lower secondary, upper secondary or tertiary educated (see table 7.3). For all urban male dependents, these rates were close to 21 per cent. Among young males they ranged from 24–8 per cent. If results are standardised by education level of job seekers, the difference in unemployment rates among lower and higher socioeconomic status households narrows. This is illustated among young dependants who were upper secondary educated (table 7.4). Smaller differences in unemployment rates are recorded between dependents in households with the lowest socioeconomic status and those in higher-status groups, especially if many of those with no recorded activity outside the workforce are assumed to be unemployed. High unemployment rates in the lower socioeconomic status groups – 20–30 per cent – suggest that many children in these households face considerable difficulty in getting jobs.[20]

Finally, if the unemployed are represented as a share of the working-age population, the share peaked among households where the head had a lower secondary education or above and was lower among households where the head was upper secondary or tertiary educated (table 7.4).[21]

Data on the ratio of the unemployed to the population shows a clear contrast between lower-status and better-off households. More educated

---

[20] Almost half of unemployed individuals with secondary schooling came from the lowest socioeconomic status groups – those in which the head had only primary schooling or low-wage incomes. However, unemployment rates were slightly lower in lower-income households.

[21] The share of those classified as 'other' (those outside the work force and reported no activity, such as schooling or housework) was also higher among the less educated.

Table 7.4. Unemployment and employment rates of upper secondary educated urban youth (ages 15–29) by education and income of household head: Indonesia, 1992

	Measures of unemployment (%)					
	% of labour force		% of population			School participation rate[c]
	Unemployed	Unemployed + other[a]	Unemployed	Unemployed + other[a]	Employment rate[b]	
Schooling of head						
<Primary	25	37	18	32	54	13
Upper Secondary	31	43	19	33	43	23
Upper Secondary	28	41	14	24	35	40
Tertiary	36	48	10	17	18	65
Income of head (Rp 000)[d]						
<Rp 50	19	37	13	26	54	11
50 – <100	31	40	24	35	54	19
100 – <200	29	41	19	32	46	25
200+	32	44	14	23	29	42
All persons	27	40	16	29	44	27

Notes: [a] [(U+O) / (L+O)] * 100, where U=Unemployed, L=Labour Force, O=Other (outside labour force); [b] (Employed / Population) * 100; [c] (Main Activity in School/Population) * 100; [d] Wage earners only (no date on incomes of self employed).
Source: CBS, National Labour Force Survey, 1992, Jakarta.

people in the former group were more likely to enter the workforce after graduating, a high proportion found themselves unemployed and they were less likely to continue their schooling to tertiary levels (see table 7.4). Alternatively, many more of those from better-off households could afford to go on to further education – around half of secondary-educated people in the highest socioeconomic classes were enrolled in tertiary institutions – and a relatively small proportion were unemployed.

A final piece of evidence challenging the luxury hypothesis indicates that long durations of unemployment were also recorded for people in low-status households. The share of long-term unemployed was close to 30 per cent among the unemployed in households in which the head had only completed primary schooling or less. Lower-economic status households did not experience shorter periods of unemployment than higher-status households.

These findings are supported by logit analysis undertaken by Manning and Junankar (1994: chapter 6), using data from the 1992 National Labour Force Surveys and focusing on urban youths (aged 15–29 years). The likelihood of someone being unemployed was related to individual and household characteristics.[22] The results showed that the probability of being unemployed was lower for the very poor, but higher for lower-income groups.

Tracer studies among secondary and tertiary graduates emphasised the interrelationship between the quality of schools, socioeconomic status of graduates and affected earnings (Strudwick 1991, REDECON 1994 and Strudwick and Cresswell 1994). Graduates from academic streams in quality public schools were more likely to go on to tertiary education and reap private benefits from higher levels of schooling. Strudwick and Cresswell (1994: 45) point out the disadvantages suffered by students from less well-off families in the diversified secondary school system.

> Access to the public schools favours those with higher socioeconomic status, resulting in enlarging, rather than reducing disparities in the provision of education. In this way the structure and policy arrangements for the current system appear to favour a decrease, rather than an increase in overall equity in society.

At university level, a sizeable fraction of all graduates found work in the first six months after completing university. Durations of unemployment, however were typically 1–2 years in duration among 20–30 per cent of graduates. One study showed that a higher proportion of graduates found jobs quickly and the period of transition from school to work was shorter among graduates from technical faculties and from the more prestigious

---

[22] These characteristics included household socioeconomic status, and the individual's age, education, gender and region of residence.

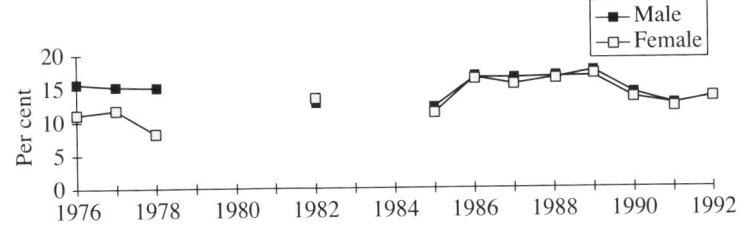

Figure 7.4 Unemployment rates among persons aged 15–29: urban Indonesia, 1976–1992
Sources: CBS, National Labour Force Survey, all years except 1982. National Social and Economic Survey, 1982 data.

universities (REDECON 1994). More females suffered long-term unemployment, although the particular university or field of study chosen probably affected this result: women were more heavily concentrated in non-technical fields of study.

Changes in youth unemployment

Given the extraordinary expansion in the supply of educated labour, one might expect that youth unemployment rates would have risen. That they did not do so has been a considerable achievement. Nevertheless, urban unemployment rates have remained high among educated youth and unemployment queues have become increasingly dominated by the educated people.

Youth unemployment has a structural rather than cyclical component. Nevertheless, there has been some variation in urban unemployment rates among young people. Unemployment rates among those aged 15–29 rose during the years of slow economic growth in the mid to late-1980s and then fell in the period of more rapid economic growth in the 1990s (figures 7.4 and 7.5).[23] Youth unemployment rates have been responsive to changes in labour demand.

There have been structural shifts, however. Unemployment rates have risen significantly among people in their twenties, females and highly educated people. These increases have in turn been counter-balanced by lower unemployment rates among the younger and less educated (appendix table 7.2).

---

[23] As noted, rates rose again in 1994–5, but this was probably partly due to definitional changes. Nevertheless, the slow-down in labour-intensive exports and rising minimum wages may also have played a part (chapter 8).

186 *Labour market structure and institutions*

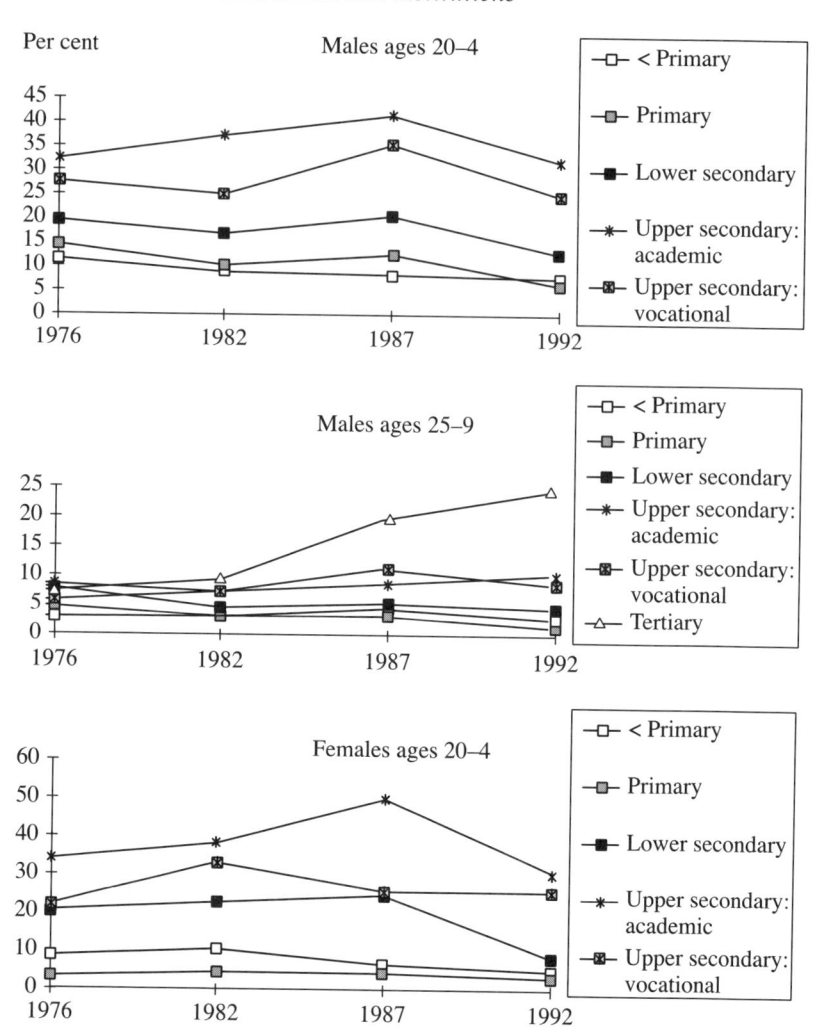

Figure 7.5 Open unemployment by age and education: urban Indonesia, 1992

Less-educated youth

Aggregate unemployment rates have not risen partly because higher unemployment among the educated has been offset by lower rates among younger people who left school earlier. In the mid 1970s, unemployment rates were similar (20–30 per cent) among young upper secondary graduates, and young male job seekers aged 15–19 who had only completed lower secondary education or less. Subsequently, unemployment halved among the group of less educated, younger job seekers. As the number graduating from senior high school rose rapidly, the less-educated appear to have been crowded out of better-paid modern sector jobs where queues were longest, and opted for work where entry was easier.

Declines in unemployment among the young, and less educated, suggests a clear bumping-up of educational requirements for modern sector jobs related to credentialism – a pattern common in other developing economies.[24] Whereas primary and lower secondary graduates could realistically aspire to gaining modern sector jobs in the 1970s – and were prepared to queue for them – the situation had changed by the 1990s. Public sector jobs were virtually closed to primary graduates from the late 1970s and to lower secondary graduates from the mid 1980s. Many modern private sector firms followed suit, even for unskilled workers.

The growth of job opportunities in low-wage, export-oriented manufacturing has probably contributed to lower unemployment among the less educated. While young primary and lower secondary graduates have been bumped-out of potential jobs in the public sector and established modern private sector firms, many have found jobs in new industries, such as clothing and footwear (White *et al.* 1992).

More-educated youth

The share of unemployed who were senior high school and tertiary graduates in their twenties rose from less than one-quarter in 1976 to nearly two-thirds of all unemployed in 1992. Among younger tertiary graduates, both unemployment rates and the share of all unemployed doubled from 4 to 10 per cent. There was a tripling of rates recorded among males and a smaller increase among females. For both sexes, the rates were approximately 20 per cent among people in their late twenties.

From the stand-point of both underutilisation of skilled manpower and social returns to investments in education, these increases represent a worrying trend, and are likely to remain an important feature of the Indonesian labour market in the 1990s.

Unemployment among tertiary graduates rose despite a shortage of certain categories of highly skilled labour. The latter led to inflows of larger numbers of foreign workers and high salaries for local personnel during the deregulation period. In part, the coincidence of unemployment and labour shortages can be attributed to the quality differences between higher education institutions. In part, it is explained by the heavy emphasis on law, social sciences and the humanities rather than on pure and applied sciences (Keyfitz 1989; Hough and Wiranta 1994).

---

[24] See especially Sabot's (1977) study of labour market adjustment in urban Tanzania.

Unemployment by gender

Total female unemployment rates have risen relative to those of males. Whereas in the latter half of the 1970s male unemployment rates were 20–30 per cent higher than among females, by the 1990s the situation was reversed.

Relatively high female unemployment has been offset by declining rates among less-educated males. In the 1970s, primary and lower secondary educated males recorded higher unemployment rates than females. Although unskilled and semi-skilled females have been preferred in labour-intensive industries, this has not been at the expense of the growth in job opportunities among less-educated males. Their participation has risen in construction and transport, in industries like chemicals, metals and machinery, and in service activities such as repair shops.

Contrary to popular views, higher female unemployment does not represent a significant disadvantage compared with rates for males from the same age–education cohorts. The higher female unemployment rates are mainly the result of a higher proportion of younger, educated females than younger males (relative to older people) entering the labour market recently. There was much less difference in age-standardised unemployment rates among educated and less-educated men and women.[25]

Nevertheless, upper secondary and especially tertiary educated women in slightly older cohorts appear to have faced greater problems than men in gaining employment. Unemployment rates in 1992 were considerably higher among female senior high graduates aged 25–35 than men. This was also true for tertiary educated women in their early thirties.[26] Less than 30 per cent of unemployed women aged 25–34 reported previous work experience. This suggests that educated women who do not get into the upper segment of the labour market quickly – partly because of maternity and child care responsibilities – face difficulties in getting jobs in competition with younger women, or men of the same age and educational status.[27]

Underemployment

Underemployment is frequently a pressing problem at early stages of development. It relates to people either working less than the desired

---

[25] For example, standardised unemployment rates among females at academic, senior high and tertiary levels (based on male age distributions) were 13 and 8 per cent respectively, only slightly higher than for males (12 and 7 per cent respectively).
[26] Among the tertiary educated people aged 30–4 male rates were 3 per cent compared with 9 per cent among females (appendix table 7.1).
[27] The break in the labour market experience puts women at a disadvantage and there is evidence of discrimination against women in recruitment for modern sector jobs, however (chapter 9).

Table 7.5. *Persons working less than 35 hours in all jobs and available for more work by major sector, employment status and region: Indonesia, 1990 (per cent)*

	Percentage working <35 hours a week				
		Total		Available for more work	
Region/		Non-agriculture			
Work status	Agriculture	Urban	Rural	Agriculture	Non-agriculture
Java					
Self-employed	41	15	25	10	6
Family workers	72	48	60	25	14
Employees	43	16	16	23	4
Total	53	19		17	5
Outer islands					
Self-employed	36	20	32	9	8
Family workers	64	54	63	16	15
Employees	19	15	22	11	4
Total	48	25		12	7

Source: CBS, National Labour Force Survey, 1990 computer tape, Jakarta.

number of hours, or working less than normal, full-time hours, especially among self-employed and family workers engaged in rural work.[28]

It is widely believed in Indonesia that underemployment is a better indicator of labour market imbalance than unemployment because official unemployment rates are so low (Arndt and Sundrum 1980; World Bank 1985). Also, notions of shared poverty (and work), and rural work shortages, are accepted as fundamental problems associated with overpopulation in Java.

But the evidence for widespread underemployment, and its association with poverty and excess pressures of labour supply, is remarkably thin (chapter 3). Table 7.1 above suggested that involuntary underemployment – in the sense of people working few hours and seeking more work at going wage rates – was not markedly more serious than unemployment. Only around 10 per cent of the workforce was affected in 1990 and 1992. The proportions were higher in agriculture (12 per cent) than in non-agriculture (7 per cent) (table 7.5), a pattern common in many developing economies (Turnham 1971; Squire 1981).

Involuntary underemployment was high in agriculture both in Java and

[28] With economic development, underemployment is expected to decline, as people move out of family work and self-employed jobs in agriculture into non-agricultural wage employment. At later stages, more flexible work arrangements may lead to an increase in those working less than a full-time working week.

in the Outer Islands (table 7.6). Voluntary underemployment was highest in agriculture in Java, where there is limited access to land and work. Although hours worked are understated in national surveys, many people in Java may not be able to get enough work outside agriculture, despite the massive changes in employment structure.

The incidence of short working hours was greatest among those frequently engaged in part-time or seasonal employment; agricultural workers, females, young and older workers and less-educated workers, primarily self-employed and engaged in family work, are in rural areas (table 7.6).[29]

Two unusual aspects of labour utilisation reported in the national surveys bear mention – the high proportion of prime-age males (approximately one-quarter) who said that they worked less than 35 hours a week in the early 1990s, and a large share of educated male employees reported working less than 35 hours. The latter amounted to over 20 per cent of upper secondary and tertiary graduates. Since these data refer to work in main jobs, they imply that educated and prime-age males are underutilised in their primary activities in Indonesia.

It is likely that many on the government pay-roll as civil servants, teachers, and health care workers, are engaged in unreported, secondary activities. Nevertheless, low levels of labour inputs and productivity in primary occupations appear to a be a key problem, as evidenced in studies of specific occupations such as university teaching (Clark and Oey-Gardiner 1991).

Declining rates of underemployment?

We could expect that the proportion of people working shorter hours would have declined as a result of the availability of more productive work, or of more complementary inputs to support work. Such a decline in underemployment should have occurred with the shift away from agriculture to a greater reliance on wage labour – especially in urban areas. This was the case in South Korea during the period of labour market transition in the 1960s and 1970s.[30]

The national data on hours worked are fragmentary and almost certainly understate female and child work. But they suggest that there has not been a significant change in average hours worked or the proportion of underemployed people (working less than 35 hours each week) (table

[29] There was no systematic difference in hours worked in all jobs between Java and the Outer Islands. However a much higher share of wage employees in agriculture in particular were recorded as working less than 35 hours in Java in 1990.

[30] For example, Kim (1986: 58) reports that the proportion of females in farm households (the largest group among underemployed in Korea) who worked less than 18 hours fell from close to 20 per cent to negligible levels over the period 1961–83.

Table 7.6. *Mean number of hours worked and percentage of people working less than 35 hours: Indonesia, 1977 and 1990*

	Mean hours worked (per week)[a]				% underemployed (working <35hrs)			
	Wage workers		Non-wage workers		Wage workers		Non-wage workers	
	1977	1990	1977	1990	1977	1990	1977	1990
Male								
Agriculture	42	43	38	36	27	25	37	39
Non-agriculture: Urban	49	46	51	48	9	10	15	17
Rural	47	46	48	45	16	15	21	23
Sub-total	48	46	50	47	11	12	17	19
All male	47	45	42	40	14	13	30	33
Female								
Agriculture	32	31	31	27	55	54	59	69
Non-agriculture: Urban	50	47	46	41	17	18	27	38
Rural	43	42	41	36	28	29	38	47
Sub-total	49	46	44	38	20	21	32	43
All female	43	43	37	31	32	28	46	59

Note: [a] Figures in parentheses represent the percentage of total workers in each group. The distributions are estimates only, based on weighted samples from the National Labour Force Survey.
Source: CBS, National Labour Force Survey, 1977 and 1990, Jakarta.

192 Labour market structure and institutions

Table 7.7. *Percentage of persons working less than 35 hours in main job by major sector and gender, 1980 and 1990*

	% working <35 hours[a] 1980	1990	% working <25 hours[a] 1980	1990
Male				
Agriculture	39	41	22	20
Urban: Manufacturing	9	8	5	4
Trade	15	15	9	7
Services	12	17	7	6
Rural: Manufacturing	22	20	13	10
Trade	28	26	17	13
Services	27	30	13	10
All non-agriculture[b]	19	18	11	8
All males	30	29	17	14
Female				
Agriculture	62	67	43	43
Urban: Manufacturing	20	17	13	10
Trade	27	27	16	16
Services	22	27	12	12
Rural: Manufacturing	46	44	27	31
Trade	40	40	26	24
Services	44	45	28	22
All non-agriculture[b]	37	36	24	21
All females	51	51	34	32
Both sexes	37	37	23	20

Notes: [a] Excludes those temporally not working; [b] Includes all non-agricultural sectors.
Sources: CBS, Population Censuses, 1980 and 1990 (Series S2), Jakarta.

7.7). Average hours worked actually fell slightly in the period 1977–90, and the proportion of underemployed and part-time workers rose.

Increased underemployment was evident among female non-wage workers, who experienced a substantial decline in average hours worked. In part, this can be attributed to a greater incidence of part-time work among female self-employed and family workers in agriculture, but it also relates to underutilisation of female family workers in all sectors. Underemployment among non-wage workers in urban trade and rural manufacturing also increased sharply.

Why did hours worked not increase and underemployment fall, as expected? Two explanations are suggested. Structural change has involved movement out of rural low-paid, self-employed activities, where workers reported as many as 12–14 hours a working day (White 1976; Sawit, Saefudin and Sri Hartoyo 1985). As the share of workers in such industries has declined, a decline in average hours worked, counterbalances the impact of long hours worked in modern manufacturing firms (White *et al.* 1992; Loc 1993).

Second, average hours worked were shorter and underemployment more prevalent among urban non-wage workers outside non-agricultural sectors, and in manufacturing and services. The increased participation of females (especially as family workers) in such activities also offset the tendency towards a rise in hours of work in other sectors.

Increased value added per worker has been principally achieved through people working in higher productivity activities (chapter 4). They used more complementary capital, skilled labour and managerial inputs, rather than worked longer hours. It was this change rather than increased hours worked by previously underemployed labour which was a major contributor to economic growth and rising incomes.

Conclusions

In the NIEs, both underemployment and unemployment declined as these countries approached the turning point. Unemployment fell from quite high levels, both in the city states of Singapore and Hong Kong and in South Korea and Taiwan during the 1960s.[31] Average hours worked rose in South Korea and Taiwan, in particular as people moved out of agriculture into manufacturing and service industries – average hours worked in manufacturing of close to 60 a week in South Korea became among the highest in the world (Amsden 1989).

Indonesia's experience differed from that of other rapidly growing economies in East Asia. Overall unemployment was initially low in Indonesia and has remained so. It has never been close to the 10 per cent levels recorded in many Latin American countries and even from time to time in some Asian countries such as the Philippines and Malaysia. Surprisingly, like unemployment, underemployment did not decline in response to rapid economic growth, despite substantial structural changes in the economy and employment.

Some of these differences can be attributed to measurement and conceptual problems. Low initial levels of unemployment can be explained partly by the low share of wage employment, and high underemployment among part-time workers in traditional sectors.

However, some of the differences with neighbouring countries are specific to the process of economic transformation in Indonesia. The dominant

---

[31] See especially Yin and Clark (1976), Chau (1976), Kim (1986) and Kuo (1983) for studies of Singapore, Hong Kong, Korea and Taiwan respectively.

role of the government in providing employment, especially for educated manpower for the first two decades of the New Order, is one. Another is the protection of modern sector activities for long periods. Slower industrial employment creation than in the NIEs, despite rapid economic growth, high rates of unemployment among educated youth, and low average hours of work in primary jobs, are problems which remain unsolved in Indonesia. The failure to adequately utilise young and educated labour can be viewed as primarily an economic problem associated with wastage of resources. It also has implications for welfare – support is required from some families for long periods of job search.

How does this persistent problem relate to more general labour market changes and structures? In the 1990s, policy makers have suggested that the main problem is lack of skills for the private sector. The Ministry of Education embarked on an ambitious programme of 'link and match', subsidising the involvement of the private sector in on-the-job training for students at final years of high school.

Yet the problem goes beyond the extent to which skills demanded in the work place are imparted through formal schooling. Three aspects of the economic and social environment explain the persistence of high unemployment among educated youth. First, the dominance of government employment and public enterprises in which educational credentials have been a basis for recruitment. Second, on the demand side, the relatively segmented structure of wages by industry and type of establishment has been a feature of Indonesia's labour market. It is not surprising that many young graduates are prepared to wait long periods in the hope of gaining wages in these firms at double or more the entry rate in non-protected industries.[32] High wages and secure employment are a feature of capital-intensive industries which receive considerable government support and often involve government participation. A powerful incentive is offered by high wages in industries like cement, pulp, fertiliser, petrochemicals, and in the minerals and oil companies (such as the state-owned oil company PERTAMINA).[33] Such employment opportunities were more extensive in Indonesia

---

[32] For example, the lowest level employees (high school graduates) received around Rp. 250,000 (excluding generous allowances) on entry into a large, state-owned cement factory with a protected market share in East Java in December 1995. Similar although slightly lower levels of entry wages was offered by a big alumina smelting firm in North Sumatra. In each of these provinces the regional minimum wage required firms to pay around Rp. 90,000–Rp. 125,000 per month, and many firms in both provinces still paid the minimum wage (field interviews and observations, November–December 1995).

[33] Many of these firms also offer a virtual guarantee of lifetime employment and automatic salary increases with seniority (Manning 1979).

because of its rich natural resource base and associated industrial structure, and because of a history of government involvement and control (Hill 1996).

Third, in comparison to other East Asian countries, there appears to be less turnover among the educated employed in modern sector jobs. This characteristic has been reinforced by the discouragement of dismissals in labour legislation.[34]

The neoclassical explanation of the labour market imbalance is relevant in the Indonesian case. Processes which underpin high unemployment imply the operation of flexible labour markets and rational choices made by many job seekers. Long periods of job search have paid off for many educated job seekers in the past, in terms of incomes earned in wage employment (Clark 1983). This, combined with relatively stable or even declining unemployment rates among specific age–education cohorts implies that unemployment should not be considered a major problem.

Nevertheless, several patterns also support the structuralist interpretation. These include consistently long search periods and high rates of unemployment among young people from lower-income households. The structure of output, employment and wages encourage high rates of urban unemployment.

The social (public) costs of unemployment must be emphasised, even if private rewards justify long periods of search for employment in the modern sector. Stable unemployment rates until very recently imply that the number of unemployed grew by over 5 per cent in urban areas and over 10 per cent among upper secondary graduates in the period 1977–92. This meant a tripling of the unemployed, and a seven-fold increase in unemployed upper secondary graduates: an absolute increase from just over 100,000 to 700,000. The scale of the problem in a country of Indonesia's size cannot be ignored, given the potential for social and political unrest associated with the concentration of underutilised young people in urban areas.

---

[34] See chapter 8 for an elaboration on this point.

Appendix table 7.1. *Unemployment rates by age and education: Indonesia, 1992*

Age/Level of schooling	Urban Male	Urban Female	Rural Male	Rural Female
15–19				
<Primary	8.8	4.0	2.2	1.5
Primary	10.6	5.4	2.9	4.2
Lower secondary	13.7	12.5	4.9	5.7
All 15–19[a]	11.5	7.4	4.0	5.1
20–4				
< Primary	7.0	4.4	1.3	1.4
Primary	6.8	3.8	2.2	1.5
Lower secondary	12.7	8.5	6.0	6.6
Upper secondary: Academic	32.0	31.3	18.5	24.9
Vocational	24.7	25.5	12.2	21.3
All 20–4	19.4	17.9	5.5	5.4
25–9				
<Primary	2.8	1.3	0.5	0.6
Primary	1.6	2.2	0.6	0.8
Lower secondary	4.7	7.5	1.2	2.2
Upper secondary: Academic	10.3	14.3	5.7	14.1
Vocational	8.9	8.3	4.2	10.4
Tertiary	24.7	21.0	20.0	20.3
All 25–9	7.3	8.3	1.6	1.9
30–4				
<Primary	0.9	1.1	0.4	0.5
Primary	1.0	0.9	0.2	0.4
Lower secondary	2.5	3.1	0.6	0.5
Upper secondary: Academic	2.8	6.5	2.9	7.7
Vocational	1.6	2.4	0.6	1.1
Tertiary	2.9	8.5	4.3	13.2
All 30–4	1.8	2.6	0.5	0.6
35+				
<Primary	0.7	0.2	0.1	0.2
Primary	0.7	0.4	0.4	0.6
Lower secondary	0.9	0.6	1.4	0.4
Upper secondary: Academic	1.0	0.6	0.9	0
Vocational	0.3	0.4	0.7	0.2
Tertiary	0.6	0.8	0.1	0
All 35+	0.7	0.4	0.6	0.2
All ages				
<Primary	1.5	0.8	0.4	0.6
Primary	2.5	2.3	1.0	1.4
Lower secondary	4.9	6.3	2.7	3.8
Upper secondary: Academic	11.7	20.6	10.0	20.0
Vocational	7.6	11.9	3.8	9.9
Tertiary	6.9	16.0	6.3	15.0
Total	5.3	6.6	1.4	1.7

Note: [a] Includes small number of upper secondary graduates.
Source: CBS, National Labour Force Survey, 1992.

Appendix table 7.2. *Unemployment rates by age and education: urban Indonesia, 1976–1992*

Age/Educational category	Males 1976	Males 1982	Males 1986[a]	Males 1990[a]	Males 1992[a]	Females 1976	Females 1982	Females 1986[a]	Females 1990[a]	Females 1992[a]
15–19										
<Primary	22.3	11.4	10.2	9.1	8.8	6.5	7.1	5.0	10.0	4.0
Primary	26.2	20.3	16.1	10.9	10.6	7.5	10.2	11.4	5.7	5.4
Lower secondary	32.3	24.2	20.3	14.3	13.7	25.9	19.9	21.6	14.3	12.5
All 15–19b	26.3	20.4	21.2	11.9	15.8	9.9	12.9	16.6	8.9	13.8
20–4										
<Primary	11.5	9.9	8.1	4.9	7.0	3.0	4.1	4.3	2.3	4.4
Primary	13.9	9.3	12.2	6.6	6.8	8.3	10.0	6.1	4.4	3.8
Lower secondary	19.5	16.7	20.3	14.4	12.7	20.7	22.5	24.9	10.2	8.5
Upper secondary: Academic	32.2	37.1	41.5	34.4	32.0	33.4	38.0	50.2	32.0	31.3
Vocational	27.6	25.1	35.1	29.3	24.7	21.9	32.9	25.5	26.0	25.5
All 20–4	18.2	17.6	26.1	21.1	19.8	14.4	18.8	24.4	18.0	19.9
25–9										
<Primary	3.0	3.2	5.5	1.7	2.8	2.0	3.3	2.0	1.7	1.3
Primary	4.7	3.4	3.6	2.5	1.6	3.4	5.9	2.0	2.3	2.2
Lower secondary	7.8	4.6	5.2	5.3	4.7	10.9	4.2	11.9	7.9	7.5
Upper secondary: Academic	8.4	7.2	8.7	12.6	10.3	5.9	11.8	13.9	14.6	14.3
Vocational	5.8	7.2	11.3	9.3	9.0	9.1	6.7	8.5	8.1	8.3
Tertiary	7.4	9.4	19.6	20.0	24.7	13.6	30.5(?)	15.6	17.8	21.0
All 25–9	5.8	4.9	7.1	7.8	7.3	5.5	6.9	7.0	7.6	8.3

Appendix table 7.2. (cont.)

Age/Educational category	Males 1976	1982	1986[a]	1990[a]	1992[a]	Females 1976	1982	1986[a]	1990[a]	1992[a]
All levels										
<Primary	5.1	3.1	2.5	1.2	1.5	1.7	2.2	1.8	1.3	0.8
Primary	7.1	4.5	4.2	2.6	2.5	5.5	5.9	4.5	2.5	2.3
Lower secondary	8.0	5.9	6.4	5.5	4.9	11.3	9.2	11.2	7.2	6.3
Upper secondary: Academic	9.7	9.3	14.8	12.9	11.6	18.6	22.5	31.0	21.1	20.6
Vocational	10.6	10.3	11.8	8.6	7.6	12.1	6.1	11.7	11.8	11.9
Tertiary	6.9	3.9	6.9	6.3	6.9	9.3	11.5	14.4	13.7	16.0
Total	6.9	5.5	6.9	5.7	5.3	5.1	6.5	8.1	6.5	6.6

Notes: [a] Diploma I and II graduates included in the secondary vocational school group. [b] Total for ages 15—19 includes a small group of upper secondary graduates with very high unemployment rates.
Sources: CBS, SAKERNAS, 1976, 1986, 1990 and 1992 and National Social Economic Survey, 1982.

8

Protecting and controlling workers in a labour surplus economy[1]

Government intervention in economic life has been an important part of national ideology in Indonesia since independence. Protection of the weak through support from the state and cooperatives is enshrined in the constitution, even if the government lacked the means, or at times the will, to follow through with policies to achieve its stated goals. A similar concern for protection of labour is reflected in labour legislation.

Especially since the mid 1980s, the New Order government has also been prepared to place greater reliance on markets to determine the allocation of goods and services. Aside from the substantial support for politically powerful groups close to the palace, government intervention has either been justified on the grounds of national interest, market failure or a desire to achieve specific distributional goals.

There is debate concerning the appropriate level of government intervention in labour markets, especially as it is often based on a non-transparent mix of efficiency, equity and political goals. The *World Development Report* on labour (World Bank 1995: chapters 11–13) emphasised the pitfalls of minimum wage legislation and job security regulation, in contrast to the more interventionist approach encouraged by the ILO. The Bank stressed the benefits of legislation improving worker safety and health and the encouragement of free unionism, alluding to the latter's role in work-place bargaining. Such an approach has been questioned, however. In an assessment of that report, Mazumdar (1996) argued that the impact of government policies needs to be viewed in the context of the segmented structure of LDC labour markets, of monopsony and of the external effects of labour policies. He also stressed the limited impact of legislation on smaller, competitive firms compared with larger, often protected establishments. Other commentators have also stressed the flexibility of implementation of labour laws in practise, especially during periods of economic downturn (Freeman 1992a).

---

[1] This chapter expands on Manning (1993).

200 *Labour market structure and institutions*

The NIEs are renowned for considerable labour market flexibility. Nevertheless, this experience offers relatively little guidance as to appropriate government intervention for later industrialisers. Labour markets have generally performed well in all the rapidly growing East Asian economies, yet the extent of government involvement has varied widely. Several propositions from the NIE experience of labour market intervention are nevertheless relevant to Indonesia.[2]

- The fostering of a productive workforce, encouraging flexible labour markets, was a key aspect in the promotion of labour-intensive investment growth. While trade unions were controlled, the state did not pursue policies which regulated labour standards extensively. Nor did it support bureaucratic systems of arbitration and conciliation, such as developed in some South Asian countries (Battacherjee 1987). Minimum wage legislation was noticeably absent in NIE labour market policies until well after they had passed the turning point.
- While the determination of private sector wages was left largely to the market – except in Singapore – the industrial relations system favoured employers in setting labour standards and resolving industrial disputes. Restrictions imposed on trade union organisations were justified by governments both on political and economic grounds.
- There is little empirical evidence of wage repression (distinguished from labour repression) in the newly industrialised economies. Some commentators have argued that the controls over trade unions and the absence of minimum wage legislation, or guide-lines regarding annual wages increases, are evidence of attempts to repress wages and labour costs (Deyo 1989). Fields (1994) however challenged the argument that attempts at wage repression were successful.[3] High wage increases often matched productivity growth, there was rapid growth in wages in less-unionised industries, and the share of wages in GDP rose.[4]
- Depending on economic and political circumstances, government involvement in the labour market varied considerably. The Singapore government intervened heavily in wage setting and industrial rela-

---

[2] Bonggano (1988), Galenson (1992), Deery and Mitchell (1993) and Fields (1990, 1994).
[3] There was a deliberate but largely unsuccessful policy to contain wages growth in Singapore in the 1970s, and before 1987 in Korea.
[4] As Lim (1978) noted in the case of Singapore, restraint of trade union action was introduced as much for political as for economic reasons. Further, the latter relate more to reduction in uncertainty in the investment climate than attempts to suppress wage costs.

tions. At the other extreme, Taiwanese and Hong Kong governments relied on market forces as the mechanism for guiding resource allocation, employment and productivity growth. Wage and industrial relations policies also experienced changes due to economic conditions, political instability and associated labour unrest.
- Changed political circumstances and tightening labour markets by the mid 1980s marked a watershed, resulting in greater union freedom and efforts at labour protection in some countries (South Korea and Taiwan).[5] The proliferation of unions and near doubling of trade union membership are evidence of an increase in the involvement of organised labour in industrial relations processes.

These propositions also apply to several ASEAN countries (Malaysia, Thailand and the Philippines). The variation in government policies towards labour in these countries has probably exceeded that in the NIEs (Sharma 1985; Galenson 1992). For example, union action and organisations were tightly controlled in Malaysia and Thailand but freer in the Philippines. Minimum wages have been in force since the 1950s in the Philippines and since the 1970s in Thailand, but there has never been a minimum wages system in Malaysia.

It could be anticipated that government intervention on the side of labour would be greater in Indonesia than in the newly industrialised economies. A closer parallel with India might be expected, given the popularist emphasis on protection of the weak against market forces and support for cooperatives in national ideology in both countries. On the other hand, the strong military government in Indonesia might be expected to have exerted tight controls over organised labour for political reasons, as in South Korea and Taiwan.

Another issue is the evolution of labour policies during the transition to export orientation and liberalisation of financial and real sectors. In a period of deregulation, we would expect that direct government intervention in the labour market to be small. Similarly, labour repression could be anticipated to have featured more prominently in labour relations, when comparative wage costs began to be perceived as critical to economic performance.

The foundations of labour policy

The setting of labour standards through legislation is the main mechanism

---

[5] See Park [Young-bum] (1992), Park [Fun-Koo] (1991).

by which the Indonesian government has sought to safeguard the welfare of wage employees.[6] The system contains both centralised and decentralised elements. Basic labour laws are extensive and apply to all employees in establishments with 25 or more workers (and some to all wage employment). At the same time, quasi-compulsory collective bargaining at the enterprise level has been viewed as an important component of the system for setting wages and working conditions in private enterprise.

A brief summary of the legislative framework is required. The first comprehensive labour law for Indonesians, adapted from the Dutch laws, was passed in 1948 and remains the basis for labour protection today.[7] The Basic Law prescribes a 40-hour and six-day working week, with a maximum of seven hours worked at normal pay per day.[8] The 40-hour working week is shorter than that prescribed in labour legislation in most countries in the region (either 44 or 48 hours).[9] The law bans all work of children below the age of 15 and night work among women was heavily restricted.[10] It guarantees women the right to take menstruation leave (two days per month) and three months maternity leave. Minimum wages were not introduced in the early laws, however, despite pressures from some of the more radical union groups.

Emphasis was placed on job security in labour legislation, with retrenchment legislation (Law No. 12, 1964) regulating procedures for dismissal of workers. All cases of retrenchment must be discussed with the worker and his/her union and the employer must gain permission for retrenchment from provincial labour disputes councils (P4D). Separation payments were also regulated under this basic law.

As in most newly independent states, successive governments guaran-

[6] The 1945 Constitution is the basis of the legal framework governing labour relations. Specifically with regard to labour the constitution guarantees 'the right to work ... to a level befitting for human beings' and the 'freedom of association and assembly'. See Articles 27 and 28 of the Constitution. However, there is no explicit mention of trade union freedoms.

[7] This was reaffirmed as Basic Law No. 1 in 1951 and several articles incorporated in the Basic Law on Manpower (No. 14, 1969).

[8] Firms may also adopt a five day, eight hour working week, like that adopted in all government offices in 1995. A second basic law (No. 14 1969) guarantees the right of persons to join unions, conclude labour agreements and achieve basic labour standards (health and safety, and workers compensation); all of these matters were regulated in subsequent legislation.

[9] A maximum of nine hours of work is permitted per day and 54 hours per week, although firms may obtain a special license (renewable each year) for working hours exceeding the maximum. Firms have little difficulty in obtaining permission to work overtime.

[10] The law limits the activities undertaken by young people aged 15–17 (such as work in mines). A later ministerial regulation (No. 1 1987) contradicts the Basic Law by stipulating working conditions for children forced to work for 'socio-economic' reasons. Women were not permitted to work at night, except with special permission from the Manpower Ministry.

teed workers the right to organise and all trade unions were registered with the Central Government. There was a strong mandatory element in the basic industrial relations legislation. Three laws formed the basis of the system, covering the settlement of labour disputes through regional and central government councils, the right to organise, bargain collectively and establish trade unions. Although labour disputes could be settled by an intermediary, they had to be referred to the regional disputes councils (and failing resolution to the central body). The right to strike was limited under the Disputes Resolution Act and subsequent legislation. Trade unions had to be registered and collective labour agreements were recognised under a basic law (No. 21 1954) and regulated by the Manpower Ministry.[11]

Trade unions and labour unrest before 1965

In 1965 the Soeharto government inherited a militant and fragmented union movement. The government approach to unions was influenced by perceptions regarding the destabilising role of the high profile union movement in the previous era of political conflict and economic stagnation and decline.[12]

Union membership mushroomed after independence and industrial unrest was a problem for governments.[13] Around half of all registered union members were in SOBSI, a left-leaning union with close ties to the Indonesian Communist Party. Organised labour was a force to be reckoned with, although one-third of union members were in the plantation sector and a majority were non-dues paying members.

Early governments found it difficult to reconcile union freedoms and industrial disputes with the needs of achieving economic stability and growth. Strike activity was frequent among the small percentage of wage employees in the firm sector. It is estimated that the 400 strikes (average) per annum which occurred in the 'normal' years of 1951–6 involved 5 per cent of all wage employees (and close to 20 per cent of

---

[11] One restriction was placed on the latter: they had to be represented in 20 provinces, 100 districts and in at least 1,000 work places.

[12] The labour movement emerged as a significant political and social force until the struggle for independence against the Dutch in 1945–9. There was no mass-based trade union organisation in Indonesia during the colonial period (Wertheim 1956; Ingleson 1981 and 1986).

[13] By the mid 1950s the union movement was estimated to be already large, with a membership of around 2 million (over half of all employees in larger establishment and public enterprises) in 13 different federations which had close links with political parties (Hawkins 1963: 261). By developing country standards, union density (the share of employees in unions) was already high (around 20 per cent).

regular employees).[14] Foreign companies were a target for labour action, although a number of strikes also occurred in state-owned enterprises (Richardson 1958: 67–9). The government was understandably quite concerned about the threat to the economy posed by labour action.

Even though most of the early Indonesian governments were pro-labour in ideology, this was not necessarily reflected in their reform programmes.[15] Increased controls – which set a precedent for later developments – came with the nationalisation of foreign interests and their takeover by the army beginning in 1957. Despite increasing anti-capitalist flavour of state ideology, the government became less pro-union (Hawkins 1963: 267).[16]

The 'Panca Sila' approach to labour policy

The changes in political and economic life after 1965 had far-reaching implications for Indonesia's industrial relations system, both in form and substance. Most important were the transformed political structure, new economic policies in favour of private enterprise and a turnabout in macroeconomic performance. Job creation became an objective of economic policy, associated with policies promoting economic growth. Emphasis on economic stability resulted in tighter labour controls, in contrast to the more open, participatory environment of the Sukarno period. Despite oscillating approaches to the role of government in economic affairs, labour protection did not feature highly in government programmes until economic deregulation in the late 1980s (table 8.1).

In this earlier period, there was conflict in government policies towards labour protection and industrial relations. The government extended tight controls over the union movement and organisation, and sought to regulate labour standards by legislation. On the other hand, it supported collective bargaining (which required active union participation) as a principal means of setting labour standards and resolving labour disputes.

[14] An average of 250,000 workers were engaged in strikes annually, out of a total of 5–6 million employees. Over half worked as casual workers in agriculture or cottage industries (Richardson 1958: 68). In 1950, the first year of independent government, and 1957 there were more strikes, associated with nationalisation and conflicts in foreign (especially Dutch) firms.
[15] There were other more pressing needs and few governments (cabinets) had the time or expertise to pass labour legislation. Thus recognition of trade unions was only given legal status in 1956 (Act No. 18) when Indonesia ratified the ILO Convention No. 98 on the right to organise (Tedjasukmana, 1961).
[16] In 1957, the government reintroduced anti-strike measures over vital industries.

Table 8.1. *Changes in labour policies and labour market developments during main periods of economic change: Indonesia, 1965–1995*

Key areas	1965–73	1973–81	1982–7	1988–92/3	1992/3–5
Political affairs	Tight controls exerted over political parties and processes	Consolidation of political controls under Soeharto and army		Campaigns for more open political system – signs of some disunity in armed forces	Tighter controls over political dissidents, Soeharto asserts control over army, Habibie is more prominent
Economic policy and performance	Rehabilitation, and deregulation of the foreign account; achievement of greater economic stability	Oil boom, rapid economic growth, especially in modern sector, and increasing government intervention	Slow-down in economic growth, fiscal stringency and beginnings of deregulation	Take-off in non-oil exports and return to rapid growth, further deregulation	Continued rapid growth, slow-down in deregulation and intensified competition with China and Vietnam in manufactured exports
Labour markets	Recovery of real wages in modern sector; strong labour supply pressures from the rural poor	Rapid non-agricultural employment and wage growth, especially in construction and services	Slow-down in modern sector employment growth and wage stagnation	Increase in manufacturing employment around major cities, real wage growth begins again	Slower manufacturing employment growth, continued real wage increase
Industrial relations	Hardly any industrial unrest; launch of cooperative 'Panca sila' framework to reduce conflict	Labour peace followed by increase in strikes 1979–82. Failed attempts to stimulate enterprise bargaining	Some success in attempts to limit labour unrest; widespread military involvement in disputes settlement	Increasing labour unrest from 1990 and continued military involvement in disputes settlement	Continued unrest 1993-4 culminating in Medan riots. Efforts made to limit military involvement in settlement of non-violent disputes

Table 8.1. (*cont.*)

Key areas	1965–73	1973–81	1982–7	1988–92/3	1992/3–5
Trade unions	'Left' oriented unions disbanded, government union (FBSI, later SPSI) formed	SPSI expands but heavily dependent on government support, some industrial branches of union active	Government exerts control over leadership and structure of SPSI through hard-line Minister of Manpower	SPSI becomes less financially dependent on government but by-passed in most labour actions. New union formed (SBM), despite government opposition	Because of domestic pressure and US threat to withdraw GSP trade rights, government does not ban independent unions, but they are not recognised and their leaders harassed
Minimum wages (MW) and labour welfare	Reaffirmation of early labour protection legislation	First regional MW introduced, but ad hoc revisions and implementation	Greater attention to labour controls than labour protection	Revamped wage policy. MW established in all provinces. Comprehensive social security and insurance law passed	Government makes MW a central plank of labour policy

Labour standards

The Soeharto government reaffirmed a commitment to basic labour standards set out in the Basic Laws of the first independent governments and extended legislation in several key areas, including health and safety, workers compensation and insurance and the conclusion of labour agreements.[17] The government also established a framework for setting minimum wages on a provincial basis.

Insurance, including accident and death insurance, and superannuation or provident funds were first regulated for establishments with 25 or more employees through a government insurance fund (ASTEK) set up in 1977. In 1992, the government took a bolder step and introduced a basic law on Worker Social Security (JAMSOSTEK), making it compulsory for all employers to participate in a national social security programme, and broadened it to include health insurance (initially only mandatory in establishments with ten workers or more).[18] Although the law was to be phased in over time, the task is enormous and implementation is problematic for a country at Indonesia's stage of development (McLeod 1993).

A second avenue for protecting workers was envisaged through collective labour agreements. These were given greater encouragement by the Soeharto government than their predecessors. However, because many firms were not unionised and workers were thus unrepresented in negotiations with management,[19] the majority of larger firms drew up company regulations (registered with the Ministry of Manpower) regarding conditions of employment.

The third channel through which the government promised to support labour incomes was minimum wages. Despite pro-labour early governments and an active union movement, minimum wage legislation was not passed until the mid 1970s. when provincial and provincial-sectoral minimum wages were initiated (McCawley and Manning 1976). A provincial focus acknowledged the variation in regional labour markets.[20]

Despite the rhetoric, however, minimum wages remained symbolic

---

[17] Government Regulation No. 14, 1969 provides for detailed legislation in these areas of labour protection.

[18] Total contributions were to amount to approximately 10–12 per cent of wages (depending on the size of health and workers compensation contributions), of which approximately 2 per cent was to be funded by workers and the remaining 8–10 per cent by employers.

[19] Despite pressure from the government, only around 4,000 out of 25,000 eligible companies concluded collective labour agreements in the 1980s. The slow pace of the spread of labour agreements led the Minister of Manpower to streamline legislation in 1986, and to encourage groups of factories in the same industry and location to sign one agreement.

[20] Minimum wages are proposed by the provincial governors (assisted by research councils) and ratified by the Minister of Manpower on the advice of the National Wages Council.

Table 8.2. *Minimum wage, and minimum physical needs (kfm), 1982–1994*

	North Sumatra	Jakarta	West Java	Central Java	South Sulawesi
Minimum wage (rp.)[a]					
1982	700	750	–	625	500
1988	1,200	1,600	750	780	1,000
1992	2,550	2,500	2,100	1,600	1,750
1994	3,750	3,800	3,600	2,700	2,300
CPI (major city, 1990=100)[a]					
1982	54	56	51	49	50
1988	89	92	89	92	84
1992	107	115	116	116	113
1994	126	140	123	129	132
Real minimum wages (1990=100)[b]					
1982	67	64	–	163	100
1988	70	83	71	109	119
1992	123	104	151	177	155
1994	154	129	244	268	174
Minimum wages as a percentage of KFM[c]					
1982	55	60	–	58	63
1988	46	66	31	35	50
1990	69	75	46	31	34
1992	83	75	70	52	50
1994	114	85	83	85	65

Notes: [a] Minimum wage 31 December each year, CPI index for December (1990 = 100); [b] Deflated by the CPI. Minimum is for high wage region in West Java; [c] KFM = Minimum physical needs (annual average except for 1994–January). Assumes 26 day working week. The KFM trends are diverse and have only weak correlation with CPI movements.
Source: Department of Manpower, unpublished data; CBS, Economic indicators, various years.

during the 1970s and 1980s. They were promulgated at different levels in a range of sectors in most provinces but revised irregularly. In many provinces there was a delay of up to three years or more in the revision of nominal wages – by which time the real value of minimum wages was eroded.[21] In real terms, the value of minimum wages declined in the five provinces for which data are available during the 1980s (table 8.2).

The Ministry of Manpower adopted a measure of minimum physical needs as the basic criteria for judging the adequacy of minimum wages.[22] However, in practice, the minimum physical needs measure was not a

[21] By early 1980, only 6 out of 27 provinces had adopted a regional minimum wage, an indication of low priority given to the policy.
[22] Data on minimum physical needs were collected on a quarterly basis in all provinces in Indonesia from the mid 1970s based on 2,100 calorie food consumption, and included basic fuel, housing, clothing and other basic expenditure items (valued at approximately Rp. 80,000–100,000 (US$ 40–50) for a single worker in the early 1990s).

benchmark for government decision-making on minimum wages, amounting to only 50–60 per cent of the minimum wage for a single worker in the same provinces in 1982. The ratio deteriorated in all provinces except Jakarta during the 1980s (table 8.2). More attention was given to the existing wage structure, the employment implications and the capacity to pay.

The industrial relations system in theory and practice

The New Order government was determined to control the trade union movement and minimise labour unrest. Three developments affected industrial relations processes:[23] the destruction of the communist party (PKI) and the ascendancy of the military, the banning of the leftist union (SOBSI) and removal of its leaders from industrial relations, and a severing of ties between unions and political parties (except the ruling GOLKAR party). There was heavy curtailment of labour rights through government controls and military intervention in industrial relations (table 8.1).[24]

After a period of political consolidation, an ideological framework of *panca sila* labour relations was agreed upon by 'approved' union leaders, government and employer representatives to guide labour management relations. Underlying this was a rejection of an adversarial approach to conflict resolution between workers and management. The emphasis was on common goals, cooperation and conciliation based on family principles (*kekeluargaan*). Indonesia followed the international trend towards tripartite and bipartite industrial relations systems and employer and union cooperation (ILO 1985; Marshall 1992).[25]

The Soeharto regime opted for a government-controlled, national trade union organisation, the All-Indonesia Labour Federation, FBSI (later the SPSI) in 1973. It was modelled on national unions in other countries, such as the National Trade Unions Congress in Singapore and the Federation of South Korean Trade Unions. Provincial and district branches of the union were formed, and industrial branches were established to represent workers in economic sectors.[26] The national body was entrusted with a

---

[23] See especially Crouch (1978) for an analysis of political changes in the first decade of the New Order.
[24] Most important among these activities was the vetting of union leaders and officials, detention of labour activists and active participation of military and police in the settlement of disputes.
[25] Tripartite refers to government, employer (organisation) and union cooperation, bipartite to union and employer cooperation.
[26] The industrial branches were disbanded in 1985 and then re-established in 1995, in response to domestic and international criticism of excessive centralisation.

Table 8.3. *Union density in selected East Asian countries, circa 1990 (% unionised)*[a]

Country	All employees	Non-agricultural employees[b]
Singapore	20	20
South Korea	17	17
Malaysia	15	14
Thailand	3	5
Indonesia	4	5

Notes: [a] Percentages of unionised employees to all wage employees. Measured as a share of the total non-agricultural workforce. Since a high proportion of agricultural and non-agricultural workers are self-employed and family workers, union density is more appropriately measured as a share of wage employees; [b] Unionised agricultural workers excluded in the case of Malaysia and Indonesia.
Source: Deery and Mitchell, 1993: pp. 81, 101, 245; Bai Moo Ki, 1993: p. 90; Indonesia, Ministry of Manpower, unpublished data, 1992.

coordination role, determination of policy and support for the establishment of enterprise unions and the completion of collective labour agreements.

Since its establishment in 1973, the SPSI has become a large organisation. Membership amounted to approximately one million in the early 1990s, and unions were represented in approximately one-third of all larger enterprises.[27] However, only around 3–5 per cent of all employees and 5–10 per cent of manufacturing employees were nominal members of a union in the early 1990s, a level of unionisation lower than during the Sukarno period.

Union density, the proportion of workers who were union members, was low even by East Asian standards around 1990, although this is a crude measure of effective labour representation. Among wage employees, union density was around 4–5 per cent compared with 15–20 per cent in neighbouring countries (South Korea, Malaysia and Singapore) (table 8.3).

Extension of labour controls
Promoting the interests of employers and workers depended on the government's willingness to allow the SPSI to develop as an independent body, and resolve disputes on behalf of its members. As in South Korea under Park in the 1970s, neither of these conditions were fulfilled by the

---

[27] The organisation was reported to have over 250 district branches spread throughout the country and approximately 9,000 enterprise units mainly in manufacturing in the early 1990s.

national trade union body. The SPSI emerged as a tool for government control of organised labour, rather than representing workers' interests in negotiations with employers.[28]

The leadership was weakened and its independence compromised from the early years, and it failed to promote labour issues at a national level.[29] Leaders were replaced by appointees more sympathetic to the government and the union's leadership was also closely vetted by the military. A large number of public sector workers, including employees in state enterprises, were excluded from the organisation, weakening its influence in modern manufacturing.

At the enterprise level, some SPSI units were active – especially those in large, established foreign and domestic firms. They negotiated working conditions through collective labour agreements, and represented workers in labour disputes. But many enterprise unions were little more than token labour organisations. Their leaders were appointed by, and came from the ranks of, management, with little support from regional branches. Those represented on the regional board of SPSI were military officials or GOLKAR party members (INDOC 1986: 9).

The SPSI's inability to effectively defend workers in industrial disputes undermined its credibility. Local police and military were actively engaged in dispute settlement, usually at the behest of employers.[30] Dissident workers and strike leaders were detained, interrogated and frequently subjected to physical abuse by the authorities.[31]

Despite all this, the new industrial relations framework was initially successful in achieving labour peace until the 1990s. From the mid 1960s through to 1978 the number of recorded strikes did not exceed 35 in any year (table 8.4).[32]

The number of strikes was tiny compared with the early 1950s, especially given a more than doubling of the industrial workforce by the 1980s. It was smaller than in South Korea or any of the ASEAN countries bar

---

[28] See especially Lambert (1994) for an evaluation of SPSI leadership and its programmes in the early 1990s.
[29] Lubis (1981: 54) coined the phrase *gerakan buruh salon* (freely translated as 'armchair' labour movement) to portray the close relations between labour leaders, business and the government. Another common term was *wakil buruh emplop* ('envelope' unionists) reflecting the pecuniary interests of union leaders in relations with government and business (INDOC 1981: 89).
[30] See especially annual reports of the Indonesian Legal Aid Institute (YLBHI) and of the Dutch based INDOC group (1981–7/8).
[31] The *de facto* military involvement in the settlement of labour disputes was formally sanctioned through Manpower Department ministerial decree (No. 342) passed in 1986.
[32] We use the term strike to describe what might be more appropriately termed protest actions (or *unjuk rasa* in Indonesian) given the short average duration of disputes, usually one day or less, and the fact that most occurred in single enterprises.

Table 8.4. *Selected data on strikes: Indonesia, 1961–1994 (per annum)*

	No. of strikes	No. of workers involved ('000)	No. of working days lost ('000)	% of all strikes in manufacturing
1961–5	40	23	42	34
1966–70	2	(0.4)	(0.4)	20
1971–5	5	1	1	75
1976–80	66	11	28	92
1981–5	112	27	142	87
1986–90	46	13	99	82
1991–4	210	100	998	n.d.
1990	61	31	307	89
1991	114	60	385	96
1992	251	102	1,019	n.d.
1993	185	100	974	n.d.
1994[a]	290	138	1,612	n.d.

Notes: n.d.=no data.
[a] To May 1994.
Sources: ILO, *International Yearbook of Labour Statistics*, various years; Ministry of Manpower, unpublished statistics; Sinaga, 1994, p. 46.

Singapore (table 8.5). Only during 1979–82, did strike action increase significantly in response to a spate of retrenchments and the rising cost of living associated with inflation. Partly in response to actions taken by a new hardline Minister of Manpower, it declined again to low numbers for the rest of the 1980s.[33]

The labour peace did not last into the 1990s, however. Strong criticism emerged, domestically and internationally, regarding the government's labour record, as manufacturing exports took off in the late 1980s. Increased strike activity followed. But rather than the customary clampdown on unions, the government responded with highly publicised efforts to raise labour standards through minimum wages.

Labour policy and industrial relations in the 1990s

There were two important developments in labour policy and industrial relations in the 1990s: an attempt by the government to implement minimum wage policy and substantial labour unrest. Both were mainly the

---
[33] The ex-security chief (KOPKAMTIB) Sudomo was appointed Minister of Manpower in 1983.

Table 8.5. *Strikes in selected countries in Asia, 1961–1993 (average per annum)*

	Indonesia	Thailand	Philippines	Malaysia	South Korea
No. of strikes					
1961–5	40	8	89	71	42
1966–70	2	15	108	55	11
1971–5	5	232	45	65	24
1976–80	66	49	54	40	104
1981–5	112	25	245	24	150
1986–90	46	9	333	13	1,541
1991–3	183	15	147	16	204
No. of strikes per 1,000 non-agricultural workers					
1966–70	0.0	0.5	9.8	10.3	4.1
1976–80	0.6	3.6	4.8	3.8	2.3
1986–90	0.2	0.3	9.3	0.7	28.5
Percentage of strikes in manufacturing					
1966–70	1	26	40	12	47
1976–80	89	79	33	61	85
1986–90	82[a]	99	55	28	46
Total non-agricultural workforce (million)[b]					
1986–90	32	9	11	4	13

Notes: [a] Percentage of strikes (not strikers);
[b] Annual average for period.
Source: ILO, *International Yearbook of Labour Statistics*, various years.

product of two forces: a larger, concentrated, better-educated and volatile workforce, especially around the capital city; and the stagnation of wages in the 1980s. This was accompanied by a belief that workers – the heroes and heroines of Indonesia's success – had been abandoned by the government to whims of market forces. A brief move towards greater political 'openness' (*keterbukaan*) and tolerance of dissent also encouraged labour action.

Dissatisfaction regarding labour standards in the new industries stirred strong nationalist reactions. The issues were raised repeatedly in the press. The views of many are well summed up in comments made by well-known writer and journalist, Mochtar Lubis, who suggested that low wages were an insult (*penghinaan*) to the Indonesians, that the law of comparative advantage was outdated (*kadaluwarsa*) and that the government should raise wages (*Problema*, No. 4 1991: 27). Other commentators have linked the denigration of national pride and standing directly to foreign investment in low-wage industries.[34] Implicit in these comments is

[34] Criticism was levelled at the Investment Coordinating Board for advertising low wages abroad to attract foreign capital (*Kompas*, 27 December 1991).

the belief that wages and working conditions were out of step with income trends in the rest of the country.

This issue was highlighted because of low wages paid in larger-scale firms engaged in exporting, and by some of the new foreign investors from Taiwan and South Korea (see chapter 6). Lower wages paid in foreign firms was a particularly sensitive issue because it was at odds with the experience of higher wages paid by foreign investors in earlier periods.[35] Long hours associated with high capital utilisation – accompanied by harsh labour management practises – added to this negative reaction to the new East Asian investors.[36]

Another factor was the concentration of establishments around the national capital from the late 1980s.[37] The close proximity of a large workforce in manufacturing meant greater exposure of poor wages and working conditions by the media. As middle incomes rose rapidly in Jakarta following deregulation, the news reports highlighted the gap between the wages of factory workers and private sector salaries.

Domestic political developments played a role in directing criticism towards labour conditions in the new industries. The early 1990s were characterised by a move towards political 'openness' (*keterbukaan*) in which labour rights and standards was a subject of heated discussion.[38] Non-governmental organisations also protested at the *de facto* operation of the industrial relations system and poor wages and working conditions.[39] Although political parties played little direct role in supporting labour action, non-government organisations helped inform workers of their rights. In addition, the Commission on Human Rights, formed in 1993, began to examine the issues of legal processes in labour disputes, including events which led to the murder of the labour activist Marsinah.

Patterns of labour unrest

The number of recorded strikes rose in the 1990s, topping 250 in 1992 and 300 in 1994. They culminated in a labour protest and riots claiming several lives, including that of a prominent local businessman, in the North Sumatran city

---

[35] See chapter 6.
[36] Korean managers in particular were criticised for their rough treatment of workers, often involving physical punishment.
[37] The Jakarta and urban West Java share almost doubled to slightly under 20 per cent of total manufacturing employment over the period 1985–90. It was heavily concentrated in the three regions – Tangerang, Bogor and Bekasi – surrounding the capital city.
[38] See Crouch (1992) and Little (1993) on the political climate.
[39] Many of these had become actively engaged in education and support activities among factory workers during the 1980s. Dissatisfied workers continued to take their grievances to the LBH which completed remarkably frank regular reports on the transgression of human rights in cases of labour dispute (see, for example, YLBHI 1991, 1992).

Table 8.6. *Causes of strikes: Indonesia, 1985–1991 (percentage)*

Cause	1985	1986	1987	1988	1989	1990	1991
Wages	58	38	32	61	69	58	67
Annual bonus (THR)[a]	6	26	19	5	–	–	9
Collective labour agreement	4	3	–	–	–	3	2
Formation of union	1	3	8	10	5	6	8
Social insurance	–	3	–	3	–	2	5
Other working conditions[b]	30	27	41	21	26	31	9
Total	100	100	100	100	100	100	100
N=	78	73	37	39	19	61	113

Notes: [a] Tunjangan Hari Raya (Idul Fitri allowance), the annual bonus for most workers;
[b] Including dismissals.
Source: Ministry of Manpower, unpublished data.

of Medan in April 1994. The involvement of the opposition union SBSI and its leader Muchtar Pakpahan, in the labour action hardened the resolve of the government in opposition to recognition of independent unions.[40]

Most of the strikes were smaller than the Medan affair. In many cases, stop-work action took a specific form. Lack of confidence in the SPSI caused protesters to bypass the normal industrial relations procedures to seek assistance from the national or regional parliaments or from the Legal Aid Institute. Strikes or *unjuk rasa* rarely lasted more than two days, although protracted 'negotiations' often occurred between management and labour representatives.[41]

A high proportion of the strikes occurred in manufacturing, and near Jakarta.[42] Many were in the export-oriented industries, especially the low-wage textiles, clothing and footwear industries (Manning 1993). Low wages and non-compliance with minimum wage regulations were the cause of most strikes (table 8.6),[43] especially in major cities where workers

---

[40] Some observers have argued that the government deliberately allowed the dispute – which began over bonus payments in one firm – to get out of hand, and thus provide it with ammunition to discredit and detain Muchtar and many of the SBSI leaders.
[41] Unpublished Ministry of Manpower data indicate an average duration of stop work action of nine hours in Jakarta and surrounding areas in 1991.
[42] Approximately 20–30 per cent of recorded strikes occurred in Jakarta and 40–50 per cent in West Java, mainly in the JABOTABEK region, and a further 10–20 per cent but rising share in the East Java industrial belt (Ministry of Manpower 1993: 33).
[43] This was especially so in 1994 when the government phased in minimum wage increases across all provinces. The increases were larger than in previous years and brought in earlier, at relatively short notice on 1 January, in the sensitive Jakarta and West Java regions. The large majority of all strikes occurred in the first three months of that year, and the intensity of strike action declined significantly after the Medan affair in April.

had a greater knowledge of regulations. Labour rights disputes, especially over the formation of trade unions, were also important.

In response to the unrest, the government liberalised some aspects of industrial relations practices in the 1990s in response to increasing domestic and international criticism of labour rights. Some of the restrictions on national union registration were removed. Company unions not affiliated with the government-backed SPSI could be registered, although they were urged to join the SPSI.[44] Employers involved in a labour dispute were no longer formally encouraged to coordinate with local security forces.[45]

A new policy towards minimum wages

Partly in response to domestic pressure to revise labour policies, the government responded with new minimum wage initiatives, despite the general move towards deregulation in other markets.

New legislation required regular revision of regional minimum wages to meet minimum physical needs in each province. The appointment of businessman Abdul Latief as Minister of Manpower, in 1993, led to large increases in minimum wages in all provinces – on average, by just under one-third in 1994 and by 21 per cent in 1995. The latter took effect in all provinces at the beginning of the budget year in April. This was no small achievement, given that minimum wages still had to be proposed by provincial governors, approved by the National Wages Council and ratified by the Minister. An associated regulation issued in 1994 required firms with 25 employees or more to pay an annual bonus to all workers equivalent to one month's wage.[46]

These developments indicated a new phase of government attempts to raise labour earnings directly and to remove one of the causes of industrial unrest. Real minimum wages rose by approximately 15 per cent in real terms nationally and by 10–20 per cent in most provinces (Jakarta 12 per cent) during 1988–94 (see table 8.2 above). This included a 25 per cent real increase in the rapidly industrialising districts of West Java surrounding Jakarta and in Bandung over the six-year period, and smaller rises in the

---

[44] By the mid 1990s, the Ministry of Manpower had registered over 1,000 new, independent enterprise unions. New unions were now only obliged to establish 100 company branches and five provincial branches to meet registration requirements.
[45] The controversial Ministerial Decision No. 342 which had supported military intervention in disputes was rescinded.
[46] The bonus had been customary in many firms, and encouraged by the authorities on a voluntary basis in previous years. The Head of the Employer's Association (APINDO) opposed the mandatory payment of bonuses and complained that the decision had been taken without consultation with employers (*Jakarta Post*, 22 September 1995).

Table 8.7. *Average annual growth of labour productivity and average earnings in manufacturing, and minimum wages: Indonesia, 1978–1992*

	1978–88	1988–92	1992–5
Labour productivity[a]	15.0	15.5	n.d.
Average earnings[b]	15.4	16.6	n.d.
Minimum wages			
Jakarta	13.0	11.2	20.3
Indonesia[c]	9.6[c]	15.1	19.7

Notes: [a] Large and medium establishments; [b] Unweighted mean of provincial minimum wages; [c] Four provinces (Jakarta, Central Java, North Sumatra, South Sulawesi).
Source: CBS, Statistical Yearbook, 1993. Ministry of Manpower, unpublished data.

other, traditionally low-wage provinces in Java. The range between the highest- and lowest-wage provinces also narrowed.[47]

Whereas average earnings and productivity growth in manufacturing outstripped that of minimum wages from 1978 to 1988, the situation changed subsequently. In the years 1988–92, the increase in real minimum wages (national average) was similar to the growth rate in average wages and productivity in manufacturing (around 15 per cent per annum) (table 8.7). After 1992, national minimum wages increased more rapidly (20 per cent per annum), and probably outstripped productivity increases.

The impact of minimum wages

Unless enforced, minimum wages have little impact on the labour market, as has been the experience in many developing countries (Watanabe 1976; ILO 1989). Their impact depends on three key variables: the relationship of minimum wages to average wages, the distribution of wages (in particular industries and regions) and implementation of the minimum wages law.

Minimum wage rates were still considerably lower than the average earnings of wage workers in Indonesia in 1992. Minimum wages were

---

[47] The legal minimum in the high-wage provinces, which was more than twice that in the Java provinces in 1988, fell to 60 per cent above those in the low-wage provinces in 1995. The coefficient of variation in legal minimum wages across 26 provinces halved from 0.31 to 0.15 over the period 1988–95.

around 50–60 per cent of average wages of all wage workers, and 60–80 per cent of average wages of less-educated and younger workers in the textile, clothing and footwear industries. It was a lower proportion of average wages in all industries in 1992 (table 8.8). Assuming that overtime and other emoluments not included in the basic pay package accounted for around 20 per cent of the workers earnings, the minimum was probably around 10 per cent above average basic earnings in the TFC industries and perhaps 20–30 per cent higher in all industries.

High statutory minimum wages relative to average earnings is not unusual in early stages of development (World Bank 1995: 75). Nevertheless, the gap between the average and minimum wage was already considerably smaller in Indonesia in 1992 than that recorded in several other developing countries, where minimum wages were typically only 20–30 per cent of average earnings.[48] A significant proportion of employees (30–40 per cent) in manufacturing earned close to or less than the minimum in the same year. This was especially the case in relatively industrialised East Java. Also it is instructive that average wages were not significantly lower in rural Java than in the major urban centres. Hence the minimum wage, insofar as it was implemented outside the cities, was likely to place pressure on basic wages in these regions also.

The stated goal of government policy has been to raise the average level of wages in the majority of enterprises, rather than ensure that lagging establishments come closer to the average. While the impact on average wages might have been limited in 1990, the impact began to have much greater effect by the mid 1990s. By 1994, minimum wages were on a par with average wages in lower wage industries and exceeded average wages among younger, less-educated females (Manning and Jayasuriya 1996).

Implementation

Unlike in the past, when the government had paid lip service to minimum wages, the policy was pursued earnestly, and received public backing from the President. The government took court action against several hundred firms for paying less than the minimum wage.[49] The fines were ridiculously small as a deterrent, but managers suffered the

---

[48] Agrawal (1995: 17) cites a World Bank study which estimated that the minimum wage ranged from 13–25 per cent of average earnings in Korea, Chile and Mexico in the early 1990s.
[49] Although there was evidence of lack of compliance. The Ministry of Manpower found most larger firms paid the minimum wage in Jakarta, but a smaller proportion did so in other Java cities of Bandung and Solo in 1990–2. The SPSI, however, claimed that the majority of larger firms broke the law in Jakarta in 1990.

Table 8.8. *Comparison of minimum wages and average wages in selected industries and regions: Indonesia, 1992*

Industry/Region	Legal minimum	Daily wage (Rp.) All workers	Daily wage (Rp.) Less educated, aged <30[a]	Minimum as a % of average wage All workers	Minimum as a % of average wage Less educated, aged <30[a]	% Workers earning <minimum wage (less educated, aged <30)[a]
1 Textiles, footwear & clothing						
Jakarta	2,500	5,362	3,684	47	68	12
Botabek[b]	2,100	3,940	3,200	53	66	10
Bandung	2,100	3,578	2,960	59	83	19
Central Java cities[c]	1,600	3,214	2,260	50	71	17
Surabaya & environs	2,250	2,933	2,054	77	110	38
Major Sumatran cities[d]	1,600–2,550	3,889	3,186	51	53	n.d.
2 All manufacturing						
Jakarta	2,500	7,603	3,534	33	71	14
Botabek[b]	2,100	5,353	3,368	39	62	11
Bandung	2,100	4,376	2,956	48	71	23
Central Java Cities[c]	1,600	4,577	2,184	35	73	16
Surabaya & environs	2,250	5,170	2,614	44	86	24
Major Sumatran cities[d]	1,600–2,550	5,690	3,431	35	58	10
Rural West Java	1,900	3,556	2,857	53	67	26
Rural Central Java	1,600	3,828	2,318	42	69	27
Rural East Java	2,100	3,025	2,178	69	96	49

Notes: [a] Proxy for unskilled labour, lower secondary educated or below; [b] Three districts adjacent to Jakarta; [c] Solo, Semarang and Yogyakarta; [d] Medan, Padang and Palembang.
Sources: CBS, National Labour Force Survey, 1992; Ministry of Manpower, unpublished data.

embarrassment or time-consuming process of attending civil courts to answer for breaches.[50]

From 1993, the Ministry of Manpower, aided by the military, mounted a spirited campaign to ensure that larger establishments adhered to the new minimum wage.[51] Violations of minimum wages were widely publicised in the media and a series of enterprise level protests drew attention to recalcitrants (Manning 1993).

In 1994 and 1995, the Minister for Manpower refused requests from business groups for dispensation or postponement of implementation in key industries, especially the garments industry which had been struggling to maintain growth from 1993.[52] Although the military had a reputation for involvement in disputes on the side of employers, it was now called on to support government minimum wage policy by helping in the interests of keeping the peace. The Medan riots of 1994 were regarded as a warning of the potential for unrest if labour demands were not taken seriously. In the Jakarta region, the military began to work with manpower officials to ensure that minimum wages were implemented.

By 1995 implementation appears to have been quite widespread in larger establishments and in the regions near Jakarta. Nevertheless, the potential impact of the legislation on wages and employment needs to be qualified. There were still reports of widespread non-compliance outside the Jakarta region.[53] Only establishments with 25 workers or more were targeted by the government (although the legislation applies to all establishments), leaving out around half of the industrial workforce. As in other countries, it is inevitable that firms tried to bypass legislation by adopting different labour recruitment strategies – increasing sub-contracting arrangements with smaller firms and utilising home-workers through putting-out arrangements (Manning and Jayasuriya 1996).

Increasing labour regulation in an era of deregulation

It might seem surprising that the government opted for increasing labour regulation through minimum wages precisely at a time when it was endeavouring to deregulate the economy. It had largely ignored calls for

---

[50] Transgressors incurred a fine of Rp. 100,000 (approximately $50), or received a short prison term.
[51] A coordinating group which included elements of the police and military was established in 1995 to ensure peaceful implementation of the new wage levels.
[52] The textile producer's association, API, in particular made strong representations for a special dispensation in early 1995.
[53] One survey in East Java in 1994 reported that 86 per cent of a sample of firms broke the law, a finding which was vigorously denied by the Ministry of Manpower (*Business Indonesia*, 1 October 1994).

minimum wages throughout the 1970s and 1980s, at times when there had been much stronger calls for government intervention in the economy. There was unqualified public support for the new policies – including from influential Indonesian economists – even though earlier experience in the NIEs suggested that deregulated labour markets contributed to economic growth and rising labour incomes.

The revamped minimum wage policy can be partly understood in the context of an increasing domestic and international focus on labour rights. Minimum wage policy was supported partly as a trade-off for government intransigence concerning union freedoms, as evidence of its commitment to labour welfare.

The threat to withdraw GSP rights
Greater international scrutiny of Indonesia's labour record began with the opening up of the economy in the 1980s. Although there was foreign criticism of Indonesia's record at the ILO annual meetings in Geneva during the 1980s, formal complaints were first issued by two major international bodies in 1987–8.[54] Repeated, strongly worded criticism of Indonesia's labour rights record was clearly embarrassing to the government.[55] One issue in particular which received much international attention in 1993–5 was the brutal murder of Marsinah, an informal labour leader from an East Java factory, in May 1993, and subsequent torture and jailing of company officials on what appeared to be trumped-up charges to cover up for alleged military involvement in the crime.[56]

The United States government announced in June 1993 that renewal of GSP (General System of Preference) rights – special trade access to a selected number of commodities to the United States market – would be made contingent on improvement in Indonesia's labour record.[57] The United States government sent teams of investigators to Indonesia in

---

[54] First was from the conservative International Confederation of Free Trade Unions (ICFTU) regarding trade union freedoms and second (resubmitted in 1988–91) from the AFL-CIO (The American Federation of Labor and Congress of Industrial Organisations) petitioning the US Trade Representative to remove Indonesia's GSP special tariff concession privileges because of its poor record on worker rights (INDOC 1989: 1).

[55] For example, in a statement from the ILO governing body in 1995, Indonesia was named – together with El Salvador and Peru – as one country involved in 'grave violations' of workers' human rights, including assassinations, torture and arbitrary detentions (*Jakarta Post*, 29 April 1995).

[56] Marsinah became a symbol of Indonesia's labour struggle among groups of labour activists, and belatedly also by the official union, SPSI.

[57] The main charges were contained in an initial petition to the US government which questioned Indonesia's labour record in all five areas under which the US government could withhold GSP trade preferences: absence of the right to organise and bargain effectively, employment of prison and child labour and inadequate labour standards.

1993–4 and continued to pressure Indonesia, although it seemed most unlikely that it would follow through with the threat of withdrawing GSP preferences.

Potentially, the direct economic costs from withdrawal of GSP preferences were small, even though the US government also threatened to withdraw investment insurance guaranteed to United States companies operating abroad by OPIC (The Overseas Private Investment Corporation).[58]

Nevertheless, the Indonesian government took the United States threat seriously.[59] Although it rejected any link between labour reforms and GSP, several industrial relations reforms and hikes in wages were introduced one month before the United States government was to announce a decision on GSP access in February 1994. The United States government, and associated human rights activists and protection lobbyists, can claim some credit – or blame if unemployment should rise – for Indonesia's new policy on minimum wages.

The challenge from independent unions

In the 1970s and 1980s, there had been no challenge to the SPSI as the only recognised union in the country, owing to tight political controls and little international exposure of Indonesia's labour record. International attention focussed more on countries in Latin America and the NIEs, the latter increasingly fanned by protectionist interests in the USA (Park 1986).

This situation changed in the 1990s with the emergence of rival union groups, first the SBM (*Serikat Buruh Merdeka*) and then the SBSI (*Serikat Buruh Sejahtera Indonesia*). From the outset the SPSI was registered to represent workers at a national and regional level. While international focus on labour rights precluded outright bans, the government gave the rival organisations no support.[60] The SBSI, under the leadership of the resourceful Muchtar Pakpahan, cleverly exploited the government's dilemma. Taking advantage of the US spotlight on labour issues, he challenged the credibility of the official union SPSI, through criticism of labour rights and standards in 1993–4, including demands for an increase in the minimum wage to Rp.7,500 per day, well over twice the prevailing rate in most provinces. In February 1994, Muchtar called the first (rather unsuccessful)

---

[58] Indonesian products sold according to GSP preferences accounted for slightly over 10 per cent of total exports to that country, or only around 3–4 per cent of total non-oil exports in 1993. The average tariff on products listed for GSP rights averaged only around 5 per cent.
[59] See especially *Warta Ekonomi*, 16 August 1993: 16–20.
[60] One potential threat has been the alliance between students and workers which was so successful in some other countries such as Korea. Several student groups announced their support for SPSI in 1993–4.

general strike held in Indonesia under the New Order as a gesture of no-confidence in the government's record.

In part, the government and military ostensibly opposed independent unions on the grounds that multiple unionism would threaten economic stability, pointing to the experience of the Seokarno era. It also stressed the danger posed by radical unions for political stability. The arguments of stressing economic disruption were far fetched, especially given the economic success of neighbouring countries with greater union freedoms, and in the light of the contribution of unions to productivity gains in countries like Malaysia (Standing 1992). Even before 1965, union contribution to economic disruption was small. It is likely to have been an issue of importance in the more competitive environment of the 1990s.

The government was concerned about the potential political challenge posed by Muchtar and the SBSI. The attempts to form rival unions in 1992–3 met with strong opposition, including harassment and imprisonment of union leaders, and the frequent disruption of meetings by security forces.[61] Despite domestic and international criticism, Muchtar was detained several times – once on the eve of the planned general strike – and he and key officials were sentenced to prison terms on charges of masterminding the Medan riots. However, given continuing public focus on labour issues through 1993–4, the government had to be seen to be taking steps to improve the situation. The challenge posed by SBSI was, indirectly, a contributing factor to the evolution of the minimum wage policy in the 1990s.

Government justification for minimum wages

Four explanations were given by the high profile Minister of Manpower for increased minimum wages (*Kompas*, 22 and 23 March 1994). First, higher wages were required to raise labour productivity. It was argued that the productivity of Indonesian workers was low because of short-sighted management practices and low-wage policies.[62]

Second, it was argued that labour costs are a small proportion of total costs, generally much less than 10 per cent even in low-wage industries. Minister Latief in 1994 is quoted as saying, 'This isn't right . . . It's too small' and later, in 1995, of increases of around 10–20 per cent 'The increase . . . will only add an estimated 1 per cent to any given company's total production costs. This will certainly not impose an undue burden on our

---

[61] The SBM broke up in 1992–3 partly as a result of pressure from the government and partly because of internal conflicts.
[62] This point is argued cogently by economist Dr Djisman Simanjuntak in an interview in the Asian *Wall Street Journal*, 19 May 1994.

industrial sector.'⁶³ On this reasoning, increases in minimum wages even of the order of 20–60 per cent per annum in 1994 would only increase total costs by around 2–6 per cent. The low share of labour costs to total costs, it was argued, contributed to a relatively inelastic labour demand curve. Increased wages would have little negative impact on employment, especially since large-scale and foreign firms were assumed to earn substantial profits which could be squeezed without affecting performance.

Third, it was also argued widely that various irregular and illegal charges (*pungli*) paid by firms were a major cause of high costs, and increased minimum wages would force establishments to conserve on these. The mechanism by which rent-seekers would accept a redistribution of their income to wage workers was not spelt out – perhaps through moral suasion combined with tougher bargaining by employers with bureaucrats.[64]

Finally, the government argued that minimum wage policies would stimulate economic activity through a spending effects flow which would benefit relatively small and informal sector establishments. Since the income elasticity of demand for food and basic needs produced locally was estimated to be high, the minimum wage policy would have a strong multiplier effect on employment.[65]

There are problems associated with these arguments. Increased minimum wages cannot be justified as a 'first-best' policy to overcome problems of low productivity and the prevalence of *pungli*, or to stimulate employment through increased spending among wage workers. Achievement of higher labour productivity depends on improvement in management, skills, and physical inputs and commitment on the part of workers. Only the latter may be affected by increased wages. The low-wage–low-productivity argument also rests on the assumption that employers are irrational in following low-wage policies, or that monopsony conditions exist which enable them to depress wages below market levels. Such arguments may be relevant, but are hard to sustain when applied to the situation in the new export industries. Many firms in these industries were concentrated in several large labour market areas where

---

[63] *Jakarta Post* (15 January 1994: 2, and 11 January 1995: 2).
[64] Critics of minimum wage policy might equally argue exactly the opposite, that increased government intervention in wage-setting mechanisms would actually increase *pungli* going to Ministry of Manpower officials and the military.
[65] The Director General for Industrial Relations heroically estimated that the new policy would increase the 'money in circulation' by around Rp. 18 trillion (around $7 billion) or more than total annual spending on civil personnel in the 1994/5 budget. Assuming generously that around 20 million wage workers outside agriculture increased their spending by Rp. 1000 per month, the first round effect of the increase would be approximately Rp. 20 billion or $9 million a month.

labour mobility was often high, and workers were well aware of alternative wage opportunities (Lok 1993).

The low share of labour in total costs can contribute to relatively inelastic labour demand curves. But, with a given technology and requirement of intermediate inputs, the ratio of labour costs to total value-added is a more relevant indicator of enterprise response to wage increases. Wage costs typically amount to approximately 20–30 per cent of value-added in relatively labour-intensive establishments. An increase in minimum wages of 20 per cent will thus raise costs by 3–6 per cent. Given the competitive nature of the labour-intensive export-oriented industries – in contrast to protected capital and resource-based industries – it is difficult to argue that substantial minimum wage increases will not affect output, investment and employment.

Impact of the minimum wage policy

Indonesia has taken a big gamble in following a concerted policy to raise minimum wages. Given the increased expectations of wage workers for continued increases in the future – at the very least in line with cost of living increases – there is little likelihood that the policy could be reversed in the medium term. Unlike in Japan, South Korea or Taiwan, there is no tradition of belt-tightening in difficult years, or a flexible wage system which rewards labour generously through increased annual bonuses in good years. So far, the major goal of the minimum wage policy has been to achieve parity with minimum physical needs. There are however strong pressures for the government to go beyond this indicator as a standard on which to base minimum wage policy.[66] Future governments may well be unable to resist pressures for further large increases.

In the mid 1990s, it was too early to estimate the overall effects on employment. Given the low levels of labour productivity relative to that of neighbouring countries, the government hopes that higher wages will force gains in productivity. Tighter labour markets appear to have contributed to substantial wage growth in the first half of the 1990s, thus lessening the potentially negative impact of minimum wages on employment (Manning and Jayasuriya 1996). Minimum wages have probably mainly affected establishments which pay wages at the lower end of the earnings distribution.

However, while there is scope for productivity gains from changes in

---

[66] It is argued the basket of goods which form the basis for the calculation of the minimum physical needs is out of date and should be reviewed, at least to provide a wage closer to the similar, but higher-value minimum 'living' needs (KHM).

management practices, the improvements would be unlikely to compensate for wage growth in most regions in 1994–5. There were some disquieting signs. Complaints were made by textile exporters in 1995, who faced increasingly stiff competition from Vietnam and China. They complained that a cost–price squeeze in some product runs was partly influenced by minimum wages. One large domestic footwear exporter which reported record profits in 1993, estimated that these could be halved in 1994, because of the near doubling of the minimum wage in regions close to Jakarta, even through market prospects were bright (*Kompas*, 16 June 1994). The decline in the rate of growth in garments and footwear exports in 1993 and the first half of 1994 was probably influenced by minimum wage increases.[67]

Other indirect evidence comes from a fall-off in foreign investment in several key export-oriented industries. This was particularly evident among South Korean investors. There was a sharp dip in the large South Korean investment in garments and footwear – the two biggest of the rapidly growing labour-intensive export industries – in the mid 1990s. South Korean investors accounted for half the number of projects from the newly industrialised economies and a slightly smaller share of all foreign investment approved by the Foreign Investment Board in these two industries in 1990–2.[68] The percentage of South Korean projects fell to closer to 10 per cent in the subsequent two years.[69]

Labour controls and state paternalism

To what extent does Indonesia fit the model of wage repression, especially bearing in mind the relative stagnation in wages during the 1980s? At first glance the stylised facts appear to fit the model. One might draw parallels between the circumstances behind the rash of strikes in Indonesia in the 1990s, and the much larger outbreak of labour unrest and associated wage demands which led to liberalisation of industrial relations in South Korea in 1987. Strikes in Indonesia could be attributed to two decades of tight controls over organised labour as workers sought to raise wages in line

---

[67] The Minister of Manpower indirectly recognised these problems when in 1995 he suggested that textile producers who faced difficulties in paying the minimum wages in Jakarta move to lower-wage regions of Java (*Jakarta Post*, 14 February 1995).

[68] Based on unpublished data from the Investment Coordinating Board (the author is grateful to Haryo Aswicahyona for help in obtaining the data). The above figures include approvals for new projects and for the extension of existing projects. Korean investment was also dominant in value terms.

[69] As a result, the total number of foreign projects approved in these two industries also fell – from an average of 40 in 1990–1 to closer to 20 each year in 1993–4. Domestic circumstances in South Korea and the targeting of South Korean firms by labour activists probably also affected this slide.

with market conditions. This interpretation is consistent with stagnant real wages and rapid growth in labour productivity which outpaced earnings in manufacturing throughout the 1980s.

Nevertheless, the wage repression model does not altogether fit the Indonesian case. First, non-agricultural wages rose rapidly in the earlier period of the 1970s, despite tight labour controls, and the increases were on a par with labour productivity growth in manufacturing (chapter 5). At the same time, real wage rates stagnated in rice agriculture. Urban wage growth was faster than might have been expected from underlying labour market conditions.

Second, the brake on wage growth in the 1980s was mainly the result of slower economic growth in the post oil-boom. The government extended controls over trade unions in the mid 1980s at a time when real wages had already begun to stagnate in manufacturing and construction.

In this period, increased labour controls were related to several factors: labour unrest at the beginning of the decade, the economic slow down and the government's goal of attracting investment into export-oriented sectors. The major concern was the investment climate and employment during the years of recession, not the level of wages. The threat of wage growth was not a serious consideration – except perhaps in the months immediately following the devaluation in 1983. Thus, restrictions were mainly aimed at maintaining security and supporting economic recovery.

Contrary to popular opinion and the findings of some case studies, wages were not generally lower in the new centres of exporting or in relatively labour-intensive export-oriented industries. In the growth areas close to Jakarta (BOTABEK) and Surabaya, wages in TFC industries were higher than in the traditional centres of manufacturing in other parts of Java, and generally higher than in the largely domestic-oriented food processing industries (table 8.9). The workforce was also better educated.

State paternalism: political masterstroke but economic question-mark

Indonesia followed the East Asian model of tight controls over trade unions and industrial relations processes. However, a heavy commitment to minimum wages was a radical departure from the policies of its successful neighbours – with the exception of Singapore and, to a lesser extent, Thailand. It is a high-risk strategy for a country where employment growth in non-agricultural sectors depends on the expansion of labour-intensive industries which, in turn, are partly dependant on labour cost advantages. Sustained income growth is still heavily influenced by the transfer of workers from low-productivity agriculture into new industries.

Table 8.9. *Characteristics of manufacturing employees in major regions: Indonesia, 1990*

	Jakarta & district[a]	Surabaya & district[b]	Bandung & district[c]	Major central Java cities[d]	Other Java	Other	Total
% of all manufacturing employees	21	10	7	6	30	26	100
Distribution by main sector (%)							
Food/beverages	8	24	4	32	27	17	19
Textiles/footwear	37	20	65	32	29	8	27
Chemicals, metals, mach.	49	42	28	29	27	32	34
Other	6	14	3	7	17	43	20
Total	100	100	100	100	100	100	100
Personal characteristics of employees							
% aged <25 years	37	38	35	33	42	39	39
% female	27	40	32	46	39	23	34
% >primary schooling	66	49	43	40	29	46	45
% working 55 hours+	8	16	14	11	24	23	18
Earnings of less educated[e]							
% earning < Rp 250/hr[f]	16	48	39	63	56	27	40
Mean (Rp '000/month)							
All sectors	94	63	67	50	67	85	81
Food/beverages	74	54	50	42	51	63	54
Textiles/footwear	91	56	67	50	45	58	63
Chemicals, metals, mach.	102	73	74	61	94	86	88

Notes: [a] Jakarta, Bogor, Tangerang and Bekasi (Jabotabek); [b] Surabaya, Malang, Mojokerto and Gresik; [c] Bandung City and District (*kabupaten*); [d] Semarang, Solo, Yogyakarta, Kudus, Tegal, Pekalongan; [e] Lower secondary school and below; [f] US$1.00 = Rp 1,900.
Source: CBS, National Labour Force Survey, 1990, data tape.

Why, then has the government moved in this direction at this critical juncture in economic transformation? Aside from disappointment with wage growth, it was a strategy aimed at defusing the issue of union freedoms and labour rights by indicating that the government was capable of delivering real gains to wage workers, even in the absence of free trade unions.

The political strategy aimed at defusing labour unrest may well have been masterly in the short term, given the apparent decline in strike activity in 1995.[70] There are however flaws in arguments which stress low wage rates as an indicator of lack of progress in labour welfare, either relative to

---
[70] After a year of record strike activity in 1994, only 31 strikes were officially recorded in the first five months of 1995 compared with 225 over the same period in the previous year (*Jakarta Post*, 27 May 1995: 1).

Table 8.10. *Monthly wages and per-capita incomes: selected East Asian economies, 1990*

	Index monthly wages (general workers)	(Indonesia=1.0) GDP/capita[a]
Singapore	11.4	19.6
Hong Kong	14.2	20.2
South Korea	9.5	9.5
Malaysia	3.9	4.1
Thailand	3.0	2.5
Philippines	2.3	1.3
Indonesia	1.0	1.0
China	1.0[b]	0.7

Notes: [a] Converted from *national currencies* according to the prevailing nominal exchange rate. GDP data calculated on a PPP basis to give a much higher relative GDP figure for Indonesia; [b] Southeast regions.
Sources: Data on Wage Rates: James Abeggleu, *Sea Change: Pacific Asia as the New World Industrial Centre*, Free Press, New York, p. 140. GDP per-capita data from World Bank, *World Development Report 1992*.

equivalent workers in neighbouring countries, or compared with other groups in Indonesia. The stage of development in Indonesia compared with other countries has necessarily meant that wage rates have risen faster in the latter. But in relation to GDP, per-capita, unskilled wage rates in Indonesia were not significantly lower than those in neighbouring countries, except the Philippines, in the early 1990s (table 8.10).

While the unit price of unskilled labour in labour-intensive industries stagnated, average earnings rose in the 1980s. The incomes of poorer sections of the community increased through the transfer of labour to new industries (Huppi and Ravallion 1991). The gap in labour incomes between agricultural and non-agricultural workers was still large and labour was utilised much more intensively in new non-agricultural industries.

Increased minimum wages deflected criticism away from the apparent government neglect of worker welfare, but it may have exacerbated inequality. If the hoped-for gains in labour productivity are not realised, fewer workers will gain access to new jobs in export-oriented industries. Those displaced will place pressure on wage rates in small-scale firms and the informal sector not covered by the legislation.

One caveat is necessary. The impact of government labour market intervention on employment and economic performance is an issue of debate among economists. Empirical research mainly in developed countries has questioned the assumed inverse relationship between minimum wages and employment.[71] Freeman (1992: 139–40) in his survey of the evidence in support of either the interventionist or deregulated labour market approach (ILO versus the World Bank prescriptions) found to his surprise that 'studies designed to support the distortionist (i.e., pro-deregulation) view of labor markets in developing countries failed to make a stronger case than they did'.

In part, the lack of a clear negative association between intervention and economic performance has been attributed to the flexibility of enforcement mechanisms.[72] Political considerations – the need for the government to be seen to be concerned with worker welfare, regardless of the outcome – have been as important as economic factors in ensuring continuation of interventionist policies. At the same time, there are obvious examples of adverse effects on employment and unemployment in countries where the minimum wages and standards have been enforced in the modern sector, such as in Papua New Guinea and Puerto Rico, or Singapore in the early 1980s.

These considerations seem relevant to the case of Indonesia. Some positive impact on labour productivity can be expected to result from the minimum wage policy, given the very low level of wages. Moreover, the impact of minimum wages may not be as severe as some anticipate, given the apparent tightening of labour markets and rise in the real earnings of casual workers in the early 1990s. It is doubtful, however, whether these developments will be sufficient to outweigh the potentially negative effects on employment.

Indonesia may well have chosen the worst option in its mix of labour protection and industrial relations. Based on a survey of international experience, the World Bank (1995: 86) argues that a free environment for union organisations and encouragement of enterprise bargaining is probably the best combination of policies to enhance productivity in rapidly industrialising economies:

> In the absence of free unions and collective bargaining, many governments feel obliged to reach out to formal sector workers through labour regulation and special privileges. This is especially true when the government needs the political support of strong urban groups in order to remain in power. One result is that labor market distortions are particularly severe in many countries that repressed labor unions.

The case of Indonesia is not mentioned in the report, but it could have been.

---

[71] See especially Card and Krueger (1994) and Dickens, Machin and Manning (1993).
[72] Further, referring to adjustment programmes in the 1980s, Freeman concluded that many labour markets were flexible enough to overcome inefficient interventions: 'many distortions were paper tigers when the crunch time came'.

9

More women in the workforce: regress or progress?

> But it seems to be a general rule in all developing economies . . . that men are quicker than women to change over from traditional to modern type occupations . . . we find more women in the bazaar and service sector than in the modern sector . . . . With economic development there is a proportional increase in the total labour force employed in the modern sector, while employment in agriculture and in some of the bazaar and service occupations declines (Boserup 1970: 184, 185).
>
> [Yet] the realities of rapid economic development have allocated the nooks and crevices to women, making it difficult for them to hold their share of productive life, defined as the ability to earn cash. (Heyzer 1989: 1109)
>
> Women in developing countries are often overrepresented in the informal sector and are so eager for jobs in the modern sector that they willingly ignore an employer's failure to implement government-legislated standards . . . . It appears, therefore, that women as a group gain much more from better access to modern sector jobs than from special standards to protect those who already have good employment. (World Bank 1995a: 73)

How have women fared in the Indonesian labour market, given the tremendous changes which have occurred over the past 30 years? Female participation, especially in modern sectors and skilled jobs, increased markedly both absolutely and relative to males. Nevertheless women's wages and working conditions are far from ideal, and often worse than males. Some of the wage and job discrimination problems which have plagued other East Asian economies are also apparent in Indonesia.

Identifying and explaining variations in female participation, occupations and wages is a major challenge for all labour market studies (Durand 1975). Boserup's (1970) study of the role of women in development emphasises discontinuity in female participation associated with the transformation from rural, agricultural to urban, industrial societies.[1] Participation tended to fall as women found it difficult to compete with males in urban labour markets. Involvement rose again as education and associated

---

[1] For a more recent statement of the hypothesis see Psacharopolous and Tzannatos (1989).

232 Labour market structure and institutions

demographic changes supported increased participation. Yet Boserup and others have noted that this tendency is not universal: urban participation rates have been much higher in some regions (Latin America and Southeast Asia) than in others. Substantial intra-regional and within country variation are also observed.

Overall participation rates rose sharply in East Asia as economic growth accelerated (Jones 1984, Khoo 1987 and Heyzer 1989). Nevertheless, the consensus has been that women have not gained much. Heyzer notes that poorer Asian women wage-earners have often been bypassed in economic development programmes. They are discriminated against in competition with males for jobs by credentialism. They are more vulnerable to technological change and have been discriminated against in wage contracts. Similarly Lim (1993) argues that women have been much more adversely affected by structural adjustment policies and industrialisation.

Other studies have emphasised that even with education, women tend to crowd into certain jobs because of enduring values regarding appropriate womens' work and because of employer discrimination (Anker and Hein 1986; Standing 1989). In the modern sector, more educated women tend to be heavily overrepresented in lower level professional occupations, such as primary school teaching, nursing and midwifery. Opportunities for advancement are blocked by their concentration in jobs with little prospect of skill improvement or promotion (Standing 1981). In part, as in industrial economies, the problem is related to the gender gap in human capital and experience. Females with the same human capital characteristics and experience are discriminated against in wage contracts. This is explained partly by social attitudes, and partly by statistical discrimination which attributes to all women qualities which employers perceive as pertaining to women as a group, regardless of individual differences (Anker and Hein 1986).

Few studies of female employment agree with the quotation from the World Bank Development Report regarding the gains from modern sector employment, which draws on research among Bangladeshi women employed in garments industries. Rather, they stress low wages and unstable employment, long hours of work and other abuses of the labour code in the modern manufacturing firms, such as electronics and garments. Quoting from Deyo (1989: 8) on the NIEs:

> East Asian development has centred until recently on rapid growth in light, labour-intensive export manufacturing. The attraction of young, low-skilled, and often female workers to employment characterized by low pay, tedium, minimal job security, and lack of career mobility encourages low job commit-

ment, high levels of turnover, and lack of attachment to work groups or firms. These conditions impede independent unionization . . . . In contrast, more skilled and secure male workers in the less dominant, heavy industry . . . are able to challenge elite policies from a greater position of strength.

Female crowding into low-wage and less-desirable jobs, both in the informal sector or in putting-out work, is considered worse in developing economies where poverty has enabled employers to exploit those less protected by the state or by organised labour.

Similar themes are dominant in research on Indonesia, although womens' important role in household budgeting and market trade in Java has also been highlighted. Participation rates have increased, but many authors question the benefits accruing to the poor. Mather (1983), Wolf (1992) and White (1993) stressed the low wages paid to young women in large, often foreign-managed factories. Others have emphasised the displacement of women from agriculture and traditional industries, wage discrimination and the fate of older, less mobile females (ILO 1993, van Velzen 1994, and Grijns et al. 1992).

These rather pessimistic conclusions are questioned in the following discussion of female participation rates, changing employment patterns and wage differentials by gender. The final section examines several broader implications of the findings regarding the relationship between rapid economic growth and female work patterns and earnings.

Female labour force participation

Increasing female participation rates (FLPs) have been a major factor driving labour force growth globally in recent decades.[2] The rising educational status of women, accompanied by declining fertility, postponement of marriage, greater access to child care facilities, and more flexible work arrangements are contributing factors.

Relatively high female participation rates in colonial times, and in the early years of independence, set Indonesia apart from most other predominantly Muslim countries (Durand 1975; Psacharopolous and Tzannatos 1989).[3] Among females aged 15 and above, they were just on 50

---

[2] Owing to conceptual and measurement problems in national surveys, participation rates vary substantially across countries, in part due to different concepts and definitions of economically active work (Anker 1983).

[3] Recorded participation (activity) rates have generally been higher in the National Labour Force Surveys than in Population Censuses. Data from the National Labour Force Surveys 1976/7, 1986/7 and 1992/3 are referred to, especially for activity rates. Data for 1971, 1980 and 1990 refer to the censuses. Both sources evidence similar trends over time (Jones 1981; Jones and Manning 1992).

234 *Labour market structure and institutions*

Table 9.1. *Labour force participation rates: selected East Asian countries, 1970/1 and 1990–1992 (age 15 and above)*

Country	1970/1	1990–2	% change
	Year[a]		
Hong Kong	42.9	48.2	12
Singapore	24.6	48.4	97
Korea	38.4	47.4	23
Malaysia[b]	38.9	45.2	16
Thailand[c]	72.8	70.1	−4
Philippines[d]	32.7	41.9	28
Indonesia: urban	26.6	36.0	35
Total	37.0	44.2 (50.4)[e]	19

Notes: [a] 1970 or 1971; 1990, 1991 or 1992; [b] 1988; [c] Ages 11+ in 1971, Ages 15+ in 1990; [d] Ages 10+ ; [e] 1992, National Labour Force Survey.
Source: ILO, *Yearbook of Labour Statistics*, various years; for Indonesia, Population Census, 1971 (Series D) and 1990; National Labour Force Survey, 1992.

per cent in 1993 in contrast to 10–20 per cent in several Middle Eastern and South Asian countries. Indonesian female participation rates were more comparable with a selection of countries in East Asia which report data to the ILO Yearbook in 1992–4 (table 9.1).[4]

Female participation rates rose in Indonesia from the early 1970s, although not as substantially as in several other East Asian countries. Overall, rates rose from 37 to 44 per cent between 1971 and 1990, or, alternatively, from 43 to 47 per cent between 1985 and 1995. The increase was much greater in urban areas (26 to 36 per cent, 1971–90).[5] Gains have been greatest in relative terms among young and less-educated groups, especially those in their twenties, and among primary and lower secondary educated women in urban areas (figure 9.1).

Increases in participation rates at younger ages largely pre-dated the recent export-oriented development (except among women aged 15–19), although improvements continued into the 1990s.[6] However, the marked

---

[4] The Indonesian rate was 50 per cent according to the 1992 National Labour Force Survey, considerably higher than evidenced in the Population Census in 1990 (44 per cent); such a difference is not uncommon in Developing economies, given the more careful recording of women's work in the more specialised labour force surveys.
[5] The 1985 and 1995 data are from the intercensal surveys.
[6] The experience of the 15–19 age group in urban areas is significant, however, since it is precisely in this age group that schooling enrolments have risen quickly, yet many of these

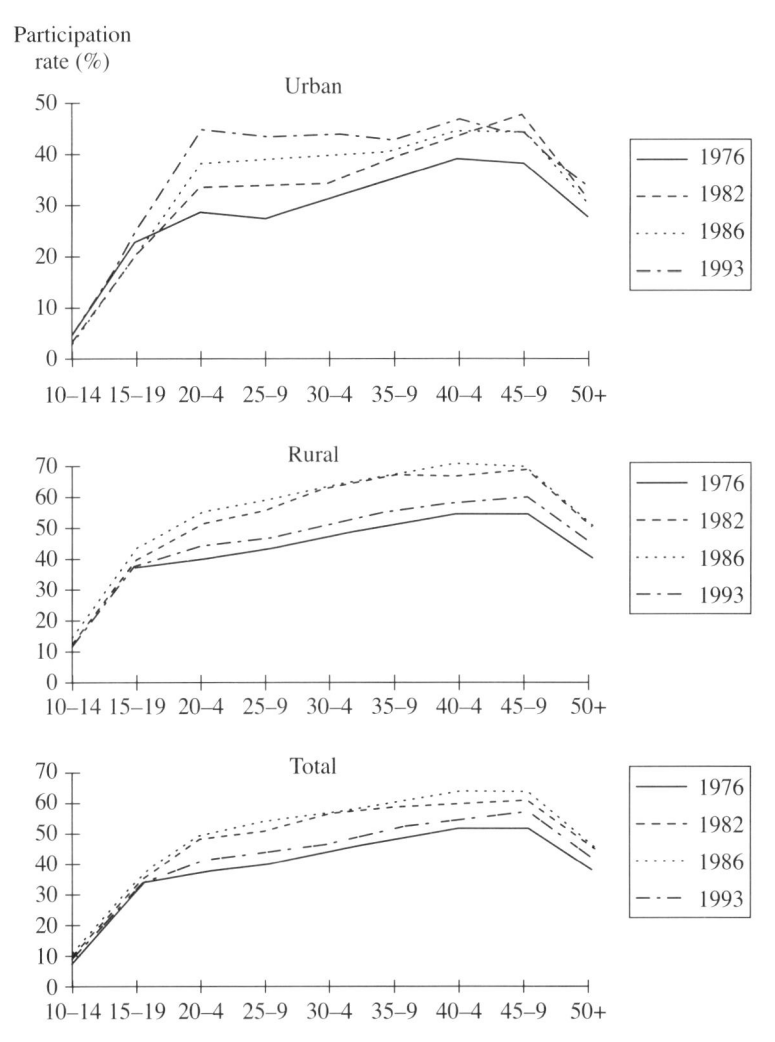

Figure 9.1 Female participation rates by age: Indonesia, 1976–1993
Sources: CBS, National Labour Force Survey, 1976, 1982, 1986, 1993; National Socio-Economic Survey, 1982.

peak in participation rates among young urban women was a new development from the mid 1980s. It suggests that job opportunity expansion in manufacturing has contributed higher FLPs among young, single females.

A word of caution – much of womens' work, even outside the home, is missed in National Labour Force Surveys. Even in urban areas, surveys women have been employed in the new export-oriented garment factories (White *et al.* 1992; Lok 1993).

probably miss a considerable amount of work which contributes directly to household income.[7] Many middle-class women enumerated outside the work force engage in a variety of part-time income earning activities, especially activities related to events in their husbands' place of work.[8] Lower-class women are likely to be more involved in urban subsistence activities, such as cultivation of some vegetables and improvement to houses and dwellings, which contribute to income and wealth.[9] Women engaged in putting-out activities in particular are not always covered by the National Labour Force Surveys.

The U-curve hypothesis

To what extent is participation in Indonesia consistent with the Boserup conclusion of withdrawal, or exclusion, of women from labour force activities, initially, followed by increases in participation later, as the country urbanises and industrialises – the so-called 'U-curve' hypothesis?

Support for the conclusion comes from the patterns of rural compared with urban FLPs and patterns of participation by educational status. Rural rates are notoriously difficult to measure in an economy dominated by self-employed and family workers. Nevertheless, they have been consistently recorded as much higher (40–50 per cent or more) than those in urban areas. In 1993, for example, rural rates were close to 50 per cent above those in urban areas. This is in contrast to general East Asian patterns of relatively high urban and rural participation rates (Boserup 1970: 186).

But official figures tend to overstate the contrast in work force participation among females in the cities compared with the countryside. High rural activity rates to some extent reflect the structure of employment dominated by micro-enterprises and small farms which are more marked in Java than in any other Southeast Asian regions – partly a response to historically severe labour supply pressures. Female engagement in these activities has different social and economic implications to those arising from their engagement in full-time wage work such as in factories or plantations.

Since the early 1970s, Indonesia has exhibited a U pattern of participation rates by education, especially in urban areas (figure 9.2).[10] Rates were high among females with no formal schooling, fell among lower secondary

[7] For example, in Jakarta women frequently interpreted census questions on work to apply only to work outside the home (Raharto 1993: 40).
[8] These include catering for special occasions, as well as sales of cloth and jewellery.
[9] Evers (1989: 163) reports on a survey which estimated that 'urban subsistence' activities accounted for over 20 per cent of household incomes of poorer households in Jakarta; the share was probably greater in other cities.
[10] Given the problems of comparing rural participation rates over time, owing to changing coverage of family workers, we concentrate the discussion on urban women.

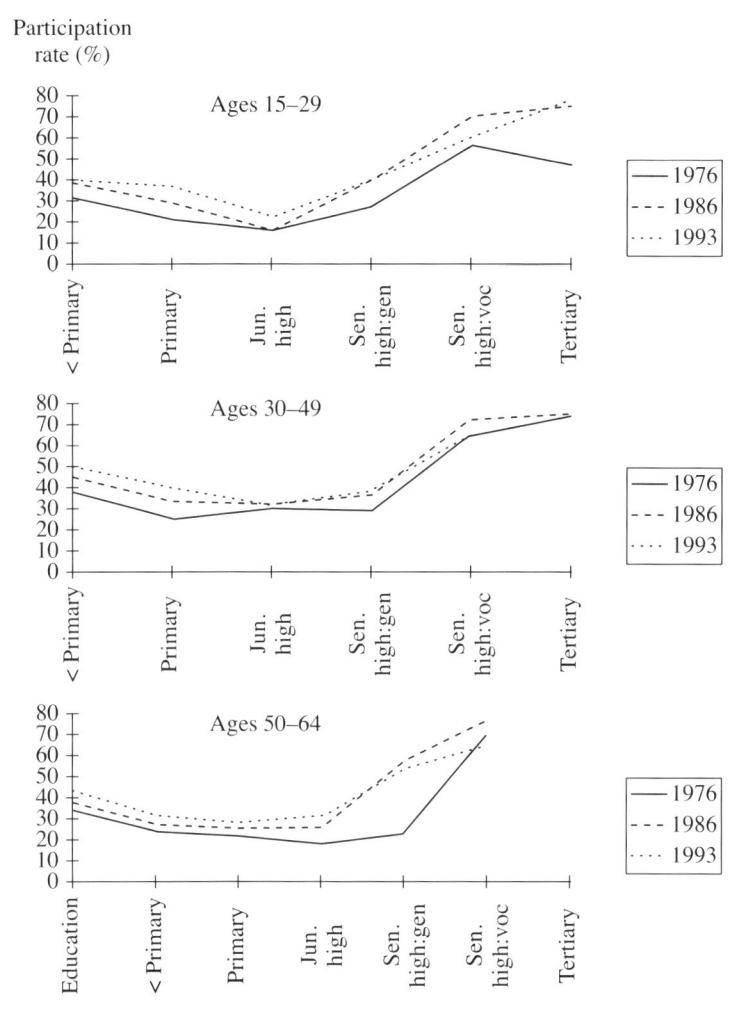

Figure 9.2 Female participation rates by education: urban Indonesia, 1976–1993
Source: CBS, National Labour Force Survey, 1976, 1986 and 1993.

graduates and then rose again among upper secondary and tertiary educated women. Relatively low FLPs among primary and junior high graduates can be attributed to two factors: reluctance of young women to take up informal jobs common among many poorer urban dwellers, and their inability to compete with more educated people for formal sector jobs. Jellinek (1991: 88–91), for example, describes how young womens' employment prospects in Jakarta in the late 1970s and early 1980s were affected by these factors.

238 *Labour market structure and institutions*

> Just as the public service was becoming more popular [due to wage increases], it became more difficult to enter. In the kampung, only five educated young people with a senior high school certificate (SMA) were able to get government jobs in the late 1970s. . . . Upward mobility into employment in the multinational factories seemed possible only for young persons whose parents could pay for their education and then support them while they searched and applied for jobs. (p. 90).
>
> By the 1970s, children whose parents had arrived in the city in the 1950s and 1960s and found employment in the informal sector did not wish to follow in their parents' footsteps. . . . They aspired for secure and better paid jobs in government or private offices or factories rather than the hard, arduous and insecure work on the streets. (p. 91).

As Jellinek implies, many less-educated job seekers had little prospect of modern sector jobs. The public sector was largely closed to lower secondary graduates by the 1980s and the substantial expansion of employment in labour-intensive exporting had not begun.

However, by the 1990s rapid economic growth was associated with a rise in urban participation among all schooling groups, at young ages in particular. While still low among less-educated women, participation rates rose in the 1980s.[11] Younger, secondary educated women took advantage of employment opportunities in a wide range of sectors, in addition to the new export-oriented manufacturing industries.

In part, women who entered the labour force in the 1990s with a primary or lower secondary education were of a different socio-economic group to young women with similar qualifications two decades earlier. Secondary graduates in particular were now being increasingly drawn from lower-income households.

Determinants of participation rates

In many societies, participation has been higher among young, unmarried women, inversely related to the number of children living at home and positively associated with education. Theoretical and empirical studies also suggest that participation rates are negatively related to household income (Sheehan and Standing 1978; Psacharopoulos and Tzannatos 1989).

Results from analysis of the determinants of Indonesian FLPs for 1992, from a probit regression equation are reported in appendix table 9.1. Four

---

[11] Owing to the rapid expansion of schooling over the past 20 years, a high proportion of people at lower levels of schooling are still at school and yet to enter the workforce. If those currently at school are excluded, the rates jumped by 20–30 per cent.

findings in particular are relevant to our discussion of relatively low but rising urban female participation rates in Indonesia.

First, the probit analysis confirmed the U-curve. Although attendance at academic senior high school did not significantly affect the probability of participation, education in vocational schools (in many cases the former teacher training schools) and at the tertiary level were highly correlated with female participation.

The contrast between the findings for upper secondary graduates from academic and vocational schools is significant. Coupled with high unemployment rates among women at this level of schooling (chapter 7), it points to the bumping up of job entry requirements for modern sector jobs. Among senior high-school graduates, competition for these jobs was much stiffer than several decades earlier. The positive and significant coefficient for vocational high-school graduates suggests that especially teacher training and home economics were highly valued in the market place.

Second, the probit analysis confirms a strong relationship between participation in the female urban work force and age, marital status and family structure in 1992. Marriage and the presence of young children were negatively associated with participation. Despite the much discussed role of extended families, the presence of young children clearly discouraged female participation in urban Indonesia.[12] It appears that declining birth rates have made a significant contribution to rising urban female participation rates.

Nevertheless, low participation rates among married women still sets Indonesia apart from several East Asian countries, such as Singapore, Malaysia and Thailand (Jones 1984). Conservative social values regarding female work outside the home, especially in key provinces such as West Java and South Sulawesi, probably influenced this outcome.

Third, women from better-off households tend to remain outside the workforce – a pattern found by Hull (1976) in an urban fringe area of Jogjakarta 20 years earlier.[13] Participation was negatively associated with both the educational achievement and the income status of household heads. The negative relationship between participation and husband's education was also found by Widarti (1991: 245) among married women in Jakarta in 1985.

The results suggest that income rather than educational status of the

---

[12] See also Widarti (1991: 242).
[13] Although participation through home production and home-based trading was undoubtedly more extensive among middle-class households than shown in the National Surveys (Evers 1989).

240 *Labour market structure and institutions*

head was the primary factor which discouraged participation among urban women. In the equation for women whose husbands were wage earners only, the coefficients for dummy variables representing the household head's income were negative and highly significant, whereas the coefficients for dummies for the head's education were negative but not significant. Non-participation in the work force, particularly as a wage worker, remains an important indicator of social status.

Finally, region of residence and associated ethnic values, also influenced female participation. East Java, Indonesia's second largest and one of its more dynamic provinces, was selected as the reference group. The probability of female participation was much higher in the major cities and urban areas in Central Java and Bali than in most other regions. It was significantly lower in all other Outer Island groups of provinces, including the regions with a high proportion of Christians in Eastern Indonesia (East Nusa Tenggara, North Sulawesi, Maluku and Irian Jaya). Perhaps surprisingly, the probability of participation was also lower in the greater Jakarta region (JABOTABEK) and West Java (see also Jones 1986).

Two conclusions emerge from the pattern of FLPs across regions. First, high rates in several of Indonesia's traditionally poorest regions (some of which, such as Bali, now have a much lower incidence of poverty) have been a feature of labour markets since the Suharto government came to power. Participation rates were especially high in the densely populated provinces of Eastern Inner Indonesia, stretching from Central Java to West Nusa Tenggara, an area which accounted for 40 per cent of Indonesia's population. Higher rates in these regions applied especially to urban areas.

Most of these provinces have a long tradition of female involvement in work inside and outside the home. It seems that economic need has played an important role in influencing participation rates. However, high FLPs compared with some other poor provinces are no doubt also related to values, social structure, rapid expansion of female education (especially Jogjakarta) and labour demand (especially Bali) in recent years.

Second, low participation rates in the JABOTABEK region were unexpected, given the tremendous expansion of female employment in labour-intensive industries in this region. In part, the rates can be explained by the fact that many of the workers in the new industries were temporary migrants from West and Central Java rather than residents of Jakarta. Historically low participation rates among the native *betawi* women of Jakarta and the predominantly Sundanese population from West Java who reside in the JABOTABEK region also help explain low FLPs in and around the capital city (Jones 1977, 1986).

However, caution should be exercised in attributing variations in provincial participation rates either to socio-cultural indicators, or to economic progress. The variations implied by the probit analysis defy simple generalisation. FLPs were both high and low (more than one standard deviation above or below the mean) in predominantly non-Muslim and in Muslim provinces, in low- and high-income provinces, in rapidly and slower-growing provinces, and in both more- and less-urbanised provinces in 1990. Clearly, a range of interactive demographic, social, economic and cultural explanations are at play.

To sum up, two opposing forces have tended to influence the trend of rising female participation rates. On the one hand, the population has become more urbanised. The redistribution of females away from rural areas – where rates have traditionally been high – has tended to put a break on the growth of the female labour force, exacerbated by rising school enrolments. Yet rapid growth in female schooling has meant that many more educated women were better equipped and motivated to enter the workforce.

It is still too early to tell how many of the younger, better-educated cohort will continue to participate in the work force as they grow older. It seems likely that many of the above changes are genuine cohort effects.[14] Socio-demographic characteristics of younger women are vastly different from several decades ago: they marry later, have fewer children, are more likely to move for work, and are better educated. Alternatively, some changes may only apply while women are young. The tendency for new manufacturing industries to employ mainly young female workers (see below) would suggest that participation rates will fall among the current cohorts of younger women as they get older, marry and have children.

Changing patterns of employment

To what extent did the increase in participation among females result in marginalisation of women, either absolutely or relative to males? Were poor women, who made up the overwhelming majority of female workers when Soeharto came to power, indeed mainly restricted to the 'nooks and crevices' in the workforce (to use Heyzer's words)?

In part, of course, womens' gains and losses depend on the changing structure of work. Total female employment rose faster than that of males over the period 1971–90 (3.5 compared with 2.9 per cent per annum), despite increasing female unemployment rates (chapter 7). The ratio of

[14] Effects which signal change in the behaviour of a particular birth cohort or cohorts, which mark them apart from their predecessors.

1971   1990

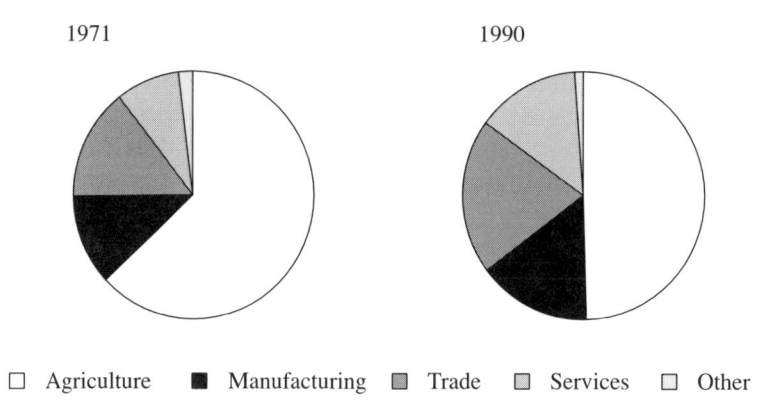

☐ Agriculture ■ Manufacturing ▨ Trade ▨ Services ☐ Other

Figure 9.3 Percentage distribution of female employment by sectors: Indonesia, 1971 and 1990
Notes: Services includes government, community and social services; other includes mining, public utilities, construction, transport and business services (all small employers of female labour).
Source: CBS, Population Censuses, 1971 (Series C) and 1990.

female to male employment rose in most work statuses, occupations and sectors, as well as overall in both urban and rural areas. Women did not gain in all activities, however, nor did all groups of women gain uniformly.

Female engagement in non-agricultural employment was quite high in the 1970s, especially by the standards of poor, agricultural-based economies (Jones 1983). Throughout South Asia and Africa the agricultural share of female employment was frequently well above 70 per cent around the 1970s compared with 65 per cent in Indonesia in 1971 (figure 9.3).

Female employment was overwhelmingly non-wage and rural in 1971 (table 9.2). Non-wage employment in agriculture and in rural non-agricultural activities, accounted for just under 70 per cent of total employment. Although one should bear in mind that categorisation of women into the group of family workers often devalues their economic contribution, it is striking that in over one-half of these activities females were enumerated as (secondary) family workers or helpers in home enterprises.[15] Rural, self-employed and family work in trade and manufacturing accounted for over half of all female non-agricultural employment in 1971. Both wage and urban employment were heavily dominated by males (just under 80 per cent of both).

[15] The distinction between female self-employed and family workers is often gender biased. Although women manage and provide most of the labour in home enterprises, female participation is reported in the family worker category because ownership may be invested in male hands (see Grijns and van Velzen 1993).

Table 9.2. *Female employment by major sector and work status: urban and rural Indonesia, 1971 and 1990*

	Share (%)		Growth (% p.a) 1971–90	Sex ratio (Male=100)	
Work status/Sector	1971	1990		1971	1990
Agriculture	65	49	2.0	49	54
Wage workers	14	7	−0.2	47	47
Non-wage	51	42	2.5	49	54
Non-agriculture	35	51	5.4	52	61
Urban wage workers	6	14	8.1	30	47
Manufacturing	(1)	(4)	10.4	45	60
Services[a]	(4)	(9)	6.8	44	68
Urban non-wage	5	10	6.6	56	61
Trade	(4)	(7)	6.9	70	88
Rural wage workers	6	10	5.8	30	41
Manufacturing	(3)	(5)	6.5	56	80
Services[a]	(3)	(4)	5.1	29	49
Rural non-wage	18	17	3.3	103	89
Manufacturing	(7)	(4)	1.0	172	143
Trade	(10)	(11)	4.2	100	118
Total	100	100	3.5	49	56
N(m)	13.0	25.1	–	–	–

Note: [a] Government, community and personal services.
Source: CBS, Population Censuses, 1971 (Series D) and 1990.

Given this difference in starting points, it is not surprising that changes in the structure of employment have been much more dramatic among females. Two developments stand out. First, the ratio of females to males in wage employment increased by over 50 per cent in urban areas between 1971 and 1990 (table 9.2). Women made spectacular gains, especially in wage employment in services and manufacturing. Second, these gains were associated with a substantial increase in the employment share of the better educated females (figure 9.4).

While there still remain substantial gender differentials in formal sector wages, these employment shifts have made a major contribution to the relative earnings of females. Many new females took up higher paying, full-time urban jobs in contrast to the employment of the previous generation in part-time work in agriculture or non-wage jobs in rural areas.

How do these developments compare with those in other East Asian countries? Even though females gained relative to males in Indonesia, their gain was smaller in Indonesia than in Singapore, South Korea, Malaysia and the Philippines (appendix table 9.2). Thailand, with an already high female share, was the exception.

244 Labour market structure and institutions

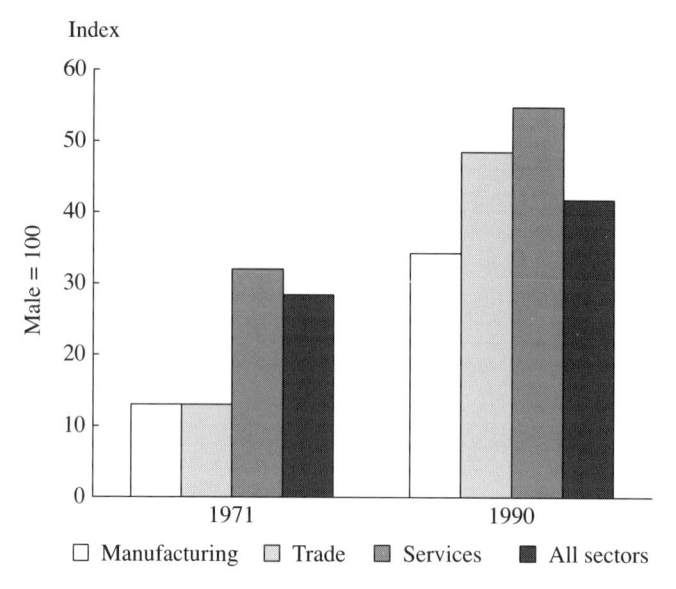

Figure 9.4 Sex ratio of employment among senior high graduates in urban Indonesia, 1971 and 1990 (male=100)

Data on total employment however tend to understate the extent of female participation and increasing involvement in the modern sector in Indonesia. First, the share of female employment was already high in Indonesia compared with other countries in 1971. Second, the share of wage jobs held by women in Indonesia rose as fast and in some cases faster than in other East Asian countries. This occurred both in all non-agricultural employment and in manufacturing, the former from a low base period share (22 per cent in 1971). Increased participation in modern industry and services was counterbalanced by slow growth in female employment in traditional manufacturing, in which females had long played a commanding role in Indonesia.

One important lesson to be drawn from appendix table 9.2 is that rapid service sector employment growth in Indonesia was certainly not unique from a regional perspective. The role of low-wage female involvement in manufacturing in East Asian development has received much attention. However, the increase in the female share of service and trade sector employment eclipsed the increase in manufacturing in almost every country. Increased female involvement in manufacturing as women moved from agriculture in developing economies is only a small part of the story of greater female involvement in the labour market.

Agricultural employment

To what extent were women pushed out of agriculture? There was no overall displacement of females compared with males in agriculture. Womens' employment share relative to that of males increased at roughly the same rate as for all jobs, both in Java and the Outer Islands (table 9.3).

Java

There are two predominant, seemingly conflicting interpretations of changes in female employment associated with rapid agricultural growth and occupational diversification. Early studies emphasised the marginalisation of women associated with new technologies and institutions introduced as part of the green revolution in rice cultivation (see chapter 6). Heyzer (1989: 1112) suggests that women have either left agriculture more rapidly than men, and/or those who remain have less remunerative jobs.

> Most studies found that here too [as in the Punjab] women are losing out on the higher productivity tasks, and are left with the more labour-intensive work, or are marginalized or displaced altogether.

In contrast, others have emphasised that females have increasingly outnumbered males in agricultural work. One report, drawing largely on studies of Java, comes to the categorical conclusion that there has been feminisation of the rural workforce arguing that '[m]odernizing and commercializing changes in agricultural technology and practices intended to raise productivity have had the impact of largely reducing paid employment of women on the one hand and increasing their unpaid labour inputs in family farms on the other' (ILO 1993: 31). Booth (1988: 187–8), writing about the period 1976–82, observes that the figures

> give little support to the argument that the new agricultural technologies have pushed females out of agriculture. Indeed in Java it appears . . . that in time women may come to dominate agricultural labour, as they do in Northeast Asia.

Naylor (1994: 524) concurs that labour market developments supported employment growth among females in both agriculture and other sectors in Java in the 1980s.

The 1971–90 intercensal data suggest however that there was neither substantial female labour displacement nor a major trend towards feminisation of agricultural employment. Rather there was a slight tendency for females to increase their share of agricultural jobs. This pattern is also observed for

Table 9.3. *Female employment by major sector: Java and the Outer Islands, 1971–1990*

Region/Sector	Share (a)	1971 (b)	Growth 1971–80	Growth 1980–90	Growth 1971–90	Sex Ratio (male=100) 1971	1980	1990
Java								
Agriculture	58	37	0.1	2.1	1.2	46	44	51
Manufacturing	13	8	3.8	5.3	4.6	90	81	112
Trade	18	12	5.0	4.0	4.5	87	101	96
Services[a]	10	6	6.7	3.9	5.3	42	48	63
All sectors[b]	100	(63)	2.6	3.4	3.0	50	50	55
Outer Islands								
Agriculture	76	29	1.8	4.2	3.1	51	49	56
Manufacturing	9	3	3.5	6.4	5.1	118	81	69
Trade	8	3	9.6	6.8	8.1	59	71	88
Services[a]	7	2	9.7	6.4	7.9	33	40	58
All sectors[b]	100	(37)	3.4	5.0	4.3	50	47	56
Indonesia	–	100	2.9	4.0	3.5	50	47	55

Notes: [a] Government, community and personal services; [b] Includes mining, construction, public utilities transport and financial services (all very small employers of female labour).
Source: CBS, Population Censuses, 1971 (Series C), 1980 and 1990, Jakarta.

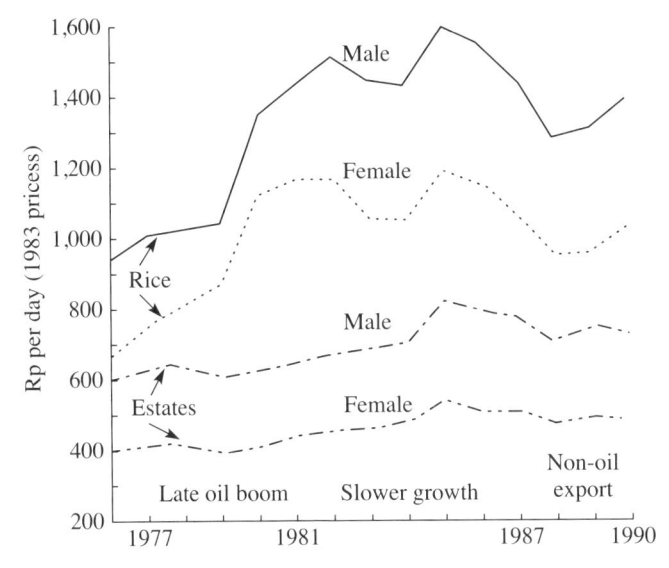

Figure 9.5 Real daily wages in rice (Java) and estate crops (Indonesia), by gender, 1976–1990 (Rp/day, 1983 prices)
Sources: CBS, unpublished data and Average Wages on Estates, various years.

the Outer Islands (table 9.3).[16] Trends in wages also suggest quite constant differentials between males and females through to the 1990s (figure 9.5).

Nevertheless, there was a fundamental difference between developments in the 1980s and the 1970s, when the most dramatic technological change occurred and there were periods of erratic agricultural growth. Macro-level data confirm the general findings from village studies that female employment grew less rapidly than that of males, especially in Java, during the 1970s. The displacement of female labour arising from new technology and labour institutions in rice farming (chapter 6) contributed to this slower rate of growth, although poor, landless males were more likely to migrate out of the village in search of work than females (Hugo 1978; Hart 1986; Manning 1988b).[17]

---

[16] The extraordinary claim of dramatically increased female shares in agriculture made in the above-quoted ILO report are based on questionable comparison of the 1961 and 1990 census results. The adoption of a six-month reference period in 1961 resulted in substantial overcounting of females in seasonal agriculture, compared with the one-week reference period used subsequently (Mertens 1978; Jones 1974).

[17] Labour-augmenting technology generally favoured males (cultivation by tractors and activities oriented to raising soil productivity).

The situation reversed during the 1980s – the macro data suggest that female employment in agriculture grew quite quickly in Java. Naylor (1994) has drawn attention to the increasing role of females on family farms, as males migrated to urban areas. While this may be true, the gender ratio in employment was still heavily in favour of males, especially if one bears in mind that most females worked fewer hours.

Naylor (1994) has also argued that induced institutional changes tended to favour females. For example, the traditional systems of *ceblokan* and *tebasan*, which gave preference to a smaller number of often male workers in rice cultivation, gave way to wage labour in many parts of Java. Contract work in planting, mainly a female activity, also spread widely.

The pattern of an increasing female share of agricultural employment in Java, began to change in the latter part of the 1980s, when young females began to play a much greater role in manufacturing employment. Direct comparisons are not possible but employment growth among females appears to have been much slower in agriculture in the second half of the 1980s and into the 1990s than in the early part of the decade.

The Outer Islands

Much less is known about employment trends by gender in the agriculturally diverse Outer Islands. Over the period 1971–90 both male and female employment increased rapidly, and in both cases agriculture dominated total job growth. Extension of land devoted to smallholder crops supported the growth of female employment. Also the expansion of small farms under the transmigration programme probably has increased female employment, as has the more recent growth in private estates.

Increased female engagement has not always been associated with rising incomes in Outer Island regions. Two examples are increased casual work in plantations struggling to cope with deteriorating terms of trade, and extreme difficulties in some isolated, agriculturally dependent transmigration settlements (World Bank 1986; Stoler 1983). Alternatively, many females were left behind to look after family farms as males migrated interregionally and abroad from poorer regions in Eastern Indonesia (Hugo 1993). Agricultural incomes per capita rose and the incidence of poverty declined in most Outer Island regions in the 1970s and 1980s. However, women faced severe employment problems in many poorer regions.

Non-agriculture

What sort of jobs did females take in the rapidly growing service and trade sectors and why did females take fewer jobs than males in manufacturing?

Table 9.4. *Employment of female professional, managerial and technical workers: Indonesia, 1971 and 1990*

	Professional	Managerial	Clerical
1 Share of non-agricultural employment			
1971	6.7	0.3	2.8
1990	9.2	0.1	6.1
2 % employed in services			
1971	97	55	65
1990	97	27	56
3 Completed schooling			
% senior high school			
1971	37	27	28
1990	77	33	69
% Tertiary			
1971	5	9	5
1990	16	53	16
4 Sex ratio (male=100)			
All employees 1971	47	6	1
1990	75	12	27
Tertiary educated 1971	29	5	13
1990	48	15	34

Wage employment was much larger in the service sector and included a substantial share of relatively educated workers in government administration and social services. Increased opportunities in the trade sector consisted mainly of non-wage jobs, mostly taken by less-educated women, and characterised by petty trade – including small stalls (*warung*), market trade and hawking.

Mainly educated women in services

In one sense educated females competed very favourably with males in services. Among professionals – a major share of educated females in services – the ratio of females to males rose by 60 per cent. A similar proportional gain was recorded among tertiary educated professionals (from a lower base, table 9.4). But educated women remained more heavily dependent than males on work in services. The significant increase in the ratio of females to males among tertiary educated, professional workers reflects the expansion of jobs for teachers at upper secondary and tertiary levels. The increase in the ratio of female to male jobs was especially marked in rural areas, where schools and health clinics mushroomed. Similarly the rise in the ratio of tertiary educated clerical females was related to the concentration of women among office workers in government administration.

Table 9.5. *Percentage of all non-agricultural employment absorbed in government, community and social services – educated, female workers: Indonesia, 1971–1990*

	Female		Male	
	1971	1990	1971	1990
Urban				
Senior high school graduates[a]	65	52	53	39
Tertiary graduates	68	66	65	59
All workers	43	37	36	28
Rural				
Senior high school graduates[a]	83	73	80	60
Tertiary graduates	75	87	74	55
All workers	16	20	32	23

Note: [a] Includes Diploma 1 and 2 graduates in 1990.
Sources: CBS, Population Censuses, 1971 (Series D) and 1990.

While the participation of educated females, especially for tertiary graduates, remained skewed in favour of services, the share of educated males in this sector declined as opportunities opened up in other areas of the economy (table 9.5). Within services, moreover, educated females gained relative to males at lower levels but were poorly represented in senior positions. By 1992 the ratio of females to males among senior high graduates in the civil service was 69 (table 9.6). But the more senior or top managerial and decision-making levels continued to be dominated by males.

Two occupations – paid household helpers and prostitutes – continued to dominate employment among less-educated women in services. Large numbers of domestics were especially evident in the bigger cities. According to the population census, domestics accounted for around 30 per cent of total female employment in Jakarta in 1971. Although the share had fallen to slightly under 25 per cent two decades later, the absolute number had almost tripled. Historically, a sharp decline in the number of persons in low status, paid household help has been regarded as one indicator of tightening labour market conditions (Boserup 1970). There was little evidence that this stage had been reached in Jakarta, let alone other urban centres in Indonesia in 1990.

Although not enumerated in national surveys, the number of prostitutes has been estimated at close to 200,000 or around 2–3 per cent of all employed females in urban areas in 1990 (Jones, Sulistyaningsih and

Table 9.6. *Female participation in civil service employment: Indonesia, 1978–1992*

	1978 %	1978 Sex ratio (Male=100)	1985 %	1985 Sex ratio (Male=100)	1992 %	1992 Sex ratio (Male=100)
Level						
1	22	16	10	14	6	152
2	73	53	81	56	80	50
3	4	18	8	29	13	37
(3D)[a]	(0.3)	(12)	(0.3)	(16)	(0.5)	(19)
4	0.2	8	0.2	11	0.3	12
(4EF)[a]	*	(5)	*	(6)	*	(8)
All levels	99	29	99	40	100	50
Completed schooling						
Junior high	31	17	17	17	11	18
Senior high	62	49	71	60	75	69
Academy/Bachelor	5	23	5	33	7	49
Sarjana[b]	2	19	3	28	6	40
All levels	100	29	96**	40	100	50
N (000)	(412)		(848)		(2,108)	

Notes: * <0.1 per cent
** Excludes not classified
[a] Highest levels in seniority; Level 4E and F covers civil servants in senior administrative and professional jobs (professors, senior judges etc.); [b] Four/five year tertiary degree.
Source: CBS, Statistical Yearbook of Indonesia, various years.

Hull 1995). Based on a small survey in Surabaya these authors (33–34) found that most of the women were young, unmarried or divorced, from rural areas and less educated than the female population as a whole. One can only guess as to possible future trends in employment in this 'industry'.[18]

Women in trade
The role of women in trade is a vastly understudied topic. The trade sector accounted for many more new jobs for women than either manufacturing or services in the period 1971–90. The percentage of women in non-wage

[18] Economic need has repeatedly been reported as the main reason women take up prostitution. Declining poverty should therefore have contributed to declining numbers of prostitutes. However, as Jones, Sulistyaningsih and Hull (1995) note, several factors suggest that numbers may remain high for some time: the relative nature of economic needs, high earnings in prostitution, and the social, economic and cultural environment which encourage it.

jobs in trade rose from an already quite high level in rural Java, and growth was even more rapid in the Outer Islands.

Nearly 40 per cent of the increase in female non-agricultural employment in the Outer Islands over the period 1971–90 was in the trade sector (including hotels and restaurants). The expansion of roads and subsequent beginning of more intensive rural–urban trade links in previously isolated regions has been important for trading activities throughout the Outer Islands. A wide range of trading activity ranged from specialisation in trade in agricultural products within provinces (such as in the relatively prosperous Karo Batak highlands of North Sumatra) to near subsistence roadside stalls involving the poorer women in isolated villages. The new transmigrant sites opened opportunities for rural trade, and the wives of plantation workers, many from Java, have also been heavily engaged in trade in urban and rural areas Sumatra (Stoler 1983).

Trade in Java remained largely a rural occupation, mostly small in scale and employing mainly older and less-educated women. Petty trading alone accounted for well over half of female non-agricultural occupations recorded in rural areas in 1985. In the early 1970s, these activities were for the most part close to the top of the occupational ladder in terms of earnings per hour among females, in contrast to the very low earnings in rural cottage industries (White 1976; Hart 1986).

The majority of petty trade activities in 1985/6 were conducted on a full-time basis, were non-seasonal in nature, had been operating for some years and made a valuable contribution to poverty alleviation among poorer households (Alexander and Booth 1992: 297–9). This challenges the common view that these were largely itinerant activities conducted on a part-time basis by underemployed labour, and hampered by a shortage of capital and poor organisational skills.[19]

However, as many cottage industries declined and more women crowded into trade, this privileged position may have been eroded, especially among poorer households in the 1980s. One study of rural trade in Jatinom District, Central Java found that earnings from trade were a major source of income among all socio-economic groups (Effendi 1991: 244–8). However, absolute earnings were substantially higher among women in better-off families, who owned the larger stalls and shops. Mainly female stall owners and hawkers earned among the lowest incomes among non-agricultural workers in Jatinom in the late 1980s. Average household expenditures were significantly lower than for the total population, and

---

[19] Alexander challenges the contemporary validity of Geertz's (1963) much earlier characterisation of Javanese petty traders as lacking in the capital and organisation which would enable them to expand to compete with larger Chinese enterprises.

well below those in other divisions of cottage industry (Alexander and Booth 1992: 299).

There has been some cause for concern about the capacity of this sector to continue to provide sufficiently remunerative jobs for rural women. Alexander (1992: 310–11) draws attention to the disappearance of a wide range of key commodities in rural trade in competition with factory products. Copperware and *batik* are given as prime examples. There was also centralisation of distribution in shops and greater standardization of rural commodities. This process had already begun in the 1970s (Anderson 1978) but was counterbalanced in its effects by the stimulus to trade from rising rural incomes and expenditures.

These worrying aspects of womens' employment opportunities in rural trade were counter-balanced by the rapid growth in family and small businesses in towns and cities. Increased trading was an important part of the expansion of the informal sector, especially during the growth oil-boom period from the mid 1970s to mid 1980s. Many women who found it hard to make ends meet in rural Java, both in agriculture and in traditional industries, moved into petty trade in the growing cities.[20] Jellinek (1991) describes how women in an urban *kampung* in Jakarta survived through petty trade during the good times of the 1970s, but suffered during the years of slower economic growth in the 1980s.

Generally, incomes have been found to be low compared with many other informal sector occupations, although a small number of women with greater access to capital, earned relatively high incomes from trading. For example, at the height of the oil boom in 1979–80, Guinness (1986: 63–4) found 63 small stalls serving 464 households – a phenomenal ratio of one stall for 7–8 households – in a relatively poor urban kampung in Jogjakarta (Central Java).

> Because there are so many, each concentrates on particular items, such as *bakmi* noodles, fruit and bread, fried cassava and *tahu* (soya cakes), raw vegetables and spices, rice cigarettes and kerosene. While some stalls sell only one or two items, sometimes from tables set outside the house on the pathway, others sell a wide selection of goods. Many stall operators are single women, either divorced, separated or widowed, who have children to look after . . . . Others are older women, often assisted by their retired husbands, with whom grandchildren are often left in charge.

He noted that only a very few stalls grew to much larger size, hampered by competition, daily consumption needs of the family (eating into

---

[20] Lehrman (1983), Chandler (1984) and Hetler (1989). See Alexander and Booth (1992) for a survey.

working capital) and the failure of many poor customers to fulfil their debts for goods purchased on credit.

Nevertheless, Guinness also notes that their incomes and social status within the village were higher than mostly casual wage workers. Their net incomes were reported to be around Rp. 1,000 per day, which compared favourably with wage labour incomes (around Rp. 400–600) in factories. Several other studies return similar findings. However, traders' earnings and livelihood were often less stable, especially in the larger cities where transport congestion had seriously begun to threaten the existence of many small traders by the 1980s.

While many women in urban trade activities in Java earned low incomes relative to other urban occupations, their incomes were not necessarily low compared with incomes in their home villages. Studies point to the importance of remittances from urban trade for the economic welfare of households in the village. In a poor village in Wonogiri, Central Java where many women sold herbal medicines or *jamu*, 'households receiving remittances from short-term circular migration tend, on average, to have raised household income and living standards quite rapidly compared with those 10 years ago' (Hetler 1989: 72). Families without remittances or access to land and other village resources tended to fall behind in the midst of comparative affluence created by remittances.

A final feature of female engagement in trade relates to rapid employment growth in shops, restaurants and supermarkets, especially in major cities. Sales and shop workers alone accounted for over 10 per cent of female workers in Jakarta in 1990. Most employees were relatively young (aged less than 30) and secondary educated. Nonetheless, all female wage employees in trade, restaurants and hotels accounted for less than 15 per cent of employment in the urban trade sector in 1992. The sector was dominated by older, less-educated women who worked mainly on food stalls and in small shops: even in urban areas this latter group accounted for over 60 per cent of growth in female jobs in the trade sector in the 1980s.

Manufacturing
The employment and earnings structure differed quite considerably in manufacturing where younger, relatively educated females found most of the jobs. In the period 1971–90, a large part of the growth in female wage employment growth in manufacturing occurred in Java where manufacturing has been traditionally concentrated and where labour-intensive export industries were also concentrated (table 9.3 above). Female wage employment in manufacturing also rose quickly in the Outer Islands, although the latter occurred mainly in Bali and North Sumatra.

The pattern of female involvement in manufacturing was very different among wage and non-wage workers. The former worked mainly in factory environments whereas the latter were concentrated in cottage industries. Despite recent rapid growth in female employment in the TFC industries, wage employment in all manufacturing has remained predominantly male (the ratio of females was 63 to 100 males in 1992). Non-wage employment, on the other hand, consisted mainly of women. The former was predominantly urban and the latter mainly rural.

Wage employment of females in manufacturing largely consists of young, unmarried women. The fall in the share of female wage workers relative to males at older ages is striking. Just under 75 per cent of all female wage employees in manufacturing were aged less than 30 (table 9.7).[21] However, at ages 30–49 the ratio of females to males fell to just over 60 in TFC and food industries, and was close to 20 for females aged 50 and over in urban Indonesia (table 9.7).

As in other East Asian countries, the preference for women in these industries has been attributed to a range of factors: women are frequently said to show greater application, to have specific skills in areas such as sewing, to be more easily controlled and managed, and to be prepared to accept lower wages. Harassment and poor working conditions are common among young females, especially in illegal or semi-legal, medium- and small-scale establishments (Grijns et al. 1992). But strikes and stop-work actions in the early 1990s were mainly in the TFC industries where young women held most of the jobs (chapter 8). The ferocity of stop work actions in large, female-dominated plants – such as in the giant Great River Industries (in 1995) and the more diversified Gajah Tunggal (1991) plants in the Greater Jakarta region – attests to the fact that young females are by no means a docile, easily exploited work force in the export-oriented industries.

Although female work outside the home has been a long tradition in Central and East Java, conservative social values discouraged young females in some regions from leaving their villages to work in manufacturing in the early years of expansion of large-scale factory employment. In some cases, traditional village patriarchs controlled recruitment and helped supervise women working in modern factories (Mather 1983).

How have females fared in self-employed work, largely small-scale and

---

[21] For example, the ratio of females to males in wage employment in textiles was 168 in the Jakarta and environs (JABOTABEK) and over 200 in urban East Java among women aged less than 30 in 1992. See also White et al. (1992) regarding the preference for young females, especially in large-scale TFC factories in the environs of Jakarta and Wolf's (1992) research among young village women in textile and beverage plants near Semarang in Central Java.

Table 9.7. *Female employment in major industries: Indonesia, 1992*

	Industry				
	Food	Textiles	Wood	Other	Total
Wage employment					
Age <30	24.9	56.1	23.0	33.7	36.3
30–49	13.3	12.7	3.9	11.9	11.5
50+	2.4	1.4	1.0	2.2	1.7
Sub-total	(40.6)	(70.2)	(27.9)	(47.8)	(49.5)
Non-wage employment					
Age < 30	22.0	13.3	26.6	18.3	19.0
30–49	26.0	12.0	27.8	22.4	21.2
50+	11.4	4.5	17.7	11.8	10.3
Sub-total	(59.4)	(29.8)	(72.1)	(52.5)	(50.5)
Total	100	100	100	100	100
N (000)	1,123	1,119	516	976	3,733
Sex ratio (male=100)					
Wage: age <30	127	144	37	56	87
30+	66	64	8	24	36
Non-wage	175	310	88	116	138
N (000) Both sexes	1,988	1,905	1,567	2,577	8,037
Main location (% distribution)					
Jakarta and environs	10	55	3	32	100
Other Java/Bali	34	27	15	24	100
Outer Islands	23	31	15	31	100

Source: CBS, National Labour Force Survey, 1992.

cottage industries in Java? The ratio of females to males in non-wage manufacturing fell from 172 to 143 between 1971 and 1990, indicating that males made inroads into this segment of manufacturing, although it still favoured female workers.

The fall in the share of female workers reflects the changing composition of small-scale industry. Most important was the decline of very low-wage home industries in which women were the main participants – especially the handloom, rattan weaving and traditional batik industries (chapter 6). The fall was even more severe in the Outer Islands – self employment and family work among women in rural manufacturing fell absolutely. Traditional weaving and other female-dominated industries appear to have found it increasingly hard to compete with factory products largely concentrated in Java.

Men have also tended to become more involved in work and management in household industries (often in joint household enterprises), such as food processing, which were formally mainly the preserve of women

(Van Velzen 1994: 98–110). Male participation increased where new product lines, new technology and longer distance marketing were introduced, or where access to credit or formal training were important.

Nevertheless, management and organisation of most small businesses remained very much in the hands of women. Van Velzen found (p. 109) that females managed one-third of all enterprises on their own, and a further 42 per cent together with their spouses in 239 food processing enterprises studied in West Java. Male-managed firms only accounted for 12 per cent of enterprises in which both sexes were involved, and less than a quarter of all enterprises run entirely by either males or females.

What are the implications for the welfare of women? The in-roads modern industry has made into the market share of small business adversely affected women. This applied especially to older, less-educated women who had less prospect of moving into wage employment or new activities. A greater male role in home industries does not seem evidence enough, however, to conclude, as Van Velzen (1994: 166) and others do, that this is a first step towards marginalisation of women. Much depends on the impact of male involvement on household income, especially that portion going to and managed by women. Where women were displaced or withdraw altogether, the increasing marginalisation hypothesis holds only if they end up in lower-income and less sought-after activities.

Wages and earnings

The extent to which growth in employment has been a mixed blessing for women depends partly on the level and trends in their wages. Real wages in a range of non-agricultural sectors where women are employed rose substantially from the 1970s, although they stagnated for several years during difficult economic times in the 1980s (chapter 5). Increases in wages in agriculture were smaller but not insignificant, and female wages on both estates and in rice rose as fast if not faster than those of males. Many more women were now in non-agricultural sectors, earning higher wages and independent incomes as wage earners than several decades ago. Those who had a secondary education or above certainly were better-off compared with many of their less-educated mothers, bearing in mind the substantial differentials in earnings by educational category.

There is also the issue of wage justice, however: the extent to which there is discrimination against women are in wage contracts, as suggested by pervasive wage differentials in Taiwan, Korea and Malaysia.[22] Large wage

---

[22] See especially Gannicot (1987), Bauer and Shin (1986) and Lee and Nagaraj (1995).

258 *Labour market structure and institutions*

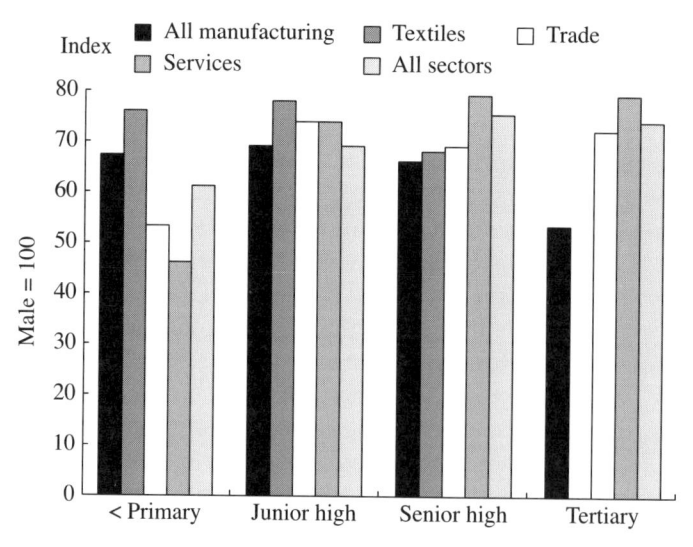

Figure 9.6 Gender gap in hourly earnings by major sector of activity in Indonesia, 1992 (male=100)
Note: Senior high includes academic stream (non-vocational); there is no data on tertiary graduates in textiles.
Source: CBS, National Labour Force Survey, 1992.

differentials were apparent in Indonesia in the 1990s. Overall, less-educated males earned 40–60 per cent more than less-educated females. The gap was smaller (on average 10–30 per cent) but still sizeable between the better more educated men and women (figure 9.6).

Among less educated women, the differentials were greater in non-agriculture (10–20 per cent) and were particularly marked in services, reflecting the low hourly wages of household servants.[23] But, even in manufacturing, men received substantially higher wages.

A slightly different pattern is evident among educated females. Hourly earnings differentials were generally lower among younger persons, especially in social and community services, and greater in manufacturing and government administration.

Among younger people, greater competition from better educated women tended to reduce wage differentials between the sexes in the 1990s. Notwithstanding their role in managing traditional businesses, female involvement in management in modern business and in higher-paid

---

[23] The earnings data understate the total value of the pay package of mainly female workers in this occupation; most household servants receive substantial payments in kind, including food and board, which are not recorded in the monthly earnings data.

professional occupations is a phenomenon largely of the past decade. Higher enrolment rates in tertiary education and involvement in the growing information technology sectors and banking indicates stronger female competition in prized private sector jobs.[24]

A second explanation for the sex differentials in earnings is different occupations taken by men and women on entry to the labour market. For example, in manufacturing, a steeper age earnings profile among men was related to the concentration of men in career-oriented jobs, such as engineering and accountancy, which led to managerial roles.[25] Similarly, the lower salaries of older, tertiary educated women in government administration are related to female recruitment into lower-level administrative jobs, or less well-paid professional occupations such as high school teaching.

A final explanation for the earnings differentials relates to an age composition effect. Women leave the work force at younger ages than men, and do not always reap rewards from seniority and experience, especially in manufacturing.

Earnings functions and relative endowments by gender

Some of the factors accounting for these earnings differentials were estimated with the aid of earnings functions, run separately for males and females. The equations provided a remarkably good estimate of earnings (appendix table 9.3).[26]

Coefficients for schooling, especially upper secondary and tertiary, were highly significant. They were generally larger among females, especially senior high, vocational school graduates. This partly reflects the narrower range of formal sector occupations held by more educated females, especially in the public sector.

Coefficients of industry and regional group dummy variables were generally positive. Wage rates were relatively low in the Central and East Java heartland where wage employment is much more widespread than in most Outer Island provinces. These coefficients were generally larger and more significant for males than females, especially in manufacturing,

---

[24] By the 1990s, significant numbers of Indonesian women were at least branch managers or senior executives in major companies. See *Asian Wall Street Journal*, September 8, 1993.
[25] Such patterns are prevalent in many developed and developing countries, related both to intermittent labour force commitment among women and discrimination in favour of men in promotion to more senior supervisory and management positions (Psacharopolous and Tzannatos 1989).
[26] Separate equations run for various groups of non-wage earners produced consistent results.

government administration and other services, and in the resource rich and more-developed Outer Island provinces.

Among women, negative coefficients were recorded for wage workers in trade, hotels and restaurants and personal services. This points to the importance of focussing on services, in addition to manufacturing, in discussions of low wage packets dominated by women.

The Blinder (1973) approach was used to calculate the extent to which wage differentials estimated by the earnings functions could be explained by the different endowments or attributes of males compared with females.[27] This poses the question: what would the estimated level of female earnings have been if females were endowed with the same characteristics as males? The difference between this estimate of average earnings and that produced by the regression equation provides an approximation of the extent to which wage differentials can be attributed to endowment differences between men and women.[28] The residual can be attributed to unmeasured attributes, including discrimination in the labour market. Approximately 30–40 per cent of the predicted difference in hourly earnings could be explained by different endowments/characteristics (table 9.8).

Four variables contributed to the advantage which endowments gave males in wage outcomes: the higher proportion of males at prime ages who graduated from non-vocational senior high schools, worked in North Sumatra or in the resource rich provinces outside Java, and who were employed in 'other' industries (mainly mining, construction and transport). Female endowments gave them a significantly higher wage on only one variable: graduation from vocational high schools.

The residual difference in earnings by gender can partly be attributed to characteristics not included in the equation. In particular, data on occupation and years of experience (proxied by age in our equations) were not available in the data sets used. Nonetheless, given that a significant residual remained, it seems likely that forms of wage discrimination were important in the labour market.

There is a consensus from several studies of wages in other countries that the occupational mix between the sexes accounts for a substantial

---

[27] To do this, coefficients from the separate male and female regression equations were multiplied by the estimated means values of each explanatory variable for females and males respectively; the results summed (together with the constant) to produce a second estimate of earnings for each of the sexes. The methodology used here follows the Blinder (1973) technique for estimating gender discrimination in wage equations. See also Lee and Nagaraj (1995) and Oaxaca (1973).

[28] Endowment is here interpreted broadly to include place of residence and industry of employment in addition to age and education.

Table 9.8. *Decomposition of hourly earnings differentials: Indonesia, 1992*

	Equation	Value in logarithms	Value in Rupiah	%[b]
1 Males average earnings (a) observed		6.338	624	
(b) predicted	$\Sigma b_m X_m$		565	
2 Females average earnings (a) observed		5.992	405	
(b) predicted	$\Sigma b_f X_f$		400	
(A) Wages according to the male earnings structure				
3 Females, predicted wages based on males coefficients	$\Sigma b_m X_f$	6.198	492	
4 Total gender differential in predicted earnings (1b–2b)	$\Sigma b_m X_m - \Sigma b_f X_f$	0.432	165	41
5 Differential if male regression coefficients applied ('endowment' differences, 1b–3)	$\Sigma b_m(X_m - X_f)$	0.140	74	(45)
6 Residual (occupation and discrimination, 4–5)	$\Sigma(b_m - b_f)X_f$	0.292	91	(55)
(B) Wages according to the female earnings structure				
7 Males, predicted wages based on Females coefficients	$\Sigma b_f X_m$	6.184	485	
8 Total gender differential in predicted earnings (1b–2b)	$\Sigma b_m X_m - \Sigma b_f X_f$	0.432	165	41
9 Differential if female regression coefficients applied ('endowment' differences, 7–2b)	$\Sigma b_f(X_m - X_f)$	0.192	85	(52)
10 Residual (occupation and discrimination, 8–9)	$\Sigma(b_m - b_f)X_m$	0.248	80	(48)

Notes:[a] Explanatory variables expressed in terms of natural logarithms and corrected to rupiah by antilogs for equations 1–3, and calculated from these rupiah values subsequently; [b] Total percentage differential between male and female predicted wages, and relative contribution to the differential (for rows 5 and 6, 9 and 10).
Source: CBS, National Labour Force Survey, 1992.

share of the gender earnings differential.[29] Occupational data are not available in any national data sets which include earnings, so this hypothesis is not directly testable for Indonesia.

Occupational segregation

Data from the 1985 Intercensal Survey suggest very substantial occupation crowding in Indonesia.[30] Petty trade accounted for almost half of all female non-agricultural employment; maids and primary school teachers a further 17 per cent (table 9.9). The top ten non-agricultural jobs accounted for over 80 per cent of all female employment.

Unlike in some Latin American countries (Terrell 1992), males were also heavily concentrated in a small number of non-agricultural occupations. The ubiquitous trader category, covering a multitude of activities for an occupation recorded at a five-digit level of disaggregation, was the major occupational category with just under 20 per cent of all non-agricultural employment. The top ten occupations accounted for just over half of all male employment. In only two of these – trading and primary school teaching – was the male share of employment less than their share in all non-agricultural employment relative to females. If the trader group are excluded, the difference between the share of males and females in the top five and ten occupations for each gender was even smaller.

This pattern is broadly reflected in the changing occupational structure over time. National Census data for Jakarta suggest that the five main occupations among females and males in 1980 and 1990 remained relatively stable (table 9.10). Although there are pitfalls in comparing occupational categories over time in Indonesia, the pattern of considerable concentration is evident for both sexes.

It seems reasonable to conclude that occupational crowding among females may not have been the major explanation for wage differentials by gender. Different occupational distributions would not have accounted for the substantial unexplained wage differentials identified.[31] Among the ten occupations identified in 1985, only two occupations among females (house-

---

[29] See especially an excellent survey article by Terrell (1992) and Chapman and Harding's (1986) paper on Malaysia. Lee and Nagaraj (1995) incorporated occupation into their equation and found that it accounted for almost the same amount of variation in earnings as endowments in Malaysian manufacturing.

[30] The 1985 Intercensal Survey provided data on occupation and included some general observations on occupational bunching, although there are problems with the overall reliability of occupational data collected from the censuses (Godfrey 1987).

[31] This conclusion is of course tentative, bearing mind that the data on occupational distributions are taken from different years (in Indonesia as a whole in 1985, and Jakarta in 1980 and 1990) and hence cannot be directly compared with the wage data.

Table 9.9. *Ten major non-agricultural occupations by gender: Indonesia, 1985*[a]

Major female occupations	Distribution %	Cum. %	% of all workers female	Representation[b]
1 Traders	38.3	38.3	49	1.5
2 Paid household help	9.5	47.8	88	2.8
3 Primary school teachers	7.3	55.1	51	1.6
4 Tailors	3.8	58.9	59	1.8
5 Basket weaving	3.0	61.9	78	2.4
6 Weaving operators	3.0	64.9	80	2.5
7 'Other' clerical	2.9	67.8	19	0.6
8 Other textiles	2.2	70.0	68	2.1
9 Sales employee/assisant	2.0	72.0	30	0.9
10 Book keepers	1.9	73.9	25	0.8
Other	44.5	100		
N^c: Non-agricultural	28,786		32	
Agricultural	16,056		20	
Total	44,842		26	

Major male occupations	Distribution %	Cum. %	% of all workers male	Representation[b]
1 Traders	19.3	19.3	51	0.8
2 Drivers	6.2	25.8	100	1.5
3 'Other clerical'	6.3	32.1	81	1.2
4 Bricklayers	4.6	36.7	98	1.4
5 'Other' construction	4.4	41.1	96	1.4
6 Government officers	3.5	44.6	90	1.3
7 Primary teachers	3.4	48.0	49	0.7
8 Carpenters	3.1	51.1	99	1.5
9 *Becak* drivers	2.8	53.9	100	1.5
10 'Other' services	2.6	56.5	93	1.4
Other	26.1	100		
N^c: Non-agricultural	60,095		68	
Agricultural	65,092		80	
Total	125,187		74	

Notes: [a] Excludes family workers ('earnings' workers only). This explains the low share of females in agriculture; [b] Defined as female (male) share in occupation relative to their share in all non-agricultural occupations; [c] Total sample (unweighted).
Source: CBS, Intercensal Survey, 1985.

Table 9.10. *Five major occupations by gender: Jakarta, 1980 and 1990*

	1980		1990	
Gender/occupation[a]	% Distribution	% Female[b] (male) in occupation	% Distribution	% Female[b] (male) in occupation
Female				
Paid household help	30.8	86	24.3	89
Sales/shop assis.	20.6	30	14.3	32
Clerical, book keeper[c]	9.4	23	13.1	30
Tailors	6.6	49	11.4	57
Teachers	4.6	51	5.1	53
Sub-total	72.0		68.2	
Other	31.2		38.6	
Total	100	26	100	31
N (000)	502		894	
Male				
Sales/shop assistant	17.8	70	13.2	68
Clerical, book keeper[c]	11.0	77	13.5	70
Drivers & related	10.6	100	10.3	99
Bricklayers	7.6	99	6.6	99
Machine fitters, assemblers	2.9	97	3.9	97
Sub-total	49.9		47.5	
Other	50.1		57.3	
Total	100	74	100	69
N (000)	1,426		2,038	

Notes: There are a number of apparent inconsistencies in the coding of occupations in the 1980 and 1990 Censuses. The occupations in the table include the top five occupations for both males and females excluding working proprietors in trade which clearly received different treatment in the two censuses. [a] All occupations based on 3-digit classification; [b] The female share in each occupation for the five main female jobs, and similarly for males in the main male jobs; [c] Clerical and book keeper/cashier combined.
Source: CBS, Population Census, 1980 and 1990 (data analysed by Nima Singarimbun).

hold servants and basket weavers) were clearly low wage. Thus we probably need to search elsewhere for a considerable part of the unexplained residual identified in the gender wage regressions. Statistical or other discrimination is likely to have been an important source of the variations, especially regarding promotion and job descriptions in formal sector wage jobs.

Conclusions

How has increasing participation benefited women and their households, if at all, and does greater involvement indicate regress rather than progress? How have females performed relative to males in the labour market?

Women increased their participation substantially, although not to the extent in other East Asian countries. Both increased and changing patterns of engagement have been extraordinarily broad-based – in terms of the educational, industrial and occupational distribution of women's employment. Increased participation occurred at all ages, among all educational classes and in almost all wage and non-wage segments of the labour market, and in both urban and rural areas, within and outside Java.

Two aspects of increased female labour market involvement bear on the questions raised above. The first relates to the extent to which the changing composition of employment has benefited women. The second deals with the extent to which women have gained absolutely, and relatively to males, in new (and traditional) jobs.

Shifts in the composition of the labour force have been the main channel through which women have gained as a result of rapid economic growth. As in other rapidly growing East Asian countries, the rising share of educated women in government employment, manufacturing and other services – combined with continuing high-wage premiums for schooling – has been the single most important change. From a situation where most formal sector jobs were held by educated males, females with a high school education or more have close to doubled their participation in the modern sector. The growth of services, buttressed by the prudent use of public funds during the oil boom, played the major role in providing better jobs for females. The boom provided opportunities for many young women to continue schooling and later work as teachers, health care workers and civil servants.

Access to higher levels of education for women has been much closer to the East Asian pattern than the South Asian. Yet, in some respects Indonesian women remain at a disadvantage. Although female schooling has improved dramatically relative to that of male, the gender gap remains substantial compared with some neighbouring countries such as Malaysia, the Philippines and Thailand.[32]

The second important structural shift was the decline in the agricultural share of female employment. This mirrored changes taking place in the labour market generally. While escape from agriculture and rural poverty often meant long hours of work under sub-standard factory conditions, it also meant more regular work and higher incomes.

Greater female access to rural trade appears to have made a considerable contribution to poverty alleviation. Manufacturing wages barely

---

[32] Although secondary school enrolment rates were lower in Thailand than in Indonesia in the 1980s, the gender gap was much smaller in Thailand. It narrowed rapidly in Indonesia but in 1990 the ratio of female to male enrolments was 84 compared with 94 in Thailand.

covered subsistence costs in many cases, but wage income allowed young females to help dampen the impact of shocks to their households from seasonal aberrations, enterprise failure and personal loss.[33]

For much of the period under examination, the increase in women's participation was not associated with a dramatic increase in employment in low-wage manufacturing export industries. Rather, it involved an increase in female engagement in wage employment in services and in the informal economy, especially in the growing number of urban centres. In part, supply pressures played a role in this shift. Females were most affected by declines in traditional industries and technological change in agriculture.

How did women fare in specific occupations? Outcomes were for the most part positive in terms of participation. Nevertheless, there are major questions regarding their position relative to males. Gender-based earnings differentials remained substantial across sectors and educational categories. Females had become more prominent in the business and the professions, and there are some highly placed women in most spheres of Indonesian public life. But there are questions regarding progress to higher levels in government and the private sector, where endowments are similar to or superior to those of men.

Underrepresentation of women at senior levels in government may well be the result of career and family choices. These issues are not well researched and the data base on earnings and occupation are weak at a national level. In one sense, a broadening of the occupational base has been relatively easy in a rapidly growing economy, starting from such a low base. Achievement of greater parity with men in more specialised skill-intensive occupations is likely to be a much more demanding task. Changes in the composition of employment will play a less dramatic role in job growth among both sexes in the future. Other issues have also begun to come into focus as better education supports a broadening of horizons. These include sexual harassment, discrimination against married women in the work place and the absence of maternity leave in many private sector firms.

Two final points are worth stressing. First, a focus on future challenges as society modernises would include an analysis of factors which have contributed to past successes as well as failures. There is a general tendency to view all capitalist economic growth as inimical to women's

---

[33] Wolf's (1992: 180–91) moving account on this issue notes that young factory women in Central Java frequently borrowed from their parents for daily needs. At the same time they saved 30–40 per cent of their low wages which were mostly spent on consumer durables and gold, and for emergencies and life-cycle events.

participation. The fact that many women have made extraordinary advances compared with their parents' generation is surely an important starting point for policy formulation.

Second, studies of females in the work force frequently ignore the fact that some of the problems faced by women are equally faced by men. Crowding into low-paid occupations has affected men in a similar way – if not to the same extent. Oversupply in the informal sector, in low-paid jobs in manufacturing and in services, is a general characteristic of the Indonesian labour market. It has relatively little to do with discrimination against females – except in the sense that some jobs such as driving (including low-wage *becak* or trishaw driving) and construction work are socially deemed male, irrespective of earnings. For many, raising household incomes from the participation of all household members in the labour force, and through improvements in human capital, irrespective of gender, remains the real challenge.

Appendix table 9.1. *Probit estimates of the determinants of female labour force participation (LF): Urban Indonesia, 1992 (All women aged 15–64, wage earner households)*[a]

Variables		Estimate	T-ratio	Chi-square
Intercept		8.440	16.71	279.2
AGE		−0.290	27.62	764.6
AGE[b]		0.004	25.87	670.3
EDUC 1	Junior high	−0.582	12.34	151.9
EDUC 2	Senior high (academic)	0.140	2.75	7.7
EDUC 3	Senior high (vocational)	1.585	28.73	822.8
EDUC 4	Tertiary	1.923	20.00	398.7
MAR	Married	−1.501	32.13	1,028.7
CHILD	One or two children aged <10yrs	−0.152	4.56	20.8
CHILD	Three children aged <10yrs	−0.420	3.81	14.5
REGION 1	Jakarta and environs[b]	−0.357	5.89	34.8
REGION 2	Other West Java	−0.470	6.20	38.6
REGION 3	Central and East Java cities	0.489	4.84	23.4
REGION 4	Other C. Java	0.125	2.00	3.9
REGION 5	North and West Sumatra	−0.601	8.22	67.2
REGION 6	Other Sumatra	−0.596	9.03	81.2
REGION 7[c]	Kalimantan	−0.519	6.99	49.4
REGION 8	Mainly Christian E. Indonesia	−0.417	5.85	35.0
REGION 9	Other E. Indonesia	−0.663	9.43	89.2
HHD EDUC 1	Household head junior high	−0.738	1.43	2.1
HHD EDUC 2	H.Head senior high (academic)	−0.267*	0.49	0.2
HHD EDUC 3	H.Head senior high (vocational)	−0.070*	1.30	1.6
HHD EDUC 4	H.Head tertiary	0.106*	1.71	2.8
HHD WAGE 1	Rp. 50,000–<100,000	−0.527	6.43	41.2
HHD WAGE 2	Rp. 100,000–<200,000	−0.046	13.16	173.2
HHD WAGE 3	Rp. 200,000+	−1.425	17.11	289.7

Notes: * Coefficients not statistically significant at 5 per cent level or better.
Log Likelihood   −11,746
Pearson Chi-square   21,488
L.R. Chi-squared   23,454
Sample Size   21,500

[a] The equation was estimated with intercept dummies for all variables except current age. These dummies are referred to in the text where relevant.
[b] The JABOTABEK region.
[c] More than 50% of the urban population Christian (East Nusa Tenggara, East Timor, Maluku, Irian Jaya and North Sulawesi).
Source: CBS, National Labour Force Survey, 1992.

Appendix table 9.2. *Percentage share of females in total employment by sector: selected East Asian countries, 1970–1991/2*

Sector/year[a]		Singapore	South Korea	Malaysia	Philippines	Thailand	Indonesia
(A) ALL EMPLOYMENT							
All sectors	(Circa) 1970	24	35	30	31	47	33
	(Circa) 1990	40	41	35	37	47	36
	Index 1990 (% 1970=100)	(167)	(117)	(117)	(119)	(100)	(109)
Agriculture	1970	–	41	37	19	50	33
	1990	–	45	35	26	47	35
	Index 1990	–	(110)	(95)	(137)	(94)	(106)
Non-agriculture	1970	24	29	23	45	38	34
	1990	40	39	35	46	46	36
	Index 1990	(167)	(134)	(152)	(102)	(121)	(106)
Manufacturing	1970	36	36	29	55	43	49
	1990	44	42	46	46	50	45
	Index 1990	(129)	(117)	(160)	(84)	(116)	(92)
Trade	1970	10	38	18	58	54	44
	1990	40	53	39	67	54	51
	Index 1990	(400)	(139)	(217)	(116)	(100)	(116)
Services[b]	1970	27	29	30	56	36	28
	1990	48	44	40	56	52	35
	Index 1990[a]	(179)	(151)	(134)	(100)	(144)	(125)
(B) WAGE EMPLOYMENT							
Non-agriculture	1970	26	27	–	37	30	22
	1990	43	38	35	40	41	30
	Index 1990[a]	(165)	(141)	(–)	(108)	(137)	(137)
Manufacturing	1970	34	35	–	37	38	34
	1990	45	43	42	39	50	41
	Index 1990[a]	(132)	(123)	(–)	(105)	(132)	(121)
(C) FEMALE SHARE OF TOTAL EMPLOYMENT GROWTH IN MANUFACTURING 1970/1–1990/2		49	46	62	30	57	42

Notes: [a] All countries 1970 except Indonesia 1971; all countries 1991/92 except Thailand 1990 and Malaysia 1988; [b] Government, community and social services (ISIC code 9).
Source: ILO, *Yearbook of Labour Statistics*, 1993 and 1989/90.

Appendix table 9.3. Regression results of log earnings equations by gender: Indonesia, 1992

Variables	MALE B coefficient	T-ratio	(Mean)	FEMALE B coefficient	T-ratio	(Mean)
Dependent variable						
LWHR Ln wage per hour			(6.437)			(6.005)
Constant	5.397			5.172		
Independent variables						
AGE						
AGE 2 Age 30–49 years (<30, 50+=Control)	0.22	36.39	(0.511)	0.23	21.42	(0.381)
Age squared						
AGESQ	0.0001	49.04	(1,312.41)	0.0001	18.07	(1,084.34)
COMPLETED SCHOOLING (Primary=Control)						
ED2 Lower secondary school	0.2	22.75	(0.161)	0.37	21.24	(0.097)
ED3 Upper second. general school	0.42	45.4	(0.169)	0.65	37.03	(0.127)
ED4 Upper second. vocational school	0.49	51.18	(0.153)	0.84	50.78	(0.196)
ED5 Academy and University	0.88	72.41	(0.086)	1.09	50.76	(0.079)
INDUSTRY (Agriculture=Control)						
IND2 Food	0.13	6.78	(0.027)	0.03	1.39	(0.056)
IND3 Textile	0.12	6.52	(0.034)	0.04	1.73	(0.068)
IND4 Wood+other manufacturing	0.22	17.79	(0.109)	0.08	3.83	(0.084)
IND5 Trade	0.15	10.16	(0.067)	−0.04	1.6	(0.079)
IND6 Financial services	0.44	21.74	(0.026)	0.39	11.19	(0.024)
IND7 Government administration	0.39	33.58	(0.226)	0.35	16.95	(0.205)
IND8 Social and community services	0.19	15.02	(0.105)	0.009	0.49	(0.128)
IND9 Other services	0.11	7.66	(0.055)	−0.32	−16.97	(0.112)
IND10 Other sectors	0.32	30.69	(0.212)	0.34	10.05	(0.024)
REGION (Other Java=Control)						
REG2 JABOTABEK	0.43	40.68	(0.125)	0.49	28.99	(0.119)
REG3 Bandung	0.21	12.18	(0.034)	0.26	9.95	(0.039)

REG4	Surabaya	0.21	12.55	(0.036)	0.15	6.38	(0.049)
REG5	Other West Java	0.21	16.8	(0.074)	0.21	10.58	(0.07)
REG6	North Sumatra	0.27	18.03	(0.067)	0.32	12.62	(0.041)
REG7	Resource rich region	0.47	37.04	(0.067)	0.38	14.82	(0.039)
REG8	Other Sumatra	0.22	20.06	(0.095)	0.22	12.16	(0.095)
REG9	Other Kalimantan	0.36	26.24	(0.058)	0.29	11.79	(0.044)
REG10	South Sulawesi	0.23	12.02	(0.027)	0.29	9.34	(0.026)
REG11	Other Sulawesi	0.19	13.31	(0.049)	0.15	5.83	(0.041)
REG12	Bali	0.22	12.82	(0.034)	0.25	10.17	(0.042)
REG13	Maluku and Irian Jaya	0.43	24.78	(0.034)	0.41	13.73	(0.028)
REG14	Least Indonesia	0.09	6.67	(0.057)	0.09	4.16	(0.046)
		N of cases=30,852			N of cases=13,629		

IV

Lessons from Indonesia

10

Rapid economic growth and labour outcomes

Lessons from Indonesia

Indonesia has experienced a transformation of labour markets, reflecting dramatic changes in social and economic life over three decades. In concluding the story, we focus on two sets of issues: the role of labour market transformation in structural change and development in Indonesia, and the lessons from the Indonesian experience for understanding labour market transitions in East Asia.

Although the emerging structure of labour markets is only one indicator of economic advancement, it is contended that labour market dynamics provide valuable insights for an assessment of changes in welfare and productivity. Constraints to both labour supply and demand pose major obstacles to structural change, as do imperfections in markets for goods and services, and other factors of production.

We take the following points into account in evaluating the significance of labour market transformation for structural change

- Access to work, improvements in wages and greater security of employment are fundamental to improved living standards in poor countries where income from physical labour is a major component of household incomes.
- The distribution of these changes across specific population subgroups – by gender, region and class – is critical to improvements in income distribution.
- Rising labour productivity, associated with shifts in the structure of work, better incentives and work place reforms, which are fundamental sources of improvements in total factor productivity and economic growth.
- Enhancement of the skill composition of the workforce also has a basic influence on the quality of work – more brain than brawn – as well as contributing to higher and more stable incomes.

- The rising wages and skills of the workforce improves bargaining power with employers and the choice of jobs.
- Effective enterprise-based unions contribute to productivity and counter the monopsonistic power of employers under conditions of elastic labour supply.

All of these changes contribute to greater economic choice and freedom, and at least in the longer term can be expected to feed into processes of social and political change.

Three general conclusions are important for the assessment of the contribution of labour market change to development in Indonesia during the Soeharto era. First, economic growth and associated policies have been favourable to labour, in terms of improved welfare, security and equity. This assessment challenges the view among many observers – both within and outside Indonesia – that labour has been left behind in the process of development. As in other East Asian countries, the present generation of workers have borne a substantial burden of dislocation and relocation as a consequence of shifts in employment across jobs, industries and regions. Tight political controls have limited the voice of many who have had justifiable greivences, be they insecure informal sector workers or wage employees suffering from the arbitrary actions of employers. But, compared with the parlous wages and working conditions which existed in the 1960s, we conclude that economic growth and labour market transformation have benefited the large majority of Indonesian workers and contributed to the remarkable decline in poverty.

Second, we have stressed that unfavourable labour supply market conditions – the concentration of workers in low-productivity jobs, rapid labour force growth and low levels of human capital – were the major factors which constrained wage growth, rather than political controls exerted over organised labour, or government neglect. These adverse labour supply conditions help explain why labour incomes remained low compared with the more advanced economies in developing East Asia. By the mid 1990s this backlog of low-productivity workers was much smaller, and labour force growth rates had also begun to slow. This has created the necessary conditions for more rapid and sustained wage growth than in the past.

Third, we have argued that government policies both encouraged and hindered the process of labour market change and of improvements in labour welfare. On the positive side, prudent macroeconomic policy, economic liberalisation, encouragement of agriculture, and investment in human resources made a major contribution to employment expansion, and wages and productivity growth. On the negative side, employment expansion was less rapid in manufacturing than in the NIEs and labour market transition was delayed as a result of the delayed shift away from ISI policies.

Having established a framework for examining labour market issues in the earlier chapters of the book, these conclusions are supported by the analysis in chapters 4–9. We found that intersectoral labour shifts and improvements in human capital have been a major source of rising wages and labour incomes, starting from a position of extreme labour surplus in Java and a national employment structure dominated by agriculture and low-productivity jobs (chapters 4 and 5). Despite high rates of unemployment among young educated people in the cities, rapid economic growth meant more and better-paying jobs for both formal and informal workers.

New wage and non-wage jobs compare favourably with the low and uncertain incomes faced by a majority of rural workers 30 years ago, although employment and income security is still a luxury for a relatively small proportion of the workforce. High rates of urban unemployment were mainly related to segmented wage and employment structures, rather than to slow growth in labour demand relative to supply (chapter 7). Underemployment had not fallen much in terms of conventional indicators, but the shift of many workers out of low productivity jobs largely contributed to overcoming the much greater challenge of poverty alleviation.

One feature of labour market change in Indonesia was the broad spread of jobs and wages growth across sectors, rural–urban boundaries and regions (chapter 6). In this respect the Indonesian experience appears to have differed from other large resource rich countries such as Brazil and also perhaps from China in recent years (Savedoff, 1995; Jian, Sachs and Warner, 1996). Wage differentials narrowed between agriculture and other sectors, the town and the countryside and across provinces. This is notwithstanding the very high wage incomes earned by scarce highly skilled manpower, and even by unskilled workers in certain protected sectors.

In the 1990s, female participation in the workforce played a much more important role in the more skilled segments of the labour market (chapter 9). Improvements in education relative to men contributed to a narrowing of the gender gap in employment and wages, even though women are poorly represented in high-level positions, and significant gender–wage differentials persist.

Although labour market transformation has been by no means a smooth process, the momentum of sustained economic growth transformed the labour market, ridding it of many of the signs of classic labour surplus, which were all too obvious at the beginning of the New Order. Labour market adjustments resulting from rapid economic growth and more recent internationalisation have contributed to a more rather than a less equitable society.

Lessons from Indonesia's experience

What are the general lessons from the Indonesian story and what aspects are unique to the Indonesian case?

Six lessons were derived from our survey of labour market performance in developing economies in chapter 2. What can one learn from the Indonesian labour market experience on each of these subjects? Regarding the first lesson, economic growth and structure played a critical role in labour outcomes. Rapid economic growth underpinned the expansion of non-agricultural and wage employment, even though it was not fast enough to bring about sustained real wage growth, as had occurred in the NIEs 15–20 years earlier.

Sustained economic growth has resulted in a transformation of employment and improvement in labour outcomes over the period of the New Order. Without high rates of economic expansion, the country could not have sustained such a large increase in wage jobs in services initially, and later in manufacturing, as occurred in the 1970s through to the 1990s. It could not have supported the rise in the educational status of the population which has contributed to rising productivity, wages and labour earnings.

The second lesson from the survey of LDC labour market experience relates to the importance of macroeconomic policy. Perhaps more than any other factor, macroeconomic stability and greater opportunities for private business have been the primary forces driving the transformation of the labour market in Indonesia. Although adversely affected by interventionist policies, flows of investment were maintained, even during the oil boom years. The country also suffered an economic downturn in the 1980s. But Indonesia avoided the boom and bust cycle which caused high rates of unemployment and falling wages forced on other Third World countries during the period of inevitable structural adjustment.

In the Indonesian case, conservative macroeconomic policy played a critical role in encouraging investment and employment in all sectors. The key features were budgetary discipline, moderate inflation and an exchange rate which was adjusted, broadly, in accordance with the conditions of Indonesia's external balance.

In particular, the government handled the difficult structural adjustment problems posed by the oil boom with skill and foresight. Indonesia faced the same problems which had dogged many other countries struggling to contain the impact of windfall gains. The channelling of oil revenues to support labour-intensive agriculture, services and public works provided a stimulus to employment and supported wage growth. These policies were critical – both for educated and less-educated workers – at a time when manufacturing was unable to provide enough jobs for the rapidly growing workforce.

The government resisted – with some notable exceptions – pressures for a much higher level of domestic and foreign spending. Hence Indonesia avoided the major problems of internal and external imbalance experienced by several OPEC countries in the post-oil boom period. Although the country experienced an overvalued exchange rate after the oil price rise, this effect was relatively minor compared with the experiences of many other countries. Indonesia devalued the exchange rate on several occasions, thus avoiding harmful effects on growth and employment, especially in the 1980s, when there was a pressing need for structural change.

Two choices were particularly beneficial to labour. These were the decisions to invest heavily in agricultural development and to develop infrastructure and human capital through regional grants – the INPRES programmes in particular. The oil boom offered the possibility of raising rice production and extending communications throughout the country. Agricultural programmes were heavily concentrated in Java-Bali and enabled the seemingly 'involuted' rice sector to absorb more labour, albeit at a slow rate. Perhaps of greater significance, many workers retained a foothold in agriculture and experienced rising incomes for a period of 15–20 years at a time when there were not sufficient remunerative jobs elsewhere in the economy. While agricultural development was neglected, relatively, in much of the Outer Islands, the public works programmes stimulated trade and service activities and encouraged labour mobility.

Nevertheless, although economic policy supported employment and growth in labour welfare, it could have been more favourable to workers. Heavy protection and emphasis on relatively capital-intensive projects into the 1980s did not stimulate many jobs, wages were stagnant for an extended time period, the informal sector grew rapidly and labour was squeezed by deflationary policies. As a consequence, labour market transition was slower than in several East Asian industrialising economies, which deregulated earlier.

The Indonesian experience also confirms the third lesson highlighted in chapter 2 – that labour markets mostly work well, despite restrictive institutional arrangements. A caveat is necessary however – labour markets generally work better under conditions of rising demand for labour associated with growth. Most worthy of note was the role which rapid labour demand growth – and associated improvements in infrastructure – had in supporting labour mobility and a more integrated labour market across sectors and regions. The break-down of 'exclusionary' employment practices in rice agriculture was one powerful example of how more open labour markets can contribute to labour welfare.

At the same time, capital-intensive investment in manufacturing contributed to wide dispersion in wages. Inward-looking policies during the 1970s supported a segmented labour market with large differentials in earnings between a relatively elite workforce and the large majority of wage employees. Part of Indonesia's continuing youth unemployment problem can be attributed to the structure of incentives promoted by protected structures set up by the government during this period. Long periods of job search are a rational response on the part of young people who are willing to gamble on gaining high wage and secure jobs. This aspect of the labour market – together with widespread credentialism – contributed to a wastage of youth resources through unemployment.

Indonesia is a good example with respect to the fourth lesson, which is related to the importance of sequencing of human capital investments. That social and economic policy played a major role in supporting an improvement in job opportunities and wages may seem surprising to many readers, with the image of tight political controls imposed by the military elite which has ruled in Jakarta for 30 years. In the early years, many were sceptical that the new government could, or indeed would be motivated to effect improvements which would help the mass of Indonesian workers. This was especially felt in the wake of the demise of the populist Soekarno, the eradication of the Indonesian communist party – and one of the most powerful trade union bodies in the Third World (SOBSI) – and the bloody and potentially divisive aftermath of the counter coup, which brought the army and Soeharto to power in 1966.

Several factors hardly promoted the government's image of a champion of worker progress. These included the centralised controls which the military and the President established and maintained over political and economic decision making. Also important was its hard line stance towards any opposition – including independent trade union organisations. This scepticism was not unwarranted. This is especially true given the record for corruption and economic mismanagement which some military regimes have promoted in other parts of the world, notably in Africa and Latin America.

However, the achievement of near universal primary enrolments – from not much above 50 per cent – over a period of 30 years, supported development and labour advancement at all levels of society. Education and the associated Family Planning Programme facilitated greater control over family size and both enabled many poorer women to participate more fully in the workforce. These reforms freed poor women from the burden of repeated childbirth and onerous childcare responsibilities. Young women delayed marriage and many, primarily from the poor Java heartland, increasingly moved long distances to seek work. The emphasis on universal primary schooling was important in giving young people – mainly from villages – the confidence to move and take up more demanding jobs in towns and cities in Indonesia, or to continue their schooling. Strong state support for education and increasing opportunities in private schooling facilitated the substantial increase in enrolments at all levels.[1]

Like in the NIEs, the decision to invest heavily in education enabled many Indonesian women in particular to take up higher paying jobs. The increase in the supply of educated people was sufficiently large – and policies which stimulated the demand for unskilled labour strong enough – to prevent a general widening of earnings differentials among wage employees. These effects were not as great – especially between more- and less-educated workers – as in the NIEs, especially given the enclave nature of investments which required high wage and skilled manpower. Thus a more equal distribution of wages has tended to counterbalance forces which have contributed to a worsening of the overall income distribution.

The fifth and sixth lessons from other LDC experience dealt with the costs which workers shoulder in periods of rapid economic growth and structural adjustment, partly through the growth of casual employment and the urban informal sector. Indonesian workers experienced the backwash effects of new industries and technology on traditional, low-productivity industries. These transitional effects adversely affected employment of less-educated and older workers in industries such as textiles, although the oil boom and the green revolution ensured that most workers were able to gain new jobs at a critical transitional stage in the 1970s.

The urban informal sector grew rapidly in Indonesia during the early years of the New Order and continued to expand into the 1990s. Rapid expansion in the early years was partly related to rural labour market pressures and net labour displacement in rice agriculture, before sustained rice production growth began to swamp the backwash effects of new

---

[1] Although the variable quality of education made it more difficult for young people from lower socioeconomic groups to find better jobs, and lengthened their duration of job search.

technology. In the 1980s, the informal sector also expanded rapidly in the period of slower economic growth. In the 1990s, growth of the informal sector was slower but still significant. It was stimulated first by an increase in wage employment opportunities – the proliferation of food stalls and putting-out work – and later by a worrying slow-down in employment growth in labour-intensive industries.

New jobs have frequently been exploitative from a First World perspective. They have often involved child and female labour working long hours a day under sub-standard working conditions, or irregular incomes in sometimes uncertain work in informal jobs.

Fluctuations in economic policy and performance adversely affected labour market outcomes, especially during the years of slower economic growth in the 1980s. Long hours of work and uncertain employment, both in wage jobs and the informal sector were one cost associated with movement of rural and urban poor into higher-paid employment. The much greater mobility of labour has its down side – the hardship endured by millions of workers seeking higher-wage jobs in far off industrial centres and often commuting long distances on a daily or weekly basis to and from their village homes. Inadequate information was often exploited by intermediaries (jobbers, or *calo*).[2] We highlighted the impact of tight controls over the labour movement on labour productivity and labour rights, and the potentially adverse effects on employment of minimum wage legislation. The employment displacement effects of recent increases in minimum wages were less marked than if the policy had been introduced years earlier, but it can be expected to have a longer-term impact through reduced labour market flexibility and incentives.

However, contrary to popular opinion, wage rates do not compare unfavourably with those in neighbouring countries, if they are measured against overall levels of per-capita income. Standards of living had improved markedly, compared with conditions of poverty and insecurity which many men and women and their families faced in their villages of origin. And, even in factories close to their villages, young women gained greater independence and a voice against overbearing employers, as is described in the Wolf's (1992) absorbing account of women factory workers in Central Java in the early 1980s.

Labour rights was one area where Indonesia shared much in common with several more oppressive East Asian governments. Indonesia's policies in this area were largely driven by political considerations. The

---

[2] Although agents (jobbers) provide information on employment opportunities, they can also exploit imperfections in information and the high demand for income among villagers, especially in a society where the poor have little redress to legal and political processes.

association of free labour unions with left-wing political parties and with demands for greater political freedoms contributed to the governments' intransigence on the issue of union rights.

Earlier, when the possibility of slipping into poverty was very real for many – and the possibility of moving out of it seemed just as remote for others – restrictions on trade union freedom was accepted, grudgingly, in return for the improvements in living standards which the economic growth delivered. Such acceptance was much less evident in Indonesia in the 1990s, as workers and urban sympathisers began to weigh up the expected economic gains against the social and political costs.

Enterprise bargaining is recognised in law, and has worked well in some large, established firms since the early years of the New Order. But it is not a general feature of the industrial relations environment. Officially there is a large, well-organised union movement. But in practice, it plays a minor role in representing workers. Strong opposition to union freedoms and pluralism, and the maintenance of tight controls over the officially sanctioned union movement, has meant that most workers have no genuine worker representation. Without increased representation, it is difficult to see how significant increases in labour productivity can be guaranteed in the growing and increasingly diversified industrial sector.

To sum up, the general lesson for labour market transition from this analysis is that rapid economic growth and macroeconomic policies can have a substantial positive impact on labour welfare, especially in the early stages of development, when human resources, agricultural and regional development are emphasised. Sustained economic growth over two to three decades can promote labour welfare significantly, even where overcoming initial conditions of poverty seems an impossible task, in one generation. The message is basically an optimistic one for several of the poorer countries of Asia now seeking to emulate the Indonesian experience.

This message is important in the current debates over the directions of Indonesian development. Income distribution is a key issue, and quite rightly the focus of many observers of the accumulation of wealth among a small number of elite families. But this has not – for the most part – been the result of processes working through the labour market. Policies which seek to directly intervene in the labour market to help solve distribution issues are more likely to harm, rather than help, the employment prospects and welfare of the poor. Redistribution of income and opportunity can be much more effectively undertaken by targeting the poor through education, health and infrastructure programmes than through labour market programmes.

Implications for development theory and policy

The study has implications for development theory and policy in three specific areas: the 'surplus labour' model of development, the role of segmented labour markets during periods of rapid economic growth and the interaction between economic growth and labour market institutions.

How relevant is the modified Lewis model and notion of labour market transition to the Indonesian case? In general, the Lewis model assists the explanation of several key aspects of labour market experience. The failure of wages to rise in key sectors such as rice for extended time periods – even when economic growth was rapid as in the 1970s – is *a priori* evidence for surplus labour at prevailing wage rates. We identified the existence of low-productivity and earnings activities outside rice sector – rather than underemployment or disguised unemployment – as the major source of excess labour supply. A key part of the economic development story was the transfer of labour out of these activities and a rising share of urban wage employment.

Nevertheless, the Lewis model was challenged by the rapid rise in real non-agricultural wages during the rehabilitation and oil boom period. This was a period when other indicators – including rice wage trends – pointed to excess labour supply to the modern sector. Thus it was found that wage rate trends can vary significantly across sectors in the early stages of development, quite apart from any direct government interference in wage setting. Because of low labour mobility, rapid growth in labour demand in particular sectors or regions does not quickly transmit widely in the early stages of development. Three major explanations are suggested in the book for this outcome: the intensity of labour demand shifts in the oil boom period, government wage policies which influence the modern private sector and a catching-up process after a period of real wage decline in the modern sector.

The Lewis model – broadly conceived – seems particularly relevant to well-integrated economies (and labour markets) where two conditions hold: (i) direct government intervention in wage-setting mechanisms is minimal and (ii) international labour migration is not a key feature of development experience in the early stages of rapid economic growth. Japan, South Korea and Taiwan are all good examples. They are well suited as a guide to explaining several aspects of labour market change in Java in Indonesia. It is less relevant as a framework for examining other labour market outcomes in a large economy, where the governments' direct role in economic life is pervasive and segmented labour markets are common.

The second implication for development theory relates to the impact of rapid economic growth on labour market segmentation. While much of the Indonesian economy – the micro-enterprise sector in particular – was highly competitive, segmentation was a feature of the Indonesian labour market in the early years of rapid economic growth. In part, this resulted from a range in technologies and associated labour systems. It was also associated with poverty and labour market discrimination arising from limited choice and information.

As incomes rose, there was a decline in the extent of rural labour market segmentation. Several special kinds of labour contract – which had often varied from village to village and even within villages – began to disappear. As more labour market choices were open to poor labourers, farmers found it increasingly more difficult to recruit wage labour using discriminative contracts. They were forced to raise wages to attract labour from both inside and outside the village. Rapid economic growth also contributed to greater integration of labour markets on a regional basis, in response to improved communications, and also much greater mobility among poorer households.

However, segmentation remained a feature of the Indonesian economy, partly because of structural characteristics – high wages paid in capital-intensive resource based industries – and partly related to policy. Wage differentials across industries and firm types are closely bound up with industrial policy. Promotion and protection of capital-intensive industry in a relatively poor economy is not only a waste of resources, it also creates disequilibrium in labour markets. Firms redistribute some of their excess profits in the form of above-market clearing wages, to promote productivity and industrial peace. But high wages in protected industries raise wage expectations among other industrial workers. The government's attention to minimum wages has been influenced by such expectations among ordinary workers.

Finally, the study suggests that some labour institutions may not be greatly influenced by rapid economic growth. In particular, politics plays a critical role in determining the way in which the government responds to organised labour. Thus, despite the improvement in the education of the workforce, it is doubtful whether bargaining and cooperation between workers and managers over issues such as working conditions, health and safety and insurance has significantly increased in Indonesia over the past 30 years. Significant improvements in industrial relations are needed to promote welfare and productivity as the economy modernises.

Lack of consultation with workers may not be costly in the early stages of export orientation, when footloose industries are more dependent on 'perspiration' than on the creativity of workers. But, it is likely to run counter to efforts aimed at raising labour productivity at later stages when there is an increasing need to improve technological capacity and product quality.

Labour policies

We have already stressed the very positive role which educational expansion and public works programmes played in income and employment growth. Labour protection in policies have been less successful. In the early years they were not given heavy emphasis, despite quite far-reaching labour legislation. A large proportion of the workforce were in agriculture or the informal sector, and there were other pressing priorities. As the country industrialised, labour protection policy assumed greater significance, and there were increasing demands that labour laws be executed more extensively.

In the 1990s, the government's determination to both raise and implement minimum wages, and introduce comprehensive worker social security legislation, heralded a departure from the strategy followed in several other East Asian countries. For many, it was a sign that the regime was concerned about workers' welfare, and the reforms received widespread support in the community, even if sections of business were not altogether enthusiastic. There appeared to be little consideration of the potential impact of reforms on labour costs and employment.

One of the government's stated goals is to raise labour productivity. Two requirements for improved productivity are betterment of often abysmally low wages and greater income security. However, mandatory legislation of minimum wages is certainly not the best way to tackle the issue of low productivity. A minimum wage policy is also questionable on equity grounds because of its potential effects on employment growth and unemployment.

Owing to tightening labour markets from the early 1990s, the distortionary effects of a rigidly applied minimum wage formula may not have been as great as some earlier commentators expected. But there is still a general perception that the government can raise the overall level of wages – not just provide a safety net – by direct action. This command approach has brought results in some development programmes such as rice and family planning. But it is hardly suited to atomistic labour markets across a myriad of activities and regions. The belief that centralised government controls and direction can bring the same benefits to a complex industrial workforce – as it did to the largely agricultural workforce – without a reworking of labour institutions, is misplaced. Human resource development is viewed by some as the magic cure for low levels of productivity. But it is not a substitute for reform of industrial relations principles and practices in the interests of workers and management alike.

We argued that given the large share of the workforce still in low-productivity agriculture and the informal sector, it would be a tragedy if Indonesia's rapid manufacturing employment growth and associated gains in worker welfare were adversely affected. This will be the result if the government miscalculated on what employers are able and willing to pay, and will continue to grow in an increasingly competitive international environment. There were many signs that this was the case, as modern sector job creation slowed towards the mid 1990s.

The future

Looking to the future, three points arise from the analysis in the book. First, it is important to recognise how far Indonesian workers have come in the past 30 years, and the policy initiatives which have contributed to success. As the Soeharto era draws to a close – haltingly – and Indonesians become more exposed to international competition, there is a tendency to judge progress in terms of comparisons with neighbouring countries such as South Korea, Thailand and Malaysia. In the late 1960s, Indonesian workers started far behind these countries. While absolute gaps in wages and GDP are large, they have narrowed in relative terms. The extraordinary achievements in educational expansion and rural development, and associated poverty decline, have been fundamental to rising wages and productivity.

Second, the main labour market challenges in Indonesia in the 1990s remain similar – although certainly less demanding – to those which faced the Soeharto government in its early years. The belief among some that a leap into the technological future will help achieve parity in wages and living standards with neighbouring countries is fanciful. Raising the productivity and incomes of a high proportion of workers, who remain in low productivity agriculture and self-employed occupations, remains the major labour market challenge. Rapid employment growth will also remain the main channel through which this goal can be achieved. Public support for human resource development and training will play a critical supporting role. But this will remain complementary.

Finally, improvements in labour standards and freedoms are likely to play an increasingly important part in assisting increases in labour productivity. Delay in reforms in the area of labour freedoms is not only likely to affect the political landscape. It will also affect the pace of economic reform and development. At the same time, the introduction of new labour standards needs careful consideration in the context of Indonesia's current level of development. The extension of social security coverage to many workers may well pay off – not only in social terms but also in terms of a more motivated and committed workforce. But standards applied willy nilly from abroad are only likely to harm the employment prospects of the poor who are most in need of better jobs.

References

Abegglen, J. C. (1994) *Sea Change: Pacific Asia as the New World Industrial Centre*, The Free Press, New York.

Addison, T. and L. Demery (1988) 'Wages and Working Conditions in East Asia: A Review of Case-Study Evidence', *Development Policy Review*, 6, 371–93.

Adelman, I. and S. Robinson, 'Income Distribution and Development', in H. Chenery and T. N. Srinavasan (eds.), *Development Economics* (Volume 1), North Holland.

Adiratma, R. E. (1969) 'Income and Expenditure Pattern of Rice Producers in Relation to Production and Rice Marketed,' Ph.D. Dissertation, Institut Pertanian, Bogor.

Akerlof, G.A. and J.L. Yellen (eds.) (1986) *Efficiency Wage Models of the Labor Market*, Cambridge University Press.

Akilu, B. and J. R. Harris (1980) 'Migration, Employment, and Earnings', in G. F. Papanek (ed.), *The Indonesian Economy*, Praeger, New York.

Akita, T. and R. A. Lukman (1995) 'Interregional Inequalities in Indonesia: A Sectoral Decomposition Analysis for 1975–92', *Bulletin of Indonesian Economic Studies*, 31(2), 61–82.

Alexander J. and P. Alexander (1982) 'Shared Poverty as Ideology: Agrarian Relationships in Colonial Java', *Man* (New Series), 17, 597–619.

Alexander, J. and A. Booth (1992) 'The Service Sector', in A. Booth (ed.), *The Oil Boom and After: Indonesian Economic Policy and Performance in the Soeharto Era*, Oxford University Press, Singapore, pp. 283–319.

Amsden, A. (1989) *Asia's Next Giant: South Korea and Late Industrialisation*, Oxford University Press, New York.

Anderson, A. G. (1978) 'The Structure and Organization of Rural Marketing in the Cimanuk River Basin West Java', Rural Dynamics Series, No. 3, Agro-Economic Survey, Bogor.

Anker, R. (1983) 'Female Labour Force Participation in Developing Countries: A Critique of Current Definitions and Data Collection', *International Labour Review*, 126(2), 709–23.

Anker, R. and C. Hein (eds.) (1986) *Sex Inequalities in Urban Employment in the Third World*, Macmillan, New York.

Anker, R. M., E. Khan and R. B. Gupta (1987) 'Biases in Measuring the Labour Force', *International Labour Review*, 126(2), 151–67.

Ariff, Mohamed and H. Hill (1985) *Export-Oriented Industrialisation: The ASEAN Experience*, Allen and Unwin, Sydney.

Arndt, H. W. (1971) 'Indonesia – Five Years of "New Order"', *Current Affairs Bulletin*, Department of Adult Education, University of Sydney, 25 January 1971.

——— (1987) 'Industrial Policy in East Asia, 1950–1985', in *Industry and Development*, UNIDO, Vienna. Reprinted 1989, National Centre for Development Studies, No. 2, Australian National University, Canberra.

Arndt, H. W. and H. Hill (1988) 'The Indonesian Economy: Structural Adjustment after the Oil Boom', in *South East Asian Affairs 1988*, Institute of Southeast Asian Studies, Singapore, pp. 106–22.

Arndt, H. W. and R. M. Sundrum (1975) 'Wage Problems and Policies in Indonesia', *International Labour Review*, 112 (5), 369–87.

——— (1980) 'Employment, Unemployment and Under-Employment', *Bulletin of Indonesian Economic Studies*, 16(3), 61–82.

ARTEP (ILO) (1972) 'Manpower and Related Problems in Indonesia', Report on the Mission to Indonesia, April–May 1972, ARTEP-ILO, Bangkok.

Athukorala, P. (1993) 'International Labour Migration in the Asian-Pacific Region: Patterns, Policies and Economic Implications, *Asian-Pacific Economic Literature*, 7(2), 28–57.

Ayadurai, D. (1993) 'Malaysia', in S. Deery and R. Mitchell (eds.), *Labour Law and Industrial Relations in Asia: Eight Country Studies*, Longman Cheshire, pp. 61–95.

Azis, I. J. (1996) 'Eastern Indonesia in the Current Policy Environment', in C. Barlow and J. Hardjono (eds.), *Indonesia Assessment 1995: Development in Eastern Indonesia*, Research School of Pacific and Asian Studies, Australian National University, Canberra and Institute of Southeast Asian Studies, Singapore, pp. 75–122.

Baer, W. and M. E. A. Herve (1966) 'Employment and Industrialization in Developing Countries', *Quarterly Journal of Economics*, 80(1), 88–107.

Bai, Moo Ki (1985) 'The Turning Point in the Korean Economy', *Developing Economies*, 20(2), 117–39.

——— (1993) *Korea's Trade Movement in Transition*, Korea Labor Institute, Seoul.

Bairoch P. and J. M. Limbor (1968) 'Changes in the Industrial Distribution of the World Labor Force', *International Labour Review*, 98(4), 311–36.

Balisacan, A. (1993) 'Agricultural Growth, Landlessness, Off-Farm Employment and Rural Poverty in the Philippines', *Economic Development and Cultural Change*, 41(3), 533–63.

——— (1994) *Poverty, Urbanization and Development Policy: a Philippine Perspective*, University of the Philippines Press, Manila.

Banerjee, B. and J. B. Knight (1991) 'Job Discrimination and Untouchability', in N. Birdsall and R. Sabot (eds.), *Unfair Advantage*, The World Bank, Washington, DC.

Bardhan, P. and A. Rudra (1981) 'Terms and Conditions of Labour Contracts in Agriculture: Results of a Survey of West Bengal', *Oxford Bulletin of Economics and Statistics*, 43 (February), 89–111.

Bardhan, P. K. (1984) *Land, Labour and Rural Poverty: Essays in Development Economics*, Oxford University Press, Delhi.

Barker, R., R. W. Herdt and B. Rose (1985) *The Rice Economy of Asia*, Washington, DC, Resources for the Future.

Barlow, C. (1985) 'Changes in the Economic Position of Workers on Rubber Estates and Small Holdings in Peninsular Malaysia', Working Papers in Trade and Development, Division of Economics, Research School of Pacific Studies, Australian National University, Canberra.

Barlow, C. and C. Condie (1986) 'Changing Economic Relationships in Southeast Asia, and their Implications for Small Farmers', *Outlook on Agriculture*, 15(4), 167–78.

Barlow, C. and J. Hardjono (eds.) (1996) *Indonesia Assessment 1995: Development in Eastern Indonesia*, Research School of Pacific and Asian Studies, Australian National University, Canberra and Institute of Southeast Asian Studies, Singapore.

Barlow, C. and S. Jayasuriya (1987) 'Structural Change and its Impact on Traditional Agricultural Sectors of Rapidly Developing Countries: The Case of Natural Rubber', *Agricultural Economics*, 1, 159–74.

Barlow, C. and T. Tomich (1991) 'Indonesian Agricultural Development: The Awkward Case of Smallholder Tree Crops', *Bulletin of Indonesian Economic Studies*, 27(3), 29–55.

Battercherjee, D. (1987) 'Union-type Effects on Bargaining Outcomes in Indian Manufacturing', *British Journal of Industrial Relations*, 25(2).

Bauer, J. and Young-Soo Shin (1986) 'Female Labor Force Participation and Wages in the Republic of Korea', Working Paper No. 54, East–West Population Institute, East–West Centre, Honolulu.

Bautista, R. (1993) 'Trade and Agricultural Development in the 1980s and the Challenges for the 1990s: Asia', *Agricultural Economics*, 8, 345–75.

(1992) *Development Policy in East Asia: Economic Growth and Poverty Alleviation*, Institute of Southeast Asian Studies, Singapore.

Behrman, J. R. and A. B. Deolalikar (1995) 'Art There Differential Returns to Schooling by Gender? The Case of Indonesian Labor Markets', *Oxford Bulletin of Economics and Statistics*, 57(1), 97–117.

Berg, E. J. (1969) 'Wages Policy and Employment in Less Developed Countries' in A. Smith (ed.), *Wage Policy Issues in Economic Development*, Macmillan, London, pp. 294–337.

Berry, A. (1975) 'Unemployment as a Social Problem in Columbia: Myth and Reality', *Economic Development and Cultural Change*, 23(2), 276–91.

(1978) 'A Positive Interpretation of the Expansion of Urban Services in Latin America, with Some Columbian Evidence', *The Journal of Development Studies*, 14(2), 210–31.

Berry, A. and R. H. Sabot (1978) 'Labour Market Performance in Developing Countries: A Survey', *World Development*, 6, 1199–242.

Bertrand, T. and L. Squire (1980) 'The Relevance of the Dual Economy Model: A Case Study of Thailand', *Oxford Economic Papers*, 32(3), 480–511.

Bhagwati, J. (1993) *India in Transition: Freeing the Economy*, Clarendon Press, Oxford.

Binswanger, H. P. and M. R. Rozenweig (1981) *Contractual Arrangements, Employment and Wages in Rural Labour Markets*, The Agricultural Development Council, New York.

Birdsall, N. and R. Sabot (1993) 'Virtuous Circles: Human Capital Growth and

Equity in East Asia', Background paper for the *East Asian Economic Miracle*, World Bank, Washington.

Blaug, M. (1974) *Education and the Employment Problem in Developing Countries*, ILO, Geneva.

Blinder, A. S. (1973) 'Wage Discrimination: Reduced Form and Structural Estimates', *Journal of Human Resources*, 8(4), 436–55.

Bliss, C. and N. Stern (1978) 'Wages and Nutrition', *Journal of Development Economics*, 5(4) 331–98.

Bloom, D. and R. Freeman (1986) 'The Effects of Rapid Population Growth on Labour Supply and Employment in Developing Countries', *Population and Development Review*, 12(3), 381–414.

Boediono, W., W. McMahon and D. Adams (1992) 'Education, Economic, and Social Development', Second 25 Year Development Plan and Sixth 5 Year Development Plan, Background Papers and Goals, Department of Education and Culture, Jakarta.

Bongnanno, M. (1988) 'Korea's Industrial Relations at the Turning Point', KDI Working Paper No. 8816, Korean Development Institute, Seoul.

Booth, A. (1988) *Agricultural Development in Indonesia*, George Allen and Unwin, Sydney.

—— (1992a) 'Introduction', in A. Booth (ed.), *The Oil Boom and After: Indonesian Economic Policy and Performance in the Soeharto Era*, Oxford University Press, Singapore, pp. 1–38.

—— (1992b) 'Income Distribution and Poverty', in A. Booth (ed.), *The Oil Boom and After: Indonesian Economic Policy and Performance in the Soeharto Era*, Oxford University Press, Singapore, pp. 323–62.

—— (1993) 'Counting the Poor in Indonesia', *Bulletin of Indonesian Economic Studies*, 29(1), 53–84.

—— (1994) 'Survey of Recent Economic Developments', *Bulletin of Indonesian Economic Studies*, 30(3), 3–40.

—— (ed.) (1992) *The Oil Boom and After: Indonesian Economic Policy and Performance in the Soeharto Era*, Oxford University Press, Singapore.

Booth, A. and P. McCawley (1981) 'The Indonesian Economy Since the Mid-Sixties', in A. Booth and P. McCawley (eds.), *The Indonesian Economy During the Soeharto Era*, Oxford University Press, Kuala Lumpur, pp. 1–22.

Booth, A. and R. M. Sundrum (1981) 'Income Distribution', in A. Booth and P. McCawley (eds.), *The Indonesian Economy During the Soeharto Era*, Oxford University Press, Kuala Lumpur, pp. 181–217.

—— (1985) *Labour Absorption Agriculture: Theoretical Analysis and Empirical Investigations*, Oxford University Press, Oxford.

Boserup, E. (1970) *Woman's Role in Economic Development*, St Martin's Press, New York.

BPS (Biro Pusat Statistik) (1991) *Statistik Upah Buruh Tani di Pedesaan 1980–1990*, BPS, Jakarta.

Brand, W. (1968) 'The Manpower Situation in Indonesia', *Bulletin of Indonesian Economic Studies*, 11, 48–72.

Breman, J. (1980) 'The Informal Sector', in *Research, Theory and Practice*, Erasmus University, Rotterdam.

Budhisantoso (1975) 'Rice Harvesting in the Krawang Region (West Java) in Relation to High Yielding Varieties', Working Paper No. 6, Centre of Southeast Asian Studies, Monash University.
Calmfors, L. (1994) 'Active Labour Market Policy and Unemployment: A Framework for the Analysis of Crucial Design Features', Labour Market and Social Policy Occasional Paper No. 15, OECD, Paris.
Campbell, B. O. (1993) 'Development Trends: A Comparative Analysis of the Asian Experience', in N. Ogawa, G. W. Jones and J. Williamson (eds.), *Human Resources in Development along the Asia-Pacific Rim*, Oxford University Press, Singapore, pp. 66–126.
Card, D. and A. B. Krueger (1994) 'Minimum Wages and Employment: A Case Study of the Fast-Food Industry in New Jersey and Pennsylvania', *American Economic Review*, 84, 792–3.
CBS (Central Bureau of Statistics) (Indonesia) (1972) *The Population of Indonesia*, Population Census 1971, Series C, Jakarta.
  (1974) *The Population of Indonesia*, Population Census 1971, Series D, Jakarta.
  (1976–78, 1986–94) *The Labour Force Situation in Indonesia*, Annual Publications based on the National Labour Force Survey (SAKERNAS), Jakarta.
  (1978) *The Labour Force in Indonesia*, Intercensal Population Survey (SUPAS) 1975, Jakarta.
  (1983) *The Population of Indonesia*, Population Census 1980, Series S2, Jakarta.
  (1984) *The Labour Force Situation in Indonesia*, National Socio-Economic Survey (SUSENAS), Jakarta.
  (1987) *The Population of Indonesia*, Intercensal Population Survey (SUPAS) 1985, Series S5, Jakarta.
  (1996) *The Population of Indonesia*, Intercensal Population Survey (SUPAS) 1995, Series S5, Jakarta.
  (various years) *Statistical Yearbook of Indonesia*, Jakarta.
  (various years) *Economic Indicators*, Jakarta.
  (various years) *Average Wages on Estates*, Jakarta.
  (various years) *Survey of Large and Medium Manufacturing Establishments*, Jakarta.
Chandler, G. (1984) 'Market Trade in Rural Java', Monash Paper on Southeast Asia – No. 11, Centre of Southeast Asian Studies, Monash University.
Chandrakirana K. and I. Sadoko (1994) 'Dinamika Ekonomi Informal di Jakarta: Industri Daur Ulang, Angkutan Becak dan Dagang Kakilima', Center for Policy and Implementation Studies, Jakarta.
Chapman, B. J. (1984) *Streetfoods in Indonesia. Vendors in Urban Food Supply*, EPOC, Bogor.
Chapman, B. J. and J. R. Harding (1986) 'Sex Differences in Earnings: An Analysis of Malaysian Wage Data', *Journal of Development Studies*, 21, 362–76.
Chau, L. C. (1976) 'Industrial Growth and Employment in Hong-Kong', *Philippine Economic Journal*, 15(1–2), 82–138.
Chenery, H. B., S. Robinson and M. Syrquin (1986) *Industrialization and Growth: A Comparative Study*, Oxford University Press, New York.
Cho, Yong Sam (1963) *Disguised Unemployment in South Korean Agriculture*, University of California Press, Berkeley.

Clark, D. H. (1983) 'How Secondary School Graduates Perform in the Labor Market: A Study of Indonesia', World Bank Staff Working Paper No. 615, Washington.

(1994) 'Labour Markets for D3 and S1 Graduates', Unpublished Paper, Jakarta.

Clark, D. H. and M. Oey-Gardiner (1991) 'How Indonesian Lecturers have Adjusted to Civil Service Compensation', *Bulletin of Indonesian Economic Studies*, 27(3), 129–41.

Collier, W. L. (1981) 'Agricultural Evolution in Java', in Gary E. Hansen (ed.), *Agricultural and Rural Development in Indonesia*, Westview Press, Boulder, Colorado, pp. 147–78.

Collier, W., Soentoro, G. Wiradi and Makali (1974) 'Agricultural Technology and Institutional Change in Java', *Food Research Institute Studies*, 8(2), 169–94.

Collier, W., Soentoro, K. Kidayat and Y. Yuliati (1982) 'Labour Absorption in Javanese Rice Cultivation', in W. Gooneratne (ed.), *Labour Absorption in Rice-Based Agriculture: Case Studies from Southeast Asia*, ILO-ARTEP, Bangkok, pp. 3–65.

Collier, W. L. et al. (1982) 'Acceleration of Rural Development in Java', *Bulletin of Indonesian Economic Studies*, 18(3), 84–101.

Collier, W. L. et al. (1993) 'A New Approach to Rural Development in Java: Twenty Five Years of Village Studies', Unpublished paper, Jakarta.

Colter, Y. (1982) 'Pendapatan dan Kesempatan Kerja Buruh Migran di Mariuk dan Tambakdahan, Kecamatan Binong, Subang', Unpublished Masters Thesis, Bogor Agricultural University (IPB), Bogor.

(1984) 'Ciri-Ciri dan Pola Tenaga Kerja Migran Dari Daerah Pedesaan', Rural Dynamics Series No. 24, Agro-Economic Survey, Bogor.

Corden, M. (1984) 'Booming Sector and Dutch Disease Economics: Survey and Consolidation', *Oxford Economic Papers*, 35, 359–80.

Corden, W. M. (1981) 'Booming Sector and Dutch Disease Economics: A Survey', *Oxford Economic Papers*, 36, 359–80.

Corden, W. M. and P. Warr (1981) 'The Petroleum Boom and Exchange Rate Policy in Indonesia', *Ekonomi dan Keuangan Indonesia*, 29(3), 335–59.

Cox-Edwards, A. and S. Edwards (1994) 'Labour Market Distortions and Structural Adjustment in Developing Countries', in S. Horton, R. Kanbur and D. Mazumdar (eds.), *Labor Markets in an Era of Adjustment* (Volume I: *Issues Papers*), EDI Development Series, The World Bank, Washington, DC.

Cremer, G. (1990) 'Who Are Those Misclassified as Others? A Note on the Indonesian Labour Force Statistics', *Bulletin of Indonesian Economic Studies*, 26(1), 69–91.

Crouch, H. (1978) *The Army and Politics in Indonesia*, Cornell University Press, Ithaca.

(1992) 'An Ageing President, An Ageing Regime', in H. Crouch and H. Hill (eds.), *Indonesia Assessment 1992: Political Perspectives on the 1990s*, Department of Political and Social Change, Research School of Pacific Studies, Australian National University, Canberra, pp. 43–62.

Dapice, D. O. (1980) 'An Overview of the Indonesian Economy', in G.F. Papanek (ed.), *The Indonesian Economy*, Praeger, New York, pp. 3–55.

David, C. C. and K. Otsuka (1994) *Modern Rice Technology and Income Distribution in Asia*, Boulder, London, chapters 1–2 and chapter 12.

Davis, K. (1984) 'Wives and Work: The Sex Role Revolution and its Consequences', *Population and Development Review*, 10(3), 397–417.
de Soto, H. (1989) *The Other Path: The Informal Revolution*, Harper and Row, New York.
de Wit, Y. B. (1973) 'The Kabupaten Programme', *Bulletin of Indonesian Economic Studies*, 9(1), 65–85.
Deane, P. (1965) *The First Industrial Revolution*, Cambridge University Press, London.
Deery, S. and R. Mitchell (eds.) (1993) *Labour Law and Industrial Relations in Asia: Eight Country Studies*, Longman Cheshire, Melbourne.
Deyo, F. C. (1989) *Beneath the Miracle: Labour Subordination in the New Asian Industrialism*, University of California Press, Berkeley.
Deyo, F. C., S. Haggard and H. Koo (1987) 'Labour in the Political of East Asian Industrialization', *Bulletin of Concerned Asian Scholars*, April-June.
Dhanani, S. (1994a) 'Employment, Remuneration and Training in a 1994 Tracer Study of Technical Graduates in Indonesia', Jakarta.
 (1994b) 'Unemployment and Underemployment in a Growing Economy: Evidence from Indonesian Labour Force Surveys 1976–1993', Technical Report. No. 45, Jakarta.
 (1994c) Unemployment and Underemployment in Indonesia in the 1980s, Unpublished paper, Jakarta, March.
 (1994d) 'Kebutuhan Pelatiham di Sektor Industri Pengolahan: Hasil Temuan Survai di Sektor Industri Pengolahan Tahun 1992', Seminar paper presented at the Workshop on Vocational Training, Labour Markets and Economic Development in Indonesia, Bali 10–12 February 1994.
Dick, H. (1982) 'Survey of Recent Economic Developments', *Bulletin of Indonesian Economic Studies*, 18(1), 1–38.
 (1993) 'Manufacturing', in H. Dick, J. J. Fox and J. Mackie (eds.), *Balanced Development: East Java in the New Order*, Oxford University Press, Singapore, pp. 230–55.
Dickens, R., S. Machin and A. Manning (1993) 'The Effect of Minimum Wages on Employment: Theory and Evidence from Britain', Centre for Economic Performance, London School of Economics, Discussion Paper No. 183.
Dréze, J. and A. Mukerjee (1989) 'Labour Contracts in Rural India: Theories and Evidence', in S. Chakravarty (ed.), *The Balance between Industry and Agriculture in Economic Development*, Proceedings of the Eighth World Congress of the International Economic Association (Delhi), St. Martin's Press, New York, pp. 233–65.
Durand, J. D. (1975) *The Labour Force In Economic Development*, Princeton University Press.
Edgren, G. (1979) 'Fair Labour Standards and Trade Liberalisation', *International Labour Review*, 118(5), 523–44.
 (1984) 'Spearheads of Industrialisation or Sweatshops in the Sun: A Critical Appraisal of Labour Conditions in Asian Export Processing Zones', in E. Lee (ed.), *Export Processing Zones and Industrial Employment in Asia: Papers and Proceedings of a Technical Workshop*, Asian Employment Programmeme, ILO, Bangkok.

Edmundson, W. C. (1976) 'Land, Food, and Work in East Java', New England Monographs in Geography No. 4, University of New England, Armidale.

(1994) 'Do the Rich Get Richer, Do the Poor Get Poorer?', *Bulletin of Indonesian Economic Studies*, 30(2), 133–48.

Effendi, T. N. (1991) 'The Growth of Rural Non-Farm Activities at the Local Level: A Case Study of Causes and Effects In A Subdistrict of Upland Central Java', Thesis submitted for degree of Doctor of Philosophy, School of Social Sciences, The Flinders University of South Australia, Adelaide.

Effendi, T. N. and C. Manning (1993) 'Rural Development and Nonfarm Employment in Java', in B. Koppel, J. Hawkins and W. James (eds.), *Development or Deterioration: Work in Rural Asia*, Lynne Rienner Publishers, Boulder, pp. 211–48.

Eicher, C. and L. Witt (eds.) (1964) *Agriculture in Economic Development*, McGraw-Hill, New York.

Elson, R. E. (1984) *Javanese Peasants and the Colonial Sugar Industry: Impact and Change in an East Java Residency 1830–1940*, Oxford University Press, Singapore.

Evers, H.-D. (1989) 'Urban Poverty and Labour Supply Strategies in Jakarta', chapter 7 in G. Rodgers (ed.), *Urban Poverty and the Labour Market: Access to Jobs and Incomes in Asian and Latin American Cities*. ILO, Geneva.

Fane, G. (1994) 'Survey of Recent Economic Developments', *Bulletin of Indonesian Economic Studies*, 30(1), 3–38.

Fane, G. and T. Condon (1997) 'Trade Reform in Indonesia 1987–95', *Bulletin of Indonesian Economic Studies*, 32(3), 33–54.

Fei, J. C. H. and G. Ranis (1964) *Development of the Labour Surplus Economy: Theory and Practice*, Homewood, Illinois.

Fields, G. S. (1990) 'Labor Standards, Economic Development and International Trade', in S. Herzenberg and J. F. Perez-Lopez (eds.), *Labor Standards and Development in the Global Economy*, Bureau of International Labor Affairs, US Department of Labor, Washington, DC, pp. 19–34.

(1994) 'Changing Labor Market Conditions and Economic Development in Hong Kong, the Republic of Korea, Singapore, and Taiwan, China', *The World Bank Economic Review*, 8(3), 395–414.

Fields, G. S. and H. Wan Jr (1989) 'Wage Setting Institutions and Economic Growth', *World Development*, 17(9), 1471–93.

Fong Chan Onn (1989) 'Wages and Labour Welfare in the Malaysian Electronics Industry', *Labour and Society*, 14 (special issue on *High Tech and Labour*), 81–102.

Frank, C. R. (1968) 'Urban Unemployment Economic Growth in Africa', *Oxford Economic Papers*, 20(2).

Freeman, R. (1992a) 'Labor Market Institutions and Policies: Help or Hindrance to Economic Development?', *Annual Proceedings of the World Bank Conference on Development Economics 1992*, World Bank, Washington DC, pp. 117–56.

(1992b) 'Does Suppression of Labor Contribute to Economic Success? Labor Relations and Markets in East Asia', Background paper for the *East Asian Economic Miracle*, World Bank, Washington DC.

Frenkel, S. (1993). 'Organised Labor in the Asia-Pacific Region: A Comparative

Study of Unionism in Nine Countries', Cornell International Industrial and Labor Relations Report No. 208, ILR Press, Ithaca.
Furnivall, J. S. (1939) *Netherlands Indies: A Study of a Plural Economy*, Cambridge University Press, London.
Galenson, W. (1992) *Labor and Economic Growth in Five Asian Countries: South Korea, Malaysia, Taiwan, Thailand and the Philippines*, Praeger, New York.
Gannicot, Ken (1987) 'Women, Wages and Workers: Some Evidence from Taiwan', *Economic Development and Cultural Change*, 34(4), 721–30.
Garnaut, R. (1977) 'Resource Trade and the Development Process in Developing Countries', in L. B. Krause and H. Patrick (eds.), *Mineral Resources in the Pacific Area*, Papers and Proceedings of the Ninth Pacific Trade and Development Conference, Federal Reserve Bank of San Francisco, San Francisco, California, pp. 135–73.
 (1980) 'General Repercussions of the Resources Boom in the Segmented Indonesian Economy', in R. Garnaut and P. McCawley (eds.), *Indonesia: Growth and Poverty*, Australian National University, Canberra, pp. 413–26.
Garnaut, R. and C. Manning (1974) *The Transformation of a Melanesian Economy: Irian Jaya*, ANU Press, Canberra.
Geertz, C. (1963) *Agricultural Involution*, University of California Press, Berkeley.
Gelb, A. and Associates (1988) *Oil Windfalls: Blessing or Curse*, Oxford University Press, Oxford.
Ghose, A. K. (1980) 'Wages and Employment in Indian Agriculture', *World Development*, 8, 413–28.
Ginanjar K. (1994) 'Berbagai Pokok Strategi Pembangunan Nasional Dalam Rangka Mengatasi Pengangguran', Paper presented at the *National Seminar on Unemployment*, Jakarta, May 3–4.
Godfrey, M. (1987) 'Planning for Education, Training and Employment in Indonesia', Summary Report, ILO/UNDP Project INS/84/006, Jakarta.
 (1992) *Wage Statistics for Employment Monitoring and Labour Market Analysis*, ILO-UNDP-Department of Manpower, Jakarta.
 (1993) *Labour Monitoring and Employment Policy in a Developing Economy: A Study of Indonesia*, ILO-ARTEP, New Delhi.
Gray, C. (1979) 'Civil Service Compensation in Indonesia', *Bulletin of Indonesian Economic Studies*, 15(1), 85–113.
Gregory, P. (1980) 'An Assessment of Changes in Employment Conditions in Less Developed Countries', *Economic Development and Cultural Change*, 28(4), 673–700.
Gregory, R. G. (1991) 'Jobs and Gender: A Lego Approach to the Australian Market', in K. W. Clements, R. G. Gregory and T. Takayama (eds.), *International Economics Postgraduate Research Conference Volume*, Supplement to the Economic Record, Economic Research Centre, Department of Economics, University of Western Australia, Perth, pp. 20–40.
Grijns, M. and A. van Velzen (1993) 'Working Women: Differentiation and Marginalisation', C. Manning and J. Hardjono (eds.), *Indonesia Assessment 1993 – Labour: Sharing in the Benefits of Growth?* Political and Social Change Monograph, Research School of Pacific Studies, Australian National University, pp.214–28.

Grijns, M., S. Machfudz, P. Sajogyo, I. Smyth and A. van Velzen (1992) 'Gender, Marginalisation and Rural Industries. Female Entrepreneurs, Wage Workers and Family Workers in West Java, Indonesia', West Java Non-farm Sector Research Project, Bandung.

Guinness, P. (1986) *Harmony and Hierarchy in a Javanese Kampung*, Oxford University Press, Singapore.

—— (1990) 'Indonesian Migrants in Johor: An Itinerant Labour Force', *Bulletin of Indonesian Economic Studies*, 26(1), 117–31.

Gunawan, M. et al. (1977) *Penyediaan dan Kebutuhan Tenaga Kerja di Sektor Pertanian: Tahap II 1976/77*, Rural Dynamics Study, Agro-Economic Survey, Bogor.

Gunawan, M., R. Nurmanaf and M. Husein Sawit (1979) 'Penyediaan dan Kebutuhan Tenaga Kerja di Sektor Pertanian: Tahap IIV1978/79', Rural Dynamics Study, Agro-Economic Survey, Bogor.

Habir, A. D. (1993) 'The Emerging Indonesian Managerial Élite: Professionals and Patriarchs', *Southeast Asian Affairs*, Institute of Southeast Asian Studies, Singapore, pp.161–82.

Hadiz, V. R. (1992) 'The Political Significance of Recent Working Class Action in Indonesia', Paper presented at the Centre of Southeast Asian Studies Annual Winter Lecture Series, Monash University, Melbourne, July 22.

—— (1993) 'Workers and Working Class Politics in the 1990s', in *Indonesia Assessment 1993 – Labour: Sharing in the Benefits of Growth?*, Political and Social Change Monograph, Research School of Pacific Studies, Australian National University, pp. 186–202.

Hansen, B. (1969) 'Employment and Wages in Rural Egypt', *American Economic Review*, 59(3), 298–313.

Harberger, A. C. (1988) 'Growth, Industrialization, and Economic Structure: Latin America and East Asia Compared', in H. Hughes (ed.), *Achieving Industrialization in East Asia*, Cambridge University Press, Cambridge, 164–94.

Hardjono, J. (1986) 'Transmigration: Looking to the Future', *Bulletin of Indonesian Economic Studies*, 22(2), 28–53.

—— (1987) *Land, Labour and Livelihood in a West Java Village*, Gadjah Mada University Press, Yogyakarta.

—— (1993) 'From Farm to Factory: Transition in Rural Employment in Majalaya, West Java', in *Indonesia Assessment 1993 – Labour: Sharing in the Benefits of Growth?*, Political and Social Change Monograph, Research School of Pacific Studies, Australian National University, pp. 273–89.

Harris, J. and M. P. Todaro (1970) 'Migration, Unemployment and Development: A Two-Sector Analysis', *American Economic Review*, 60(1), 126–42.

Hart, G. (1986) *Power, Labor and Livelihood: Processes of Change in Rural Java*, University of California Press, Berkeley.

Hasibuan, S. (1968) 'Political Unionism and Economic Development in Indonesia: A Case Study of North Sumatra', Unpublished Ph.D. Thesis, University of California, Berkeley.

Hawkins, E. D. (1963), 'Labour in Transition', in R. McVey (ed.), *Indonesia*, Human Relations Area Files Press, New Haven, pp. 248–71.

Hayami, Y. and M. Kikuchi (1981) *Asian Village Economy at the Crossroads: An Economic Approach to Institutional Change*, University of Tokyo Press, Tokyo.
Hetler, C. B. (1989) 'The Impact of Circular Migration on a Village Economy', *Bulletin of Indonesian Economic Studies*, 25(1), 53–76.
Heyzer, N. (1987) *Women Workers in Southeast Asia: Problems and Strategies*, Asian and Pacific Development Centre, Kuala Lumpur.
—— (1989) 'Asian Women Wage-Earners: Their Situation and Possibilities for Donor Intervention', *World Development*, 17(7), 1109–23.
Heyzer, N. (ed.) (1988) *Daughters in Industry: Work, Skills and Consciousness of Women Workers in Asia*, Asian and Pacific Development Centre, Kuala Lumpur.
Hidayat (1979) *Pengembangan Sektor Informal Dalam Pembangunan Nasional: Masalah dan Porspek*, Pusat Penelitian Ekonomi dan Sumber Daya Manusia, Fakultas Ekonomi, Universitas Padjadjaran, Bandung.
Hill, H. (1980) 'Choice of Technique in the Indonesian Weaving Industry', Ph.D. Thesis, Australian National University, Canberra.
—— (1989) *Unity and Diversity: Regional Economic Development in Indonesia since 1980*, Oxford University Press, Singapore.
—— (1990) 'Indonesia's Industrial Transformation', *Bulletin of Indonesian Economic Studies*, 26(2 and 3), 75–110.
—— (1992) 'Regional Development in a "Boom and Bust Petroleum Economy": Indonesia since 1970', *Economic Development and Cultural Change*, 40(2), 351–79.
—— (1994) 'The Economy', in H. Hill (ed.), *Indonesia's New Order: The Dynamics of Socio-Economic Transformation*, Allen and Unwin, Sydney, pp. 54–122.
—— (1995) *Southeast Asia's Emerging Giant: Indonesian Economic Policy and Development Since 1966*, Cambridge University Press, Cambridge.
—— (1996) *Southeast Asia's Emerging Giant: Indonesian Economic Policy and Development Since 1966*, Cambridge University Press, Cambridge.
Hill, H. (ed.), (1991) *Indonesia Assessment 1991*, Political and Social Change Monograph 13, Australian National University, Canberra (Special Topic: Higher Education in Indonesia).
Ho, S. (1982) 'Economic Development and Rural Industry in South Korea and Taiwan', *World Development*, 10(11), 973–90.
Horstmann, K. and W. Rutz (1980) *The Population Distribution in Java 1971: A Map of Population Density by Sub Districts and Its Analysis*, Institute of Developing Economies, Tokyo.
Horton, S., R. Kanbur and D. Mazumdar (eds.) (1994a) *Labor Markets in an Era of Adjustment*, vols I and II. The World Bank, Washington DC.
Horton, S., R. Kanbur and D. Mazumdar (1994b) 'Labor Markets in an Era of Adjustment: an Overview', in S. Horton, R. Kanbur and D. Mazumdar (eds.), *Labor Markets in an Era of Adjustment,* vol. I: *Issues Papers*, EDI Development Series, The World Bank, Washington DC, pp. 1–59.
Hough, J. and S. Wiranta (1994) 'Labour Market and Higher Education Graduate Employment in Indonesia', *Masyarakat Indonesia*, 21(1), 33–52.
Hughes, H. (1988) *Achieving Industrialization in East Asia*, Cambridge University Press, New York.

Hughes, H. and B. Woldekidan (1994) 'The Emergence of the Middle Class in ASEAN Countries', *ASEAN Economic Bulletin*, 11(2), 139–49.

Hugo, G. (1978) *Population Mobility in West Java*, Gadjah Mada University Press, Yogyakarta.

—— (1983) 'Road to Transport, Population Mobility and Development in Indonesia', in G. Jones and H. V. Richter (eds.), *Population Mobility and Development*, Development Studies Monograph No. 27, Australian National University, Canberra.

—— (1985) 'Structural Change and Labour Mobility in Rural Java', in G. Standing (ed.), *Labour Circulation and the Labour Process*, Croom Helm, London, 46–88.

—— (1993a) 'Indonesian Labour Migration to Malaysia: Trends and Policy Implications', in *Southeast Journal of Social Science*, 27(1), 36–70.

—— (1993b) 'International Labour Migration', in *Indonesia Assessment 1993 – Labour: Sharing in the Benefits of Growth?*, Political and Social Change Monograph, Research School of Pacific Studies, Australian National University, pp. 108–26.

Hugo, G., T. D. Hull, V. J. Hull and G. W. Jones (1987) *The Demographic Dimension in Indonesian Development*, Oxford University Press, Singapore.

Hull, T. (1991) 'Population Growth Falling in Indonesia: Preliminary Results of the 1990 Census', *Bulletin of Indonesian Economic Studies*, 27(2), 137–42.

Hull, V. (1976) 'Women in Java's Middle Class: Progress or Regress', Working Paper Series No. 3, Population Institute, Gajah Mada University, Yogyakarta.

Huppi, M. and M. Ravallion (1991) 'The Sectoral Structure of Poverty During an Adjustment Period: Evidence for Indonesia in the mid-1980s', *World Development*, 19(12), 1653–78.

Hüsken, F. (1979) 'Landlords, Sharecroppers and Agricultural Labourers: Changing Labour Relations in Rural Java', *Journal of Contemporary Asia*, 9(2), 140–51.

Hussmanns, R., F. Mehran and V. Verma (1990) *Surveys of Economically Active Population, Employment, Unemployment and Underemployment: An ILO Manual on Concepts and Methods*, International Labour Office, Geneva.

Hymer, S. and S. Resnick (1969) 'A Model of an Agrarian Economy with Nonagricultural Activities', *American Economic Reviews*, 59(4), 493–506.

ILO [International Labour Office] (1970) *Towards Full Employment*, Geneva.

—— (1971) *Matching Employment Opportunities and Expectations: A Programme of Action for Ceylon*. Geneva.

—— (1972) *Employment, Incomes and Inequality*. Geneva.

—— (1985), *Innovative Approaches to Industrial Relations in ASEAN*, ILO-UNDP, Geneva.

—— (1987) *World Labour Report*, vol. I–II, Geneva.

—— (1989) *World Labour Report*, vol. IV, Geneva.

—— (1992) *World Labour Report*, vol. V, Geneva.

—— (1993) 'A Comprehensive Women's Employment Strategy for Indonesia', ILO/UNDP TSSI Mission, Bangkok.

—— (1995) *World Labour Report*, Geneva.

—— (various years) *Yearbook of Labour Statistics*, Geneva.

INDOC (The Indonesian Documentation and Information Centre) (1981–1987/8),

Indonesian Workers and Their Right to Organise, Leiden. (Main report in May 1981 and annual updates with the same title to 1986 and for 1987–8.)

Indonesia Central Bureau of Statistics, National Family Planning Coordinating Board and Ministry of Health (1995) *Indonesia: Demographic and Health Survey 1994, Preliminary Report*, Macro International Inc, Jakarta.

Indonesia. Department of Manpower (1993a) *Manpower and Employment Situation in Indonesia 1993*, Department of Manpower/UNDP/ILO, Jakarta.

Indonesia. Department of Manpower (1993b) *Data Ketenagakerjaan*, Jakarta.

Ingleson, J. (1981) 'Worker Consciousness and Labour Unions in Colonial Java', *Pacific Affairs*, 54(3), 485–501.

—— (1986) *In Search of Justice: Workers and Unions in Colonial Java, 1908–1926*, Oxford University Press, Singapore.

James, W. E. (1995) 'Survey of Recent Developments', *Bulletin of Indonesian Economic Studies*, 31(3), 3–38.

James, W. E., S. Naya and G. M Meier (1989) *Asian Development: Economic Success and Policy Lessons*, The University of Wisconsin Press, Madison.

Jayasuriya, S. and C. Manning (1990), 'Agricultural Wage Growth and Rural Labour Market Adjustment: The Case of Java 1970–1988', Working Papers in Trade and Development No. 90/2, The Australian National University, Canberra.

Jayasuriya, S. and I. Ketut Nehen (1989) 'Bali: Economic Growth and Tourism', in H. Hill (ed.), *Unity and Diversity: Regional Economic Development in Indonesia since 1980*, Oxford University Press, Singapore, pp. 331–49.

Jayasuriya, S. and R. T. Shand (1986) 'Technological Change and Labour Absorption in Asian Agriculture: Some Emerging Trends', *World Development*, 14(3), 415–28.

Jellinek, L. (1991) *The Wheel of Fortune: The History of a Poor Community in Jakarta*, University of Hawaii Press, Honolulu.

Jian, T., J. T. Sachs and A. M. Warner (1996) 'Trends in Regional Inequality in China', NBER Working Paper No. 5412, New York.

Jiminiz, R. T. (1993) 'The Philippines', in S. Deery and R. Mitchell (eds), *Labour Law and Industrial Relations in Asia: Eight Country Studies*, Longman, Cheshire, pp. 208–40.

Johansen, F. (1993) *Poverty Reduction in East Asia: The Silent Revolution*, World Bank, Washington, pp. 1–24.

Jones, G. W. (1974) 'What Do We Know About the Labour Force in Indonesia', *Majalah Demografi Indonesia*, 1(2), 7–36.

—— (1977) 'Factors Affecting Labour Force Participation of Females in Jakarta', *Kajian Ekonomi Malaysia*, 14(2), 71–93.

—— (1981) 'Labour Force Developments Since 1961', in A. Booth and P. McCawley (eds), *The Indonesian Economy During the Suharto Era*, Oxford University Press, Kuala Lumpur, pp. 218–61.

—— (1983) *Structural Change and Prospects for Urbanization in Asian Countries*, Papers of the East–West Population Institute No. 88, Honolulu.

—— (1984) 'Links between Urbanization and Sectoral Shifts in Employment in Java', *Bulletin of Indonesian Economic Studies*, 20(3), 120–57.

(1986) 'Differentials in Female Labour Force Participation Rates in Indonesia: Reflection of Economic Needs and Opportunities, Culture or Bad Data?', *Majalah Demografi Indonesia Nomor*, 26(2), 1–30.

(1988) 'Economic Growth, Changing Employment Structure and Implications for Educational Planning in ASEAN Countries', NUPRI Research paper Series No. 47.

(1993) 'Dilemmas in Expanding Education for Faster Economic Growth: Indonesia, Malaysia and Thailand', in N. Ogawa, G. W. Jones and J. Williamson (eds.), *Human Resources in Development along the Asia-Pacific Rim*, Oxford University Press, Singapore, pp. 229–58.

(1994) 'Labour Force and Education', in H. Hill (ed.), *Indonesia's New Order: The Dynamics of Socio-Economic Transformation*, Allen and Unwin, Sydney, pp. 145–78.

Jones, G. W. and B. Supraptilah (1976) 'Underutilisation of Labour in Palembang and Ujung Pandang', *Bulletin of Indonesian Economic Studies*, 12(2), 30–57.

Jones, G. W. and C. Manning (1992) 'Labour Force and Employment During the 1990s', in A. Booth (ed.), *The Oil Boom and After: Indonesian Economic Policy and Performance in the Soeharto Era*, Oxford University Press, Singapore, pp. 363–410.

Jones, G. W. and S. G. M. Mamas (1996) 'The Changing Employment Structure of the Extended Jakarta Metropolitan Region', *Bulletin of Indonesian Economic Studies*, forthcoming.

Jones, G. W., E. Sulistyaningsih and T. H. Hull (1995) 'Prostitution in Indonesia', Working Papers in Demography No. 52, Research School of Social Sciences, The Australian National University, Canberra.

Junankar, P. N. (1988) *Very Long Term Unemployment*. Commission of the European Communities, Luxembourg.

Keyfitz, N. (1985) 'An East Javanese Village in 1953 and 1985: Observations on Development', *Population and Development Review*, 11(4), 695–719.

(1989) 'Putting Trained Labour Power to Work: The Dilemma of Education and Employment', *Bulletin of Indonesian Economic Studies*, 25(3), 35–56.

Khan, A. R. (1994) 'Stabilisation, Structural Adjustment and the Labour Market: Issues and Evidence from Asia', in R. Islam (ed.), *Social Dimensions of Economic Reforms in Asia*, ILO, Geneva.

Khoo, Siew-Ean (ed.) (1987) *Women's Economic Participation in Asia and the Pacific*, Economic and Social Commission for Asia and the Pacific, United Nations, Bangkok.

Kim, J. H. (1986) *Wages, Employment and Income Distribution in South Korea: 1960–83*, ARTEP-ILO, New Delhi.

Klinger, G. D. (1993) 'Labour in Mining: The Kaltim Prima Coal Experience', in *Indonesia Assessment 1993 – Labour: Sharing in the Benefits of Growth?*, Political and Social Change Monograph, Research School of Pacific Studies, Australian National University, pp. 173–85.

Korns, A. (1987) 'Distinguishing Signal from Noise in Labor Force Data for Indonesia', Development Studies Project, Research Paper No. 1, Jakarta.

(1988) 'Wage Data at BPS', DSP Research Paper No. 4, Jakarta.

Korns, A. et al. (1994) 'Kumpulan Paper Mengenai Evaluasi Data Tenaga Kerja', DSP Working Paper, Jakarta.
Krongkaew, M. (1994) 'Income Distribution in East Asian Developing Countries: an Update', *Asian-Pacific Economic Literature*, 8(2), 58–73.
Krueger, A. O. (1981) *Trade and Employment in Developing Countries*, University of Chicago Press, Chicago.
Krugman, P. 1994. 'The myth of Asia's miracle', *Foreign Affairs*, 73(6): 62–78.
Kuo, S. (1977) *Labour Absorption in Taiwan, 1954–1971*, Council for Manpower Studies Reprint Series No. 7, School of Economics, University of Philippines, Diliman.
— (1983) *The Taiwan Economy in Transition*, Westview Press, Colorado.
Kuznets, P. W. (1976) 'Labour Absorption in Korea Since 1963', *Philippine Economic Journal*, 15(1–2), 36–81.
Kuznets, S. (1957) 'Quantitative Aspects of the Economic Growth of Nations: Industrial Distribution of National Product and Labor Force', *Economic Development and Cultural Change*, 5(4), 3–111.
— (1965) *Economic Growth and Structure: Selected Essays*, W. W. Norton, New York.
— (1982) 'The Pattern of Shifts of Labor Force from agriculture 1950–70', in M. Gersovitz et al. (eds.), *The Theory and Experience of Economic Development: Essays in Honor of Sir W. Arthur Lewis*, George Allen and Unwin, London, pp. 43–59.
Lambert, R. (1994) 'Authoritarian State Unionism in New Order Indonesia', Paper Presented at the 8th AIRAANZ Conference, Sydney.
Lee, K.-H. and S. Nagaraj (1995) 'Male-Female Earnings Differentials in Malaysia', *The Journal of Development Studies*, 31(3), 467–80.
Lee, Won-Duck (1990) 'Economic Growth and Earnings Distribution in Korea', Working Paper No. 90–03, Korea Labor Institute, Seoul.
Lehrman, C. (1983) 'Sex-Differential Patterns of Circular Migration: A Case Study of Semarang, Indonesia', *Peasant Studies*, 10(4), 251–69.
Lewis, W. A. (1954) 'Economic Development with Unlimited Supplies of Labour', *The Manchester School of Economics and Social Studies*, 22, 139–91.
Liddle, R. W. (1993) 'Politics 1992–1993: Sixth Term Adjustments in Rural Formula', in C. Manning and J. Hardjono (eds.), *Indonesia Assessment 1993. Labour: Sharing in the Benefits of Growth?*, Department of Political and Social Change, Research School of Pacific Studies, Australian National University, Canberra.
Lim, L. L. (1988) 'Labour Markets, Labour Flows and Structural Change in Peninsular Malaysia', in Pang Eng Fong (ed.), *Labour Market Developments and Structural Change: The Experience of ASEAN and Australia*, Singapore University Press, Singapore, pp. 100–38.
— (1993) 'The Feminization of Labour in the Asia-Pacific Rim', in N. Ogawa, G. W. Jones and J. Williamson (eds.), *Human Resources in Development along the Asia-Pacific Rim*, Oxford University Press, Singapore, pp.175–206.
Lim, L. Y. C. (1978) 'Women Workers in Multinational Corporations: The Case of the Electronics Industry in Malaysia and Singapore', Michigan Occasional Paper No. 9, University of Michigan.
Lin, Ching-yuan (1988) 'East Asia and Latin America as Contrasting Models', *Economic Development and Cultural Change* (Supplement), 36(3), S153–98.

Little, I. M. D., D. Mazumdar and J. M. Page Jr (1987) *Small Manufacturing Enterprises: A Comparative Study of India and Other Economies*, published for The World Bank, Oxford University Press.

Lluch, C. and D. Mazumdar (1985) *Wages and Employment in Indonesia*, World Bank, Washington DC.

Lok, H. P. (1993) 'Employment in the Garment Industry: an employer's perspective', in C. Manning and J. Hardjono (eds.), *Indonesia Assessment 1993 – Labour: Sharing in the Benefits of Growth?* Political and Social Change Monograph, Research School of Pacific Studies, The Australian National University, pp. 155–72.

Lubis, M (1981) 'Keadaan Buruh Kita Dewasa Ini: Sebuah Tinjauan Hak Asasi Manusia', *Prisma*, 10(1), 48–55.

Mackie, J. A. C. (1967) 'The Government Estates', in T. K. Tan (ed.), *Sukarno's Guided Indonesia*, The Jacaranda Press, Brisbane, pp. 58–72.

Mackie, J. and A. MacIntyre (1995) 'Politics', in H. Hill (ed.), *Indonesia's New Order: The Dynamics of Socio-economic Transformation*, 1–53.

Manning, C. (1971) 'The Timber Boom with Special Reference to East Kalimantan', *Bulletin of Indonesian Economic Studies*, 7(3), 30–60.

(1979), 'Wage Differentials and Labour Market Segmentation in Indonesian Manufacturing', Unpublished Ph.D. Thesis, The Australian National University, Canberra.

(1980) 'Fringe Benefits in Manufacturing: Efficiency or Welfare?', *Bulletin of Indonesian Economic Studies*, 16(2), 54–82.

(1987) 'Rural Economic Change and Labour Mobility: A Case Study from West Java', *Bulletin of Indonesian Economic Studies*, 23(3), 52–79.

(1988a) 'Employment Creation in Rural Java: Lessons from the Green Revolution and Oil Boom', *Population and Development Review*, 14(1), 47–80.

(1988b) *The Green Revolution, Employment, and Economic Change in Rural Java: A Reassessment of Trends Under the New Order*, Institute of Southeast Asian Studies, Flinders University of South Australia.

(1992) *The Forgotten Sector: Service Sector Employment in Indonesia*, ILO and Department of Manpower, Jakarta.

(1993) 'Industrial Relations and Structural Change during the Suharto Period: An Approaching Crisis?', *Bulletin of Indonesian Economic Studies*, 29(2), 51–95.

(1994a) 'What has Happened to Wages in the New Order?', *Bulletin of Indonesian Economic Studies*, 30(3), 73–114.

(1995) 'Approaching the Turning Point?: Labor Market Change under Indonesia's New Order', *Developing Economies*, 33(1), 52–81.

(1996a) 'Labour Markets and Human Resources in Developing East Asia: Different Solutions to Different Problems', in R. Wooley *et al.* (eds.), *Asia Pacific Economic Cooperation: Theory and Practise*, JAI Press, Tokyo.

(1996b) 'Labor Standards and Economic Development: The Indonesian Case', in J. E. Lee (ed.), *Labour Standards and Economic Development*, Chung-Hua Institute for Economic Research, pp. 249–72.

Manning, C. and M. Papayungan (1984) 'Pendahuluan', in *Analisa Ketenagakerjaan di Indonesia Berdasarkan Data Sensus penduduk 1971 dan 1980*, Jakarta, Biro Pusat Statistik, Book 1, 1–56.

Manning, C., H. Hill and Y. Saefudin (1988) 'Indonesia: Employment Problems, Prospects and Policies', Unpublished report prepared for the Country Economic Report, World Bank Mission, Jakarta.

Manning, C. and P. N. Junankar (1994) *Unemployment in Indonesia: a Focus on Urban Youth*, Report prepared for the Ministry of Manpower, Republic of Indonesia, ANUTECH Pty Ltd, Canberra.

Manning, C. and S. Jayasuriya (1996) 'Survey of Recent Developments', *Bulletin of Indonesian Economic Studies,* 32 (2), 3–43.

Manning, C. and Pang Eng Fong (1990), 'Labour Market Trends and Structures in ASEAN and the East Asian NIEs', *Asian-Pacific Economic Literature*, 4(2), 59–81.

Manning, C., A. Maude and D. Rudd (1990) 'Outer Eastern Indonesia: An Exploratory Survey of Population Dynamics and Regional Development', Discussion Paper No. 22, Centre for Development Studies, Flinders University, Adelaide.

Manusphaibool, S. (1993) 'Thailand', in S. Deery and R. Mitchell (eds.), *Labour Law and Industrial Relations in Asia: Eight Country Studies*, Longman Cheshire, pp. 241–69.

Marshall, R. (1992) 'The Future of Government in Industrial Relations', *Industrial Relations*, 31(1), 31–50.

Mather, C. (1983) 'Industrialization in the Tangerang Regency of West Java: Women Workers and the Islamic Patriarchy', *Bulletin of Concerned Asian Scholars*, 15(2), 2–17.

Mazumdar, D. (1981) *The Urban Labor Market and Income Distribution: A Study of Malaysia*, Oxford University Press.

— (1989) 'Microeconomic Issues of Labor Markets in Developing Countries: Analysis and Policy Implications', Economic Development Institute (EDI) Seminar Paper No. 40, The World Bank, Washington DC.

— (1993) 'Labor Markets and Adjustment in Open Asian Economies: the Republic of Korea and Malaysia', *The World Bank Economic Review*, 7(3), 349–80.

— (1996) 'Labor Issues in the World Development Report: A Critical Assessment', *International Monetary Issues,* UNCTAD, Geneva, April.

Mazumdar D. and M. H. Sawit (1986) 'Trends in rural wages, West Java 1977–83', *Bulletin of Indonesian Economic Studies*, 22(3), 93–105.

McCawley, P. (1979) 'Industrialisation in Indonesia: Developments and Prospects', Occasional Paper No. 13, Development Studies Centre, The Australian National University, Canberra.

— (1981) 'The Growth of the Industrial Sector', in A. Booth and P. McCawley (eds.), *The Indonesian Economy During the Soeharto Era*, Oxford University Press, Kuala Lumpur, pp. 62–101.

— (1988) 'Investasi dan kesempatan kerja di daerah pedesaan', *Prisma*, 17(1), 27–33.

McCawley, P. and C. Manning (1976) 'Survey of Recent Developments', *Bulletin of Indonesian Economic Studies*, 12(3), 1–49.

McCawley, P. and M. Tait (1979) 'New Data on Employment in Manufacturing, 1970–1977', *Bulletin of Indonesian Economic Studies*, 15(1), 125–36.

McGee, T. G. (1987) 'Urbanisasi or Kotadesasi: The Emergence of New Regions of

Economic Interaction in Asia', Paper presented for Environment and Policy Center, Honolulu East-West Center.

McLeod, R. (1993) 'Workers' Social Security Legislation', in *Indonesia Assessment 1993 – Labour: Sharing in the Benefits of Growth?*, Political and Social Change Monograph, Research School of Pacific Studies, Australian National University, pp. 88–107.

McMahon, W. and Boediono (1991) *Education and the Economy*, Education Policy and Planning Project, Department of Education and Culture, Jakarta.

McMahon, W.W. and Boediono (eds.) (1992) *Education and the Economy: The External Efficiency of Education*, Ministry of Education and Culture, Jakarta.

Mertens, W. (1978) 'Population Census Data on Agricultural Activities in Indonesia', *Demografi Indonesia*, 5(9), 9–44.

Michaely, M., D. Papageorgiou and A. M. Chokski (1991) *Liberalising World Trade: Lessons of Experience in the Developing World*, Basil Blackwell, Oxford.

Minami, R. (1973) *The Turning Point in Japanese Development: Japan's Experience*, Kinokuniya Bookstore, Tokyo.

Mincer, J. (1985) 'Intercountry Comparisons of Labor Force Trends and of Related Developments: An Overview, *Journal of Labor Economics*, 3(1), S1–S33.

Mintoro, A. (1984) Distribusi Pendapatan (Income Distribution), in F. Kasryno (ed.), *Prospek Pambangungan Ekonomi Pedesaan Indonesia*, Yayasan Obor, Jakarta, pp. 263–301.

Moir, H. (1975) *The Jakarta Informal Sector*, LEKNAS, Jakarta.

Morawetz, D. (1974) 'Employment and Implications of Industrialization in Developing Countries: A Survey', *Economic Journal*, 84(335), 491–542.

Morley, S. A. (1982) *Labor Markets and Inequitable Growth: The Case of Authoritarian Capitalism in Brazil*, Cambridge University Press, Cambridge.

Mortimer, R. (ed.) (1973) *Showcase State: the Illusion of Indonesia's Accelerated Modernisation*, Angus and Robertson.

Murray, A. (1987) 'No Money No Honey: A Study of Street Traders and Prostitutes in Jakarta', Ph.D. Thesis, Australian National University, Canberra.

Murtopo, A. (1975) *Buruh dan Tani*, Center for Strategic and International Studies, Jakarta.

Myint, Hla (1968) *The Economics of the Developing Countries*, Hutchinson and Co., London.

Myrdal, G. (1968) *Asian Drama: An Inquiry into the Poverty of Nations*, 3 Volumes, Pantheon (Random House), New York.

Nasution, A. (1991) 'Survey of Recent Developments', *Bulletin of Indonesian Economic Studies*, 27(2), 3–43.

Naylor, R. (1990) 'Wage Trends in Rice Production in Java: 1976–1988', *Bulletin of Indonesian Economic Studies*, 26(2), 133–56.

(1991) 'The Rural Labor Market in Indonesia', in S. Pearson, W. Falcon, P. Heytens, E. Monke and R. Naylor (eds.), *Rice Policy in Indonesia*, Cornell University Press, Ithaca.

(1992) 'Labour-Saving Technologies in the Javanese Rice Economy: Recent Developments and a Look into the 1990s', *Bulletin of Indonesian Economic Studies*, 28(3), 71–92.

(1994) 'Culture and Agriculture: Employment Practises Affecting Women in Java's Rice Economy', *Economic Development and Cultural Change*, 42(3), 509–37.
Neary P. J. and S. van Wijnbergen (eds.) (1986) *Natural Resources and the Macro Economy*, MIT Press, Cambridge, MA.
Norlund, I., P. Wad and V. Brun (1984) *Industrialization and the Labour Process in Southeast Asia*, Repro Series, University of Copenhagen, Copenhagen.
Oaxaca, R. (1973) 'Male–Female Wage Differentials in Urban labor Markets', *International Economic Review* (Philadelphia), 14(3), 693–709.
OECD (1993) *Employment Outlook*, OECD, Paris.
Oey-Gardiner, M. (1993) 'A Gender Perspective on Indonesia's Labour Market Transformation', in C. Manning and J. Hardjono (eds.), *Indonesia Assessment 1993. Labour: Sharing in the Benefits of Growth?*, Department of Political and Social Change, Research School of Pacific Studies, Australian National University, Canberra.
Ogawa, N. G. W. Jones and J. Williamson (eds.) (1993) *Human Resources in Development along the Asia-Pacific Rim*, Oxford University Press, New York.
Ogle, G. (1990) *South Korea: Dissent Within the Economic Miracle*, Zed Books, London.
Ohkawa (1972) *Differential Structure and Growth*, Kinokuniya Bookstore, Tokyo.
Oshima H. T. (1988) *Economic Growth of Monsoon Asia: A Comparative Survey*, University of Tokyo Press, Tokyo.
  (1971) 'Labor Force Explosion and the Labor-Intensive Sector in Asian Growth', *Economic Development and Cultural Change*, 19(2), 161–85.
  (1976) 'Labor Absorption in East and Southeast Asia: Summary, Perspective, Prospects', *Philippine Economic Journal*, 15(1–2), 3–36.
Oshima H. T. and W. H. Lai (1976) 'Labor Absorption in Taiwan', *Philippine Economic Journal*, 15(1–2), 139–82.
Paauw, D. S. (1963) 'From Colonial to Guided Economy', in R.T. McVey (ed.), *Indonesia*, Human Relations Area Files, New Haven, pp. 155–247.
Pang Eng Fong (1988) 'Development Strategies and Labour Market Changes in Singapore', in Pang Eng Fong (ed.), *Labour Market Developments and Structural Change: The Experience of ASEAN and Australia*, Singapore University Press, Singapore, pp. 195–242.
  (1994) 'An Eclectic Approach to Turning Points in Migration', *Asian and Pacific Migration Review*, 3(1), 81–92.
Pang Eng Fong (ed.) (1988) *Labour Market Developments and Structural Change: The Experience of ASEAN and Australia*, Singapore University Press, Singapore.
Pangestu, M. and I. J. Azis (1994) 'Survey of Recent Economic Developments', *Bulletin of Indonesian Economic Studies*, 30(2), 3–37.
Papanek, G. F. (1974) 'The Poor of Jakarta', *Economic Development and Cultural Change*, 24(1), 1–27.
  (1980) 'The Effect of Economic Growth and Inflation on Workers' Income', in G. F. Papanek (ed.), *The Indonesian Economy*, Praeger, New York, pp. 72–120.
  (1985) 'Agricultural Income Distribution and Employment in the 1970s', *Bulletin of Indonesian Economic Studies*, 10(2), 119–25.

Papola T. S. (1992) 'Labour Institutions and Economic Development: the Case of Indian Industrialisation', in T. S. Papola and G. Rodgers (eds.), *Labour Institutions and Economic Development in India*, International Institute of Labour Studies, Geneva, pp. 17–48.

Park, F. K. (1987) 'Labor Rights and International Trade: A Developing Country View', Korean Development Institute Working Paper No. 8707, Korean Development Institute, Seoul.

— (1991) 'Emerging Issues of Industrial Relations and Labor Markets In Korea', in Chung-hoon Lee and Fun-Koo Park (eds.), *Emerging Labor Issues in Developing Asia*, Korean Development Institute, Seoul.

Park, Se-II (1980) Wages in Korea: Determination of the Wage Levels and Wage Structure in a Dualistic Labor Market, Unpublished Ph.D. thesis, Cornell University.

— (1988) 'Labour Issues in Korea's Future', *World Development*, 16(1), 99–119.

Park, Young-Bum (1992) 'State Regulation, the Labor Market and Economic Development: South Korea', Paper presented at the Workshop on *Labour Institutions and Economic Development*, Denpasar (Bali).

Park Young-Ki (1993) 'South Korea', in S. Deery and R. Mitchell (eds.), *Labour Law and Industrial Relations in Asia: Eight Country Studies*, Longman Cheshire, pp. 137–71.

Patten R. et al. (1980) 'An Experiment in Rural Employment Creation: The Early History of Indonesia's Kabupaten Development Programme', in G.F. Papanek (ed.), *The Indonesian Economy*, Praeger, New York, pp.155–82.

Pelzer, K. J. (1963) 'Physical and Human Resource Patterns', in R. T. McVey (ed.), *Indonesia*, Human Relations Area Files Press, New Haven, pp. 1–23.

Penny, D. H. and M. Singarimbun (1973) *Population and Poverty in Rural Java: Some Economic Arithmetic from Sriharjo*, Cornell University, Ithaca.

Pernia, E. M. (1993a) 'Urbanization, Population Distribution and Economic Development in Asia', Report No. 58, Asian Development Bank, Manila.

— (1993b) 'Economic Growth performance of Indonesia, the Philippines, and Thailand: The Human Resource Dimension', in N. Ogawa, G. W. Jones and J. Williamson (eds.), *Human Resources in Development along the Asia-Pacific Rim*, Oxford University Press, Singapore, pp. 159–74.

Pinto, B. (1987) 'Nigeria During and After the Oil Boom: A Policy Comparison with Indonesia', *The World Bank Economic Review*, 1(3), 419–45.

Pitayanon, S. (1988) 'Labour Market Changes and Economic Development in Thailand', in Pang Eng Fong (ed.), *Labour Market Developments and Structural Change: the Experience of ASEAN and Australia*, Singapore University Press, Singapore, pp. 243–77.

Poapongsakorn, N. (1993) 'Transformation in the Thai Rural Labor Market', in B. Koppel, J. Hawkins and W. J. (eds.), *Development or Deterioration: Work in Rural Asia*, L. Rienner, Boulder, pp. 167–210.

Portes, A. and L. Benton (1984) 'Industrial Development and Labor Absorption: A Reinterpretation', *Population and Development Review*, 10(4), 589–611.

Portes, A. and R. Schauffler (1993) 'Competing Perspectives on the Latin American Informal Sector', *Population and Development Review*, 19(1), 33–61.

Prebish, R. (1959) 'Commercial Policy in the Underdeveloped Countries', Papers and Proceedings, *American Economic Review*, 49, 251–6.
Psacharopolous, G. and Z. Tzannatos (1989) 'Female Labor Force Participation: An International Perspective', *World Bank Research Observer*, 4(2), 187–202.
Raharto, A. (1992) 'The Context of Women's Work Decisions in DKI Jakarta, Indonesia', Ph.D. Thesis, Australian National University, Canberra.
   (1993) 'The Context of Women's Decisions in DKI Jakarta', Ph.D. Thesis, Australian National University, Canberra.
Ranis, G. (1992) 'Labor Markets, Human Capital and Development Performance in East Asia', Background paper for the *East Asian Economic Miracle*, World Bank, Washington DC.
REDECON (1994) *Studi Pelacakan Lulusan Perguruan Tinggi di Indonesia*, Department of Education and Culture, Jakarta.
Richardson, H. J. (1958), 'Indonesian Labor Relations in their Political Setting', *International Labor Relations Review*, 12(1), 56–78
Riedel, J. (1988) 'Economic Development in East Asia: Doing What Comes Naturally', in H. Hughes (ed.), *Achieving Industrialization in East Asia*, Cambridge University Press, New York, pp. 1–38.
Rietveld, P. (1986) 'Non-agricultural Activities and Income Distribution in Rural Java', *Bulletin of Indonesian Economic Studies*, 22(3), 106–17.
Rodgers, G. (ed.) (1989) *Urban Poverty and the Labour Market: Access to Jobs and Incomes in Asian and Latin American Cities*. ILO, Geneva.
Ross, A. M. (1966) *Industrial Relations and Economic Development*, Macmillan, London.
Rosenzweig, M. R. (1988) 'Labor Markets in Low-Income Countries', in H. Chenery and T. N. Srinavasan (eds.), *Development Economics* (vol I), North Holland, pp. 713–62.
Rucker, R. L. (1985) *A Preliminary View of Indonesia's Employment Problem and Some Options for Solving It*, United States Agency for International Development, Jakarta.
Sabot, R. H. (1977) 'The Meaning and Measurement of Urban Surplus Labour', *Oxford Economic Papers*, 29(3), 389–411.
Sandbrook, R. and R. Cohen (1975) *The Development of an African Working Class*, Longman, London.
Savedoff, W.D. (1995) *Wages, Labour and Regional Development in Brazil*, Averbury, Aldershot.
Sawit, H. M. (1980) *Masa Depan Usaha Kerajinan Rakyat: Kasus di Pedesaan DAS Cimanuk, Jawa Barat* [Prospects for Cottage Industries: The Case of Villages in the DAS Cimanuk Region West Java], Agro-Economic Survey, Bogor.
Sawit H. M., Y. Saefudin and Sri Hartoyo (1985) 'Activities non Pertanian Pola Musiman dan Peluang Kerja Rumah Tangga di Pedesaan Jawa', in Mubyarto (ed.), *Peluang Kerja dan Berusaha di Pedesaan*, BPFE, Yogyakarta, pp. 145–212.
Scherer, P. (1982) 'Survey of Recent Developments', *Bulletin of Indonesian Economic Studies*, 18(2), 1–34.
Schultz, T. P. (1990) 'Women's Changing Participation in the Labor Force: A World Perspective', *Economic Development and Cultural Change*, 38(4), 457–88.

Schultz, T. W. (1964) *Transforming Traditional Agriculture*, Yale University Press, New Haven, CT.
Sen, A. K. (1966) 'Peasants and Dualism With or Without Surplus Labor', *Journal of Political Economy*, 74(5), 425–50.
Shand, R.T. (ed.) (1986) *Off-Farm Employment in the Development of Rural Asia*, National Centre for Development Studies, Canberra (2 Volumes).
Shari, I. and Mat Zin Ragayah Haji (1990) 'The Patterns and Trends in Income Distribution in Malaysia, 1970–1987', *The Singapore Economic Review*, 35(1), 101–23.
Sharma, B. (1985) 'Aspects of Industrial Relations in ASEAN', Occasional Paper No. 78, Institute of Southeast Asian Studies, Singapore.
Sheehan, G. and G. Standing (eds.) (1978) *Labour Force Participation in Low-Income Countries*, ILO, Geneva.
Siamwalla, A. et al. (1993) 'Agriculture', in P. Warr (ed.), *The Thai Economy in Transition*, Cambridge University Press, Cambridge, pp. 81–118.
Singarimbun, M. (1992) *Renungan Dari Yogya*, Balai Pustaka, Jakarta.
— (1993) 'The Opening of a Village Labour Market: Changes in Employment and Welfare in Sriharjo', in *Indonesia Assessment 1993 – Labour: Sharing in the Benefits of Growth?* Political and Social Change Monograph, Research School of Pacific Studies, Australian National University, pp. 261–72.
Sjahrir, K. (1993) 'The "Informality" of Employment in Construction: The Case of Jakarta', in C. Manning and J. Hardjono (eds.), *Indonesia Assessment 1993 – Labour: Sharing in the Benefits of Growth?*, Political and Social Change Monograph, Research School of Pacific Studies, Australian National University, pp. 240–60.
Sobary, M. (1987) 'Between "Ngoyo" and "Nrimo": Cultural Values and Economic Behaviour among Javanese Migrants in Tanjung Pinang', Working Paper No. 43, Centre of Southeast Asian Studies, Monash University, Melbourne.
Soehoed, A. R. (1967) 'Manufacturing in Indonesia', *Bulletin of Indonesian Economic Studies*, 8, 65–84.
Squire, L. (1981) *Employment Policy in Developing Countries: A Survey of Issues and Evidence*, Oxford University Press, Oxford.
Squires, D. and S. Tabor (1994) 'The Absorption of Labor in Indonesian Agriculture', *The Journal of Institute of Developing Economies*, 32(2), 167–87.
Sri Hartoyo and Makali (1978) 'Perkembangan Tingkat Upah dan Kesempatan Kerja Buruh Yani di Pedesaan Jawa', *PRISMA*, 7(3), 35–45.
Sri Hartoyo, Makali and Soentoro (1984) *Perubahan Pola Pengeluaran Rumah Tangga di Pedesaan Jawa*, Rural Dynamics Survey, Bogor.
Standing, G. (1981) *Labour Force Participation and Development*, ILO, Geneva.
— (1989) 'Global Feminization through Flexible Labor', *World Development*, 17(7), 1077–95.
— (1992) 'Structural Adjustment and Labour Flexibility in Malaysian Manufacturing', in Lee Kiong Hock and Shyamala Nagaraj (eds.), *The Malaysian Economy beyond 1990: International and Domestic Perspectives*, Malaysian Economics Society, Kuala Lumpur, pp. 202–38.
Steele, R. M. (1980) 'Origins and Occupational Mobility of Lifetime Migrants to

Surabaya, East Java', Unpublished Ph.D. Dissertation, Department of Geography, The Australian National University. Canberra.

Stiglitz, J. E. (1973) 'Alternative Theories of Wage Determination in LDCs: The Efficiency Wage Model', Cowles Foundation Discussion Paper 357, Economic Growth Center, Yale University, New Haven.

Stoler, A. L. (1977) 'Rice Marketing in Kali Loro', *American Ethnologist*, 4(4), 678–98.

—— (1983) 'In the Company's Shadow: Labor Control and Confrontation in Sumatra's Plantation History, 1870–1979', Ph.D. Dissertation, Columbia University, Ann Arbor.

Strudwick, J. (1991) *A Tracer Study of Graduates from the HEDS Project Institutions*, USAID, Jakarta.

Strudwick, J. and A. M Cresswell (1994) *Secondary Education Outcomes in Indonesia*, USAID, Jakarta.

Sundrum, R. M. (1986) 'Indonesia's Rapid Economic Growth: 1968–1981', *Bulletin of Indonesian Economic Studies*, 22(3), 40–69.

—— (1988) 'Indonesia's Slow Economic Growth: 1981–1986', *Bulletin of Indonesian Economic Studies*, 24(1), 37–72.

—— (1990) *Income Distribution in Developing Countries*, Routledge, Melbourne.

Suryadi, A. and A. Salim (1995) 'Kesenjangan Struktur Persediaan dan Permintaan Tenaga Kerja Terdidik', *PRISMA*, 22(8), 67–85.

Sussangkarn, C. (1993) 'Labour Markets', in P. Warr (ed.), *The Thai Economy in Transition*, Cambridge University Press, Cambridge, pp. 355–400.

Tabor, S. R. (1992) 'Agriculture in Transition', in A. Booth (ed.), *The Oil Boom and After: Indonesian Economic Policy and Performance in the Soeharto Era*, Oxford University Press, Singapore, pp. 161–203.

Tan, T. K. (1967) 'Sukarnian Economics', in T. K. Tan (ed.), *Sukarno's Guided Indonesia*, The Jacaranda Press, Brisbane.

Tedjasukmana, I. (1961) 'The Development of Labor Policy and Legislation in the Republic of Indonesia', Unpublished Ph.D. Thesis, Cornell University, Ithaca.

Terrell, K. (1992) 'Female–Male Earnings Differentials and Occupational Structure', *International Labour Review*, 131(4–5), 387–404.

Thamrin, J. (1993) 'Labour in Small-Scale Manufacturing: The Footwear Industry in Java', in *Indonesia Assessment 1993 – Labour: Sharing in the Benefits of Growth?*, Political and Social Change Monograph, Research School of Pacific Studies, Australian National University, pp. 139–54.

Thee Kian Wie (1991) 'The Surge of Asian NIC Investment into Indonesia', *Bulletin of Indonesian Economic Studies*, 27(3), 55–88.

Timmer C. P. (1993) 'Rural Bias in the East and South-east Asian Rice Economy: Indonesia in Comparative Perspective', *Journal of Development Studies*, 29, 149–76.

Tjandraningsih, I. et al. (1991) 'Tenaga Kerja Pedesaan pada Industri Besar Sepatu Olahraga untuk Ekspor', West Java Rural Nonfarm Sector Research Project, Working Paper Series No. B-20, Institute of Social Studies, Bandung.

Tjondronegoro, Sediono M. P. (1977) 'Bawon dan faktor-faktor sosial ekominya', *Masyarakat Indonesia*, 5(2), 139–60.

Todaro, M. P. (1976) *Internal Migration in Developing Countries: A Review of Theory, Evidence, Methodology and Research Priorities*, ILO, Geneva.

Tokman V. E. (1984) 'Employment Crisis in Latin America', *International Labour Review*, 125(5), 587–595.

Turner, H. A. (1965) 'Wage Trends, Wage Policies and Collective Bargaining: The Problems of Underdeveloped Countries', Occasional Paper No. 6, Department of Applied Statistics, University of Cambridge.

Turnham, D. (1993) *Employment and Development: A New Review of Evidence*, Paris, Development Centre, OECD, Paris (chapters 1–3).

[with I. Jaeger] (1971) *The Employment Problem in Less Developed Countries. A Review of Evidence*, OECD Development Centre Studies, OECD, Paris.

Udall, A. T. and S. Sinclair (1982) 'The "Luxury Unemployment" Hypothesis: A Review of the Recent Evidence', *World Development*, 10, 49–62.

United Nations (1980) 'Patterns of Rural and Urban Population Growth', *Population Studies* No. 68, New York.

US Department of Labor (1992) *Foreign Labour Trends: Taiwan 1991*, Washington DC.

US Embassy (1994), 'Labor Trends in Indonesia', Unpublished Report, Jakarta.

van Diermen, P. (1995) 'Systems of Enterprises: A Study of Small-Scale Garment and Wood Furniture Enterprises in Jakarta', Ph.D. Thesis, The Australian National University, Canberra.

van Velzen, A. (1994) '"Who's The Boss?" Marginalisation and Power in Food-Processing Household Enterprises, West Java, Indonesia', Thesis submitted for degree of Doctor of Philosophy, University of Amsterdam.

Visaria, P. (1981) 'Poverty and Unemployment in India: An Analysis of Recent Evidence', *World Development*, 9(3), 277–300.

Wade, R. 1990. *Governing the Market: economic theory and the role of government in East Asian industrialisation*, Princeton University Press, Princeton.

Warr, P. G. (1984) 'Exchange Rate Protection in Indonesia', *Bulletin of Indonesian Economic Studies*, 20(2), 53–89.

(1986) 'Indonesia's Other Dutch Disease: Economic Effects of the Petroleum Boom', in J. P. Neary and Swedar van Wijnbergen (eds.), *Natural Resources and the Macro Economy*, MIT Press, Cambridge MA, pp. 288–320.

(1992a) 'Exchange Rate Policy, Petroleum Prices, and the Balance of Payments', in A. Booth (ed.), *The Oil Boom and After: Indonesian Economic Policy and Performance in the Soeharto Era*, Oxford University Press, Singapore, pp. 132–58.

(1992b) 'Agriculture's Relative Decline and the Problem of Labor Absorption: Evidence from Indonesia', *Southeast Asian Journal of Agricultural Economics*, 1(1), 11–24.

Watanabe, S. (1976) 'Minimum Wages in Developing Countries: Myth and Reality', *International Labour Review*, 113(3), 345–58.

Webb, R. C. (1977) 'Wage Policy and Income Distribution in Developing Countries', in C. R. Frank and R. C. Webb (eds.), *Income Distribution and Growth in the Less Developed Countries*, Brookings Institution, Washington DC, pp. 215–52.

Weeks, J. (1971) 'Wage Policy and the Colonial Legacy – A Comparative Study', *Journal of Modern African Studies*, 9(3), 361–87.

Wertheim, W. F. (1956) *Indonesian Society in Transition*, Van Hoeve, Bandung.

White, B. (1976) 'Population, Employment and Involution in a Javanese Village', *Development and Change*, 7, 267–90.

(1979) 'Political Aspects of Poverty, Income Distribution and their Measurement: Some Examples from Rural Java', *Development and Change*, 10(1), 91–114.

(1986) *Rural Non-farm Employment in Java: Recent Developments, Policy Issues and Research Need*, Institute of Social Studies-UNDP/ILO.

(1991) Economic Diversification and Agrarian Change in Rural Java, 1900–1990, in P. Alexander, P. Boomgaard and B. White (eds.), *In the Shadow of Agriculture: Non-farm Activities in the Javanese Economy, Past and Present*, Royal Tropical Institute, Amsterdam.

(1993) 'Industrial Workers on West Java's Urban Fringe', in *Indonesia Assessment 1993 – Labour: Sharing in the Benefits of Growth?*, Political and Social Change Monograph, Research School of Pacific Studies, Australian National University, pp. 127–38.

White, B. and G. Wiradi (1989) 'Agrarian and Nonagrarian Bases of Inequality in Nine Javanese Villages', in G. Hart, A Turton and B. White (eds.), *Agrarian Transformations: Local Processes and the State in Southeast Asia*, University of California Press, Berkeley, pp. 266–302.

White, B. and Makali (1979) 'Wage Labour and Wage Relations in Javanese Agriculture. Some Preliminary Notes from the Agro-Economic Survey', Unpublished Paper, The Hague.

White, B. *et al.* (1992) 'Workshops and Factories: Dynamics of Production Organisation and Employment in West Java's Rural Footwear Industries', Paper presented at the 9th Biennial Conference of the Asian Studies Association, July 6–9 1992.

Widarti, D. (1991) 'Determinants of Female Labour Force Participation and Work Patterns: The Case of Jakarta', Ph.D. Thesis, School of Social Sciences, The Flinders University of South Australia, Adelaide.

Williamson, J. G. (1993) 'Human Capital Deepening, Inequality, and Events along the Asia-Pacific Rim', in N. Ogawa, G. W. Jones and J. Williamson (eds.), *Human Resources in Development along the Asia-Pacific Rim*, Oxford University Press, Singapore, pp. 129–58.

Wolf, D. (1992) *Factory Daughters: Gender, Households Dynamics, and Rural Industrialization in Java*, University of California Press, Berkeley.

Woo, W. T., B. Glassburner and A. Nasution (1994) *Macroeconomic Policies, Crises, and Long-Term Growth in Indonesia, 1965–90*, The World Bank, Washington DC.

World Bank (1981) 'Indonesia: Selected Issues of Industrial Development and Trade Strategy', Report No. 3182–IND, Washington DC.

(1984) 'Indonesia: Selected Aspects of Spatial Development (A Main Report and Four Annexes), Annex 2, Demographic Patterns and Population Projections', Report No. 4776–IND, Washington DC.

(1985) *Employment and Income Distribution in Indonesia*, Washington DC.

(1986) *Transmigration in Indonesia*, Washington DC.

(1990) *World Development Report 1990*, Washington DC.

(1991) *Indonesia: Employment and Training*, Washington DC.

(1991) *World Development Report 1991*, Washington DC.

(1993) *The East Asian Economic Miracle: Economic Growth and Public Policy*, Oxford University Press, Oxford.

(1994) *World Development Report 1992*, Oxford University Press, Washington DC.
(1995a) *World Development Report: Workers in an Integrating World*, Washington DC.
(1995b) *Labor and Economic Reforms in Latin America and the Caribbean*, Regional Perspectives on World Development Report, Washington DC.
(1995c) *Indonesia Labor Market Policies and International Competitiveness*, Washington DC.
World Bank (various years), *World Development Report*, Oxford University Press, New York.
World Bank (various years), *World Tables*, Washington DC.
Yin, K. F. and D. H. Clark (1976) 'Labour Absorption and Economic Growth in Singapore', in *Philippine Economic Journal*, 15(1–2), 314–42.
YLBHI (Yayasan Lembaga Bantuan Hukum Indonesia) (1991) *Laporan Keadaan Hak Asasi Manusia di Indonesia 1990*, Jakarta.
(1992), *Demokrasi Masih Terbenam: Catatan Keadaan Hak-Hak Asasi Manusia di Indonesia 1991*, Jakarta.
Yusuf, V. (1991) 'Pembentukan Angkatan Kerja Industri Garmen Untuk Ekspor: Pengalaman dari Bandung – Jawa Barat', West Java Rural Nonfarm Sector Research Project, Project Working Paper Series No. B-13, Institute of Social Studies, Bandung.

Index

A-sector, 87
Abdul Latief, 172, 216
Aceh, 165
Addison, 25
Africa, 16, 49, 161, 242, 280
Age
   differentials, 34
   decline, 127
Agriculture, xvii, 6, 10, 12, 16–17, 18, 21, 26–8, 50, 52, 55, 60, 61, 65, 71, 78, 84, 88, 92–3, 96, 101
   in Java, 50, 190
   Javanese, 102
   peasant, 22
   Share in, 15
   value added, 22
Agricultural
   cycle, 54
   development, 61
   employment, 88
      share of, 12, 87
      growth, 90, 92, 96, 98, 101–3, 106–7, 112, 161, 163
      slow down, 111
   growth, 15
   modernisation, 22
   productivity, 28
   wages rate, 4
Akita, T., 78
Alexander, J., 252–3
Amsden, A., 193
Anderson, A.G., 253
Anker, R., 232
Arndt, H.W., 48, 57, 67, 116, 189
Ariff, M., 26
ASEAN, 201, 211
   economies, 4, 26
Asia, 8, 34, 49
   East and South, 26
ASTEK, 207

Baer, W., 13
Bai, M.K., 132

Bali, 78, 156, 159, 161, 164, 171, 240, 254, 271, 279
Bandung, 117, 126, 143, 147, 216, 271
Banerjee, B., 29
Bangkok, 73
Bangladesh, 8, 51
Bardhan, P.K., 28–9
Barker, R., 50–1
Barlow, C., xix, 26, 39, 62, 163
batik, 51, 171, 253
Battacherjee, D., 200
Bauer, J., 25
Bautista, R., 62
becak, 149, 263, 267
Bengkulu, 156
Benton, L., 31
Berg, E.J., 137
Berry, A., 31, 88
Bertrand, T., 54, 173
betawi, women, 240
Bhagwati, J., 28
Blaug, M., 173
Blinder, A.S., 260
Boediono, 181
Booth, A., 28, 51, 62, 64, 70–1, 92, 167, 252, 253
Boserup, E., 231, 250
BOTABEK, 227
Brand, W., 172
Brazil, 7, 58, 277
Breman, J., 181
Budhisantoso, 142
Burma, 48

Ceblokan, 248
Chile, 31
China, 8, 15–16, 48, 59, 78, 167, 205, 226, 277
Christian, 240
Clark, D.H., 181, 190, 195
Collier, W., 91, 143, 145–7
Colombia, 31
Colter, Y. 145
Comparative advantage, 24, 82
Condon, T., 72

315

Construction, 110
Construction, employment, *see* employment
  index of labour productivity, 96
  jobs created, in the, 94
  rural, 107
  urban, 107
Corden, W.M., 32–3
CPI, 208
  Indonesia, 127
Cresswell, 184
current account, 68
de Soto, H., 31
de Witt, Y.B., 71

Demand for labour, 165
Demery, 25
Demographic, 78
  condition, 45
Dependency ratio, 23
Deregulation, 8, 68–70, 114, 123–4, 126, 201, 204–5, 216, 220, 230
Devaluation, 67, 69, 123, 129–30
Deyo, F.C., 24, 200, 232
Dhanani, S., 179
Dick, H., 164
Dréze, J., 29
Durand, J.D., 231, 233
Dutch Disease, 32, 72
Dutch, 57

East Asia, 3, 5, 7, 12–13, 20, 64, 72, 114, 145, 193, 232, 275
East Asian, 4, 6–8, 10, 20–1, 24, 34–5, 39, 46, 57, 66, 75, 167, 173, 182, 195, 210, 214, 227, 233, 236, 239, 243–4, 255, 265, 286
  countries, 82, 99, 106, 276
  economies, 8, 200
  governments, 67
  miracle, 64
East Java, 78, 221
East Kalimantan, 78, 158
Eastern Indonesia, ???
Economic growth, 3
Edgren, G., 25
Education, 3
Effendi, T.N., 148, 252
Employers, monopsonistic, 9
Employment, 12–13, 15–16, 18–19, 21, 23, 25, 26–8, 31, 34, 36, 39–40, 48, 51–4, 56, 62, 71, 77, 82, 84–8, 91–3, 95, 97–8, 100, 104–7, 108–9, 111, 116, 122, 137–8, 143, 148–9, 164, 166, 170, 178, 183, 189, 193–5, 201, 220, 224–5, 227, 229–31, 237–8, 241, 243–6, 248, 250, 254, 257, 262, 265, 275–6, 277–8, 279, 282, 288

  contracts, 116
  creation 16, 71, 88, 193
  elasticity, 86, 94
    in services, agricultural, 86
  expanded, 105
  expansion, 111, 276–7
  factory, 146, 255
  female, 75, 232, 241–8, 255–6, 265
    wage, 254
  female non-agricultural, 40, 252, 262
  female professional, 249
  government, 265
  growth, 17, 22, 27, 30, 40, 72, 84–5, 87, 89, 91–6, 98–9, 100–1, 103–4, 106, 111–12, 122, 132, 142, 155, 164, 205, 244, 248, 282, 286–7
  higher earnings, 143
  in agriculture, 27, 99
  in Indonesia, 107
  in Java, 97
  informal, 42
  informal sector, 148
  low wage, 266
  manufacturing, 88, 108
  modern sector, 40, 55–7, 116
  national, 277
  national and regional, 45
  non-wage, 84
  non-agricultural, 14–15, 22, 54, 78, 97, 103, 109, 241
  non-farm, 42
  non-wage, 85, 95, 97, 102, 176, 255, 256
  opportunities, 22, 48, 72, 109, 238, 253
  policies, 16, 124
  productive, 20
  prospects, 283
  ratio female to male, 242
  rural, 53, 95–6, 105, 143, 149, 162
    Java, 54
  services, 92, 106
  sex ratio, 244
  share, 84
    female, 269
  stability, 149
  structure, 8, 10, 49, 57, 78, 85, 96, 98, 122, 167, 190, 243, 277
    in Java, and Indonesia, 113
  systems, 138
  total, 14, 27, 56–8, 88–9, 95–6, 98–9, 103, 109, 112
    female, 241–3, 250
  trade, 164
  trends, 14, 106, 114
  undifferentiated, 4
  urban and rural, 103

urban, 97, 145, 162, 242
wage, 101, 256–7
Europe, Western, 7
Exchange rate, 33, 40, 68, 70, 278
  depreciation of, 130
  flexible, 132
  nominal, 129
  overvalued, 105, 279
  real, 40, 69, 123, 129–30

Family Planning, programme, 281
Family workers,
  and self employed, 95, 103, 114, 236
  enumerated, 242
  female, 192
  in agriculture, 192
  on small farms, 89
  participation of female, 193, 242
Fane, G., 72
FBSI, 206, 209
Fei, J.C.H., 34
Female,
  self-employed, 52
  workers, 241
  single, 235
Fields, 9, 23–4, 114, 200
Fiscal policy, 27
Flores, 81
Female Labour Force Participation (FLP), 236–8, 240–1
Formal sector, 84, 145
Frank, C.R., 16
Freeman, R., 12, 23–5, 42, 199, 229
Furnivall, J.S., 45, 56–7

Gajah Tunggal, 255
Galenson, W., 6, 20, 57, 88, 114, 201
Gannicot, Ken, 25
Garnaut, R., xix, 33, 67
GDP, 6, 14, 17, 21, 23, 58–9, 63, 65–6, 89, 229, 287
  growth, 18, 19, 21
  non-oil, 120
  per capita, 14, 60
  structure of, 16
  total, ???
Geertz, C., 50
Gelb, A., 32–3, 71
Geneva, 221
Gini index ratio, 74, 167–8
GOLKAR, 209, 211
Government
  intervention, 20, 67, 284
  regulation, 28
Gray, C., 57, 116
Great River Industries, 255

Gregory, P., 16
Grijns, M., 233
GSP, 206, 221–2
Gudang Garam, 147
Guiness, P., 81, 253

Habibie, 69, 82, 205
Haggard, S., 24
Hansen, B., 54
Harberger, A.C., 30
Hardjono, J., 148
Harris, J., 36
Hart, G., 54, 102, 121, 143, 247, 252
Hawkins, E.D., 51, 121, 204
Health, 3
Hein, C., 232
Herdt, R.W., 50–1
Herve, M.G.A., 13
Heyzer, N., 231–2, 245
Higgins, 45
Hill, H., xix, 26, 56, 59, 61–3, 66–7, 94, 120, 123, 128, 148, 156, 163, 167, 195
Ho, S., 148
HongKong, 7, 20, 22, 81, 193, 200
Horton, S.R., 12, 23, 31
Hough, J., 187
Hugo, G., 78, 81, 142, 148, 247, 249
Hull, T., 239, 251
Human capital, 5, 9, 28, 36, 72, 82, 267, 276–7
  investment, 23, 41
Human resources, 6, 41, 72
Huppi, M., 229

ILO, 17, 19, 30–1, 199, 209, 217, 221, 230, 233
India, 8, 15, 16, 29, 40, 48, 64, 78, 201
INDOC, 211
Indonesia, xvii, xviii, 3, 5, 6–10, 15, 20, 22, 27, 29, 32–5, 38, 45–6, 48–9, 51, 56–7, 59, 62, 64, 66–7, 71–3, 75, 78, 81–4, 89, 93, 96–7, 99, 100–1, 103, 109, 112, 114–15, 121, 131–2, 141, 155, 158, 163, 166, 168, 176, 178, 182, 189, 193–4, 200–1, 212–13, 217, 223, 226, 229–30, 233, 236, 239–40, 243–4, 246, 250, 255, 258, 261–3, 269–70, 275–82, 284, 288
  eastern, 156, 240
Indonesian, female, 233
Industrial relations, 10
Infant mortality, 46–7
Informal sector, 16, 30, 39, 42, 84, 91, 112, 142, 145, 164, 181, 238, 267, 276, 279, 281–2, 286–7
INPRES, 71–2, 94, 279
Irian Jaya, 79, 156, 240, 271

JABOTABEK, 146, 240, 270
Jakarta, 7, 73, 78, 79, 81, 117, 127, 143, 146–7, 156, 164–5, 209, 214–17, 220, 237, 239–40, 250, 254, 262
Jambi, 156
James, W.E., 26–8, 63
JAMSOSTEK, 207
Jamu, 254
Japan, 37, 284
Jatinom, District, 252
Java, 7, 26, 28, 48–55, 60, 62, 68, 73–5, 77–80, 87, 89, 91–2, 94–5, 96–7, 101–3, 106–8, 117, 121, 124, 131, 137–8, 141–3, 145, 147–9, 155, 158–9, 161, 163, 189, 233, 245–6, 248, 252–4, 256, 279, 284
  Central, 148, 163, 240, 252–4, 282
  Central and East, 255, 259
  East, 146, 161, 240
  flow to, 155
  population, 46
  rural, 168
  village, 55
  West, 142, 144–5, 148, 216, 239–40, 257, 271
Jayasuriya, S., 26, 39, 123, 218, 220, 225
Jellinek, L., 237
Jian, T., 277
Jogjakarta, 146–7, 164, 239–40, 253
Jones, G., 75, 77, 163, 232, 239–40, 250
Junankar, P.N., 184

Kalimantan, 62, 78, 156, 159, 171
  Central, 156
  East, 79
  other, 271
Kampung, 253
Kanbur, 12, 23, 31
Karo Batak, 252
Kediri, 147
Kedokan, 115
Kekeluargaan, 209
Keterbukaan, 213–14
Keyfitz, N., 187
KFM, 208
Khoo, S.E., 232
Kim, J.H., 94
Klaten, 148
Knight, J., 29
Koo, H., 24
Kompas, 226, 223
Krongkaew, M., 64, 155, 167
Korea, see South Korea
Kretek, 56, 147, 170
Krueger, A.O., 23
Krugman, P., 4
Kuala Lumpur, 73

Kuo, S., 22, 94
Kuznets, S., 12–13, 39, 84

Labour, 3, 8, 12–13, 132, 137, 176, 177, 201, 210, 225, 275, 279
  absorption, 31, 106
  action, 114, 204
  advancement, 281
  agreement, 203, 207, 210, 215
  collective, 211
  allocation, 137
  condition, 25, 214
  contracts, 137, 147
  controls, 204, 210, 226–7
  demand for, 10, 280
  displacement, 122, 281
  dispute, 203–4, 211, 216
  earnings, 116, 126–7, 144, 167–8
  elastic supply of, 119
  exchange, 53
  family, 102, 137
  female, 245, 282
  freedoms, 9, 287
  income, 3, 9, 27, 40, 48, 116, 207, 221, 229
  inputs, 146, 190, 245
  institutions, 6, 247, 285, 286
  management, 214
  migration, 16, 79, 81, 284, *see also* migration
  organisation, 137, 211
  outcomes, 3, 275, 278
  peace, 205, 211–12
  policies, 138, 201, 205, 286
  record, 212, 221–2
  regulation, 220, 230
  shortages, 22, 33, 143, 146, 187
  skilled, 33, 38, 94, 193
  unrest, 201, 203, 205, 212, 214, 226–8
  unskilled, 24, 33, 38, 94, 117, 124, 229, 281
  welfare, 48, 88, 228, 276, 279, 283
Labour absorption, 8, 32, 84, 89, 96
Labour cost, 200, 223, 225, 227
Labour demand, 25, 29, 32, 36, 50, 54, 82, 114, 122–4, 130–1, 137, 156, 172–3, 220, 224, 240, 284
Labour force, 14–16, 77–9, 85, 89, 98, 160, 172, 175, 231, 236, 238, 265, 267
  expansion, 98
  female, 75, 78, 241, 268
  growth, 13, 20–1, 75–7, 81, 145, 159, 161
  participation, 83
  rural, 77
  urban female, 160

Labour-intensive, 25, 32, 39–41, 56, 66, 95, 99, 105, 108, 116, 128, 132, 143, 150–1, 154–5, 167, 188, 196, 200, 225, 226–7, 229, 238, 245, 254, 279
  growth, 22
  industries, 100, 154, 240, 282
  manufacturing, 70, 138
  products, 63
  promotion, 22
  structure, 57
  vegetable, fruit and livestock, 22
  wages in, 130
Labour laws, 202, 286
Labour legislation, 29, 199, 202, 286
Labour market, 3–5, 8, 10–11, 14, 20, 25–7, 30, 32, 34, 39–41, 49, 53–5, 72, 74, 78, 98, 112, 118, 122–4, 130, 137, 142, 147–9, 155, 166, 168, 173, 177–8, 188–9, 195, 199, 200–1, 205, 217, 224–5, 230–1, 240, 244–5, 258–9, 264–5, 276–7, 279–80, 283–4
  adaptation, 45
  adjustment, 5, 11, 19, 31, 42, 45, 48, 100, 112, 156, 278
  challenge, 8, 10, 12–14, 19, 20, 45, 48, 287
  change, 4, 6–7, 10, 15, 34, 42, 46, 141, 277, 284
  condition, 13, 33, 117–18, 167, 227
  controls, 24
  deregulated, 23, 221, 230
  discrimination, 285
  distortions, 230
  dynamics, 38, 43, 61, 275
  flexible, 8, 12, 24, 29, 41, 195, 200
  fragmented, 165
  imbalance, 42, 173
  imperfect, 137
  in Indonesia, 12, 34, 59, 91, 139, 187, 194, 267, 285
  intervention in, 9, 23, 29, 32
  in LDCs, 199, 278
  national, 120, 165
  outcome, 9, 17, 19, 23, 27, 39–40, 114, 174, 284
  regional, 155, 167, 207
  rural, 26, 28, 54, 122, 141–2, 144, 146, 281
  structure, 6, 8, 12, 23, 28, 155–6, 275
  transformation of, 6, 10, 12, 20–1, 26, 30, 33–4, 111 275–7
  transition, 6, 20, 23, 25, 34, 39, 41, 112, 114, 190, 275, 277, 279, 283
  urban, 131, 146, 231
Labour market segmentation, 20, 42, 137, 173, 281, 285
Labour mobility, 5, 41, 72, 78, 137–8, 166, 225, 280, 284

Labour productivity, 12–14, 17, 21, 35, 96, 99, 100, 112, 115, 217, 223, 225–7, 229–30, 275, 282–3, 286–7
Labour protection, 25, 35, 41, 199, 201, 204, 230, 286
Labour rights, 7, 12, 25, 209, 214, 216, 221–2, 228, 282
Labour standards, 25, 201, 204, 207, 212–13, 287–8
Labour supply, 23, 26–7, 29, 34, 36, 38, 40–2, 53–4, 62, 72, 75, 114, 117, 131, 137, 142, 147, 152, 156, 159, 165, 173, 189, 205, 275–6, 284
  elastic, 6, 26, 34–6, 122
  unskilled, 33–4
Labour surplus, 3, 14, 16, 28–9, 34–5, 37–8, 91, 99
Lampung, 78–9, 156, 158–9, 163
Land reform, 22
Land surplus, 26
Latin America, 16, 29–32, 49, 64, 84, 97, 141, 193, 222, 232, 262, 281
Lewis, W.A., 28, 34, 119
  model, 284
Life expectancy, 46–7
Lim, 25, 27, 30, 39
Link and match, 194
Lluch, C., 117
Lok, H., 225
Lombok, 81
Lubis, M., 213
Lukman, R.A., 78
Luzon, 26

M-sector, 85, 87–8, 93, 97
  employment, 87
  growth, 112
  job, 96
  rural employment, 92
  urban employment, 92
Mackie, J., 56
Macroeconomic, 9, 69
  balance, 30
  management, 7, 15, 27, 31, 40, 68
  performance, 204
  policy, 26, 40, 123, 132, 276, 278
  reform, 106
  stability, 278
Majalaya, 148
Malaysia, 6–7, 27, 39, 46, 59, 64, 66, 81, 85, 108, 115, 132, 147–8, 174, 193, 201, 210, 223, 239, 243, 257, 265, 269
Maluku, 156, 240, 271
Manning, C., 20, 27, 57, 62, 95, 102, 122–3, 127, 144–5, 148, 152, 184, 207, 218, 220, 225, 247

Manpower, 172
  educated, 25
  Minister of, 172
  Ministry of, 207
  quality, 45
  skilled, 33, 128
Manufacturing, 5, 8, 10, 12–13, 27, 63
Manufacturing employment, 17, 52, 55, 87, 92–3, 106–8, 151, 163
  growth, 17, 78, 104, 138, 173
Marsinah, 214, 221
Mather, C., 233, 255
Mazumdar, D., 12, 23–4, 31, 35, 117, 132, 137, 150–1, 199
McCawley, P., 70, 207
McGee, T.G., 142
McLeod, R., 207
McMahon, W.W., 181
Medan, 215, 220, 223
  riots, 205
Meier, G.M., 26–8
Mexico, 7
Middle East, 147
Migrant, 158
  labour, 54
  rural–urban, 31
Migration, 74, 79–80, 142, 145, 149, 158–60
  illegal, 81
  inter-regional, 155
  international, 81
  net lifetime, 160
  rural urban, 145
Minami, R., 38
Minimum wage, 32, 34–6, 111, 116–17, 124, 131, 199–200, 201–2, 206–9, 212, 216–20, 224, 226, 229–30, 282, 285, 286
  legislation, 199–200
  policy, 212, 225
  real value of, 208
  regulations, 215
Mintoro, A., 145, 147
Minimum Physical Need, 208
Modern sector, 37–8, 49, 187
Morawetz, D., 13
Morely, 58
Mukerjee, A., 29
Muslim, 233, 241
Myint, H., 26
Myrdal, G., 13, 181

National Wages Council, 216
Naya, S., 26–8
Naylor, R., 147, 245, 248
Neary, P.J., 32
New Order, 3, 8, 11, 71, 79, 82, 108, 121, 124, 137, 155, 158, 172, 193, 199, 209, 223, 227–8, 281, 283
Ngobjek, 57
Ngompreng, 57
NIEs, 4, 6, 8, 19–27, 30–1, 39, 59, 66, 88, 114, 193, 200–1, 221–2, 232, 277–8, 281
Nigeria, 7, 33, 58
Non-tariff barriers, 70
Nusa Tenggara, 78–9, 155–6, 240

Oey-Gardiner, M., 190
Ohkawa, K., 138
Oil boom, 10, 30–3, 59, 63, 67–8, 70–2, 100, 102–3, 107, 120–3, 125, 129, 131, 138, 143–4, 149, 152, 155, 165, 205, 278–9, 281, 284
OPEC, 32, 222, 279
Oshima, H.T., 13, 22, 26

Paauw, D., 46
Pakistan, 8, 28, 64
Pancasila, 204–5
  labour relation, 209
Pakpahan, M., 215, 222–3
Pang Eng Fong, 20, 25, 27
Papanek, G.F., 148
Papua New Guinea, 230
Park, 25, 210, 222
Participation rates, 233–4, 238, 240
  female, 78, 231, 233, 239–41, 251, 266–7, 277
  male, 257
Patten, R., 94
Penghinaan, 213
Penny D., 51, 53–4
Pernia, E., 73
PERTAMINA, 68, 194
Phillipines, 27, 46, 81, 85, 99–100, 132, 193, 201, 229, 243, 265, 269
Pinto, M., 33
Pitayanon, S., 27
PKI, 209
Population, 8, 13–14, 46–7, 49, 63–4, 72–4, 79, 81, 157, 240, 252, 275
  concentration, 78
  density, 73, 78
  growth, 26, 72–5, 79, 145
  rural, 78
  urban, 73
  working age, 73–4, 177–8
Portes, A., 31
Poverty, 5, 49, 60, 63, 78, 189, 240, 249, 276, 282, 283, 285
  decline, 25, 64, 69, 287
  incidence, 7, 63, 142, 166
  rural, 49, 265

Poverty alleviation, 3, 25, 252, 265, 277
Poverty line, 64, 68
Primary health care, 72
Primary products, 62
Primary schooling, 23
Probit, estimates, 268
Problema, 213
Psacharopolous, G., 233, 238
Puerto Rico, 230
Pungli, 224
Punjab, 245
Purchasing power parity, 14, 64

Ranis, G., 34
Ravallion, M., 229
REDECON, 184–5
REPELITA, II, 71
RGDP, 156, 158–9, 161, 163
  per capita, level of, 157–8
Riau, 158, 165
Richardson, H.J., 204
Riedel, J., 30
Rietveld, P., 145
Rodgers, G., 31, 174, 181
Rose, B., 50–1
Rudra, A., 29

S-sector, *see* Services, 87, 95–7, 103
  trade and transport, 110
Sabot, R.H., 31
Sachs, J., 277
Saefudin, Y., 144, 148, 192
Sasak, 81
Saudi Arabia, 81, 147
Savedoff, W.D., 277
Sawah, 51
Sawit, M.H., 144, 192
SBM, 222
SBSI, 215, 222–3
Schauffler, R., 31
Services, 95, 97, 103, 110, 125, 165, 249–50
Sex Ratio, 243, 249, 251
Sharma, B., 201
Sheehan, G., 238
Shin, Young-Soo, 25
Singarimbun, M., 46, 51, 53, 146
Singapore, 7, 20, 22–4, 81, 115, 193, 200,
    209–10, 212, 227, 230, 239, 243, 269
Sjahrir, K., 116
Sobary, M., 163
SOBSI, 203, 209, 281
Soeharto, 3, 6, 10, 20, 28, 34, 45, 67, 70, 72,
    116, 167, 203, 205, 207, 209, 240–1,
    276, 281, 287
Soehoed, 56
Soekarno, 46, 55, 57, 223, 281

Southeast Asia, 26–7, 51, 73, 167
South Asia, 8, 28, 46, 49, 59, 84, 161, 233,
    242, 265
South Korea, 4–5, 7, 20–3, 21, 25, 46, 59, 62,
    66, 73, 85, 93, 99–100, 115, 132, 148,
    152, 193, 201, 209–11, 214, 243, 257,
    269, 284, 287
SPSI, 206, 209–11, 222
Squire, L., 54, 173–4
Sri Hartoyo, 144, 192
Sri Lanka, 176
Sriharjo, 146–7, 51
Standing, G., 223, 232, 238
Stoler, A.L., 249
Strikes, 213, 215
Strudwick, J., 184
Sub-Saharan Africa, 16, 19
Sulawesi, 62, 147, 155, 159
  Central, 62
  North and South, 79
  North, 158, 240
  other, 271
  South, 239
Sulistyaningsih, E., 251
Sumatra, 62, 78–9, 156, 161
  North, 156, 171, 252, 254, 260, 271
  South, 156, 158–9
  West, 79
Sundrum, R.M., 28, 57, 59, 116, 120, 189
Surabaya, 147, 164, 227, 251, 271
Sussangkarn, C., 39

Tabor, S.R., 62, 71, 102, 107–8, 111
Tahu, 53
Taiwan, 5, 7, 20, 21–3, 25, 59, 66, 85, 93, 115,
    193, 201, 257, 284
Tebasan, 248
Tempe, 53
Terrel, K., 262
Textiles, footwear and clothing (TFC),
    108–9, 227, 255
Thailand, 27, 39, 46, 59, 64, 65–6, 73, 115,
    155, 174, 201, 227, 239, 265, 269,
    287
Timmer, P., 61
Todaro, M., 36
Tokman, V.E., 30–1
Tomich, T., 62, 163
Trade union, 24, 200, 203, 206, 227, 281
  freedom, 115, 283
  intervention, 35
  membership, 201
Transmigration, 78–9, 108, 111, 145, 159, 161,
    163
  programme, 78
Tukang, 94

Turner, H.A., 137
Turnham, D., 13, 173, 176, 181
Tzannatos, Z., 233, 238

U curve, 236, 239
Underemployment, 4, 13, 54, 172–4, 188–90, 192–3, 277, 284
  involuntary, 175, 189
  rural, 22
Unemployment, 4–5, 42, 12–13, 19, 84, 172–5, 177–81, 183–8, 193–5, 230, 281, 284
  disguised, 34
  female, 188, 241
  global, 172
  luxury, 181–2
  male, 188, 196–8
  rural, 22
  urban, 30, 31, 161, 173, 277
Unemployment rate, 15, 27, 42, 161, 176, 182, 185, 188, 239
Union, freedoms, 25, 221, 223, 228
United States of America, 221–2
Unjuk rasa, 215
Urbanisation, 15, 84
Uruguay, 31

van Velzen, A., 233, 257
van Wijnberg, S., 32
Venezuela, 31
Vietnam, 205, 226
Visaria, P., 181

Wages, 3, 5, 13, 15, 23, 25, 32, 34–6, 39, 42, 50, 82, 89, 95, 98–9, 116, 119, 120–1, 123, 124, 130–1, 137–9, 144, 149, 152, 165–6, 170, 195, 200–2, 205, 213, 214–15, 217–18, 220, 225, 228, 231, 233, 242, 243, 244, 247, 257–8, 261, 265, 267, 275–6, 287
  agricultural, 116
  construction, 118
  contract, 232, 257
  daily, 133, 149
  efficiency, 35, 137
  equation, 121
  female, 120, 254–5, 257
  government, 16, 116–17
  nominal, 125, 133
  outcomes, 29, 117, 260
  real, 28, 30, 33, 38, 81, 115, 118, 120–1, 123, 126, 131–3, 146, 152, 165, 205, 227, 257
  reservation, 35, 150
  rice, 117, 284
  rigidity, 29
  unskilled, 38, 131, 168
Wage adjustments, 41
Wage costs, 127, 129–31
  real rupiah, 129–30
Wage determination, 29, 35–6, 126
Wage differential, 25, 29, 34, 37–8, 57, 138–40, 149, 153–4, 164, 257–8, 260, 277, 285
Wage discrimination, 10, 41, 260
Wage earners, 137–8, 167–8, 257
Wage employment, 26, 31, 53, 55, 84, 89, 91, 97, 102, 106, 109, 114, 181, 243, 249, 255, 259, 266, 278, 281–2
Wage employees, 52, 89, 109, 202, 210, 276
Wage gap, 34, 141
Wage growth increase, 12, 20–1, 30–1, 36, 41, 57, 66, 102, 114–15, 118–20, 124, 131, 141, 149, 152, 167–8, 200, 205, 212, 226–8, 238, 257, 265, 278–9, 281, 285
Wage income, 167, 169, 277
Wage indexation, 32
Wage policies, 224, 284
Wage rates, 28–9, 75, 116–17, 122, 141, 259, 282
Wage repression, 200, 227
Wage structure, 4, 10, 138, 155
Wage trends, 38, 117, 131, 227
Wage workers, 9, 24, 137, 175, 218, 224, 228, 240, 243, 260
Wan, H., 9, 23
Warner, A.M., 277
Warr, P.G., 33, 67, 71, 123
Warung, 51
Watanabe, S., 217
Webb, R.C., 141
White, B., 50, 51, 53, 54, 102, 145, 187, 192, 193, 233, 252
Widarti, D., 239
Williamson, J.G., 23
Wiranta, S., 187
Wolf, D., 233, 282
Women, 231–2, 236, 243, 251, 257–8, 265
  Bangladeshi, 232
  educated, 241, 249
  Indonesian, 281
  marginalisation, 245
  middle class, 236
  urban, 235
  wage-earners, 232
Work force, 8, 14, 85, 138, 173, 227, 236, 267, 275–6, 286, *see also* Labour force
  female urban, 239
  urban, 77
  non-wage, 92
Workers, 3–4, 7, 12, 36, 48, 78, 116–18, 128, 138, 144–5, 148, 163, 167, 210, 213–14, 215, 223, 225, 230, 252, 276, 279, 281, 283, 286
  agricultural, 88, 112, 190

casual wage, 254
construction, 122
educated, 36, 49, 56–7, 79, 139, 141, 152, 158, 173, 249
female, 24, 241, 250, 256
foreign, 81
home, 220
industrial, 7, 31
informal sector, 143
landless, 142
less educated, 139, 148–9
less skilled, 165
low income wage, 127
low productivity, 276
manufacturing, 150
non-wage, 55, 103, 192–3, 255
prime-age, 23
production, 153, 154
professional, 249
protection of, 29, 39
public sector, 211
underemployed, 131
unskilled, 41, 116, 118, 149, 152
urban, 95
white collar, 57
Workers rights, 25, 41, *see also* Labour rights
World Bank, 6–7, 9, 15, 17, 24–5, 31, 39, 63, 88, 108, 111, 115, 163, 181, 189, 199, 230, 249